How Societies Work

How Societies Work

Class, Power, and Change in a Canadian Context

Fourth Edition

Joanne Naiman
Professor Emerita, Ryerson University, Toronto

Fernwood Publishing
Halifax and Winnipeg

Cover Design: John van der Woude
Text Design: Brenda Conroy
Printed and bound in Canada by Hignell Book Printing
This book is printed on paper containing 100% post-consumer fibre.

Published in Canada by Fernwood Publishing
Site 2A, Box 5, 32 Oceanvista Lane
Black Point, Nova Scotia, B0J 1B0
and #8 - 222 Osborne Street, Winnipeg, Manitoba, R3L 1Z3
www.fernwoodpublishing.ca

Fernwood Publishing Company Limited gratefully acknowledges the financial support
of the Government of Canada through the Book Publishing Industry Development
Program (BPDIP), the Canada Council for the Arts and the Nova Scotia
Department of Tourism and Culture for our publishing program.

Library and Archives Canada Cataloguing in Publication

Naiman, Joanne, 1946-
How societies work: class, power, and change in a Canadian context /
Joanne Naiman. — 4th ed.

Includes bibliographical references and index.
ISBN 978-1-55266-269-4

1. Sociology. 2. Canada--Social conditions—1991-. I. Title.

HN103.5.N35 2008   301   C2007-907466-9

Contents

Preface xi
    To the Professor xii
    To the Student xii
    Acknowledgements xiii

Getting the Most from Your Textbook and Your Course xiv
    As Soon as You Buy Your Text xiv
    Reading Each Chapter xiv
        Surveying the Chapter xiv
        Making Your Mark xv
        Reading for Meaning xv
        Studying Effectively xv
    Getting the Most Out of Each Class xv
        Before Class xvi
        During Class xvi
        After Class xvi
        Check Out Student Services xvi
    The Punchline xvi

1   Sociology and the Study of Society 1
    What Is Society? 3
        Society as Structure 3
        Relations of Power 5
        Society as Process 6
    Where Does the Individual Fit In? 7
        Society and Individual Freedom 8
    Sociology and Science 9
        The Inevitability of Bias in Science 11
        Science and Materialism 12
        Science and Dialectics 14
    Theories: Why Is There More Than One Explanation of Human Behaviour? 15
        The Major Sociological Frameworks 18
    The Boundaries of Sociology 22
    Conclusion 23
    Key Points 24
    Further Reading 25

2   Is Human Behaviour the Result of Our Biology? 26
    Do Humans Have Instincts? 27
    The Popularity of Biological Determinist Arguments 29
        From Theory to Practice: The Eugenics Movement 32
    Genetics and "Inherited Tendencies" 34
    The Process of Evolution 35

Humans and Evolution 37
Humans as Social Animals.. 43
Conclusion 43
Key Points 45
Further Reading... 46

3 Culture, Society, and History 47
Understanding Culture 48
Is There a Canadian Culture? 51
Toward a Dialectic of Culture 54
Foraging Societies: The First Socioeconomic Formation 56
What Foraging Societies Tell Us 60
The Decline of Foraging and the Development of Farming 61
The Beginning of Structured Social Inequality 62
Horticultural Societies 64
Agrarian Societies 66
Power and Structured Inequality 68
Key Points 69
Further Reading... 70

4 The Basis of Modern Societies 71
The Roots of Capitalism: Feudalism 72
Commodity Production and the Growth of Markets 73
The Decline of Feudalism 73
New Class Relations: The Rise of Agrarian Capitalism
and Growth of Capitalist Markets 74
Accumulation of Capital 75
Advances in Technology and the Growth of the Labour Force ... 76
Political Transformation in Europe and the Rise of Nation-States ... 77
Changing World View 78
What the Transition to Capitalism Teaches Us 79
The Development of Capitalism in Canada 80
Capitalism Explained 82
Profit: The Driving Force of Capitalism 84
The Hidden Source of Capitalist Profits 85
The Rise of Monopoly Capitalism 86
The Crisis of Overproduction 89
The Growth of the Paper Economy 91
Social Production versus Private Ownership 92
In Whose Interests? 92
The Changing Face of Capitalism 94
Capitalism as a Global System 94
The Transnational Corporation 96
Power in Capitalist Societies 96
Key Points 97
Further Reading... 98

5   Analyzing Social Class 100

Class and Socioeconomic Status: What's the Difference? 101

Canada: A Middle-class Society? 104

The Structure of Classes 106

The Owning Class 108

Class Consciousness in the Owning Class 112

What Is the Working Class? 114

Class Consciousness in the Working Class 116

How Important Is the Variable of Social Class? 119

Key Points 120

Further Reading 121

6   Living in Capitalist Societies 122

Isn't Bigger Better? 123

The Restructuring of Work 124

Decline in Real Wages 127

The Growing Intensity of Labour 128

Are New Technologies the Problem? 129

Worker Alienation 131

The Decline of Small Business and the Family Farm 133

The Culture of Capitalism 135

The Culture of Consumerism 137

"We" versus "Me" 139

From the "Me Generation" to the "iGeneration" 141

Consequences 145

Key Points 146

Further Reading... 146

7   The Social Construction of Ideas and Knowledge 148

Liberalism: "We" versus "Me" Revisited 150

Liberalism and the Market 152

Liberalism and Ideas 153

Ideology, Culture, and Socialization 154

Mass Communications in Canada 156

Ownership and Control of the Media 158

The Myth of Objectivity 161

The Role of the Government 165

The Education System 165

Education in the Twenty-first Century 167

Ideas and Power 171

Key Points 172

Further Reading... 173

8   The Role of the State..175

The Separation of the Private and the Public Spheres.................................... 176

Understanding the Modern State: Two Views 176

Democracy in Capitalist Societies 179

The Meaning of Democracy 179

The Need for Democratic Forms 181
Limits to Democracy 183
The Accumulation Function of the State 184
Money Coming In: The Tax System 184
Money Going Out: The Growth of Corporate Welfare 188
Money to the Military 190
Coercion: The Repressive State Apparatus 192
What Is Fascism? 197
Key Points 199
Further Reading 200

9   Neoliberalism and Globalization 201
The Erosion of the Commons 201
The Growth of the Welfare State 202
Neoliberalism and the Decline of the Welfare State 205
Selling the Corporate Agenda to Canadians 210
Globalization and the Changing Role of the State 211
The United States as Global Superpower 212
The Role of Global Institutions 213
The World Trade Organization 213
The United States as Global Police Officer 215
Globalization: Growing Tensions 219
Toward the Future: Globalization & the Changing Role of the Nation-State ... 222
Key Points 223
Further Reading 224

10 Inequality of Wealth and Income 225
Symbolic Markers of Social Inequality 228
Inequality in Canada: The Growing Gap 229
Explaining Social Inequality 232
The Degree of Social Mobility in Canada 234
Education and Meritocracy 236
Poverty in Canada 238
Who Are the Poor in Canada? 240
Why Does Poverty Exist? 241
Can Poverty Be Eradicated? 243
Why Poverty Affects All of Us 245
Reflections from Working with the Women at the Ottawa Council
for Low Income Support Services ... And the Poor Get Prison 247
Inequality on a Global Scale 248
Key Points 251
Further Reading 252

11 Race and Ethnicity 253
What Is Racism? 254
The Roots of Racism 258
A History of Racism in Canada 260
Aboriginal Peoples 261
Blacks in Canada 264

Immigration from the Nineteenth to the Twenty-first Century 265
The Liberal Perspective: Focusing on Culture 267
The Class Perspective: The Structural Basis of Racism 269
    Extra Profits from Discrimination... 269
    The Ideology of Racism 270
The Struggle for Racial Equality: How Far Have We Come? 271
    The First Nations Struggle 273
    The Issue of Gender 274
The Outlook for the Future 275
Key Points 276
Further Reading... 277

12 Gender Issues 278

Gender Inequality in the Twenty-first Century 279
Is Biology Destiny? 281
Feminist Theories of Gender Inequality 283
    Culture as the Basis of Gender Inequality: The Liberal View 284
    Structural Analyses of Power: Radical Feminism and Marxism 286
The Roots of Gender Inequality 289
Gender and Power 292
How Far Has the Struggle for Gender Equality Come? 296
The Outlook for the Future 299
Key Points 301
Further Reading... 302

13 Looking Toward the Future 303

Will Capitalism Last Forever? 304
The Contradictions of Capitalism 306
    Growing Social, Political, and Economic Instability 307
    The Limits of Growth 309
    The Consequences of Perpetual Growth 310
Will Canada Become Part of the United States? 313
The Changing Nature of Classes 315
Where Is Capitalism Headed? 316
Modern Social Movements for Change... 318
    Organizing for Change 319
    Populist Movements 321
    New Social Movements: "A Better World Is Possible" 322
Conclusion 324
Key Points 325
Further Reading... 326

Finding Useful Resources on the Web 327
Glossary..329
References 338
Name Index 352
Subject Index 357

Preface

There is no getting around it: Introductory textbooks are both hard to read and hard to write. They cover a vast range of complex topics. The users generally have little or no background in the social sciences, yet are suddenly expected to grasp not only a new way of seeing the world, but also the many details about various theories and historic events. As soon as students begin to wrap their head around a certain topic—say the genetic basis of human behaviour—it's on to the next chapter and a completely different topic. So many topics, so little time. Those who teach introductory courses know the challenge of making the complexities of social analysis meaningful to students without trivializing or oversimplifying.

I began to write this book back in 1994, thinking that it would be a breeze— I'd taught introductory sociology for so long that I naïvely thought I'd just take my course notes and quickly convert them into a text. Two years later, the task was completed and the first edition of this book was published. Without a doubt, the person who learned the most from that book was me. Each subsequent edition of the book has been both a challenge and an adventure.

My goal has always been to make the book interesting to students and relevant to their lives. Of course, I've also brought the contents of each new edition up to date, providing both new data and current social thought. For this edition there have been some substantial changes made to the book. The chapter order has been altered slightly, with the chapter that explains social class (Chapter 5) now preceding the chapter that details life in modern capitalism (Chapter 6). Chapter 9 has been renamed to more closely reflect its content. I have also reduced the amount of material on the history and political economy of capitalism; in its place I have expanded the sociological analysis of the culture of capitalism (Chapter 6). In addition, a number of new topics have been added, including White privilege and Islamophobia (Chapter 11), a brief history of feminism (Chapter 12), the shift from the "me generation" to the "igeneration" (Chapter 6), and the implications of climate change (Chapter 13). I've also briefly introduced more ideas of classical social thinkers such as Max Weber, Adam Smith, Ferdinand Tönnies, John Locke, George Herbert Mead, and Charles Horton Cooley.

New for this edition is an introductory section called "Getting the Most from Your Textbook and Your Course." My many years as a teacher of first-level students helped me understand that poor grades can often be the result of deficiencies in basic reading and study skills; this section makes some suggestions to help students succeed academically. Also added as an aid to students are four questions at the start of each chapter that lay out some of the main topics to be discussed.

Overall, the book has been made more student-friendly. Many new boxed inserts have been added to provide more down-to-earth examples of theoretical content. The list of definitions has been expanded. Several chapters, such as Chapter 1, have been reorganized to make the contents easier to understand. The language throughout the text has been simplified wherever possible, and some topics have been deleted. My son—now a university student—was one of my most important editors. Whenever he said, "Mom, no one's going to understand that point" or "Mom, that's got to go," I took it out or rewrote it.

To the Professor

I have received a great deal of feedback from colleagues and students over the four editions of this book. While I often initially resisted suggestions for change, it usually turned out that the criticisms were valid. I retired from full-time teaching in 2004. In some ways it made revising this book more difficult, as I no longer have regular student input. However, being out of the classroom has allowed me to see the book from a different point of view. In the past I would cover a topic from the perspective of my own teaching methods and course content. For this edition I saw the book in more universal terms. As a result, some topics suddenly *did* seem too complex or detailed for first-level students. I hope my new approach has made the book more accessible to them. As always, some worthwhile topics could not be included simply because of length restrictions. I would hope that professors who use this book do not feel bound by either the book's contents or its order.

Although not all instructors use the "Think About It" questions with their classes, I have left them in for this edition. From a pedagogical point of view, I find their greatest value is that they slow readers down for a brief moment, forcing them to ponder a point or consider its implications.

To the Student

The book you are about to read is the result of the many years I spent teaching introductory sociology courses. I think you will find that it is different from most other introductory sociology textbooks. For starters, it assumes that the majority of you will not be pursuing careers in sociology. As a result, you're likely to be more interested in understanding the social world than the field itself. Thus this book does not deal extensively with either social theory or methodology.

Most introductory textbooks offer what I refer to as the "smorgasbord" approach to learning: put everything on the "table" and let the student have a "taste" of a wide array of theories and topics. However, if you think of the times you have actually eaten this kind of buffet meal, you will probably agree that the quantity of food usually surpassed its quality; you put too much on your plate; it all dissolved into a gigantic mush; and you ended up with indigestion. In contrast, this book will attempt to give you a selective "meal," but hopefully a memorable one.

You are about to embark on an adventure in learning. Chances are, the orientation of this book is new to you, and its approach may challenge many of your taken-for-granted assumptions about the world. As noted in the first chapter, this is exactly what sociology is meant to do—it should shake us up. Keep in mind that this is not a theology textbook, and you are not expected to become a "believer." Sociology is about learning to ask the right questions, to be sceptical, and to weigh and judge different social analyses. Most importantly, sociology is a field that challenges students to engage with their social world. As this book makes abundantly clear, the world we live in today was made by those who came before us, but the future is in our hands. In order to change the world we must first understand how it works. This book is a small attempt to start you on that path.

Acknowledgements

I would like to thank the following individuals for their assistance over the course of the various editions of the book: Greg Albo, Mary-Ellen Belfiore, Jane Bouey and the staff at Co-Op Books, Mike Burke, Bill Burgess, Bill Carroll, Scott Couling, Slobodan Drakulic, Shannon Daub, Michael Davis, Carolyn Egan, Louis Feldhammer, Judy Fudge, Harry Glasbeek, Keith Hampson, Paul Idahosa, Maureen Hynes, John Huot, Jan Kainer, Mustafa Koç, Elsha Leventis, Debby Littman, Michael Mandel, Stephen McBride, David McNally, Jeff Miller, Colin Mooers, Joey Noble, Michael Ornstein, Murray Pomerance, John Sakeris, Alan Sears, Erika Shaker, Cheryl Teelucksingh, Gary Teeple, Barbara Tessman, Wendy Thomas, Kaari Turk, Vappu Tyyskä, John Shields, Eric Tucker, and Fiona Whittington-Walsh.

For this edition I would like to thank Sian Reid at Carleton University and anonymous reviewers whose many suggestions for change helped make this a better book. Thanks, too, to everyone at Fernwood who worked on this book: Beverley Rach, Jesse Rach-Sharpe, Debbie Mathers, Jessica Antony, John van der Woude and particularly Brenda Conroy for her excellent copyediting. Special thanks go to Errol Sharpe. Errol, you were right: I was always meant to be part of the Fernwood list, and it's a pleasure to be working with an independent Canadian press once again.

And of course, thanks to Neil for all his help over the years, especially his willingness to do more than his share of domestic chores, and to Daniel for perpetually challenging my point of view. Daniel, as always, this book is dedicated to you, in the continuing hope that together we can help make the world a better place.

Getting the Most from Your Textbook and Your Course

Students today pay a lot of money for their textbooks and often put a great deal of time into reading them. However, many have not acquired the skills that allow them to do this in an effective manner. Similarly, many students attend class regularly, but often retain little of what was transmitted there. Often it is the students who spend the most time reading or studying who actually get the poorest marks. Here are some guidelines to help you get the most out of this textbook and your course. If you are having trouble with any of the activities listed below—such as marking your text or taking notes in class—be sure to see your professor or teaching assistant immediately. Most welcome student interest and will try to help you improve your skills.

As Soon as You Buy Your Text

At the beginning of the term, make an overall survey of your text. Look at the Table of Contents to see how the book is organized and what topics are covered. Read the short Preface to get the author's personal introduction. Look at the study aids that are contained in the book, i.e., the Glossary and Index at the end of the book, and the short summaries and suggested readings at the end of each chapter. Pick a topic or two that interest you and read a few pages to get used to the writing style.

Reading Each Chapter

Too often students read a textbook as if it were a novel. They just pick it up, sit back in a comfy chair, read the required pages, and then put it down. This is not a particularly useful way to read a text. A few extra minutes doing one or more of the following at each reading will help you get much more out of it.

Surveying the Chapter

A quick "pre-reading" of each chapter will give you a general idea of what will be in it. Carefully read the questions at the beginning of the chapter to get a sense of what the chapter will be about. Also look at the chapter headings and first few sentences in each section. Ask yourself these questions: What is the main topic of this chapter? What are some of the key topics to be discussed in it? How is it connected to earlier chapters?

Making Your Mark

Marking your text in some way has two important purposes: first, it forces you to slow down and look for key points; second, it highlights these points for quick review when it comes time to reread material for a test or essay. There are different ways to mark your text—you can use any or all of the following:

- Underline or highlight key words and sentences.
- Make marginal notes of questions or ideas that occur to you as you read.
- Make brief summaries in your own words after you finish each section—these only take a few minutes, but make excellent study sheets for tests and exams.

Whatever your system, be selective. Underline or note only key points—if you mark everything, you have defeated your purpose. If you do find yourself marking almost everything, it probably means you're having trouble distinguishing the major points from the examples or the minor points. You may need to get help from your professor or teaching assistant.

Reading for Meaning

Try not to read too much at one time. After a while your brain will go numb and you will not absorb anything you are reading. Perhaps change to another course for a while before returning to your sociology material. Always try to take a ten-minute break for every hour you read. Minimally, after reading each section, put the book down for a moment and ask yourself, "What was the main point here?" If you can't answer this question, you clearly need to re-read that section.

Studying Effectively

If you have followed the above, studying for your test and exam will be much easier. When it comes time to study, again do a quick overview of a chapter to remind yourself of the content. Re-read your notes and/or underlined sections. Make a study sheet (if you haven't developed one before) with key words that might be on the test, or key points. Writing it down will help you retain it.

Reading is a very passive activity; teaching is an active one—you will learn more if you teach material to someone else. It helps if you can study with a friend and ask each other questions, go over material together, or do quizzes. If working with a friend is not possible, learn to talk to yourself out loud, as if you were, indeed, teaching the material to someone else. It may at first feel awkward to do this, but you will retain much more of the material this way.

Getting the Most Out of Each Class

It costs a lot of money to attend college or university. Try to get your money's worth. For starters, try to attend your classes as often as possible. If you miss too many classes in a row, you will have a hard time getting back into the material. If you miss the occasional class, try to get the notes as soon as possible from a classmate. Don't assume everything in the course is in the text. Some teachers will enhance the text, while others will cover extra material that is not covered in the text.

Try to sit toward the front of the class. Let's face it, few students feel comfortable at the very front of the class; however, although it may be cool to sit near the back corner with your buddies, it will almost certainly guarantee that your mind will wander. If you are going to take the time to come to a class, why not try to get the most out of it? Remember: the most expensive seats for a play or a concert are the ones near the front.

Students generally have heavy workloads, making it very easy to get behind in their reading. Try your best to keep up. Not only will classes be more worthwhile, but you will also simply have an easier time studying for tests and exams, as well as writing essays.

Before Class

Try to make sure you have done the assigned reading. If possible, take a quick look at your notes from the previous class—perhaps while you are waiting for the class to start.

During Class

Taking good notes during the class will also enhance learning. Watch for the main topic, key points, and the organization of ideas. Your professor will give you clues: voice emphasis; writing on the board; repetition of an idea; opening and closing of the lesson. Make notes that highlight the key ideas, and make sure these key ideas are distinct from examples provided by the professor.

After Class

If you quickly re-read your notes on the day you have taken them, you will be able to see if you have left anything out or if your notes make sense. It will also help you retain classroom material. If there are any problems, talk to your professor or teaching assistant at the next class.

Check Out Student Services

Most colleges and universities offer short courses in such things as note-taking, studying for multiple-choice exams, reducing stress, and so on. Find out what is being offered this semester and see if you can benefit from them.

The Punchline

At first glance all of the above might seem pretty time-consuming. Ironically, a few minutes spent before and after each class—as well as before and after each reading of your text—will actually save you time in preparing for your test, essay, and exam (or at least make your time more efficient). Few students will follow all of the above suggestions, but try a few in each of your courses and see which ones work best for you.

1 Sociology and the Study of Society

In This Chapter

- What is sociology and why is it worth studying?
- What do we mean by "society"?
- How do sociologists actually study social behaviour?
- Why are there different and sometimes conflicting theories about how societies work?

All of us are fascinated about why we behave the way we do. We currently live in a world that places tremendous emphasis on the individual, including personal motivation, feelings, opinions, values, and beliefs. As a result, we tend to explain human behaviour by focusing on the individual psychological component. Yet a moment's reflection tells us that there is something beyond the individual involved in our behaviour. For example, how did you decide what to wear today? In one sense, it was clearly an individual choice. But that choice was not made in a vacuum.

The next time you're sitting in a class, check out what the other students are wearing; chances are that you'll be amazed at the degree to which most of you, making individual choices, came to school dressed in a similar fashion. Obviously, something affected the way each of you made those individual choices. That "something," put simply, is what sociologists refer to as society. A **society** consists of a group of people within a limited territory who share a common set of behaviours, beliefs, values, material objects (together referred to as culture), and social institutions that exist as a coherent system.

When most of us try to conceptualize the notion of society, it is common to think of it as a kind of space that is inhabited by the individuals who live in it. However, it is important to note that, whatever society is, it is not simply "out there." It is also in us; indeed, it might be said that it *is* us. This is what makes the study of society so intriguing. Individuals create society, but society, in turn, creates them. Sociologists, therefore, have to disentangle the complex relationships between individuals and their social world.

If you want to see the way our social world imposes on us, try this experiment. While standing and talking to a friend, ever so slowly begin to move

1

toward her or him. Your friend will unconsciously move back to adjust the conversational distance. If you do this slowly for a few minutes, you will likely find you've moved your friend right across the room! This is because in every society there are accepted distances for social conversation. No one ever sat us down and taught us these "rules," but, somehow, most of us seem to know them. We become aware of these practices only when someone violates these expectations or we are in a culture other than our own.

The social world affects us in all our behaviours, including that most personal and private of human behaviours, suicide. When people hear about someone who has ended their life, it is common to wonder about the cause of such drastic behaviour. Usually, the focus is on the feelings and personal state of the individual at the time of death—whether the person was depressed, lonely, on drugs, insecure, afraid of failure, and so on. Sociologists, on the other hand, focus on general patterns, or regularities, in this behaviour. Because such an apparently private individual act consistently reveals itself to be patterned, it is of interest to sociologists.

At the end of the nineteenth century, a French sociologist named Émile Durkheim (1858–1917) published what has become a classic study of suicide. The data gathered by Durkheim revealed some fascinating patterns. If suicide were based primarily on individual motives, then it should be random—that is, showing no particular pattern—in the population. Yet Durkheim found patterns of suicide that were consistent through time and in different countries. For example, men were more likely to end their own life than women, single and divorced individuals more likely than married people, city people more than country people, and Protestants more than Catholics or Jews (Durkheim [1897] 1951). More recent data indicate that increases in the unemployment rate can be correlated to the rate of suicide. Certain occupations rank higher than others in rates of suicide. And in Canada, Aboriginal peoples have suicide rates much higher than those of the non-Aboriginal population.

Think About It

Sociologists, like all scientists, are interested in collecting data, but they are also interested in explaining their findings. Can you think of any reasons that Aboriginals in Canada might have high suicide rates?

We must always be cautious about how we interpret statistics on suicide, since many suicides are not reported. However, it can certainly be said that something about the social world and our place in it—such as our gender, our religion, or our economic position—does seem to affect our most intimate selves, even though we may not be consciously aware of it. As the rest of this book will demonstrate, we cannot fully comprehend any human behaviour outside of the society of which it is a part.

The fact that sociology tries to make sense of the very world in which we live is what makes it such an interesting discipline, although this also makes it much more challenging. When we study chemistry or accounting, we are unlikely to have strong personal feelings about chemicals or numbers. In contrast, most of us have strong emotions and opinions about our social world. In addition, many of the issues raised by sociologists are no different than those discussed in the popular media. As a result, those who teach sociology face a particular challenge: our students not only have strong feelings about many topics under discussion—such as crime, gender and racial inequality, the "war on terrorism," or the nature of the media—but also often feel they are already well informed about them. It is therefore not surprising that students sometimes have a hard time with sociology, which offers a new way of looking at familiar matters. Sociology is particularly challenging since it forces us to re-examine ourselves, our strongly held beliefs and values, and the social institutions to which we belong. To put it bluntly, sociology is meant to shake us up.

Of course, critically examining our taken-for-granted assumptions about the world can be a little scary. Why then should anybody engage in this activity? Put differently, aside from trying to get a good mark on a course you happen to be taking, is there any reason to bother reading this book? The answer lies in the quote from James Baldwin, a renowned Black American writer who died in 1987. As we shall see in Chapter 2, being human means, in part, having the unique capacity for

> People who shut their eyes to reality simply invite their own destruction.
> —James Baldwin

abstract thought that allows us to assess the past and ponder the future. All of us know that today's world is complex and sometimes frightening. To understand this world and perhaps to change it requires using all the tools at our disposal.

But what exactly is this field called sociology? Surprisingly, this is not an easy question to answer since, as we shall see, there are debates within the field about what ought to be the central area of study, what methods ought to be used, and what theoretical frameworks ought to be employed. These debates have led to different schools of thought within the field. In its broadest sense, we can say that sociology is the systematic study of human society and the behaviour of people in society. We should begin, then, with a more detailed discussion of the meaning of society.

What Is Society?

Society as Structure

A few years ago I joined a choir. Several people in the choir are outstanding singers while a few others can barely carry a tune; together we usually sound really good. If one or two are not singing well, it's hardly noticeable, but when a lot of us don't follow the music, we sound terrible. Our director arranges the music so that the four parts will sound harmonious; he also conducts to ensure that we are all in the correct key and singing together.

There are about eighty people in the choir, with about forty coming to the weekly practices. A number of committees have been created to carry out different tasks, including one to select the songs, another to do general administration, one for fundraising, and a committee that deals with personal disputes. When somebody joins the choir, they are given an information pamphlet that lays out the expectations for choir membership. Twice a year there is a general meeting where members can air their concerns and collective issues are debated.

The choir is able to achieve its goals because it is structured; that is, it is more than simply forty individuals singing. The choir works only if we sing together, and in harmony. Moreover, we have to work collectively over time to achieve our goal. To do that, we need some form of organization that not only allows the main task to be accomplished, but also ensures that the "behind the scenes" tasks get done as well. To do all this, we have to set rules and see that members follow them. It is also important to note that the structure exists outside of the members in it; although membership is always changing, the structure remains basically the same.

Societies are like a choir in many ways. As with a choir, the sum is always more than the individual parts. In order to survive and carry out their daily activities, people have to organize themselves into some kind of structure, and they have to construct rules for their behaviour. These structures can vary from the very simple to the very complex, and once they come into being, they can exist for very long periods of time. One key goal of sociology, then, is to systematically study and analyze the various elements that constitute a society's structure and the relationships among these elements. If society is the term generally used to describe the structure of our social world, then culture—to be examined in Chapter 3—is the term used to describe its contents. In actual practice, the terms society, social structure, and culture are often used interchangeably within the social sciences; some anthropologists try to combine the concepts by using the term **sociocultural system**.

Think About It

Are you involved in any groups that require an organizational structure to accomplish their goals? Do you think that these groups could survive without this structure?

While the social world is real and does have a real effect on us, we must be careful not to oversimplify by turning the abstract concept of society into a concrete entity with human-like characteristics. For example, we sometimes hear statements such as "Society teaches men how to behave," or "Society led her to a life of crime." But what do these statements mean? Has "society" ever shown up at your doorstep or given classes telling you what to do? How can something abstract actually "do" anything?

Terms such as *society* and *sociocultural system* are just code words for the complex ways humans live in social groups. In reality, it is individual human beings, interacting with each other, who both create and change their social world. If we actually want to understand why men and women behave differently, or why certain individuals break the law, we need more careful consideration of the issues. We must examine how and why certain forms of social organization and culture came into existence, how they affect different individuals within a particular society, and how they change over time. In addition, the role of social institutions such as the family, schools, and the media have to be examined.

Relations of Power

In order to fully make sense of any society, we have to understand the relationships of power that are found within it. **Power** is the ability of an individual or a group to carry out its will even when opposed by others, and although we all feel its effects, it is hard to actually locate both what it is and where it is. Power is largely a result of the control individuals or groups have of a society's resources, including its "human resources." It exists within personal relationships—which we might term **proximal relations of power**—and at a more abstract level in society as a whole—which we might term **distal relations of power** (adapted from Smail 1999). All of us are affected by both types of power throughout our lives.

We first experience power inequities in the sphere of proximal relations—specifically the family—where, as children, we learn that parents have more control over us than we do over them, and that they also have greater control over the family resources. "You're not the boss of me!" says a defiant five-year-old when told that it is bedtime. Of course, to every child's chagrin, parents *are* the bosses and, indeed, are legally obligated to be so. In the same way, professors are the "bosses" of their students: they have certain power over the students, for in the end they can pass or fail them. We can speak of parent, child, teacher, or student as a **status**, or position within the social structure; statuses can be ranked in relation to each other. Those with higher statuses have more privileges and power than lower-status individuals. All humans hold many different statuses in their lifetime, often concurrently.

Think About It

Can you name some of the statuses you hold at the moment?

When we are small, the power our parents have over us seems monumental, and many of us can't wait to be out of their control. In reality, however, the power that parents have over children—as with all proximal relations of power—is actually quite small when placed within an entire social system. It exists only for a certain period of time, over a small number of individuals, and over certain matters. Parents who go beyond what is deemed to be acceptable—by molesting their child, for example—may well find themselves in prison. Likewise, your professors may seem to be very powerful individuals relative to the powerlessness you feel as a student. However, the power your professors have exists only in a particular time and place. Once a course is over, the power largely vaporizes.

Moreover, once professors step out of the classroom there is a complex chain of authority that has power over them. And, in the scheme of things, the power held within an educational institution is small relative to the distal power wielded by, say, governments or major corporations.

Although distal relations of power often have more serious consequences for our lives, they are very hard for us to see and therefore oppose. Moreover, as Smail (1999) argues, we live in a society that teaches us to look inward to our own individual failings or to nearby proximal relations of power when we experience the negative consequences of distal relations of power, rather than outward to the broader social system. For example, if we apply for a job and fail to get it, we are more likely to blame ourselves than to link it to such abstract things as government policies, discriminatory hiring practices, or corporate globalization. A key task for sociologists, then, is to examine relations of power—particularly in the distal sphere—and to link them to the life experiences of individuals.

American sociologist C. Wright Mills (1916–62) differentiated what he called "personal troubles of milieu" from "public issues of social structure" (Mills 1961, 8). For him, the **sociological imagination** is the ability to go beyond the personal issues we all experience and connect them to broader social structures. If one person is barely getting by, that's their problem; if, as in Canada,

> Neither the life of an individual nor the history of a society can be understood without understanding both.
> —C. Wright Mills

millions are living in poverty, that's a social issue. If a young person can't afford university tuition, that's a personal problem; if many young people either don't go to university because of the high cost or come out with a large amount of debt, then it's a social issue. Expressed somewhat differently, the sociological imagination is the ability to link distal relations of power to our immediate life situations.

Society as Process

Much of what social scientists do involves taking a "snapshot" of a society or an element of it at a particular moment in time in order to study it. This can certainly be useful. For example, a sociologist might want to discover the extent of unemployment in Canada or of suicide among indigenous peoples. Data will be collected and then analyzed, so that conclusions about these behaviours can be drawn. However, the real world is not a snapshot but more like a moving picture. At the very same time that they display a constancy and set of recurring patterns, societies are also in the process of change. The notion that things can be simultaneously consistent yet changing requires some explanation.

In our daily life we experience repetitive patterns and a high degree of consistency. Indeed, we would have difficulty surviving from moment to moment if this were not so. In this sense, barring sudden major social or physical upheavals, the social world remains fairly constant over time. This is the order that allows humans to function. Those who have survived war or natural disasters know how stressful it is to live through a breakdown in the social order.

And yet, at the very same time that our social world is ordered, it is simultaneously in flux and change. New technologies regularly alter the way we work and the way we live; new values and beliefs arise and come into conflict with older ones; governments create new laws and reorganize structures of governance; social institutions such as families and schools change their form. Thus, at the same moment that societies display repetitive patterns, they are also being altered. In pre-industrial societies, change occurred quite slowly; today's world, in contrast, changes substantially even within a single lifetime. Sociologists, then, have the difficult task of not only explaining the ordered patterns in society but also analyzing a social world that changes over time.

Where Does the Individual Fit In?

Talk of a society that affects our behaviour without our realizing it may leave the impression that humans are simply robots controlled by unseen and unknown forces. However, accepting the notion that we are part of a social world does not deny the possibility of individual free will. Any one of us, at any time, can act in ways that go against the expected patterns—usually referred to as **norms**—of behaviour. The data indicate, however, that human behaviour is astonishingly patterned. It is these patterns that sociologists study, and on the basis of past patterns they try to predict future behaviours. As in the physical sciences, sociology deals in patterns and probabilities. The predictions it makes are not about specific individuals but rather about social groups.

Think About It

Most of us expect others to act in very predictable ways, whether it is a friend, family member, or total stranger. For one day, have fun trying to imagine all the people you meet acting in totally unexpected ways; for example, imagine a store clerk telling you the details of his hernia operation, a woman on the bus breaking into song, or your professor showing up for class in a bathing suit. Have you observed unexpected behaviours in the past? How did they make you feel?

Even though human behaviour is fairly predictable, each of us can break expected patterns at any time. For example, some young people come from traditional backgrounds where marriages are arranged by parents. For many, that will be satisfactory, but some may find this unacceptable and will insist on finding a partner of their own choosing, often at the price of ending their relationship with their family or community. Humans are social and act in patterned ways, but there is no requirement that we act in those ways. On the other hand, the need to belong and fit in with our social groups—from close family and friends to much larger religious or national groupings—makes it extremely difficult for most of us to be nonconformists. It is amazing, then, that even when the price is incredibly high (sometimes death), some people under certain conditions choose to go against established expectations. These nonconforming behaviours can become the basis for broader social change.

In sum, we can speak of a society as a system, and social behaviour as having predictable patterns, while at the same time acknowledging the possibility for individual behaviours, or what is referred to as *human agency*. Although some early sociologists proposed mechanistic views of our social world, we now know that society is not like a clock with all the pieces fitting neatly together to make the whole work. As we shall examine in more detail throughout this book, while all societies display a certain degree of coherence, they also contain many stresses and strains. It is these tensions within a society that ultimately give rise to change. Sometimes these changes occur at an extremely slow pace, while at other times they occur incredibly quickly. A major goal of sociology is to study past patterns, to detect the current strains, and, within limits, to predict the future direction of social change.

Society and Individual Freedom

Because the period in which we live puts so much emphasis on the individual, it might seem that society is nothing but a negative, constraining element, limiting our individual freedom. For example, many of us oppose censorship because we feel that it is an outside force restricting our freedom of expression. Freedom, in this construct, is the removal of social constraints, which allows individuals to do as they please.

It is certainly true that all societies have expected rules of social behaviour, and those who disobey certain of these rules may be severely punished. However, society can also be a liberating force. The commonly shared rules of our social world allow us to function as individuals in our daily lives. Imagine, for a moment, a world without rules. Would anyone dare get in a car? Obviously not, for we could never be sure, from moment to moment, what the other drivers would do. Would they stop or go on a red light? Would they drive on the left or right side of the road? Would they drive as if they were in a game of bumper cars? The constraints of society that limit what we can do also limit what others can do. The assumption that most people will act as they should reduces our level of insecurity and allows us to get on with our lives.

We can see that social expectations are as much a comfort as a constraint by the fact that so many of us cling to them. Every December large numbers of Canadians (many of whom are not even Christian) happily drag freshly cut evergreens into their living rooms and decorate them with brightly coloured balls and lights. People do it not because they have to but because they want to. Not only do customs and traditions give us comfort, they also provide ready-made solutions to many decisions we must make every day—how to dress, what way to eat, what to do when someone dies, and so on. In this way, today's social world is built on the sociocultural world of our ancestors.

Think About It

Some of you may come from backgrounds where family members are upset by your modern ways. Try to sociologically explain their feelings regarding your attitude toward their culture and traditions.

In reality, the tension is not between the individual and society, but between the various individuals and groups within a society. For example, suppose your sociology professor feels that all students have to master both a second language and advanced statistics as a minimal requirement for passing the course. This would mean that most of the students in the class would fail. Here the freedom of your professor to set course requirements would obviously come into direct conflict with the freedom of the students to pass the course and ultimately get their degree. In this situation, the chair of the department or the dean would have to be brought in to negotiate a resolution to this problem.

In the real world, the rights, beliefs, and values of various groups and individuals are always coming into conflict and must be resolved either informally or formally. For example, the Supreme Court of Canada and the Canadian government were forced to grapple with the complex question of whether gays and lesbians should have the right to civil marriage. On one side were those Canadians who wanted marriage to retain its traditional definition; on the other side were those who argued that all individuals, regardless of their sexual preference, should have the right to marry. In 2004 the Court, basing its decision on the Canadian Charter of Rights and Freedoms, ruled that same-sex marriages already being performed in eight provinces and one territory were legal and had to be recognized. In July 2005, gay marriage received parliamentary approval and Canada became the fourth country in the world to recognize gay marriages.

There can be no question that all of us, at times, feel constrained by the rules of social behaviour and that many of us rebel against at least some of them some of the time. Moreover, under certain conditions—for example, in Nazi Germany—societies can become very repressive, with the rights of large numbers of people constrained. However, the notion of free-floating individuals who function without any social constraints is a purely mental construct. From the moment we are born, we are, of necessity, part of a social world; none of us can ever be free of it. It is for this reason that a careful examination of that world is so essential to understanding human behaviour.

Sociology and Science

Humans have thought about and interpreted human behaviour since they were first capable of reflective thought. Then, as now, people likely got together to chat and gossip about each other, and to try to make sense of their social world. With the origins of writing and the increase in human knowledge, people in many parts of the world began to record their thoughts about the nature of the human condition. Many of these thoughts can be found in religious texts. Others were written by philosophers or historians, and the writings of such great thinkers as Aristotle, Plato, or Ibn Khaldun are still read today. But while these writings may have been interesting and informative, they do not constitute what is formally referred to as sociology. The roots of modern sociology lie in nineteenth-century Europe and are linked to the growth of science in the preceding few centuries.

All of us have taken science courses in elementary and high school, but when asked to define the term *science*, few of us can do so. This is because, in part, the scientific way of seeing the world is so widespread today that most of us take it for granted. But in sixteenth-century Europe, a religious world view rather than a scientific one was dominant. At that time, the Catholic Church was a very powerful institution that promoted belief in a world ordered and understood only by God. Most people at that time were illiterate and made sense of what they saw around them either through religious precepts or common-sense folk wisdom.

In sixteenth and seventeenth century Europe and England, philosophers began to develop a new way of understanding the world. This scientific world view recreated the systematic thought about the universe that had been lost since the time of the ancient Greeks and Romans. Science is rooted in two key elements: first, knowledge must be based on empirical observation, that is, on data that can be observed through the senses; second, information must be analyzed through logic and rational thought. English essayist Sir Francis Bacon (1561–1626) was one of the earliest to synthesize these notions, but it was Isaac Newton (1642–1727) who is most connected with the development of the modern scientific method. But science was much more than simply a method. It was also a totally new way of seeing the world, one that believed that both the physical and social environment could be altered by humans through the thoughtful application of reason.

This was the world in which the field of sociology began, predominantly in England, France, and Germany, where industry was developing rapidly, cities were expanding, and the new scientific world view had firmly taken hold. The methods of science not only were employed in the world of industry and commerce, but also came to be used in the study of human beings. Attempts to utilize science in the study of the human body, mind, and social behaviour all advanced during this period.

However, none of these developments took place in a neutral context. The period that we now refer to as the Industrial Revolution brought with it great social dislocation, increasing disparities between rich and poor, and growing oppression of peoples around the world. For those who were benefiting from the new economic order, the new social sciences became a means of justifying the current social arrangements. For the disadvantaged, the new tool of social science was seen as a way to change the world. Thus, from the very outset, there was a tension in sociology about the ultimate use of social analysis.

One of the earliest social theorists to try to apply scientific principles to social analysis was a Frenchman named Auguste Comte (1798–1857). He is remembered today primarily because he coined the term sociology (after he discovered that the term "social physics," his first choice for the new science, had already been used). Comte was among the first intellectuals since the time of ancient Greece to emphasize the importance of empirical observation of the external material world in the study of social phenomena. Today most social theorists would consider Comte's attempts to apply the methods of the physical sciences to the social world too mechanical and simplistic. Nonetheless, he laid out many of the basic tenets for social science that remain valid to the present day.

Sociology as a field has changed a great deal since Comte's time, and the meaning of what constitutes a "science of society" continues to be debated. North American sociology of the twentieth century became much more focused on quantitative analysis and proximal social relations while European sociology remained closer to philosophy, focusing on broader social questions. From the 1950s onward, a distinctively Canadian sociology began to flourish, and sociology departments expanded across the country. The 1970s saw the growth of a feminist orientation, which examined and critiqued the systematic domination of males in both society and the field of sociology itself. Since that time, sociology has expanded even further, with new frameworks adding to our understanding of the social world.

Think About It
When I attended university in the 1960s, almost all our sociology textbooks were from the United States and were written by men. Do you think it matters who writes a textbook?

The Inevitability of Bias in Science

It is generally assumed that the value of science lies primarily in its objectivity; that is, we believe that science is free from bias. In one respect this is true—legitimate science must base its conclusions on observable information that can be evaluated by others. For example, to link cigarette smoking to lung cancer, one cannot simply assert, "I'm sure there's a connection." Data must be provided and other competent scientists must assess the methodology and the conclusions. Early sociologists such as Durkheim and Max Weber (1864–1920), trying to build a legitimate science of society, thought that the social world had to be studied in a neutral or non-biased way. However, no knowledge—not even scientific knowledge—can be totally unbiased, since it is always collected by humans with already formed opinions, who decide what to study, how to study it, and so on.

Students have often told me that my course is biased. Of course it is, as is every course you will ever take, any book you will ever read, and any newscast you will ever watch. In order to teach a course, a professor has to decide what material to include and what to leave out, which books or articles to assign, what order to present the material in, and so on. The reason we seldom notice these biases is either because they are in fields we know nothing about, or because the biases match our own. We most commonly notice bias only when it conflicts with our own views.

Does this mean that we can know nothing for certain because everyone has a personal opinion and therefore objective reality does not exist outside of our own individual perceptions of it? Most scientists reject this view. The role of science is to validate or invalidate individual observations of the world. A piece of information can be true or false regardless of the bias of the observer. Put differently, information can be biased and true or biased and false. While sociology cannot, therefore, be value free, it must nonetheless satisfy the rigours of scientific investigation. Moreover, whether it is academic writing or material from the mass media, all information should be examined with a critical eye. This is particularly true now that anyone can post material on the Internet. It is always wise to consider where the data came from, how they were collected, how the research was funded, how the information is being presented, and so on.

Think About It

In 2006, some ten thousand scientists in the United States signed a statement protesting political interference in the scientific process. The American Union of Concerned Scientists claimed that scientists working in U.S. government agencies were being asked to change data to fit policy initiatives in areas such as global climate change, international peace and security, and water resources. Why might governments pressure scientists this way?

Science and Materialism

In the previous section, it was noted that a core belief of all science is that knowledge is based on empirical observation, or that which we can observe through our senses. However, philosophers have long debated the relationship between the external, material world (the objective) and the world of the mind, or spirit (the subjective). Indeed, the question of what is real, how our senses affect perception, and how ideas in turn affect external reality long predates the growth of science. Social scientists are faced with particular dilemmas. Do they focus on the human thoughts that give rise to social behaviour, or do they concentrate on studying the ways the social world affects our thoughts and feelings?

While these questions may seem to be of the abstract "which came first, the chicken or the egg" variety, they ultimately determine the direction of social analysis. In reality, of course, the two spheres influence each other in a never-ending relationship, but one is prior to and more important than the other. This book will argue that there is a real world that exists beyond our sense perceptions of it. While our sense perceptions may affect how we perceive this external world, and under certain conditions may even change it, we must always begin with the notion that there is an "out there" that is indeed out there and is able to be affected by our perceptions.

Philosophical materialism is an analytical framework that asserts that

Box 1.1 Idealism vs. Materialism in Social Analysis: An Example

We currently live in a world that tends to focus on individual ideas, beliefs, and attitudes as a key explanation for social behaviour, rather than on the material roots of these behaviours. This can have major implications for both social analysis and social policy, as can be seen in the following concrete example (reported in the *Toronto Star,* 14 January 1998). There are many people in Canada who do not work for a living, a concern for the individuals involved and society as a whole. A two-year program in Nova Scotia, costing $12.5 million, tried to help approximately 1600 individuals get off welfare and into the workforce. Although the program was originally touted by the Nova Scotia government as a great success, an independent review concluded that the program did nothing to end long-term dependency on welfare. Given the large expenditure of money with no positive outcome, the government tried to discover why the program hadn't worked.

Some of the program's counsellors—using an idealist analysis—concluded that the failure was probably due primarily to the poor attitudes of the recipients, who were lacking in motivation and wanted to stay home with their friends. However, a materialist analysis helps us spot some objective causes for the project's failure. First, it was noted in the newspaper article that continuing high unemployment rates were probably a factor as there weren't enough jobs for everyone who wanted one. Second, some of the recipients had real reasons for not being able to work—some were single mothers who may not have had adequate childcare, while some other recipients were disabled. Last—and perhaps most important—companies were originally given a wage subsidy from the government to hire the welfare recipients on the condition the jobs would exist after the subsidy ended. More than half the companies did not follow this requirement. Thus, even if recipients had the right attitude there were other concrete factors that put limits on their ability to find employment.

the material world is primary, and that the mind or consciousness is a property of matter. Within the social sciences, materialism focuses on the primacy of external, objective phenomena rather than on internal, subjective ones. The opposite of materialism is **philosophical idealism**. Idealism assumes that mind, idea, or spirit is primary and is the basis for the material world.

It is important not to confuse the philosophical notion of materialism with the moral term materialistic, which refers to someone who lacks ideals or lofty goals but, rather, is interested in the satisfaction of material pleasures. The same confusion of philosophical idealism with the term idealistic must also be avoided. Adherents of philosophical materialism may have no difficulty in devoting themselves to noble causes or ideals, just as philosophical idealists may demonstrate a high degree of crass, materialistic behaviour.

Perhaps we can begin to understand materialism by using a concrete example. Suppose we want to discover what causes thunderstorms. One idealist explanation might be that thunderstorms are caused by the anger of the gods. Materialists, on the other hand, try to explain thunderstorms as being a result of natural or physical forces. In antiquity, materialists believed that thunderstorms were caused not by the anger of the gods, but rather by material particles banging together in the clouds. The materialist approach, which constitutes the basis of all science, does not guarantee that errors will not be committed. It is quite possible to be a materialist and be wrong, as can be seen in the ancient view of thunderstorms. In fact, science is full of errors, such as the Ptolemaic assumption, which endured for centuries, that Earth was the centre of the universe. Unlike idealism, however, philosophical materialism is open to constant testing by observation and experience through time for verification and validation. This, in fact, is the core underpinning of the scientific method.

Although all science is ultimately materialist in its analysis, we must be careful not to treat the material world in an overly mechanical fashion. Such was the case with Isaac Newton and the entire Newtonian framework for analysis and the early social scientists who drew on this model. Although they focused on the material world, theorists who adopted mechanical explanations saw the world as a strictly deterministic machine, governed by fixed laws. This simplistic view of the social world denies human agency. In the case described in Box 1.1, for example, it would be wrong to entirely exclude the attitudes of long-term welfare recipients as one part of a complex problem. Thus, for materialism to be truly useful, it must not be mechanical, but rather dialectical.

Science and Dialectics

The concept of **dialectics**, that change is a result of internal stresses, is an old one, going back as far as Heraclitus, approximately 2500 years ago. The ideas of Heraclitus did not reappear until the modern era. Karl Marx (1818–83) and Friedrich Engels (1820–95), drawing on the work of German philosopher Georg Wilhelm Friedrich Hegel (1770–1831) as well as new advances in the physical sciences, developed the modern concept of dialectics. The principles of dialectics are similar to many non-European world views that have also existed for thousands of years. They may be briefly listed as follows:

- Everything is related. Nothing in the universe is isolated, but, rather, all things are dependent on everything else. The particular nature of the relationship may be direct and significant or relatively indirect and less significant, but it is always there. It follows, therefore, that nothing can be understood in isolation.
- Change is constant. Nothing in the universe is final, absolute, eternal, perfect, and immutable. Everything is in the continual process of becoming and passing away. But the replacement of old forms by new ones always preserves the viable elements of the earlier form in the later one.
- Change proceeds from the quantitative to the qualitative. Generally, the way things change is gradual, with the relatively slow accumulation of modifications through time. At a certain point, these cumulative or quantitative changes achieve a radically different nature resulting in a distinctly new quality. An easy example is the bringing of water to the boil. If we start, at sea level, to heat water at 20 degrees Celsius, it will get hotter and hotter

through a gradual process (quantitative change). However, at 100 degrees, the water no longer simply gets hotter, it actually begins to convert to a different form of matter, a gas (qualitative change). This example also helps us understand that both types of change are necessary, but that one is the ultimate outcome of the other.

- Change is the result of the unity and struggle of opposites. Most of us are taught that things are either one thing or another: they are alive or dead, true or false, in motion or at rest, good or evil, and so on. Dialectics, on the other hand, emphasizes the unity of opposites—that is, things can embody within them two opposing tendencies at the same time. In other words, there are opposing tendencies within societies, and it is the tensions, or irresolvable contradictions, that can often become the basis for social change.

The last principle noted above is probably the most important for understanding our social world, yet also the most difficult to understand due to its abstract nature. This is because we tend to think in a linear, rather than dialectical, fashion, and we also tend to think that humans act in rational ways. In reality, humans—in seeking what they need or want—often end up with the very opposite of what they seek. For example, many people travel the world in search of places that are not popular tourist destinations. But such visits to out-of-the-way places have often done something none of these people intended: they have opened these places to the very tourism they detest. These contradictory tendencies are not uncommon in society; thinking dialectically helps us look for such complexities.

Think About It

Can you think of any other examples where an individual or group of individuals, in seeking what they need, may actually achieve the very opposite of what was intended?

If you have found the above sections explaining the concepts of dialectics and materialism difficult to grasp in the abstract, don't despair—these philosophical terms are, indeed, hard to understand except as they are applied to real situations. These terms will re-appear in later chapters of the book, so when you see these terms again, a quick re-reading of this section may help make these abstract concepts easier to comprehend.

Theories: Why Is There More Than One Explanation of Human Behaviour?

Most of us believe that the world is made up of "facts" that, like apples on a tree, are just waiting to be picked. Once we have a basketful of facts, we can put them all together into a coherent bundle known as "the truth." Since most of us accept such notions, it can be confusing to discover that there is more than one explanation, or theory, for the same set of phenomena. Put differently, there are a number of competing broad theoretical frameworks (sometimes called *paradigms*) that explain the same facts in different ways. Indeed, the theory used may even affect which facts get picked.

The term *theory* can be a confusing one, because in everyday language we often think of it as meaning "something that has not yet been proven." For example, if someone offers us a solution to a problem and we are not sure the proposal will work, we may say, "Well, that's a good idea, in theory." In the world of science, a theory starts out as a framework for analysis, a proposal to explain something observed in the world. But most often in science, a good theory already has sufficient supportive evidence (the "data") that we can consider it to have been proven. For example, although we still speak of Einstein's theory of relativity or Darwin's theory of evolution, the supportive evidence for these theories is so extensive that they may therefore be designated as true or factual. Of course, unlike religion, science never considers truth to be eternal or absolute; all notions of reality are able to be modified as new facts are discovered.

A simple analogy can help make sense of how science works. All of us have seen movies or television shows that have as the central plot a mystery or crime that needs to be solved. Let's imagine that a theft has occurred, and the police have to find the robber. First, they have to be materialists and find some clues. Once they have the data (in this case, the clues), they can hypothesize about who did it and build a theory to explain how the crime occurred. If the clues are good and they build their theory well, they are likely to find the perpetrator. This is exactly what science does—it constructs a hypothesis, gathers data to confirm or deny the hypothesis, and builds a theory to explain the data.

In the physical sciences, it is common for a single theory or explanatory framework to dominate until a better explanatory framework comes along. For example, it was long believed in medicine that stomach ulcers were primarily the result of stress. It wasn't until 1982 that an independent-thinking Australian physician offered a new explanation after he found a previously undetected bacterium, H. pylori, in tissue biopsies taken from people with ulcers. In this way, a new theory—drawing on new data—replaced a long-accepted one.

However, in the social sciences there are normally a number of theories competing with each other at the same time. This occurs for a number of reasons. First, societies are complex entities that are full of contradictory elements (see Figure 1.1). As a result, not everyone approaches society in the same way. Some sociologists try to focus on broad social or cultural phenomena, while others focus on personal social relationships. Some focus on the structures themselves, while others focus on human perceptions of the structures. Some focus on the elements that draw humans together, while others focus on the stresses that push them apart. Some focus on how society imposes on the individual, while others focus on how the individual imposes on society.

Second, as already noted, most of us already have strong feelings and opinions about the social world in a way that few of us have about, say, ulcers. As a

Figure 1.1 Contradictory Elements in Society

Stability — Change
Individual — Social Group
Social Structure — Human Agency
Sameness — Difference
Genetic Traits — Social Learning
Personal Relationships — Broader Social Institutions
Perceptions — Behaviour

result, we do not come to the study of the social world from a neutral place. From the outset, we all bring with us our past history and a membership in various social groups, such as our religion, gender, nationality, social class, and so on.

It should not be surprising, therefore, that there are many differing—and often competing—theoretical frameworks in sociology. But rather than simply trying to explain a single social phenomenon, most social theorists—like the philosophers in centuries past— also attempt to answer some of the "big" questions: Is this a just world? How did things get to be this way? Can the world be changed? What can we expect in the future? (Sears 2005, 30). At this point in the book, it is not necessary to describe the many theories in detail; for now, a general introduction will suffice. One of the themes that will be stressed throughout this book is that ideas both arise out of the social world and have consequences for it. So it is with the various sociological frameworks. The cartoon below can help us begin to make sense of this difficult proposition.

The cartoonist has taken an "iconic" image—that is, one commonly used to visually express an abstract concept, which in this case is social inequality—and

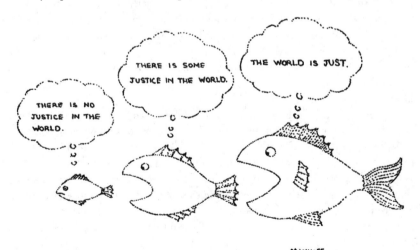

MANKOFF

made it humorous by giving the fish "human-like" moral thoughts about the justice of such inequality. However, the cartoon also has a key sociological idea embedded in it: how we see things is largely determined by our place in the world. Here structured inequality—a topic central to the field of sociology—is viewed differently depending on whether one is an eater or an eatee (the one in the middle, who is both, is, logically, ambivalent on the question).

In the human fishpond there are also different-sized fish; in other words, there are people who are situated in different places within the social structure or who identify with those situated in a place other than their own. Because all of us, including social scientists, are situated somewhere in the social structure, there can be no such thing as neutrality or unbiased social thought. (One of the fascinating questions that will be addressed later in this book is why so many human "little fish" hold the view that "the world is just.") To repeat a point made earlier, theories in sociology—as in all the sciences—have a bias, or a point of view. One of the key distinctions between schools of social thought is whether they see current social arrangements as just or unjust. We could say, then, that there are "big fish" theories, "middle-fish" theories, and "small-fish" theories. In the human fishpond, size matters.

Think About It
Which size "fish" do you think you are? Why?

The Major Sociological Frameworks

As already noted, the world of social theory can be overwhelming to the first-level student. To help us get our bearings, let us once again use the cartoon. In this hypothetical fishpond, it is easy to see that the big fish have a better situation than the small ones; as a result, they are more likely to be happy with the present scheme of things. In contrast, the small fish are more likely to be dissatisfied with the current situation and desirous of changing it (so as not to get eaten). As for the middle fish, it is likely that their commitment to the current arrangements would depend on whether, at any given moment, they are about to devour a little fish or are about to get eaten.

Earlier on we explained that societies are simultaneously ordered and changing; therefore all social theories address, at least to some extent, both the orderliness of the social world and the way it changes over time. However, if these cartoon fish were actually able to study and analyze their fishy world, it would make sense that the big fish would be interested primarily in explanations that helped maintain the arrangement in the fishpond. We might refer to these as **order theories**, since they would focus on and support the current order of things. On the other hand, the theories of the little fish would be more likely to highlight the lack of justice in the current arrangements and the ways the little fish lose out in the present situation. These theories would focus on how things have changed in the past and ways they might change in the future. Because the little fish would benefit from an alteration of the status quo, we might refer to such explanations as **change theories**.[1]

Whether acknowledged or not, all social theories either support the present social arrangements or advocate changing them. This doesn't mean that only "big fish" in human society (exactly who they are will be explained in a later chapter) actually think up the order theories themselves, and only "small fish" think up change theories. In other words, we need not be concerned with the social position of the individuals who actually develop or promote a particular analysis (we seldom know this in any case); rather, we need to assess whether a particular theory ultimately supports the present social arrangements or advocates changing them.

It is much easier for students to identify change theories than order theories. This is, in part, because we tend to notice those views that differ from our own, and change theories are not well known outside of academia in North America. All change theories are, in one way or another, informed by the ideas of Karl Marx. Marx's analysis should not be viewed as his alone. Although the name Marx and the term Marxism are often thought to reflect a single individual's ideas, they should more correctly be thought of as representing a school of thought that first developed in the mid-nineteenth century. In particular, Friedrich Engels should always be remembered when we discuss the ideas of Marx. Indeed, many of the writings often considered to be the core Marxist texts were actually written by both Marx and Engels.

Although it is sometimes thought that the downfall of most twentieth-century communist governments meant the end of Marxist thought, the ideas of Marx and Engels continue to permeate much social analysis, even among those who dispute their arguments. In fact, it has been said that most social thought of the twentieth century was little more than a debate with the ghost of Marx. Marx was not a sociologist in the official sense of the term. Indeed, since the sociology of Marx's time was fairly conservative, he would have strongly objected to this categorization. In reality, Marx was at once a historian, philosopher, social agitator, political economist, and sociologist. One writer (Collins 1994, 56) feels that it was Engels who was the more sociological writer of the two and who, in many ways, made the more lasting and solid contributions to social analysis.

> Far from being buried under the rubble of the Berlin Wall, Marx may only now be emerging in his true significance. He could yet become the most influential thinker of the twenty-first century.
> —Francis Wheen, British biographer of Marx

Like other thinkers in late nineteenth-century Europe, Marx was surrounded by a world in rapid and tumultuous social, political, and economic change. But

---

1. I have selected the word *change* because it allows readers to not prejudge either approach on the basis of name alone. Change theories are usually referred to in sociology as either conflict theories or critical theories. The problem with these terms is that both the words *conflict* and *critical* have negative connotations, while, the word *order* generally has a positive connotation.

Box 1.2 Is Our Behaviour Determined?

In order for social scientists to distinguish one theoretical approach from another and to evaluate each theory, they are given names. Sometimes the theorist chooses the name, but most often it is others who choose a name for a group of theories that share the same general approach. Sometimes the names of theoretical frameworks can get very confusing. The most straightforward frameworks are commonly referred to as *determinist* theories. These theories— or so it is argued—see a single variable as the overarching explanation to understand human behaviour; in other words, one key element determines how humans behave.

In Chapter 2, *biological determinism* is discussed. Many writers over a long span of time have written from this perspective. What they share is the view that human behaviour is primarily the result of some biological or genetic trait. The opposite of biological determinism is *cultural determinism*. These theories argue that how we behave is determined not by our biology but rather by our cul-tural and social environment. Biological determinists see human behaviour as totally the result of "nature," while cultural determinists see human behaviour as totally the result of "nurture."

Economic determinism sees all aspects of human societies—that is, the various social institutions and cultural compo-nents—as being mechanically deter-mined by the economic arrangements of that society. Karl Marx is sometimes criticized for being an economic deter-minist, although in reality his analysis was more complex than this and he fought these criticisms when he was alive. Theories that put undue emphasis on inventions and technology to explain societies and social change are referred to as *technological determinism*.

All these theories have some appeal because of their simplicity of explana-tion. In the end, however, all determinist theories are flawed in that they are not dialectical; in other words, they fail to appreciate the complexities of human social and cultural life.

---

while most of the thinkers of that period were, like the big fish, trying either to justify and maintain the social world of that period or to alter it in minor ways, Marx identified his interests with the "little fish." Thus, he tried to demonstrate how the entire social system would eventually be transformed. Moreover, while most social theory of the time placed emphasis on the world of ideas, thoughts, and feelings, Marx gave prominence to the material basis for human behaviour, primarily the economic conditions of people's lives. The general framework that draws on Marxist notions is often referred to as the *political economy* approach to sociology. In recent years others, including some feminist and anti-racist theorists, have expanded on nineteenth-century Marxist notions, making the analysis more relevant to today's world.

Order theories are harder for students to identify, not only because they seem more neutral or familiar, but also because there are so many different approaches. All such theories, however, help maintain the present social arrangements. One of the most clear-cut is that of **biological determinism**, which will be examined more closely in Chapter 2. Biological determinist theories locate the key to explaining human behaviour in some aspect of human physiology, such as anatomy, hormones, or genes. If a human behaviour is biologically based, it cannot easily be changed. It should be noted that biological determinist theories are not strictly sociological theories (they are most commonly developed by psychologists), but they find their way into all the social sciences and into the popular press as well.

Probably the best known of the order theories within the sociological tradition is that known as **functionalism**, or **structural functionalism**. This school of thought had its roots in the early sociology of Auguste Comte, Herbert Spencer, and Émile Durkheim, and became widely accepted in North American sociology following World War II and right up until the 1970s. Talcott Parsons (1902–79), an American, was probably the best-known structural functionalist of that period. Functionalist theories, to simplify somewhat, analyze the function of various elements that exist within a society. For example, it could be argued that war is functional to a society because it fuels the economy, provides employment to many young people, and unites the population against a common enemy. While such an analysis can be useful, it can also lead to the unfortunate conclusion that anything that serves a social function—as in the case of war—must be an inevitable part of that society.

There are numerous other order theories, but for the purposes of this general introduction it is not necessary to detail them at this point. The hardest of the order theories to understand are those that promote some changes to our social world, but seek only readjustments within the same basic structural arrangements. These are essentially "middle fish" theories, which argue that "there is some justice in the world." These and other theoretical approaches will be introduced and expanded upon in later chapters.

Up to this point, only theories that are generally subsumed under the term **macrosociology** have been addressed. These theories focus on the ways individual human behaviour is influenced by the broader society; that is, they concentrate on analyzing social structures. In contrast to this approach is **microsociology**, which focuses primarily on the way individual behaviour and perceptions influence society. For those sociologists who utilize this approach, human agency is primary.

Macro- and microsociology are not necessarily in opposition to each other but, rather, are two different ways of looking at social phenomena. For example, suppose we want to examine social inequality in Canadian society. Both macro- and microsociologists might be interested in this issue. Microsociologists would be interested in the "person to person" ways that inequality is maintained—for example, how forms of communication are used to signify inequalities. They would be interested in power relations primarily at the proximal level. Macrosociologists, in contrast, are more interested in the "big picture": what are the origins of inequality, and how is it maintained or eroded over time? These theorists are generally more interested in examining broad questions of distal power and control within societies as a whole. As a result, change theorists are more often connected with the macrosociological approach.

It should not be surprising that different theoretical frameworks view power in different ways. If we think of that fishpond again, it makes sense that the last thing the big fish want the other fish to know is how big they are and how much power they have. Hence, the order theories do not generally focus on the nature of power in societies or how it is unequally distributed. In contrast, change theories place more emphasis on the allocation of power in society. This is because little fish can only benefit from making other little fish aware of how little power they have relative to the big fish in the fishpond. It might be said that one of the greatest legacies of Marx is the attention he draws to the issue of distal power within societies—who has it, how they get and maintain it, who lacks it, and how those who lack it ultimately struggle to change the distal relationships of power.

However, as with our earlier discussion of society, we must be careful not to oversimplify. In the real world of theory building, things are often not clear-cut. While the various change theories address the issue of power, there are disagreements about the basis of power inequalities and the direction for change. Moreover, while all change theories may draw on Marxist theory, there can be strong disagreements among them. On the other hand, some order theories do address the issue of power and change, although they may not construct as overarching a framework as Marx's.

The Boundaries of Sociology

To this point we have been discussing sociology as if it were a well-defined discipline that can be distinguished from other disciplines. To some extent this is true: sociology has its own distinctive history, founders, theoreticians, and body of knowledge. Yet the boundaries between the various areas within the humanities and social sciences are not as clear-cut as they may at first appear. This is as it should be, because, of course, the real world is not one that is sectioned off into discrete units. Suppose you just got refused a student loan. Is that a psychological, sociological, economic, philosophical, or political issue? Depending on one's point of view, it could be any or all of them.

Although we separate elements of the physical or social world into component parts to study them, the fields of study must always be seen as somewhat arbitrary and overlapping. This book will offer a different approach than what is usually offered to first-level students. Sociology, particularly in North America, has focused to a great extent on proximal relationships, rather than on distal sources of power and broader social arrangements. In contrast to more traditional approaches, this book will venture into the spheres of genetics, anthropology, philosophy, politics, economics, and history.

A brief historic overview of human life will dominate the next three chapters. The purpose here is not to detail particular events, something that is better left to historians or anthropologists. For sociologists, looking at the broad sweep of human history allows us to find patterns—of human behaviour, of social institutions, and of social change. This helps us both make sense of current arrangements and predict what may happen to societies in future.

Conclusion

This chapter has introduced some of the many challenges sociologists face when we try to study this complex thing we call society—that is, humans living together in social groups. Like all sciences, sociology tries to find patterns in observable behaviour. However, compared to the physical sciences, social scientists have to deal with the additional complexity of studying something to which we all have strong emotional attachments. As noted in this chapter, there is no such thing as totally unbiased science. Nonetheless, sociologists must still provide concrete, reliable evidence to support or refute particular theoretical constructs and use reasonable methods to draw their conclusions.

We have seen that although there are a great many different explanatory frameworks within the social sciences, they can, in the end, all be described as order theories or change theories. The order theories, or "big fish" theories, work within the notion that "the world is just," while the change theories of the "small fish" focus on structures of power and the lack of justice in the world. We must always recall that the field of sociology is rooted in a period of intellectual curiosity and open-minded scientific investigation. Most social scientists— regardless of their theoretical approach—hope that a rational analysis of the social world will in some small way make it a better place.

> Sociology goes beyond the obvious; it asks questions when most people do not.
> —Joel Charon, *Ten Questions: A Sociological Perspective*

> …just as the whole is always more than the sum of the parts, so the amassing of small truths about the various parts and aspects of society can never yield the big truths about the social order itself—how it got to be, what it is, what it does to those who live under it, and the directions in which it is moving. These big truths must be pursued in their own right and for their own sake.
> —Paul A. Baran and Paul M. Sweezy, *Monopoly Capital*

As noted earlier in this chapter, sociology is meant to shake us up. Using primarily a change theory approach, this book will examine some of the "big" questions in the field: What does it mean to be human? How is our society organized? Why are there various forms of social inequality? Where do we fit in the global economy? How do societies change? Where are we headed? Drawing on the vision of C. Wright Mills, this book will try to help students understand the relationship between their personal problems and the wider society. The issues of culture, of society, of power, and of social change become relevant only if we can connect them with our daily life experiences. And we can hope to solve our personal problems only if we can place them within broader social institutions and structures of power.

Key Points

1. Sociology is the systematic study of human society and the behaviour of people in society. Analyzing our social world can sometimes be a difficult task because students not only have strong feelings about many topics, but also often feel they are already well informed about them.

2. Human behaviour is affected by a social world that imposes itself on us whether or not we are aware of it. However, although a society may impose itself on human behaviour, it must also be noted that societies are created and altered by humans.

3. In order to survive, people have to organize themselves into some kind of structure, and they have to construct rules of behaviour. Once they come into being, these structures can exist for very long periods of time. One key goal of sociology, then, is to systematically study and analyze the various elements that constitute a society's structure, and the relationships among these elements.

4. Society can be understood both as an ordered system, made up of identifiable cultural components and social institutions, and as an entity that is constantly changing.

5. The concept of power is central to understanding how societies work. All of us are affected by both proximal and distal relations of power. However, although distal relations of power may have more serious and negative consequences for our lives, they are very hard for us to see and oppose.

6. Although humans act in patterned ways that can be studied by social scientists, there is always room for human agency.

7. Society can be a constraining force on the individual, but it can also be a liberating force. The commonly shared rules of our social world allow us to function in our daily lives, because assuming that most people will act as they should reduces our level of insecurity and allows us to get on with our lives.

8. The roots of modern sociology lie in nineteenth-century Europe and are linked to the growth of science in the preceding few centuries. From the outset, there was a tension in sociology about the ultimate use of social analysis.

9. All knowledge has a bias embedded in it, and human understanding will be affected by where we sit in the social universe. Nonetheless, sociology must satisfy the rigours of scientific investigation by providing concrete evidence to support or refute theoretical constructs.

10. Philosophical materialism and dialectics can help us make sense of our social world by offering a basic set of tools we can use in social analysis.

11. The two major approaches in the social sciences are the order theories and the change theories. The former tend to support the status quo, while the latter try to alter it.

12. Although sociology is a distinct discipline, the boundaries between the various areas within the humanities and social sciences are not clear-cut.

Further Reading

Babbie, Earl. 2006. *The Practice of Social Research*. 11th ed. Belmont, CA: Wadsworth.
A thorough introduction to the research methods used by social scientists.

Charon, Joel M. 2007. *Ten Questions: A Sociological Perspective*. 6th ed. Belmont, CA: Thomson Wadsworth.
An easy-to-read introduction to basic questions in sociology by an American sociologist.

Collins, Randall, and Michael Makowsky. 2004. *The Discovery of Society*. 7th ed. Boston: McGraw-Hill.
A useful exploration of the main ideas and analysts who have shaped modern sociology, from the perspective of two U.S. sociologists.

Mills, C. Wright. 1967. *The Sociological Imagination*. New York: Oxford University Press.
A classic work by an American sociologist.

Morrison, Ken. 2006. *Marx, Durkheim, Weber: Formations of Modern Social Thought*. Revised edition. Thousand Oaks, CA: Sage.
An in-depth look at the key ideas of three authors whose works are the base of the classical tradition in sociological theory.

Sears, Alan. 2005. *A Good Book, In Theory: A Guide to Theoretical Thinking*. Peterborough, ON: Broadview.
Students often have a hard time grasping the concept of what constitutes a theory. This book offers a very accessible introduction to thinking theoretically.

Smail, David. 1999. *The Origins of Unhappiness: A New Understanding of Personal Distress*. London: Constable.
Written by a psychologist, this book argues that what appear to be forms of mental distress are the result of social factors. Particular emphasis is placed on the growing power of business over our culture.

2 Is Human Behaviour the Result of Our Biology?

In This Chapter

- Is there such a thing as "human nature"?
- Why are theories that see human behaviour as determined mainly by our genes so popular?
- What is the process of evolution and where do humans fit in?
- What makes us unique in the animal world?

When I introduce this chapter to students in a classroom setting, I always start with a fable. In this made-up story, I ask them to imagine two unrelated infant children—a baby boy and a baby girl—being washed up on a deserted island after a cruise ship sinks. Through an amazing set of circumstances they survive and grow. I then ask my students the following question: When they reach puberty, will these two young people mate? I have asked this question over many years. Without fail, I can be certain that the majority in every class will answer that, yes, absolutely, they will mate. When explaining why, the answer they give is always the same. They will mate, according to most students, because to do so is "instinctive," "just natural," or "human nature."

My students are not unique in responding this way. Humans have always speculated about why we do what we do, and my students' approach is one of the most common ways of explaining a human behaviour. Today the mass media frequently reinforce our belief in inborn patterns by telling us that such diverse human characteristics as sexual preference, intelligence, emotions, and behaviours such as aggression, male dominance, criminality, alcoholism, or even celebrity worship may all be genetically determined. These sorts of explanations, introduced in Chapter 1, are collectively referred to by social scientists as *biological determinism*.

Before we can proceed with an analysis of our social world, it is essential to examine whether such explanations are valid. If we accept that certain behaviours are determined by our biology, then we must accept that we cannot change them. Thus, if we argue that many of the social problems facing us today—such as war, social inequality, and criminality—are rooted in a biologically based human nature, then our ability to eliminate them is out of the question. On the other hand, if we determine that the social world is created by humans in the process of living with each other, then the possibility of altering our world becomes a possibility.

Almost all social scientists agree that humans are not born as "blank slates" capable of any behaviour under the right conditions. We, like all animal species, *are* biological entities, and our behaviour must therefore be, to some extent, limited by both our genetic matter and physical capabilities. No matter how hard we try, for example, humans cannot become airborne without the aid of technological devices, nor can we stay underwater for extended periods of time. We are not constructed to run like a gazelle or swing from trees like a gibbon. But are we "hard-wired" to act human? Can scientists identify specific behaviours that are, as most biological determinists argue, solely or predominantly the result of our genetic make-up? Is there such a thing as a human nature?

One important clue that biological determinist explanations of human behaviour have their limitations is the diversity of human social organization and behaviours. Anthropologists have undertaken field studies of many societies, and their summaries, referred to as *ethnographies*, have described many forms of human social organization and culture. Of course, in the major cities of Canada, where there are people who have arrived from every part of the globe, most of us can observe this diversity on a daily basis. Such variations in human societies—over time and across cultures—call into question the argument that our behaviour can be explained as simply the result of biology. On the other hand, there are certain similarities among all cultures. Therefore, before we can reject biological determinist arguments, we need to examine them in more detail.

Do Humans Have Instincts?

Let's begin with the argument made by my students that the fictional young boy and girl on the island would naturally have sex because it is instinctive for them to do so. An **instinct** is an inborn complex pattern of behaviour that must normally exist in every member of the species and, because it is embedded in the genetic code, cannot be overcome by force of will. It should be distinguished from a *reflex*, which is a simple response of an organism to a specific stimulus, such as the contraction of the pupil in response to bright light or the spasmodic movement of the lower leg when the knee is tapped. Instincts, in contrast, are complex sequential stimulus-response patterns; such behaviours can be easily identified in non-human animals and have been extensively studied by zoologists and biologists.

Could it be possible that at least some basic elements of human behaviour are universal and therefore must be instinctive or natural? Is there a "sex instinct"? What about the "survival instinct" or the "maternal instinct" that are so often spoken of in everyday conversations? We may all eat different foods, but we do all eat, so isn't eating instinctive? It is certainly true that, as living things, humans have a number of basic requirements: in order for our species to physically survive, we must ingest food and water and excrete wastes, we must spend some time at rest, and at least some of our species must reproduce.

But while these are general tendencies in all living things, it would be overly simplistic to speak of these as natural or instinctive. A moment's thought reveals many examples of behaviours that contradict these supposedly universal tendencies. If survival is a human instinct, how do we explain suicide? Likewise, how can we make sense of those who go on hunger strikes for a cause and refuse to eat? And if women have a maternal instinct, how is it possible that many women today consciously choose not to have children, or that some women give up their children for adoption?

Let us return to the fable about the two infants that began this chapter. Would the two infants in fact mate? When I use this story with my students, I tell it two more times, but with slight variations. The second fable is of two babies washed up on a deserted island, but this time they are brother and sister. The students become more hesitant about the sexual activity of these two. The third time, the story has both children being males. Now there is a really serious debate in the class about what will happen. What at first seemed "just natural" is, in fact, not at all easy to determine.

If we look at sexuality in our species, we find an enormous range of possibilities. Some of us prefer members of our own sex, some prefer members of the opposite sex, some prefer self-stimulation, some are turned on by inanimate objects, and some prefer animals of one sort or another. Some people have sex as frequently as possible, while others are interested in having sex only occasionally. Some of our species engage in sexual acts only after they have been legally or religiously sanctioned through marriage, while others have sex only outside of marriage. Some people, for religious, political, or personal reasons, decide not to have an active sex life at all.

In addition, a moment's thought tells us that we don't actually have sex every time we feel the biological urge. Thus, while it can be assumed that everyone (or almost everyone) at your college or university has sexual feelings—and many may be thinking sexual thoughts all day long—there aren't masses of students and faculty having sex all over the campus. In order to live together, humans had to bring such "natural" urges under social control.

The notion of a natural sex drive or a sex instinct that mechanically leads to a behavioural outcome does not adequately explain sexual behaviour in our species. The same can be said of other behaviours commonly deemed to be "just natural." The key question, then, is not whether we have universal, inborn tendencies; rather, it is how members of a species, all bringing with them the same basic genetic matter, end up displaying a variety of behavioural outcomes. No other species displays this kind of diversity.

Humans are *of* the animal world, but unique within it. Only humans have the ability to alter nature in complex ways and to transmit, through language, new ideas and accumulated knowledge through generations. This makes us the most flexible and adaptable of all species. We are the only species capable of conscious thought and abstract reasoning, able to look back on the past and plan for the future. Whatever genetic push exists in our species toward certain types of behaviour is highly generalized. In other words, while all members of our species may carry genes with a tendency to push behaviour in certain directions, there nonetheless remains a range of possible behavioural outcomes.

Because it is so much a part of our common-sense understanding of human behaviour, many of us have a problem giving up the notion of human instincts. Sometimes it is argued that, while we all have certain instincts, we are able, under particular conditions, to reject or repress them. Thus, in this line of reasoning, students don't have sex every time they feel the urge because they have learned to repress their feelings; it would be socially embarrassing if they didn't. Similarly, some might argue that a man who takes his own life has successfully repressed his survival instinct, or a woman who gives up a child for adoption has repressed her maternal instinct.

The problem with such arguments is that they simultaneously explain everything and nothing. If we can overcome our nature or instincts by force of will, how do we know which behaviours are the instincts and which the rejection of the instincts? How do we know we don't have a jumping-up-and-down-stark-naked-and-shrieking instinct that we have all repressed because it is so embarrassing? Or perhaps we all have a nose-picking instinct, which most of us repress because it is so disgusting. But late at night, while we're alone studying and there's no one around, out pops the instinct!

Arguments that focus on the centrality of human instincts are an example of biological determinist explanations of human behaviour. In the end, focusing on the biological *alone* is neither useful nor adequate in explaining human behaviour. That is not to say that there is no biological or genetic component to human behaviour; this is as false and simplistic as the opposite argument. As previously noted, humans *are* biological beings and do bring with them at birth a range of potentials, both at the level of our species and as individuals. Unfortunately, only some of us have the capacity to become a talented pianist, a brilliant scientist, or an amazing hockey player. If we think dialectically, we can appreciate that human behaviours are the result of a complex interplay of biological elements and social learning, with each feeding back on and altering the other in a never-ending process.

Think About It

Can you think of human behaviours not mentioned here that are frequently said to be "just natural"? Why do you think this is such a common explanation?

The Popularity of Biological Determinist Arguments

Sociologists study not only human behaviour, but human ideas as well. One fascinating question is why ideas retain their popularity even when proof of their legitimacy is weak or absent entirely. For example, it is interesting to ask why so many people read their horoscopes when there is no substantive evidence to

Box 2.1 Can We Identify Criminals by Their Appearance?

Many years ago, a friend told me the following story: One afternoon he visited an acquaintance and was returning home on his bicycle. Suddenly a police car pulled up in front of him. He was told to get off his bike, was thrown against the police car, and had his arm twisted behind his back. He was held in this uncomfortable position while the police asked him many questions about where he had been and where he was going. After holding him for some time, they let him go. As a university graduate and government employee, he was furious about the way he had been treated. The next day he called his local police station to complain and insisted he be told why he had been stopped. The police officer eventually explained that there had been a theft of some musical equipment in the neighbourhood, and he fit the description of the thief. He was a Black male.

Although almost all policing agencies deny that there is such a thing as racial profiling, most people of colour have experienced it. The term "Driving while Black" is a term used, with humour, to describe the "crime" that seems to result in many people of colour being pulled over by police officers when they are in their cars. Racial profiling means that people get targeted on the basis of perceived membership in a group associated with particular stereotypes rather than anything they have done (Sears 2005, 79). Following the destruction of the World Trade Center in 2001, the tendency for policing agencies to engage in racial profiling increased. People who fit some vague stereotypic description of a "terrorist" because of their country of origin or particular physical characteristics such as dark skin might find themselves stopped for questioning by security officials, unable to fly on an airplane, refused entry into a country, or even arrested.

support the validity of astrological predictions. Likewise, the question arises as to why biological determinist theories keep reappearing—not only in the popular press, but also within social science itself—even though such approaches have long been discredited. Again and again these theories have been critiqued for their shoddy science (see, for example, Richardson and Spears 1972; Montagu 1975; Chase 1977; Blum 1978; Lawlor 1978; Gould 1981; Lewontin et al. 1984; Mensh and Mensh 1991; Hubbard and Wald 1993; Lewontin 2001). What will be argued here is that these theories remain popular not because of their academic credibility, but rather because they help maintain the belief that our current social arrangements are unchangeable.

Among the earliest theorists to formulate a biological explanation of human behaviour was Cesare Lombroso, an Italian physician who, in the late nineteenth century, argued that criminals could be identified by certain physiological characteristics. According to Lombroso, certain body markers reflected the fact that "born criminals" were evolutionary throwbacks to our apelike past. As a result, Lombroso felt criminals would display this apishness not only in their behaviour but also in their appearance. Among the characteristics Lombroso thought were identifying characteristics of a criminal were a large jaw, relatively long arms, large ears, absence of baldness, darker skin, and the inability to blush. He even argued that one could identify prostitutes by their feet, which he thought were similar to apes, with the big toe widely separated from the others. Lombroso also saw some social traits as markers for criminality. It is rather humorous to note—given today's fashion—that Lombroso identified tattoos as one such marker (Gould 1981, 125–32).

While today we may laugh at the silliness of Lombroso's theory, it was taken quite seriously in its day, and Lombroso was often called in as an expert at criminal trials. Many individuals were convicted of crimes solely on the basis of Lombroso's testimony that they must be guilty since they *looked* like a criminal. Moreover, while Lombroso's theory may have been analytically simplistic, the basic assumptions of these arguments have not changed in more than a hundred years (see Box 2.1).

A recurring theme of biological determinist arguments is that social inequality is based on underlying biological differences. As a result, according to these arguments, since social inequalities are the result of individual differences that are innate, then clearly little can be done to eliminate the inequalities.

As we shall see in the next chapter, structured social inequality developed around seven to ten thousand years ago, and we can assume that there have been explanations for this inequality as long as it has existed. Prior to the modern industrial age, however, there was little expectation that there should be, or could be, equality for all. Certainly, disadvantaged groups opposed—often violently—their conditions of life. What they were generally demanding, though, were material improvements to those conditions (Lewontin 2001, 199). In contrast, the industrial era, as we shall see in the next few chapters, offered its citizenry the possibility of social equality. The great rallying cry of the French Revolution was "Liberty, Equality, Fraternity." The founding Constitution of the United States argued that "all men are created equal…." Of course, the slogans seldom fit with reality. While some people did improve their lot, most social inequality continued as before, often—as in the case of slavery—with horrific consequences.

Think About It
Biological determinist arguments began to expand at the end of the nineteenth century, primarily in the United States and Great Britain. This was shortly after slavery was abolished in both countries. What might be the link between these two developments?

By the second half of the nineteenth century, theorists began to use the developing tools of science to "prove" that structured inequalities were the result of natural biological differences between populations. Darwin's *Origin of Species*, published in 1859, provided a key analytical framework. The core of Darwin's argument revolved around the competition for survival that existed in nature. Although this work did not actually deal with our species, others concluded that, since we are part of the natural world, the competition between individuals and groups in human society must also be a biological given. Thus, some theorists explained social inequalities by arguing, as did financier John D. Rockefeller, that the richest and most powerful in any society were meant to succeed because they were most "fit"; social inequality was simply the working out of the laws of nature. Such arguments came to be known collectively as **social Darwinism**. It is worth noting that the phrase "survival of the fittest" was not coined by Darwin, as is usually assumed, but rather by Herbert Spencer, a British sociologist considered to be one of the "founding fathers" of the discipline and an early social Darwinist.

In addition to a focus on social inequality, a second underlying theme of biological determinism has been that human aggression, competition, and territoriality have a biological basis. These arguments were particularly popular in the immediate post–World War II period and were promoted by writers such as Konrad Lorenz, Robert Ardrey, Desmond Morris, and Raymond Dart. This theme can also be seen in William Golding's still-popular novel *Lord of the Flies*, about a group of British schoolboys marooned on a deserted island. Removed from the social constraints of "civilization," their "true" bestial and predatory natures, previously held in check, come out into the open.

Both the notion that inequality is the result of individual characteristics and the belief that aggression and territoriality are innate help to justify the world as it is currently structured. As all of us know, we live in a world of war, extreme social inequalities, and widespread poverty. Biological determinist arguments are "big fish" theories that argue "the world is just" by drawing our attention away from any possible social roots of human behaviour.

From Theory to Practice: The Eugenics Movement

Biological determinist arguments are not simply incorrect; they are dangerous, for they have actually been put into practice in the form of **eugenics** (from the Greek word meaning "well-born"). An examination of eugenics helps us see that social theories are not just abstract thoughts developed by professors in ivory towers; rather, theories are often used by social groups to further their aims. Eugenics started as a theory, shifted to a social movement, and later became government policy in many countries, including Canada and the United States. The argument went this way: If certain human behavioural traits are inherited, and if some of these traits are deemed by a society as negative, then it is a simple enough task to "improve" the species. For eugenicists, if adults display characteristics thought to be hereditary handicaps, such individuals should simply be sterilized. This argument was first developed in the late nineteenth century by Francis Galton, Charles Darwin's cousin.

It is not hard to see that this is a slippery slope with no end: characteristics are simply assumed to be genetically based, and the number of characteristics deemed to be inferior continually expands. For example, the Model Eugenical Sterilization Law drawn up in the United States in 1922 advocated the compulsory sterilization of all people judged to be members of the "socially inadequate classes"; these included all those with physical or mental disabilities (including epilepsy, blindness, and deafness), alcoholics, the "criminalistic," and the "dependent (including orphans, ne'er-do-wells, the homeless, tramps and paupers)" (quoted in Chase 1977, 134). While few governments actually went as far as sterilizing all these people, sterilization on the basis of criminality, epilepsy, and what was then termed "feeblemindedness" was fairly common.

In Canada, both British Columbia and Alberta passed legislation allowing for the sterilization of the "feebleminded" and the setting up of eugenics boards. Most of the victims were foster children or had been raised in institutions. Elsewhere in Canada, eugenical arguments were widely promulgated. For example, in 1935, Agnes Macphail, Canada's first woman member of Parliament, argued at a meeting of United Farm Women that it was immoral to allow "defectives" to breed (McLaren 1990, 121). After a royal commission in Ontario in 1930 recommended sterilization legislation, the province's lieutenant-governor warned of the "alarming consequences if idiots are permitted to procreate their kind" (quoted in Henton 1996).

Once one has accepted such arguments, it becomes possible to move to the next step. If characteristics are both inferior and genetically based, sterilization may not be adequate. Some individuals may escape the process and continue to "contaminate" the population. To prevent this from happening, some eugenicists argued that such inferior types should be eliminated, for their own good and the good of society. Today most of us recognize such an argument as the one adopted in Nazi Germany. Indeed, evidence detailing the horrific outcome of such theories largely discredited the eugenics movement for a long time after World War II.

However, eugenical arguments tend to reappear from time to time, albeit with some attempt to distance them from Hitler's supposed misapplication of eugenical notions. For example, in the November 1994 newsletter for Mensa, an organization for people with high IQ test scores, one author suggested that "society must face the concept that we kill off the old, weak, the stupid and the inefficient," while another proposed that most of the homeless "should be done away with, like abandoned kittens" (*Toronto Star* 11 January 1995).

> The growth of a large business is merely a survival of the fittest.... The American Beauty rose can be produced in the splendor and fragrance which bring cheer to its beholder only by sacrificing the early buds which grow up around it. This is not an evil tendency in business. It is merely the working-out of a law of nature and a law of God.
> —American financier John D. Rockefeller, 1902

> Natural Selection, otherwise known as the Rotman [School of Business] Admission Process: Species in the wild constantly find themselves in a struggle for survival. And candidates eager to join the Rotman School are no different. The competition promises to be fiercer than ever....
> —advertisement for the Rotman School of Business, University of Toronto, 2002

Box 2.2 Eugenics in Alberta

Leilani Muir spent most of her childhood living in foster homes. In 1955, when she was ten, she entered Alberta's Provincial Training School for Mental Defectives. The following year, based on the results of an IQ test and a short interview, the Alberta Eugenics Board labelled her a "moron" and approved her for sterilization. When she was fourteen she was told that her appendix was to be removed. During the operation, the surgeons—without informing her—also cut her fallopian tubes, preventing her from ever having children.

She married at twenty-five and tried to start a family. Only later did she discover why she was unable to become preg-nant. She and her husband were later divorced.

More than 2800 people in Alberta were sterilized between 1928 and 1972 before the Sexual Sterilization Act was finally repealed. In 1996, Muir and her lawyers brought her case before the Alberta Provincial Court. She was awarded $740,000 for wrongful sterilization and wrongful confinement. Over 1200 of the victims eventually brought similar suits against the Alberta government.

Sources: Alberta Online Encyclopedia; Brian Laghi, "Childless Adults Want Compensation in Alberta," *Globe and Mail*, 15 January 1996.

Genetics and "Inherited Tendencies"

The early biological determinist arguments have now been replaced by arguments focusing on genetics, with its underlying assumptions that a large proportion of human anatomy, physiology, and behaviour is "controlled" or "determined" by our genes (Lewontin 2001, 205). Thus—it is commonly believed—the Human Genome Project, a major project by geneticists to map the sequencing of DNA in the human organism, will allow scientists to "improve" individuals and societies in a way that the eugenicists never imagined.

However, even though a characteristic may be *heritable*—that is, passed on through the genes—it is still possible that the physical or social environment can have an effect on it. For example, although both body shape and height are highly heritable traits, they can nonetheless be affected by diet, general health, lifestyle habits, and so on. Obesity is a growing phenomenon around the world even though our genetic make-up has remained essentially the same. Likewise, a person may inherit a genetic predisposition toward cancer, but whether a person actually develops the disease will depend on many other factors, including some that have nothing to do with genetics, such as stress, diet, socioeconomic status, and contact with carcinogens. What is even more fascinating, evidence indicates that one's health may be related to broader social variables that are not "inside" the individual at all. For example, one economist (Chernomas 1999) discovered that the degree of inequality in a society had an effect on the overall health of a population, even for those who weren't poor.

The issues become even more complicated when we analyze behaviour rather than physiology. What does it mean to define someone as "mentally defective," "criminalistic," or "alcoholic"? Such categories are not scientifically precise; they are socially created and subjectively determined. In addition, it is simply impossible to separate out the genetic component of a particular behaviour, since the genes themselves are in constant interaction with their environment. There are simply so many possible environmental influences and such a complex interplay between environmental and inherited factors that a simplistic "cause" of the condition is impossible to detect (Hubbard and Wald 1993, 103).

Those who are identical twins, or those who know them, will agree that genetically matched individuals do not grow up to become identical people. While the number of shared traits of such individuals is greater than that of non-related individuals or even non-identical twins, identical twins are by no means a mirror image of each other, even with regard to illnesses known to be genetically transmitted. Clearly, genetics alone does not mechanically determine human characteristics. Put somewhat differently, both "nature" and "nurture" make us who we are.

Recent revelations from the Human Genome Project and the decades of research that preceded it have helped us understand that human behaviour is more complicated than the biological determinists would have us believe. The latest genetic research seems to show that our genes are not fixed and unchangeable, but rather are themselves affected by their environments, beginning in the womb (Ridley 2003, 34). Thus, modern genetics is demonstrating what most sociologists have long argued: human behaviour is the result of a complex interaction between inherited traits and social learning.

Despite growing questions about biological determinist explanations of human behaviour, such theories remain very popular. This is partially explained by the fact that such arguments are both simple and, on the surface, appear to be self-evident. For example, some might argue that although governments have spent millions of dollars trying to help the worst off in our society and to eliminate crime and gross social inequalities, crime and social inequality continue to exist. The conclusion might therefore be that the causes of crime and poverty must lie within the individual. Such arguments allow us to acknowledge social problems without having to consider the possibility of any type of social transformation. If poverty is the result of low intelligence, or criminality of a genetic predisposition, then there is no more need to waste money on social reforms. Most of us have heard such arguments so often that they simply sound correct.

Nonetheless, social science must respond to these pervasive, although incorrect, arguments. Most sociologists agree that understanding what it means to be human requires a more complex analysis of our species, as well as some examination of how our behaviour came to be less rigidly tied to its biological roots. This necessitates a brief look at the place of humans in evolution.

The Process of Evolution

While the concept of evolution will forever be connected to Charles Darwin (1809–82), many prior to Darwin—indeed, as far back as the ancient Greeks—had formulated similar notions. Darwin's contribution was that he was the first to provide a comprehensive and well-documented explanation, which he termed *natural selection*, for the way evolution occurred. The experimental work of Gregor Mendel (1822–84) on heredity some years later confirmed the process and added to our scientific understanding of how species survive and change.

> Evolution, the basic organizing concept of all the biological sciences, has been validated… and may therefore be designated as true or factual.
> —Stephen Jay Gould, *"Introduction," Evolution: The Triumph of an Idea*

Darwin's greatest legacy was that he was able to provide an explanation of the process of evolution that was both materialist and dialectical. It was materialist because it explained transformations in nature totally through observable changes to the material conditions of species. Its dialectics was rooted in the notion that individual members of species could remain constant throughout their lifetime, while the species as a whole could be in the process of change. Both Darwin and Mendel discovered that what appear on the surface as opposites—*similarity* (of members of a species when compared to another species) and *variation* (of individual members within a species)—were actually two interconnected aspects of the same reality (Lewontin 2001, 68).

Think About It

Imagine a world in which everyone was the same as you. Could our species survive if we were all the same?

It is interesting to note that Darwin never actually used the term *evolution*. Prior to Darwin, evolution was thought of as a process of advancement, of movement from lower to higher, from worse to better (Gould 1977, 36). Within this framework, humans were seen as the highest form of development in a hierarchy from simpler to more complex organisms. In contrast, Darwin saw a species as well developed if it survives in its natural habitat and produces viable genetic offspring, whatever its place in the natural world. A central principle of natural selection is that the process is both random (that is, it occurs without a specific pattern) and unplanned.

It is often falsely assumed that species evolve in some kind of planned way. For example, a young children's book on dinosaurs (Watson 1980) notes that, in order to protect themselves from the bloodthirsty *Tyrannosaurus rex*, some creatures grew long legs, some learned to fly, and others took to the sea and swam. This perspective is also seen in academic literature: an introductory sociology text explains that "the savanna-dwelling apes evolved into our ancestors because the environment of the savanna forced them to develop a new set of characteristics" (Thio 1994, 41). While it might not have been the intention of the authors, such arguments leave the reader with the impression that evolution moves in specific directions as a conscious response to changing conditions.

In reality, organisms cannot plot their genetic futures. Rather, there are a number of unplanned processes that cause species to change.[1] Because there are variations in the basic genetic matter of humans, certain minor alterations might suddenly confer a benefit to the organism that contains it. This variation would then likely be passed on to offspring and might eventually spread throughout a population. This is most likely to occur where environments are changing. If certain genetic variations or new characteristics accumulate within a population to the point where the organisms contain substantially different genetic matter from the original parent generation, a new species has come into existence.

It is most easy to observe this process with regard to changes *within* species. Houseflies, for example, have developed a resistance to DDT. This pesticide was originally used to eliminate insects such as houseflies. However, because of variation within the genes that affect the sensitivity of flies to DDT, some flies were more resistant and some less. With the widespread application of DDT, the flies sensitive to this pesticide were killed—and their genes lost—while those resistant to the pesticide survived and reproduced, passing their genes on to future generations. Eventually the entire species became resistant to DDT (Lewontin 2001, 55). In the same fashion, as a result of excessive use of antibiotics, many bacterial infections in humans that were once easily eliminated with these medicines are now quite resistant to them.

In order to comprehend the full process of evolution, we must understand the vast period of time in which it normally takes place. (The above examples are interesting to us because we can observe the evolutionary process within a short period of time; however, these entail only small alterations within species.) It is also crucial to understand that the entire process of evolution is not linear; we do not begin with a single-celled organism and move neatly to multicellular organisms, up through, say, fish to reptiles to mammals to humans. Rather, we must picture evolution as a winnowing-out process, in which a vast array of varying life forms did not survive because of failure to adapt to changing environments or as a result of recurring mass extinctions. Surviving species, while genetically similar, branched and evolved in fairly distinctive ways (Gould 1989).

In the context of evolution, behaviours that are a result of instincts or inborn patterns are neither better nor worse than those acquired through learning. Each works well under certain conditions. In unchanging environments, inborn patterns confer a certain advantage—each member of the species will automatically acquire certain mechanisms required for survival. Learning, however, can be useful in changing environments.

Humans and Evolution

Humans are mammals who are members of the order Primata, the primates. This order also includes various families of monkeys, as well as the great apes— chimpanzees, gorillas, and orangutans—to whom humans are most closely

---

1 For more details on the entire process of evolution, including how species change, see "Evolution 101," a collaborative project of the University of California Museum of Paleontology and the National Center for Science Education, at <http://evolution.berkeley.edu/evolibrary/article/evo_01>.

related. Our species, *Homo sapiens*, belongs to the family Hominidae, the hominids, and is the only remaining member of this category.

Humans share certain characteristics with other primates. Indeed, recent studies have indicated that our species shares around 98 to 99 percent of its DNA with its nearest evolutionary relatives, the chimpanzees (Lemonick and Dorfman 2006). However, despite this connection, we are here today as a species because we became distinct from chimps and apes. This distinction makes us unique among living things.

As mentioned earlier, humans are the most flexible and adaptable of all species. This means that humans are not particularly well adapted for a specific environment as are most other animals. For example, think of the polar bear, with its thick non-pigmented fur and other physiological traits that allow it to survive in the extreme cold of the far north. Unfortunately, as a result of global warming, the species is now under threat because it is physiologically not well suited to the changing environment.

> To place human evolution in a time perspective, recall that life originated on Earth several billion years ago, and that the dinosaurs became extinct around sixty-five million years ago. It was only between six and ten million years ago that our ancestors finally became distinct from the ancestors of chimps and gorillas. Hence human history constitutes only an insignificant portion of the history of life.
> —Jared Diamond,
> *The Third Chimpanzee*

Humans, in contrast, have been able to find ways of surviving in almost every environment, from the Arctic Circle to the equator, from the ocean floor to outer space. This is so because hominids, in the process of evolution, gradually acquired a package of characteristics that has allowed survival under near-impossible odds. We may be quite genetically similar to chimpanzees, but just that small difference means a huge distinction in our species. What eventually became the "human package" includes **bipedalism** (standing upright on two feet), which freed the hands for the production and use of tools; an increase in the size and capacity of the brain; complex communication through language; and the control of sexuality. But these changes would have mattered little—indeed, they likely would have never occurred—if humans were not able to live together in social groups. *It is the characteristic of sharing, of both food and knowledge, that sets us apart from other species.*

A number of interrelated developments helps make sense of this uniquely human characteristic. Together these traits help explain the basis for human existence. While they are being separated out here for theoretical analysis, in reality each developed as a part of a complex package, with every element feeding back on, and reinforced by, the others. It should also be noted that all the characteristics that are part of the "human package" can be observed in their more basic form in the evolutionary ancestors of humans.

Bipedalism and Toolmaking

It has long been theorized that bipedalism evolved in our hominid ancestors after the changing ecology in Africa pushed them from a tree-dwelling existence onto open grassy plains; in this environment it was thought that bipedalism would have provided a number of survival advantages, including the ability to see predators above the tall grasses. However, science is never static and is always open to alternative explanations that can be defended with solid evidence. In 2007, a new theory—drawn from extensive observation of orangutans—proposed that our hominid ancestors may have been bipedal from the outset. When they were forced from a tree-dwelling existence, they likely found food on the forest floor. Ancestors of apes and chimps, on the other hand, became more specialized in going up and down trees; when they walked on the forest floor, they were only partially bipedal. If this theory is correct, bipedalism in our hominid ancestors probably developed around 24 million years ago, far earlier than scientists previously imagined (McIlroy 2007).

Whatever the actual process, it is clear that bipedalism was an advantage for survival once our ancestors lived on open plains called savannas, where one could be easily spotted by predators. Bipedalism, even if only temporarily, made an animal look bigger to other animals and allowed it to brandish sticks or hurl objects at its enemies. Standing upright also allowed for a wider view of the surroundings. Most importantly, bipedalism freed our hands for making and using tools. The earliest tools were probably sticks, used for digging at roots or for threatening other animals. In addition to bipedalism, other characteristics—superior eyesight with stereoscopic vision, an opposable thumb, and precision grip—made possible the full use of the forelimbs for manipulating the environment. Toolmaking eventually led to the development of hunting as an activity. It would also have encouraged communication between members, as well as some forethought and planning. All of these elements, in turn, helped develop brain function.

Meat Eating

It is also likely that we are here today as a species because our ancestors began to have meat as a more regular part of their diets. Although some apes and chimps occasionally feast on an animal, vegetarianism is the norm. Hominids, on the other hand, are omnivores; that is, they eat both meat and vegetable matter as a normal part of their diet. It is believed that for our hominid ancestors in Africa, meat may have constituted as much as 30 percent of the diet (Leakey and Lewin 1977, 159).

Hunting and meat eating did not turn our ancestors into aggressive, bloodthirsty killers. Quite the opposite—meat eating is important to our species' existence because it propelled us toward cooperation and sharing. Herbivores (non-meat eaters) can survive as individuals, tearing off leaves and berries; in contrast, hunting, especially the large-game hunting undertaken by the hominid line, requires collective planning and action. It also encourages the collective consumption of the spoils.

We now understand that meat constitutes a readily absorbed complete protein, and those of our prehuman ancestors who began to consume it would likely have had a physical advantage for survival. But far more important are the consequences of hunting with regard to social development. Leakey and Lewin argue, "The key to the transformation of a social ape-like creature into a cultural animal living in a highly structured and organized society is sharing: the sharing of jobs and the sharing of food. Meat eating was important in propelling our ancestors along the road to humanity, but only as a package of socially-oriented changes involving the gathering of plant foods and sharing the spoils" (149).

Hunting and gathering, or foraging, societies are examined in more detail in Chapter 3. However, it is worth noting at this point that hunting required a dividing up of jobs (referred to as a **division of labour**), with some members hunting and others gathering the roots, nuts, and berries that constituted the major part of the diet. This, in turn, required forms of cooperation, sharing, restraint of individual impulses, and a dependence on others that is not seen in any other species. Once this tendency to share food began, it went far beyond the mere requirements of nutrition or basic survival. In all human societies, sharing seems to be the glue that binds individuals together—it becomes a social ritual that promotes social solidarity (White 1965, 79). And it is this social solidarity that, in turn, maximizes the chances of individual survival in a very precarious world.

Think About It

What traditions exist in your ethnic or religious community that involve the sharing of food? How many holidays have the sharing of food as a central activity, even if—in theory—they are religious events?

Language and Symbols

Of course, the ability to hunt and live together in communities would have been severely limited if our prehuman ancestors were unable to communicate with each other. Other animals communicate—even insects and birds can communicate such things as readiness to mate or imminent danger. But only humans can communicate using elaborate systems of symbolization. In most non-human animals, communication systems are largely governed by instinctual processes. In other words, they are unlearned, species-wide responses to specific environmental cues, understood instinctively by members of the same species. Humans, on the other hand, communicate primarily through the use of **symbols**, which are physical, vocal, or gestural signs that have arbitrary, socially learned meanings attached to them. Some sociologists argue that our ability to create symbols, along with our social essence, is the core of what makes us human.

Words are a good example of symbols. Suppose we want to communicate to another person the notion of a small furry animal that many of us have as pets. If we speak English, we could say *cat*. But that sound is arbitrary, in the sense that there is no automatic attachment between the word and its meaning. We could just as easily say *gato* or *kedi*. Whatever the word, however, it has meaning only if the receiver has been taught beforehand to comprehend the meaning of the sound being made.

Objects can also be symbols. Think, for example, of the following diverse objects: a swastika; a gold ring worn on the third finger of the left hand; a white cloth with a stylized red leaf in the middle and two red bars on either side; a jolly fat man with a white beard and a red suit. Each of these objects has a symbolic meaning to those who have been taught to understand it. We learn the meaning of such symbols through our various social institutions, such as the family or schools. The advertising industry also creates symbols to sell products. For example, the De Beers Corporation created one of the most successful advertising campaigns in modern history by turning the diamond engagement ring into a symbol of love (Koskoff 1981).

Verbal symbols ultimately become codified into spoken and written language systems. These highly elaborate systems consist of more than strings of words; they also have a shared set of rules and structures. These systems allow humans to communicate extremely complex thoughts and to go beyond the concrete here and now. We are the only species that can assess the past or ponder the future. We can deal with reality, or we can consider the mystical. We can discuss feelings, theories, or aesthetics. And we can pass on all our ideas and knowledge to the next generation. All this is possible not simply because of our language systems, but also because of the capacities of the human brain.

A number of authors have recently argued that hominids made music before they made language, and, in fact, music may be the key to understanding how we developed language. One author (Mithen 2006) believes that before our ancestors had language, it was music that advanced their sociability. Music helped them calm a child, find a mate, and work collectively; it helped bind people together. Even today, music—especially singing together with others—is a universal component of all cultures.

Think About It

Do you like listening to music, singing, or playing an instrument? Can you explain why? What does it feel like when you sing or play in a group? Is there music that can make you cry?

Large and Complex Brain

The brain of *Homo sapiens* is unique in the animal world. It is not simply the size of the organ that makes it special—although the primate brain is distinctively large relative to body size—but rather it is its complexity that makes it unique. Within the primate line, a gradual increase in the size of the brain can be seen along an evolutionary time frame, with the brain of *Homo sapiens* the largest. In evolutionary terms, those who could come up with the best ideas for survival, and who could retain them and pass them on to offspring who could then build new ideas upon them, had the best chance of survival.

This large and complex brain allows us to communicate through language and other symbols; it also allows us to live in social groups where complex understandings of social interaction are required. Humans seem unique in having what psychologists refer to as a "theory of mind," the ability to understand what others of their species are feeling or thinking. Even those primates closest to us in evolution—the chimpanzees—seem to lack this skill. This lack of ability in modern higher primates is a clue that our hominid ancestors must have evolved a "theory of mind" after they split from chimpanzees (Zimmer 2001, 271). Clearly, superior brain function was required for those who lived sociably.

Control of Sexuality

Humans have a different pattern of sexual activity than any other mammal species. Most mammals are generally sexually inactive, copulating only when females are ovulating and capable of being fertilized. Moreover, female mammals will solicit copulation specifically when they are ovulating; in contrast, human females can never be absolutely certain that they are ovulating. Since sexual intercourse for humans occurs at any stage of the reproductive cycle, and even during pregnancy or after menopause, much of it can have nothing to do with reproduction. This is another reflection of our liberation from the purely biological. For humans, sex takes on additional social, psychological, and recreational functions that have nothing to do with conception.

Our need to form social groups, to share and cooperate, required some kind of restraint of individual behaviours, and this must have included the realm of the sexual. All societies that have been studied by social scientists seem to have rules putting some limits on sexual behaviours. Although *specific* behaviours can vary from society to society, all societies seem to tolerate or encourage some kinds of sexual behaviours while discouraging or prohibiting others. There are, however, two universal social customs relating to sexuality that are of interest to social scientists. First, humans generally have sex in private, while all other group-living animals copulate in public. The other pattern is the **incest taboo**, which forbids sexual relations between those defined as kin, or family. No one knows for certain why these two behaviours are practised in our species, and many theories to explain them have been formulated.

What is known is that extended kinship networks are essential to early human societies through their provision of mutual aid. Keeping sex private and adhering to the incest taboo clearly must have helped families remain stable, thus giving them a better chance of survival. In this way, human biology was brought under social control. Of course, despite its prohibition incest continues to occur in most societies, including our own, as does adultery. Humans don't need to create rules preventing behaviours that we have no capacity to do; the human fear and detestation of incest, as Freud noted, is proof that we have a biological capacity to engage in it.

Think About It
Try to imagine a society where everybody could have sex with anyone they felt attracted to at any time. What problems might this create for the social group?

Humans as Social Animals

Humans are, above all, a sociable species. Living together allows for the sharing of knowledge, as well as for increased protection against predators. If, as hypothesized, a climatic change in Africa led to the decline in forested areas, species that were pushed into the open grasslands would have been in competition for food with species better adapted to that environment. It is a reasonable hypothesis that the basic sociability of our prehuman ancestors is the likely reason for their survival under virtually impossible odds. This sociability was subsequently selected for over time (the most sociable individuals tended to survive and mate), pushing our prehuman ancestors even further in this direction.

Other animal species—including bees, ants, and many of the primates—live in social groups. Orangutans and chimpanzees even show some ability to transmit knowledge and skills from one generation to another, thus creating elements of culture once thought to be the exclusive domain of humans. The appearance and development of what is now termed social intelligence not only allowed hominids to live together; it likely also became part of a feedback loop that allowed our prehuman ancestors to engage in more collective activities such as hunting, to converse more, and to develop their social networks and social skills. This, in turn, likely helped hominid brains develop and encouraged more sociability.

The origins of our increasing sociability are unknown, but bipedalism may have played an important role. Unlike virtually all mammals, human females do not deliver their offspring alone; rather, they get help from other women, which probably saves the life of both mother and child. One reason that humans need help from others is because the baby emerges from the womb in a manner that makes it very hard for a woman to deliver her child alone, as she needs help making sure it is free from the umbilical cord and mucus (*Toronto Star* 2 February 2003, A18). In addition, the length of time that infants need to be cared for and fed is much greater than for other species. This longer period of dependency probably led to an increase in the need for food sharing and long-term male-female bonding. Strong bonding would also have developed between offspring and their mothers, as well as bonding between siblings (Ehrenberg 2001).

Conclusion

This chapter has shown that, although humans are part of the animal world, we are unique within it. Humans are born in a pronounced state of physical immaturity, and we have an extremely long dependence period relative to our lifespan. Whether we want to or not, we can survive only by becoming part of

Box 2.3 Being Human Means Being Social

Think back to high school, a time when all of us were trying to make sense of who we were and where we fit in. Do you remember how strongly you felt about acceptance and how much you feared rejection by others? The biggest fear for most of us—greater perhaps than failing grades—was the fear of rejection, the fear of being laughed at by others, the fear of humiliation. Most of us think that we were the only ones feeling this way, but as we get older we usually discover that almost all of us—even the kids we thought were popular—were very insecure. We all want to belong, and it doesn't feel good to be an outsider.

The need to be accepted by others does not disappear as we enter adulthood, and the fear of being socially rejected remains strong. Many social scientists and psychoanalysts, including Freud, have written about the issue of shame. Shame is a consciousness or awareness of something said or done—whether real or not—that might result in dishonour, disgrace, or condemnation. All of us feel ashamed from time to time, although some people have trouble letting go of these negative feelings.

Although technologies have changed over the centuries, the need for social contact has not. Whereas our ancestors would interact almost exclusively in a face-to-face way, today we chat or text-message on cellphones and communicate online. However, although the means of social interaction has changed, our need to connect to others has not. In fact, online social networking sites such as Facebook have allowed young people to expand their social contacts.

A number of early sociologists, part of the theoretical framework referred to as *symbolic-interactionism*, focused their writing on the ways humans develop a sense of who they are as individuals. George Herbert Mead (1863–1931) argued that all humans have a "self" that is acquired through interaction with others, the result of the unique human ability for language and reflexive thought. Charles Horton Cooley (1864–1929) created the term *looking-glass self* to describe this process. According to Cooley, other humans act as a kind of "mirror," reflecting back to us, through words and behaviour, our self-image. Just as an anorexic individual looks in a mirror and sees someone who is overweight, many of us may have a distorted view of ourselves. For example, if a parent repeatedly calls a child "stupid," she might come to believe that this is true even if she is actually very intelligent.

Neuroscience is now confirming what anthropologists and sociologists have long assumed: the human brain is hard-wired for sociability. However, this expanding science goes beyond simply proving that we are meant to be social. Research on the human body indicates that social encounters directly affect our physical and mental health. As one author (Goleman 2006, 5) puts it, "Nourishing relationships have a beneficial impact on our health, while toxic ones can act like slow poison in our bodies." Data also indicate that people with broad social networks tend to live longer lives than those with few social connections.

In this chapter we have seen that, from our very beginnings as a species, we were social beings. This is how we survived and flourished over millions of years. Our sociability, our need to belong, is as much part of who we all are as our ability to walk on two legs or to think complex thoughts. Being human *means* being social, and this is the core notion from which all sociologists, regardless of their theoretical framework, begin.

a social group for an extended period of time. Given this reality, it is absurd to envisage society as something that constrains us, or as something that controls our true selves. There is no "self" that can exist outside the social world of which it is a part. It is also senseless to imagine a "biological" human outside of a social context. From the moment of birth, our physiological selves are in constant interaction with our social world, with each acting on and affecting the other. The biological determinist assertion—that behaviours as complex as aggression, addiction, or homosexuality can be the result of a single gene or genes—is far too simplistic.

It is important, therefore, to repeat that there is no substantive proof to support such arguments. The information currently available to us from fields as diverse as anatomy, genetics, zoology, anthropology, and palaeontology negates the commonly held view that human behaviour is simply a natural expression of our biology. Rather, the overwhelming body of evidence indicates that human behaviour is the result of a complex interaction between the biological and the social. In short, humans make their own history and, in the process of so doing, create their own nature. The conclusion is clear: If we want to understand the reasons for the existence of crime, war, or social inequality, it is not our biology, but rather society and culture that must be studied.

Key Points

1. There is little evidence that human behaviour is the result of instincts.

2. Humans are of the animal world, but unique within it. Humans are the most flexible and adaptable of all species.

3. Biological determinist arguments, which see at least some human behaviour as being primarily the result of inborn characteristics, remain very popular. A substantial body of scientific research has repeatedly discredited such arguments that help to justify and maintain social inequalities.

4. The eugenics movement turned biological determinist arguments into social policy, with horrifying outcomes for many individuals. Eugenics is not only morally bankrupt, but scientifically flawed.

5. Traits may be heritable, but the environment can still have an effect. Recent studies indicate that even genes themselves may be affected by their environment.

6. In the process of evolution, our prehuman ancestors acquired a package of traits that allowed them to survive under near-impossible odds. This package includes bipedalism and toolmaking, meat eating, increase in the size and capacity of the brain, complex communication through language, and the control of sexuality.

7. Above all, humans are social animals. Being human means being social.

8. Human behaviour is the result of a complex interplay between the biological and the social. Humans make their own history and, in so doing, create their own nature.

Further Reading

Darwin, C.R. [1859] 1975. *On the Origin of Species by Means of Natural Selection or the Preservation of the Favored Races in the Struggle for Life*. New York: W.W. Norton.
This classic remains one of the most important works in modern science.

Gould, Stephen Jay. 1989. *Wonderful Life: The Burgess Shale and the Nature of History*. New York: W.W. Norton.
This work presents some key issues related to evolutionary processes, told as a detective story. Gould, who died in 2002, wrote a monthly column for *Natural History* for many years; many of these columns have been gathered into collections and published as books. All of them are highly readable and are an excellent introduction to issues of natural history and evolution.

———. 1996. *The Mismeasure of Man*. New York: W.W. Norton.
This is a revised and expanded version of the original 1981 book, which provided a detailed historical overview of biological determinist theories. Of particular interest is Gould's critique of the methods and forms of statistical analysis used by many social scientists.

Johnson, Olive Skene. 2007. *The Sexual Spectrum: Why We're All Different*. Vancouver, B.C.: Raincoast Books.
Skene—a neuropsychologist and mother of two gay sons—examines from both a professional and personal viewpoint the many elements that influence gender behaviour and sexuality.

Lewontin, Richard, Steven Rose, and Leon J. Kamin. 1984. *Not in Our Genes: Biology, Ideology and Human Nature*. New York: Pantheon.
This U.S. work not only demolishes biological determinist arguments but also shows the key role played by science in the promotion of such arguments.

Zihlman, Adrienne L. 2001. *The Human Evolution Coloring Book*. 2nd Ed. New York: HarperCollins.
An easy-to-follow book (despite the title, it was written for adults) that explains processes of evolution.

3 Culture, Society, and History

In This Chapter

- What is culture and how do we study it?
- Is there such a thing as Canadian culture?
- What did early societies look like, and what is the point of looking at societies that preceded ours?
- How did social inequality arise?

Think about women and men in the families you know. Who prepares the meals? Who takes out the garbage? Who looks after the young children? Who watches the football games on TV? Who earns the higher wages? While there are obviously differences between families, sociologists have noted certain patterns that indicate different behaviours for men and women in the household. Gender differences can be found outside the home as well. For example, men are more likely to become engineers, while women are more likely to become nurses. Social scientists have been intrigued about why these differences occur. In the previous chapter, we saw that one of the most enduring arguments to explain social behaviour is that of biological determinism. However, few social scientists accept this approach.

In 1935, anthropologist Margaret Mead in her book *Sex and Temperament in Three Primitive Societies* argued that the many differences between men and women were largely the result of social learning—an idea that was not widely accepted at the time. Her conclusion was the result of her study of three tribes in New Guinea who lived within a 150-kilometre radius, but who were relatively isolated from each other: the Arapesh, Mundugumor, and Tchambuli. The Arapesh made very little distinction between the behaviours of the two sexes, and the idealized personality type for both sexes was, by our society's standards, "feminine." Both sexes displayed a non-aggressive, nurturing personality, and differences between men and women were minimal.

In contrast, for the Mundugumor both sexes were expected to be violent, aggressive, and competitive. Sexual intercourse was a battle between partners, with each ending up battered and bruised. Infants were treated with hostility, and weaning consisted of slapping the child. The Tchambuli were different yet again. While the Arapesh might be said to behave in a way we consider typical for females, and the Mundugumor in a way we consider typical for males, the Tchambuli reversed the pattern that is considered normal in our society. Among the Tchambuli, women were the dominant and aggressive sex, made the sexual advances, and did all the trade that was necessary for the society's survival. Men, on the other hand, devoted themselves to art and ceremony, were more highly ornamented, and lived lives full of "petty bickering, misunderstanding, reconciliation, arousals, disclaimers, and protestations accompanied by gifts" (Mead 258).

Mead's study helps us understand how social scientists try to make sense of human behaviour. First, the specific details are examined and described. Then, after looking at similarities and differences between groups, a theory of behaviour is constructed. Based on her observation of the three tribes, Mead (280) summed up her analysis as follows: "We are forced to conclude that human nature is almost unbelievably malleable, responding accurately and contrastingly to contrasting cultural conditions. The differences between individuals who are members of different cultures, like the differences between individuals within a culture, are almost entirely to be laid to differences in conditioning, especially during early childhood, and the form of this conditioning is culturally determined."

Although today we would consider Mead's argument to be a cultural determinist one—because she focuses solely on social learning—it was important as a rebuttal of the biological determinist arguments of the time. It also helped raise awareness about the wide range of diversity of human cultures. Certainly Mead's observations supported the view of others in her field that human behaviour is largely the result of the process of **socialization**, by which each generation learns the cultural beliefs and patterns of those who preceded them.

Understanding Culture

Why is it common today to see flowers left by total strangers at a spot where someone has recently died a violent death? Why do Canadian business people shake hands when meeting, while the Japanese bow? Why do Sikh men wear turbans? Why do we say "thank you" when someone has done a favour for us? Why do Canadians eat with forks and knives, while the Chinese eat with chopsticks? The answer to all these questions, in a word, is culture. **Culture** is essentially the complete way of life shared by a people, including both the material and non-material elements. The non-material elements of culture include the *cognitive*, that is, the knowledge and beliefs of a people; the *symbolic*, which include verbal and non-verbal forms of communication; and the *normative*, or values, beliefs, and behavioural expectations of a people. The material elements of a culture include all of a group's material artefacts and products created by its members. The two elements are, of course, interrelated. For example, the existence of a mosque (material culture) is linked to an Islamic belief system (non-material culture).

There are four primary characteristics of culture (Sanderson 1999, 32).

First, culture is *learned*, rather than being simply the result of some biological inevitability. Second, culture is rooted in *symbols*—physical, vocal, or gestural signs that have arbitrary, socially learned meanings to them. It is symbols that are the building blocks of all cultures. Third, culture is a system *shared* by all members of a society. It is the embodiment of a collective of individuals, past and present, rather than simply the behaviour of any one of them. Lastly, the elements of culture are generally *integrated*, in that the various components fit into a coherent whole, even though there may be contradictory or conflicting elements within the whole.

In the previous chapter it was argued that humans have few if any inborn patterns, or instincts. In other words, we are not pre-programmed for survival. Rather, in the process of living together, we work out appropriate patterns for survival under certain conditions. We develop technologies, expand our means of communicating with each other, construct social institutions, develop rules of social behaviour, and create values and belief systems that allow us to live together in groups. Collectively, this socially created package is referred to as a society's culture. Once developed, these cultural elements are passed on from one generation to the next, with each subsequent generation adding to, or modifying, them.

Humans must be taught the means of survival through the process of socialization. Luckily for us, as noted in the previous chapter, we have a long period of physical dependency after birth that allows us to learn culture from the adults around us. We have no choice in the matter; without learning language and societal norms, beliefs, and values, we would not be able to survive. The culture we learn throughout childhood and adolescence is a key part of who we become. In this sense, culture is "in us" as much as it is "out there." Not surprisingly, then, most of us are deeply attached to our language and culture; for many, the fear of being separated from one's culture is equal to losing part of oneself. This helps us understand why recent immigrants to Canada so often seek out others who share their language, cultural traditions, or religious practices. Even Canadians who have simply changed locales may try to connect with others from "back home."

Think About It

Ask your parents or other relatives why they have (or have not) retained their connection to their ethnic, linguistic, or regional communities.

Despite the cultural diversity we see all around us, it must be remembered that we are all one species with the same basic needs, such as physical survival, reproduction, sexual gratification, care of the young, keeping the group together, and so on. And because our species has the ability to think abstract thoughts and ponder the past and future, all cultures address what might be termed the "existential" questions of human life, such as these: Why are we here? Why is there so much suffering in the world? Where do we go after we die? Thus, while each culture

Box 3.1 "Us" versus "Them"

To make sense of our world, humans need to sort things into categories or groups. Humans also have language, and as we sort things, we tend to name them. However, in order to name something, we not only have to understand what it is, we also have to understand what it is not. Thus, when we call something a "dog," we have to learn both what makes it dog-like as well as what makes it different from, say, a cat or a zebra. Likewise, naming the groups to which we belong involves both an understanding of our shared characteristics as well as what distinguishes us from other groups. All of us belong to many groups—family, school, neighbourhood, religion, ethnic group, region, country, and so on. But naming these groups—like naming an animal—implies that there are others not in this group. "My family" is different from "your family." If I say I am a "social worker" then it is understood that I am distinguishing myself from non-social workers. If I am a "Calgarian," I am not a Torontonian or a Montrealer. Of necessity, then, the social world always consists of "us" (my group) and "them" (those not in my group).

Not only do we name groups, but we also evaluate them. The problem with a world in which there is always an "us" and a "them" is that a simple appreciation of difference can easily escalate into something more troubling. For foraging peoples (to be discussed later in this chapter), the separation into "us" and "them" was probably helpful for survival. Groups usually kept their distance, with the result that people stayed away from those who might harm them, and competing groups didn't over-exploit the same limited natural resources.

In today's complex world, the dichotomy between "us" and "them" is seldom so benign, and it has regularly been used by those with power to promote their own interests. For example, if it is accepted that Christianity is good, then it can, theoretically, be argued that non-Christianity is bad. Such thinking in fourteenth- and fifteenth-century England and parts of Europe—exploited by the then-powerful leaders of the Catholic Church in collaboration with certain monarchs—led to the expulsion and death of many Jews. The list of other examples, both past and present, is endless. It is also worrying that many groups cling to disputes long past, with some ethnic and religious groups still seeking revenge for events that happened hundreds of years ago.

The good news is that the tension between "us" and "them" is not embedded in our genes. Rather, it is socially created and often passed down from one generation to the next. Certain groups that may seem today to be inevitably locked in their history of hatred had actually lived cooperatively for long periods of time. And some groups with recent histories of violence toward each other—such as the Catholics and Protestants of Northern Ireland—are slowly learning to live together in peace. Thus it seems possible for humans to move past the horrible consequences of a world divided into "us" and "them."

is unique, they all share certain common elements, or *cultural universals*. These universals include sports, funerals, rules of inheritance, myths and legends, music and dancing, joking, food taboos, marriage, and so on.

However, these practices and beliefs must be understood as universal only in their most general aspects. We all have to eat to survive, but what, when, and how we eat are culturally determined. A delicacy for one group of people may be inedible for another. We all have to deal with death and dying, but how we do so will vary from culture to culture. Again, what is practised in one group may be offensive to another. Once these cultural practices—as well as the beliefs and values that are connected to these practices—come into being, they take on a life of their own and are handed down from generation to generation, whether or not they any longer have direct relevance to the survival of a people. Indeed, the fact that some customs continue even when there is no longer any particular reason for them to do so tells us that we also seem to have a strong need for cultural traditions.

Embedded in all cultures is the assumption that the ways we do things—the food we eat, the beliefs we have, the way we organize ourselves, and so on—are normal and superior, while the ways of other people are strange or possibly even immoral. This tendency to see the world in terms of our own culture is referred to as **ethnocentrism**, and it exists in all societies. This universality makes sense, since no society could survive for long if most of its members continually questioned the validity of their cultural practices and beliefs. Moreover, a shared sense of superiority binds individuals in that group together. However, ethnocentrism can often turn into something more troubling (see Box 3.1).

Is There a Canadian Culture?

It is impossible to do an analysis of culture without taking a short "side trip" to assess whether there is such a thing as "Canadian culture." If one travels to France, Great Britain, China, or Iran, the people there will happily discuss their cultural traditions and what makes them distinctive. Canadians are far less certain about who they are and whether there actually is such a thing as a distinctively Canadian culture. This is largely because Canada is such a young country in relative terms.

Think About It

What can you think of that could be defined as distinctively Canadian? Remember, culture consists of both material and non-material elements. What does being Canadian mean to you? Are there any foods you would consider distinctly Canadian? Do you think that there is a distinct "Québecois" culture that is different from that of English-speaking Canada?

Our country began with the varying cultural traditions of numerous indigenous people, plus two "charter" groups that originally came from Britain and France. The twentieth century saw the arrival of immigrants from every part of the globe; each group brought with it new cultural elements. But there was no real "melting pot" in Canada as there was in the United States, and these varied traditions did not quickly join together into a single culture. Because of Canada's size and relatively small population, it remained highly regionalized. In some ways, it is still easier to identify a distinct Newfoundland culture or an

Box 3.2 Canadian Values versus American Values

It is often noted with humour that the most distinguishing characteristic of Canadians is that we spend an inordinate amount of time trying to figure out what it is that makes us distinctively Canadian. Because Canada is such a young and regionalized country, we do often wonder "Who are we?" One way to answer this question is to compare ourselves to our neighbours to the south. This is a useful exercise because in some ways Americans seem so similar to us—we dress the same, speak the same language, purchase very similar products, consume most of the same media, and so on.

In 2003, at the request of Canadian Policy Research Networks, U.S. social researcher Daniel Yankelovich put together a citizens' vision for Canada. He found a set of core values shared by Canadians across the country. Comparing these values to those in the United States, Yankelovich identified four key areas of difference:

- Role of government: Americans wanted an "arms-length" government that would let the private sector control the economy, with the government simply enforcing the law and punishing violators. Canadians wanted a more activist government that would be involved with the private sector in economic activities while also protecting such things as health care, safety, and the environment.

- Inequality: Canadians had much less tolerance for inequality than Americans.
- Morality: Americans drew a sharp line between right and wrong, legal and illegal; they felt those who crossed the line should be punished. In contrast, Canadians saw society as operating via shared norms and social pressure.
- International relations: Americans tended to be isolationists, while Canadians had a much deeper sense of global interdependence.

Michael Adams was also interested in studying what makes Canadians distinctive from Americans. He concluded that Canadian culture is distinctive in many ways from that of Americans; he also noted that both countries have their own regional differences. While he did see changes occurring in both countries—particularly among young people—he still felt that Canadians have a distinct set of beliefs and values.

Thus, while much of our culture—especially mass culture such as music and films—is very similar to that in the United States, some of our core values remain quite distinctive, and are shared by Canadians from coast to coast.

Sources: Michael Adams, *Fire and Ice: The United States, Canada and the Myth of Converging Values*. Toronto: Penguin, 2003; Carol Goar, "We Do Have Distinctive Values," *Toronto Star*, 21 April, 2003.

Acadian culture than a Canadian one. To make things even more complex, the cultures of the world are merging as a result of new technologies and globalization, with American culture dominant in this process. The United States has had a particularly strong influence on our culture, given its proximity and our shared English language.

Although there are common practices, norms, beliefs, and values that most Canadians share, these elements are by no means universal. Sometimes the differences break out into open hostilities, such as in debates about abortion, euthanasia, gay marriage, or gun control. In addition, French-speaking Canadians and the indigenous peoples of Canada have felt that their cultural traditions and languages are being eroded through the dominance of English-Canadian social institutions and an English-speaking North American culture.

Moreover, Canadian culture, like all cultures, must be viewed as fluid and malleable. Not only is culture created by humans but it is also perpetually being *re-created* by them. We are not automatons who mechanically accept and repeat what we learn from our parents and teachers. This does not mean that there are not elements of a culture that remain constant over time (some of our beliefs and patterns of behaviour are thousands of years old). Such an analysis simply implies that culture must not be studied as a closed, unchangeable system.

For example, let us examine the notion that the roles of men and women in Canadian society are largely determined by our cultural expectations regarding gender. To some extent, it can be said that this is true. Certainly the many agents of socialization—such as family, schools, religious institutions, and mass media—reinforce the traditional expectations regarding gender roles. At the same time, however, these very expectations are changing. For example, many women are still taught that certain jobs are inappropriate for their gender. Nonetheless, in spite of learning such notions, many women have decided to enter these occupations. They in turn become role models for the next generation of women, who further alter cultural expectations—and so on, in a never-ending process.

What we refer to as "Canadian culture" is an entity constantly being changed by Canadians themselves. For example, think of our flag, something most of us would consider an essential component of our culture. Yet this flag is relatively new, having been introduced—amid much controversy—in 1965. Similarly, although "O Canada" was written over a century ago, the English words were altered in 1968, and it officially became our national anthem only in 1980. Thus newer elements are constantly becoming incorporated into the older culture, and the controversies that may have surrounded their introduction are normally forgotten. Likewise, certain cultural patterns become outmoded and disappear.

Think About It

Language is an important component of culture and is always being changed by those who use it. For example, we no longer speak the English of Shakespeare's day, although we can still understand it. Listen to the way your friends and classmates speak. In what ways do you talk differently from your parents' generation? Do you find yourself laughing at their quaint expressions? Do they ever ask you to explain what you're saying?

Toward a Dialectic of Culture

We can see that humans create culture because they live together in social groups to survive. But how do these cultures arise, why are there differences between groups, and why do cultural practices and forms of social organization change? How do we identify common patterns while acknowledging distinctive elements? Put plainly, how do we make sense of a sociocultural system? Can we ever really understand how societies work? Clearly, from the title of this book you can guess that the answer is yes. But where do we begin? A number of social scientists have argued that the starting point is a society's material infrastructure, that is, how people within a society get their basic needs met.

If you ask an observant Muslim or a Jew why they don't eat pork, chances are they will tell you that, according to their religious precepts, pigs are an unclean animal. Observant Hindus, who don't eat beef, will tell you that the cow is considered a holy animal. Anthropologist Marvin Harris (1989) was fascinated by religiously based food prohibitions. All religious groups believe that their food taboos are given to them by their god or gods. However, as a social scientist and a materialist, Harris was interested in linking the origins of these religious practices, not primarily to beliefs, but rather to issues of environment and survival.

In the case of the Hindus in India, the cow was more useful if uneaten: it was an essential traction animal, and its dung could be used for fuel, building materials, and fertilizer. Those who ate their beasts during a famine would not survive for long. The question of the Jewish and Muslim prohibition of pork was particularly fascinating to Harris because other peoples in New Guinea and the South Pacific Melanesian Islands not only ate the meat but valued it so highly that they treated their pigs as family members. Harris linked the prohibition of pork to the particular ecology of the Middle East. Pig farming was poorly suited to the hot, dry climate of the region, making pigs costly to raise and in direct competition for resources required by humans. Since they were a tempting source of protein and fat, the best guarantee for limiting pig farming was to forbid the consumption of pig flesh.

According to Harris, the construction of certain food taboos can help increase the likelihood of survival. For the Hindus of India, where the cow performed essential functions, it could not be eaten. It therefore came to be revered. Among ancient Jews and other peoples of the Middle East, for whom the pig served no useful function but instead constituted a threat, pork came to be defined as unclean and an abomination.

This is not to say that those who practise such food prohibitions see their behaviour from a materialist viewpoint; in fact, they rarely do. However, social scientists look for the underpinnings of human behaviour. It should also be noted that shared eating patterns are both a way to bind people together and to distinguish them from others. The fact that modern Jews, Muslims, and Hindus in completely different geographic and cultural environments continue to adhere to food taboos is an indication that economic factors alone do not explain them.

Nonetheless, a materialist analysis helps us understand the roots of many cultural practices.

If we return to Mead's study, which opened this chapter, the patterns of each culture make more sense if we understand them within particular material conditions. That is not to say that these patterns are mechanically determined by the conditions, but simply that such arrangements are a key variable that must be considered if we are to understand the workings of society. This can be seen most clearly by comparing the Arapesh to the Mundugumor. The Arapesh survive by planting small gardens, primarily for yams. The Arapesh do not privately own the land, and, indeed, almost all the garden work and house building is done cooperatively (Mead [1935] 1963, 16–23). Within this type of economic relations, a gentle, non-competitive, "feminine" personality type makes sense.

Compare this way of life to the Mundugumor. Unlike the Arapesh, they have private ownership of land and obtain their existence mainly through raids on neighbouring bands. There is inequality of material goods and wealth, and there is what is known as a "big man" political system, with one man having greater prestige and power due to greater wealth. Within this context, the aggressive, competitive "masculine" personality of the Mundugumor seems appropriate.

In a similar fashion we can see how the economic structure of Canadian society can be linked to many aspects of Canadian life, including the "ideal" personality type and the dominant value system. Given the emphasis on the marketplace, on profit, and on perpetual economic growth in societies such as ours, it is not surprising that competition, hard work, individual enterprise, and personal accumulation of wealth are highly valued in our culture. While these values may seem natural and eternal to the reader, we shall soon see that such ideals are not universally admired.

Karl Marx tried to explain how societies and cultures worked by focusing on what he called their **mode of production**. This term draws attention to the fact that the way humans get the things they need for survival—their food, clothing, and shelter—must be central to how they organize their societies and construct their cultures. Marx emphasized a society's *economy*, which is the organized production, distribution, and exchange of goods and services. In turn, a society's economy must be linked to three other interconnected factors (Sanderson 1999, 43): in the process of acquiring and distributing their means of existence, humans must work with what nature provides (*ecology*) and the characteristics of their own population (*demography*) to develop their tools and methods of survival (*technology*). And since humans are social animals, they must pursue their survival by entering into certain social relations with each other. A society with a specific mode of production can more precisely be referred to as a **socioeconomic formation**.

There are certainly other ways of looking at culture and society. However, the emphasis on a society's material infrastructure, that is, its mode of production, reminds us that the basis of all social life is physical survival. Humans must obtain the basics of life—food, clothing, and shelter—before they can do anything else, and they do so by working together in social groups. If used in a dialectical rather than mechanical fashion, the concepts of mode of production and socioeconomic formation can help us understand the common underpinnings of societies at their most general level, without denying the uniqueness of each society's history and culture.

Every culture seems to have some way of acknowledging the importance of ancestors, via traditions such as worshipping their spirits or giving a newborn the name of a relative. Clearly, humans understand that, in some way, we are all linked to our past. Likewise, a full understanding of today's social world requires that we examine its social and cultural roots. We discussed earlier how science seeks patterns; that is, it seeks to draw out the general from the specific. Sociologists must therefore become historians, not to study the specific details of our past, but to look for the broad patterns of change that have brought us to our current social arrangements. This brief overview will focus on the major modes of production, and how they have changed over time. In turn, we shall see how each transformation from one socioeconomic formation to another has led to widespread social change.

Foraging Societies:
The First Socioeconomic Formation

Until around 10,000 years ago, every human who had ever lived obtained their food by foraging, that is, by hunting and gathering. What did these foraging societies look like? In fact, we can't know for certain. The problem is that, while our preliterate ancestors have left remains of their skeletons and their material culture, they didn't leave behind any written record of their social lives.

Fortunately, foraging as a dominant mode of production continued in some societies right into the twentieth century, and some of you reading this book may be the modern descendants of these people, as they include most of the First Nations in Canada. The records of early traders and explorers as well as the more recent (and more precise) studies of anthropologists have helped describe a general pattern of life for foraging people. Since foraging societies, despite their many differences, seem to share certain common elements, it can be assumed that the earlier foraging societies were in general fairly similar.

Because foraging peoples produced no food of their own, they were totally dependent on what nature provided. All that was obtained from gathering and hunting was immediately consumed; in other words, no surplus was produced. Nomadic bands moved from place to place, drawing on the resources of one locale until they were depleted and then moving on to the next. A band might eventually return to its original point of settlement after the resources had replenished themselves and then start a new round of movement. For those foragers who lived off non-depleting abundant resources (such as fish), settled villages and some economic surplus became possible.

Most foraging people survived primarily by gathering fruits, nuts, berries, and roots. One anthropologist (Lee 1968) has estimated that modern foraging societies obtain about 65 percent of their diet from gathering. (Obviously, in certain environmental conditions there is less gathering. For example, the Inuit of the Arctic traditionally relied much more on hunting.) However, in spite of the fact that gathering was the more regular source of caloric intake, hunting was the more valued activity in foraging societies. This is likely connected to the fact that meat is both a more readily absorbed source of protein and a means of increasing the sociability of the population. It was also likely to be more valued because it was scarce.

Let us construct a composite picture of the typical hunting and gathering society of the past. Foraging people lived together in small groups (referred to as local bands) of approximately fifty to eighty people. Each band existed as a fairly autonomous self-sufficient unit, although bands were commonly connected through ties of marriage to a broader network of bands. This wider network shared the same general cultural patterns and was part of a common language group, although there may have been local variations. It was not uncommon for people to move from one band to another, often on a day-to-day basis.

Kinship was the central organizing feature of foraging people. When it came time to marry, most groups practised **exogamy**; this meant that marriage partners had to be sought outside the local band. Aside from the important consequence of keeping the gene pool open, the practice of exogamy served the vital purpose of maintaining kin links with neighbouring bands. This helped minimize tensions between bands in possible competition for resources, allowed for movement of individuals between bands, and increased the likelihood of sharing and cooperation.

Foraging peoples relied on simple but effective technology to obtain food, build their dwellings, and so on. Because all possessions had to be carried to the next site, hunters and gatherers had little in the way of personal possessions. The main productive forces, the land and natural resources, were not privately owned.

The division of labour—that is, how various tasks in a society are divided up—was a simple one, with the only division being that of sex and age. Everyone contributed to the essentials of survival except the very young and the very old. The **gender division of labour**—that is, assigning different tasks to men and women—varied from society to society, although big-game hunting was almost always a male activity, and women were more often food collectors. However, most animals that were regularly caught were relatively small, and women did, at times, participate in hunting them.

The differing tasks assigned to men and women were not primarily linked to differences in strength (for example, food gathering is often a strenuous task, especially when combined with the carrying of young children and necessities such as water or firewood). Rather, the fact that women gestate, bear, and suckle their young would likely have constituted a central organizing feature of foraging societies. It makes sense that there would have been a survival advantage at this stage of technological development for women (at least of childbearing age) to engage in tasks that were less risky and more compatible with pregnancy and lactation.

Having men and women perform different tasks in foraging societies served the important functions of making the two sexes interdependent for economic survival, as well as of maximizing group solidarity. The gender division of labour, by reducing contact between the sexes—contact that might have led to sexual liaisons—may also have decreased social tensions and the number of unwanted children. Whatever its functions, the gender division of labour did not seem to lead to male dominance. Women's role in foraging societies—as the main economic providers, as the likely inventors of the earliest tools and other technological innovations, and as the bearers of children—meant that status inequalities between men and women were not dramatic. In other words, men and women were essentially equal in early foraging societies.

In this context, most anthropologists feel that warfare among early hunters and gatherers was relatively low. Even those anthropologists, such as Marvin Harris (1991), who believe that warfare did occur fairly frequently among foraging peoples acknowledge that various social constraints made it less frequent and less deadly than what appears after the development of agriculture. It is not that foragers were naturally peaceable people, but rather that, under conditions of economic scarcity, fighting battles would have been highly risky for group survival. In a world where every adult member had to participate in getting food or in other essential activities, the loss of even a few band members could have tipped the balance of survival. Those individuals who could live together in relative harmony had a better chance of surviving and passing on their cultural patterns.

Within bands, relations were maintained largely through a generalized set of social obligations binding band members to each other. No major inequalities existed in these societies; the few differences that existed were of prestige due to a special skill or talent rather than heredity, and brought no special privileges or power. Even in bands that had a "headman," he could attempt to influence others but could not compel them to do his bidding. Decisions were commonly arrived at by consensus.

Anthropologists have noted that modesty and humility are essential behaviour expectations in foraging societies. For example, Richard Lee extensively studied the !Kung of southern Africa (the exclamation mark stands for a clicking sound in their language). He found that the most serious charges one could level against another were those of stinginess or arrogance. To be stingy meant not sharing one's goods with others. Arrogance was considered an even worse offence. To limit such behaviour, writes Lee (1978, 888), "levelling devices are in constant daily use, minimizing the size of others' kills, downplaying the value of others' gifts, and treating one's own efforts in a self-deprecating way. 'Please' and 'thank you' are hardly ever used in their vocabulary."

Of course, disputes between individuals did occur on occasion. Hunters

Box 3.3 Foraging, Kinship, and Sharing

Perhaps the most striking characteristic of the North American Indians was the strength of the kinship and tribal ties that bound the individual to the group as a whole. Among both agriculturalists and hunter-gatherers, these ties were stronger than among contemporaneous Europeans, Asians, or Africans. At a time when most English peasants had already lost access to lands once owned by the village in common, all lands (and waters) cultivated, hunted, fished, or otherwise used by Indian villages were still deemed the common property of all village members. Even when a family was allotted a plot of land for its crops, that grant was always temporary and did not bar other villagers from using it for other purposes, such as gathering wild berries or felling trees for canoes.

Group possession of the land implied group rights to its bounty. All had a claim to the harvest, just as all partook of the yield of the hunt. Of course, small items that a person produced independently usually belonged to that individual alone. But this rule, too, was applied loosely, for possessions were often given away as tokens of mutual obligation. "Although every proprietor knows his own," one Englishman noted, "yet all things (so long as they will last) are used in common amongst them: a bisket cake given to one; that one breaks it equally into so many parts, as there be persons in his company, and distributes it." This cultural trait shocked European observers, who had grown accustomed to the possessive ways and values of early capitalist society. A French cleric reported that the Micmac Indians of Nova Scotia were "so generous and liberal towards one another that they seem not to have any attachment to the little they possess, for they deprive themselves thereof very willingly and in very good spirit the very moment they know that their friends have need of it." Another Jesuit discovered that in Iroquois territory,... there were no poor houses "because there are neither mendicants nor paupers as long as there are any rich people among them. Their kindness, humanity, and courtesy not only make them liberal with what they have but cause them to possess hardly anything except in common. A whole village must be without corn before any individual can be obliged to endure privation."

These customs were sustained by religious views that saw human beings as but temporary custodians of the world and everything in it. A century later, another European missionary described the belief among the Delaware Indians that God "made the Earth and all it contains for the common good of mankind.... Whatever liveth on the land, whatsoever groweth out of the earth, and all that is in the rivers and waters... was given jointly to all, and everyone is entitled to his share."

The very organization of Indian society guaranteed that the distribution of wealth would be roughly but strenuously egalitarian. This economic equality reinforced the individual's sense of group identity and the utter necessity of group membership. The tribe could therefore shape personal conduct without recourse to elaborate legislative, judicial, or executive regulation. Behaviour dangerous or unacceptable to the society was quite effectively limited by public disapproval, denunciation, ridicule, or—most dramatically—by expulsion from the group itself.

Source: Copyright © 2000 by Bedford/ St. Martin's. From *Who Built America?* Volume One by American Social History Project. Reprinted with permission of Bedford/St. Martin's.

and gatherers were human after all, and conflicts could arise, even in societies that emphasized cooperation and sharing. However, in foraging societies it was important to minimize tensions that could threaten group solidarity. If disputes could not be settled informally, elders might be called upon to help negotiate a resolution; when disagreements could not be resolved, one of the parties involved simply moved to another band.

Think About It

Students frequently write in essays that some component of our society (such as war or social inequality) has existed "throughout history." When students talk of the past, how far back in history are they usually going?

What Foraging Societies Tell Us

For about 99 percent of our species' life we hunted and gathered; all of us have foragers for ancestors if we trace our lineage back far enough. If anything is "natural" to humans, we should see it in this socioeconomic formation. However, unlike the image presented by most biological determinists, humans living in these kinds of societies have not displayed the behaviours of competition, dominance, or aggression. Nor do we see warfare or structured inequality as a major social pattern. On the contrary, we see women and men working together in small cooperative units to obtain the things they need to survive.

The examination of foraging societies allows us to understand the way in which the economic arrangements of a society provide the base for the other components of a sociocultural system. Knowing that these societies were at subsistence level—that people hunted, gathered, or fished with basic tools, and that there were cooperative relations of production in which no one privately owned the means of production—helps us make sense of the total life pattern, or culture, of foraging people. That is not to say that every foraging culture throughout history has been identical, but rather that there is a similarity in all of them. In a world centred on cooperation and sharing, where productive property is not privately owned and there are no major social cleavages due to unequal access to resources, certain values and behaviours are likely to dominate. Such societies tend to emphasize the notion of *reciprocity* as well as the notion of *redistribution* (Polanyi 1957, 68). Reciprocity means that each member of a society has duties and obligations to all others. The notion of redistribution means that the community transfers wealth to those who have less.

The study of foraging societies also helps us understand that hierarchical structures and inequalities of wealth and power have *not* been the components of most societies down through the ages. In fact, for most of human history people seem to have lived in relatively cooperative, egalitarian societies. Two questions now need answering. First, given that this socioeconomic formation seemed to work for humans for such a long period, why did we cease being hunters and gatherers? Second, since it is obvious that most people today live in societies structured quite differently from the foraging societies, how did we get from there to here?

The Decline of Foraging and the Development of Farming

Some foraging societies were so well adapted to their environment that they continued to exist right into the twentieth century, and, were it not for their contact with more developed socioeconomic formations, they might have continued ad infinitum. But those societies that survived until recent times were geographically isolated. The majority of hunting and gathering societies transformed themselves much earlier. The shift to domesticated plants and animals as the major food source, sometimes referred to as the **Neolithic Revolution**, began at varying times around the globe. Few events in the history of our species can match this development in its importance. Over time, humans gained an increasing measure of control over the natural environment and were no longer simply dependent on the ups and downs of nature. It is impossible to overstate the changes in human social organization that came about as a result of the shift to farming and herding.

Although we cannot know for certain, the sea change that affected human patterns of life forever was probably the result of a number of factors. These included population pressures, the decline in availability of wild foods, and the cumulative development of new technologies. Climate change led to the increasing availability of wild plants that could be domesticated. Once food producers began to increase in numbers, it is also likely that they either displaced or killed hunter-gatherer populations (Diamond 1999, 109–113).

Three of the most important changes that resulted from the cultivation of plants and the herding of animals were the further growth of human populations, the greater permanence of settlements, and the possibility of a stable economic surplus, that is, of acquiring more than was immediately consumed (Lenski and Lenski 1978, 205). Settling in one place and producing regular surpluses in turn allowed for increased specialization of tasks as more and more people no longer had to be food producers. Increased specialization led to new technological innovations, greater surplus, greater specialization, and so on, in a never-ending process.

These changes occurred independently at different times throughout the world; to some extent, the term Neolithic Revolution gives the false impression that it was a one-time event. The widespread adoption of agriculture probably occurred first in the area that is now Iraq around eight to ten thousand years ago, about a thousand years later in the New World, and about three thousand years after that in China and Southeast Asia. It may have begun as late as the year 500 in parts of the eastern United States and in southern Africa.

While it may appear to us that farming was just a logical development on the road to greater prosperity, hunters and gatherers likely took to it gradually and hesitantly. It may seem obvious that farming means increased control over one's environment, the possibility for producing surplus, and greater productivity of labour output, but the reality for early garden farmers was a life with more work and restrictions on their freedoms. Plant cultivation, certainly at the beginning, usually meant hard work for small (and eventually diminishing) returns, in addition to the necessity of being tied both to the physical place and to cultivation cycles. That the domestication of plants and animals does eventually come to replace foraging worldwide must reflect its necessity for survival.

Farming is usually divided into two forms: *horticulture*, or garden farming, which is labour intensive, utilizing only basic technology such as the digging stick or hoe; and the more advanced form of *agriculture* (also referred to as agrarianism), in which the new technology of the plough is utilized. Societies that survive through the herding of animals and do little or no farming are known as *pastoral societies*. Pastoralism developed around 3000 to 3500 years ago in areas where farming was either difficult or impossible.

The Beginning of Structured Social Inequality

The key to understanding the rise of structured inequality lies in the gradual development of private property. But what exactly is private property? Some people would argue that all those things owned by individuals—whether it is their house or a factory—are forms of private property. However, forms of property vary. A house is actually part of one's *personal possessions*, while a factory is *productive property*, part of the means of production. The **means of production** includes all the things that humans use to produce what we need, including tools, natural resources, the land on which production occurs, and the buildings where production takes place.   ·

Why should we bother to distinguish between the two forms of property? The answer to this question lies in the fact that only productive property gives one power. If you own a factory, you gain control over others—you can hire or fire them and gain control over the productive process. You can expand the factory or shut it down and move it to another city or country. Personal possessions do not give that kind of power; at best, if one is rich and can acquire valuable possessions, one can gain status. The question of property is often confusing because people who own productive property usually have enough wealth to have valuable personal possessions as well.

Today we live in a world where private ownership of productive units seems natural, as does the notion that people in any society will compete with each other to attain the power and wealth that come with such ownership. It is therefore surprising to learn that for most of human history our species did not have a developed concept of private ownership of the means of production. However, as this chapter demonstrates, once a surplus comes to be produced, advances in technology and the expansion of the division of labour enlarge inequalities between individuals. Eventually private property—mainly land—comes to be in the hands of some whose ownership or control allows them to be completely removed from production. It also enables them to accumulate great wealth. Others not so fortunate are forced, in one way or another, to be the producers.

Once forms of structured social inequality come into existence they become, to a fair degree, self-perpetuating. This is mainly due to the fact that advantaged individuals are highly motivated to maintain, and even enhance, their position.

On the surface, it appears as if property relations are between humans and things—you own or you don't own something. In reality, property relations are between people. The only reason individuals need to identify an object as belonging to them is so that others will know it is not theirs. Someone shipwrecked on a deserted island does not need to assert ownership of the land. A property relationship, therefore, is between an owner and a non-owner.

As private property expands, some people are able to take that which has been produced by others and keep it for themselves. This process takes on different forms through history, but its essence remains the same: workers produce a surplus beyond their own requirements, and a large part of that surplus is privately appropriated by non-producers as a result of their ownership or control of some form of property. In classical Marxist analysis, each of these groups, which has a distinct relation to the means of production, is referred to as a **social class**.

The issues of structured inequality and social class are among the most controversial in sociology. In later chapters we will discuss at length the ongoing debate about the meaning of social class and the many complexities of class analysis; for the present, however, the above definition will prove sufficient and useful. In societies where private appropriation of surplus occurs, there are always *at least* two major classes: a relatively large subordinate class that produces the surplus and a relatively small appropriating class that, through ownership or control of the means of production, gets to keep all or part of that surplus. There are usually minor classes within a society as well. The reason that the owning class is always much smaller than the productive class is quite simple—until recently, at least, limited technologies meant that there had to be a large number of workers to produce what was required for everyone's survival.

Think About It

Why would the majority of people have let a few others have a position of dominance over them, a position that allowed such individuals to take much of what they produced away from them?

To understand how social inequality arose, we need to briefly examine the gradual transition of societies from egalitarian foraging societies to class-based agrarian forms. This development occurred over thousands of years and at different speeds in different parts of the world. In this chapter we will examine how inequalities began, and in the next chapter we will conclude our historical overview by looking at how we changed from agrarian societies to ones dominated by technology and the marketplace.

Horticultural Societies

Horticultural societies can be divided into two types: simple and advanced (or intensive). Advanced horticultural societies experience greater productivity as a result of the use of a hoe and the practice of certain techniques, including basic irrigation, fertilization, and metallurgy. As technologies advance, productivity increases. This, in turn, leads to increased population size, greater surpluses, and increased societal divisions, both in occupational specialization and unequal allocation of power, privilege, and prestige.

While foraging societies are usually egalitarian and have no formally structured leadership, simple horticultural societies more often show evidence of formalized political leadership. Inequalities become even more pronounced in advanced horticultural societies, and we sometimes see the appearance of monarchs. Social inequalities are thus beginning to appear.

The question, of course, arises as to why humans allowed social inequality to develop. Why couldn't our species farm and have increased surpluses and more complex forms of social organization while retaining egalitarian relations of production? The most likely answer is that societies that developed greater inequalities at that stage of production seemed to have had an improved chance of survival. Early horticulturists didn't hold meetings to decide whether they should retain cooperative forms of production or move in a different direction; social inequality appeared on the scene because, at that time, it worked. The development of a political structure with one or more people in control seems to have improved labour productivity and helped increase chances of survival.

That is not to say that the growth of social inequality must be seen as a positive thing. Obviously, it meant the betterment of some at the expense of others. Friedrich Engels ([1884] 1972, 129) spoke of the rise of structured social inequality as creating a world in which "every step forward is also relatively a step backward, in which prosperity and development for some is won through the misery and frustration of others."

Societies often have more than one form of property relation within them and therefore have different methods of extracting surplus. However, one form usually dominates at a particular point in time. Although some forms are more repressive than others, the private appropriation of surplus, regardless of its form, always requires some degree of coercion, or force. Otherwise, to put it simply, why would those who produce or create surpluses for others keep on doing this?

In foraging societies everyone contributed their labour except the very young and the very old. In agrarian societies, some people came to be excused from work. Most likely, the first people to be freed from productive activity were those who had some connection with the supernatural or who had special knowledge and skills related to production or warfare. Such individuals became leaders in their society and were able to obtain surplus through forms of tribute and, later, via taxation. The majority were probably willing to support this regular payment as an early form of insurance policy. For example, a family might be prepared to give a weekly tribute to their temple priest if they felt the priest had the ear of the gods, which would guarantee a good harvest the following season. Once structured inequality came into being it did, to some extent, take on a life of its own. For those who had more than others, there was an increasingly vested interest in maintaining, or even expanding, the inequality. The more institutionalized the inequality became, the more difficult it was to imagine any alternative.

In societies that produce a small or irregular surplus, the surplus is taken by the headman, but is not used solely to satisfy his personal needs and desires. In fact, those who are the best at giving their wealth away are the most respected. The best-known of these "giveaway" patterns are the *potlatch* ceremonies of the Aboriginals of the northwest coast of North America. In all such giveaway ceremonies, held every few years, elaborate feasts are held in which chiefs attempt to validate and protect their position by giving away as much food and other goods as possible to neighbouring bands. The guest leaders and their followers, after being laden down with an embarrassment of riches, vow to hold even bigger feasts and give away even more to show their superiority.

Such practices, seen from the point of view of our acquisitive society, might seem strange and contrary to the supposedly natural tendency to accumulate material wealth. However, anthropologists have explained such behaviours as a cultural practice that maximizes the chances of survival for the entire community under certain ecological and social conditions. Simple horticulturists—as well as some foragers—can produce a surplus, but the surplus is unpredictable and likely to decline over time, since improved economic conditions raise population size. For such societies, the occurrence of giveaway feasts serves a number of important functions that enhance survival. They mainly act as a means of redistributing surpluses among neighbouring groups, thus maximizing each group's chances of making it through lean times that result from regional and seasonal variations in resources. Giveaway feasts also push individuals to be more productive, hence providing a margin of safety in crises such as war or crop failures (Harris 1989, 118).

This does not mean that those who held potlatch ceremonies consciously noted the advantages of their activities. In a manner similar to the food taboos mentioned earlier in the chapter, these cultural practices were tied to deeply felt spiritual beliefs. Social scientists, on the other hand, are interested in understanding why certain behavioural patterns seem to appear in certain times and places but not in others. By linking these ceremonies to the survival needs of those who practised them, a materialist analysis can help us make sense of this particular social behaviour.

Warfare also becomes increasingly common once a regular surplus is produced, and it is often connected to the giveaway feasts. With a surplus, warfare becomes more feasible and more profitable. Defeating the enemy can mean acquisition of both material goods and land. Warfare also serves as a means of controlling excessive population growth in circumstances where population grows faster than the capacity to feed everyone. In this context, good warriors come to be highly valued, and leadership is often connected to the bravest and most successful in battle. Since women, due to their reproductive capacity, are almost universally prohibited from battle, it is likely that the growth of warfare lowered women's status and increasingly excluded them from circles of power.

All these tendencies become even more evident in advanced horticultural societies, where hoe technology and other developments allow even greater surpluses to be accumulated either through production or seizure. The unequal distribution of resources—material, political, and symbolic—continues to grow, although the redistributive ethic is retained. This limits the degree to which chiefs can use surplus for their own ends. Greater inequalities between groups either by gender, geographical origin, or occupational specialization are in evidence.

As farming advances, certain kinship groups acquire a great deal of land that also gives them power; with this land comes a need to have some organized way to defend and protect it. As a result, more complex military and administrative structures develop over time. But how are they financed? Usually some of the surplus is taken from subordinate groups, commonly via taxation. The institution that carries out such activities in a society is known as the *state*, and advanced horticultural societies show the beginnings of state structures. For the first time in human history, there comes to be a rigid separation between those who are producers and those who produce nothing, but keep for themselves that which is produced by others.

Humans and the cultures that they construct are essentially conservative; that is, whatever exists in the present is, wherever possible, an elaboration or alteration of what existed in the past. And yet horticultural societies are not simply foraging societies where people happen to farm. Once surpluses are regularly produced, societies begin to change from cooperative egalitarian forms of social organization to social forms with private appropriation of wealth, formalized leadership, and structured inequalities. These changes, in turn, lead to changing values, beliefs, and behavioural patterns. In other words, changing the economic arrangements of a society changes its cultural components as well. These cultural components then further alter economic elements within a society.

Agrarian Societies

Over time, a series of inventions and discoveries—including the plough, the harnessing of animal energy, irrigation systems, crop rotation, the smelting of metals, the wheel, and the sail—all bring about major transformations in production, transportation, and communication (Lenski 1966, 190). As a result, the amount of surplus produced increases substantially over what is possible in horticultural societies. These developments lead to even greater population size, increased social densities, growing need for large-scale projects such as irrigation, and more internal and external conflicts. Such conditions require increasing the degree of organization, leadership, and social control. The need for increased coordination and increased productivity leads to the centralization of power in the hands of a few.

The growth in size and complexity of societies, the growing centralization of power, and the gradual erosion in importance of kin networks eventually lead to the disappearance of the redistributive ethic common to horticultural societies. This paves the way for the emergence of major social inequalities, which become embedded in changing social institutions. Power that has previously been invested in leaders as a result of personal qualities is gradually replaced by dominance based either on inheritance or the seizure of power. It can be said that at this point a new form of society appears on the scene. This major transformation is not the result of some clever design or of a collective decision on the part of the participants; rather it arises out of the cumulative changes within the societies themselves.

Agrarian systems represent a *qualitative* change from what preceded them. Kinship now takes an increasingly secondary role to other social alliances and networks that often span whole societies or even empires. Divisions within agrarian societies increase, not only on ethnic, gender, and geographical lines, but in occupational differences as well. Most importantly, with the disappearance of the redistributive ethic, the separation between those who own or control productive property and those who don't becomes sharper and more extreme.

Slavery in Agrarian Societies

Slavery is the most direct way to appropriate the surplus produced by someone else; workers are themselves considered a form of property, owned by the master, and all the surplus they produce, save the barest minimum necessary to keep them alive, is taken from them. Slaves in antiquity were almost always obtained by conquest, which made it easier to see a slave as "the other," a thing less than human. Because they were owned as property by their master, slaves had almost no control over any aspect of their lives.

Some slavery began to appear in early horticultural societies, but it is in the agrarian empires of ancient Athens and Rome that we see a fully institutionalized system for the large-scale employment of slave labour: on the estates, in mines and quarries, and in building, manufacturing, and transportation. Although there were various ways to appropriate the surplus, slavery was the defining form, broadly integrated into the political and ideological spheres of society.

While slavery is the most direct way of appropriating surpluses from workers, it is always a highly unstable form of surplus extraction. This is largely because it is so oppressive, and because there is no incentive—except punishment—for the slave to work harder. While various forms of slavery have continued until the present day in many parts of the world—with many millions of individuals still living today in various states of enslavement—there are relatively few moments in history where slavery has been the *dominant* form of surplus extraction. The more common form of surplus appropriation in agrarian systems, discussed at greater length in the next chapter, involves a class of landlords who force another class of dependent economic producers to transfer the surplus to them via some combination of taxation, forced labour services, or rent (paid in goods or money).

The development of social classes inevitably leads to what is referred to as **class conflict** or class struggle. This struggle occurs because the interests of the owning and producing classes are in direct opposition to each other, since the greater the amount of surplus that goes to one class, the less the amount that goes to the other. It is important to note that this struggle is of a *structural*, not personal, nature. It has nothing whatever to do with whether people like or don't like each other. In many cases, members of structurally opposed classes can actually be very close, as was sometimes the case between domestic slaves and their masters.

Such personal relations do not minimize the fact that their class interests are directly opposed. The tensions between opposing classes can often be held in check for long periods of time, but the underlying structural conflict remains just below the surface, always ready to emerge under certain conditions. We can see this struggle reflected in such things as peasant and slave revolts or, in industrial societies, labour strikes. Marxists argue that this irresolvable tension between opposing classes is one of the main forces for societal change.

Power and Structured Inequality

Structured social inequality means not only the unequal distribution of resources, but also the consequent unequal distribution of power. The increased complexity of the division of labour and the growth of the state leads to increased hierarchies of power and status. One clear example, to be discussed in more detail in Chapter 12, is the erosion of women's position inside and outside the family, which gives men increased power over them. But the greatest power in any society is held by those who own or control the means of production and, as a result, are able to extract surpluses from large numbers of people who must do their bidding in order to survive. Later in the book we will see how this economic power is also linked to political power and the power over ideas.

It is for this reason that any understanding of the cultural patterns within a society must begin with an investigation of its economic arrangements, in order to determine which individual or group of individuals dominates within that society. Once we have discovered who controls the major means of production in any society, we will have a key tool for making sense of the other elements within that society. That is not to say that the economic arrangements mechanically determine a society's culture. However, the historical analysis provided in this chapter makes clear that the economic relationships in a society are primary in affecting who has power. In turn, the individuals who hold power are most able to shape a society's norms, beliefs, values, and social institutions.

Such analysis also helps us understand the underlying tensions between those who have power and those who lack it, and it is these tensions that ultimately pave the way for social change. If Mead and others are right, our culture determines not simply what we do, but also who we are. The issue of power, then, is of more than simply academic interest. If we want to fully understand our own society—indeed, if we want to understand ourselves—we must determine which people hold power, how they came to get it, and how that power is maintained.

Key Points

1. Humans are cultural animals. In order to survive together under particular conditions, we develop technologies, social institutions, means of communication, rules of social behaviour, values, and belief systems.

2. Socialization is the process of learning our society's cultural components.

3. All cultures believe that the way they do things is normal and superior, while the ways of others are strange or even immoral. This tendency is referred to as ethnocentrism.

4. Components of culture remain relatively stable over time, even as they are simultaneously being altered and reworked by humans. New cultural elements are always appearing, while some traditional elements may disappear. In complex societies such as ours, there is no single culture to which all Canadians adhere.

5. The central organizing element of all cultures is their economic arrangements, that is, the way people get the basic necessities of life.

6. A society's economic underpinning is referred to as its mode of production. A society with a specific mode of production is referred to as a socioeconomic formation.

7. Foraging societies constituted the first socioeconomic formation. Such societies, with subsistence-level economies, were small, kin-based, and nomadic. The division of labour was simple and there was no private ownership of the means of production. There was no structured inequality and warfare was rare.

8. With the eventual production of surpluses, cleavages within societies began to appear. In early surplus-producing societies, the surplus was redistributed in occasional lavish feasts. With the production of regular surpluses, warfare became more common.

9. As private property developed, one group of people was able to permanently take and keep what another group produced. In classical Marxist analysis, these groups, each of which has a distinct relation to the means of production, are referred to as social classes.

10. In societies where private appropriation of surplus occurs, there are always at least two major classes: a superordinate class that, through ownership or control of the means of production, appropriates the surplus and a subordinate class that produces the surplus.

11. The first and most direct form of surplus appropriation was that of slavery.

12. Structured social inequality means both unequal allocation of resources and unequal distribution of power.

Further Reading

Adams, Michael. 2003. *Fire and Ice: The United States, Canada and the Myth of Converging Values.* Toronto: Penguin.
The author—using extensive data—concludes that Canadians, regardless of age or region, retain a distinct Canadian culture and are, to some extent, showing increasing divergence from the values held by Americans.

Berreby, David. 2005. *Us and Them: Understanding Your Tribal Mind.* New York: Little Brown.
While not an academic, Berreby undertakes a serious yet highly readable analysis of why humans have a need to identify with groups, and the implications this has for both individuals and societies.

Ferguson, Will, and Ian Ferguson. 2001. *How to Be a Canadian.* Vancouver: Douglas and McIntyre.
A light-hearted examination of what the authors think it means to be a Canadian.

Harris, Marvin. 1989. *Cows, Pigs, Wars and Witches: The Riddles of Culture.* New York: Vintage Books.
Although he can be overly deterministic at times, this American anthropologist writes fascinating materialist explanations on the "riddles of culture."

Leacock, Eleanor Burke. 1981. *Myths of Male Dominance.* New York: Monthly Review.
This book is an interesting and informative collection of articles written by Leacock, an American anthropologist, over a thirty-year period. One of the articles is a critique of Margaret Mead's *Male and Female*, published fourteen years after her earlier work quoted in this chapter, by which time she was advocating a biological determinist view of gender roles.

Sasson, Jack M., ed. 1994. *Civilizations of the Ancient Near East.* New York: Charles Scribner's Sons.
An extensive examination of the development of some of the world's earliest civilizations, with contributions by many authors.

4 The Basis of Modern Societies

In This Chapter

- What kind of society preceded ours?
- How did capitalism develop?
- What exactly is capitalism?
- How has capitalism changed over time?

In the previous chapter we discussed foraging, horticultural, and agrarian societies. Obviously, such terms do not describe Canada today. Some social scientists might refer to Canada as an industrial society, focusing on the way we produce the goods we require. Others might refer to it as an urban society, in contrast to the rural-based societies of the past. Yet others, focusing on how our political system differs from earlier forms, might refer to Canada as a democratic society. All these descriptions would be valid. However, in the last chapter we addressed the centrality of a society's mode of production, which includes both the technology and the relations between people in the process of production. If we utilize this approach, we will see that Canada is a capitalist form of society. In order to better understand what this means, we need to first understand the historical roots of capitalist socioeconomic formations.

Studying our past is an essential part of the sociological imagination. Just as we can learn a great deal about individuals by examining their past experiences, we can really only understand societies through an examination of their roots. This is particularly important since capitalism—the socioeconomic formation in which we live—gives the appearance of being both eternal and unchangeable. This chapter demonstrates that capitalism is not a natural and inevitable outcome of human existence; rather it should be seen as the result of certain events that occurred in the past few centuries in one small part of the globe.

The past hundred years, the century or so which has seen the world-wide expansion of industrial capitalism, have... brought about social changes more shattering in their consequences than any other period in the whole previous history of humankind.
—British sociologist Anthony Giddens, 1982

The Roots of Capitalism: Feudalism

Most of us are familiar with images of the Middle Ages from childhood fairy tales—a time of queens, kings, castles, and knights in armour. Much of Western literature, art, architecture, beliefs, and religious practices have their origins in that period. And yet, aside from these mythical childhood images, few of us know anything about what life was really like at that time. The Middle Ages of Western Europe are commonly dated from around the fifth century until the sixteenth century. The dominant socioeconomic formation that developed during this period is usually referred to as *feudalism*.

Feudalism was an agricultural system that grew out of the ruins of the old slave societies, especially in what are now France, Germany, Italy, and Great Britain.[1] The classical age of feudalism occurred between the tenth and thirteenth centuries. Feudalism was a complex system—social, economic, and political—of duties and obligations between individuals. Since this was a system of private ownership of the productive units, there was an appropriating class of owners, the *nobility*, and a producing class of *serfs*, or peasants. There were also minor classes such as artisans, soldiers, and clergy, and there was a hierarchy of wealth and power *within* the two major classes.

In feudal societies, the land was divided into manors or estates that were held by royalty and then parcelled out to lords or knights. Almost all social relationships were tied to these estates, which could not be bought or sold in the way we know it; other than through inheritance, land could be acquired only through seizure, through bestowal, or through marriage. Virtually all that was produced was consumed locally.

In the early form of feudalism, the feudal lord acquired the surplus primarily from forced agricultural service. Serfs worked most of the week on the lord's land and a small part of the week on either their own allotment of land or the commons land, which was land held for public use. Everything produced on the former went to the lord, while that produced on the latter was directly consumed by the peasant. Why did the peasant agree to this state of affairs? It was mainly because of various *non-economic forms of coercion*—in other words, via the use of political, legal, or military force. Bad things would happen to you if you didn't fulfill your obligations to the lord of the manor.

Think About It

Many people today work at jobs they hate. They don't appear to be coerced. Why then do they continue to do it?

The rent system gradually began to replace the system of forced agricultural service. At this point the peasants worked their own parcel of land and

---

1. European feudalism will be discussed here because central Europe and England are where capitalism developed. However, it should be noted that feudal forms have existed in most other parts of the world and remnants can still be observed in what is often referred to as the Third World, or less-developed countries.

were required to give the lord a portion of what they produced. By the end of the fifteenth century, money payment largely replaced both agricultural service and rent in the form of goods. Over time, both lord and peasant were increasingly drawn into markets and a money economy. The growth of a new type of market—a capitalist market—is key to an understanding of how feudal relations of production declined over time.

Commodity Production and the Growth of Markets

Humans have probably always engaged in some form of trade with each other. At first, trade must have been sporadic and achieved through some kind of barter system. However, the barter system is impractical as markets develop, because it requires that the seller and buyer need each others' goods. A **market** exists when people offer goods and services for sale to others in a more or less systematic and organized way. The concept of the market embodies not simply a physical place but rather a set of social relationships organized around the buying and selling of objects. An object that is produced specifically for exchange is referred to as a **commodity**.

Early feudal Europe had little in the way of markets. However, the increase in trade, in part a result of new technologies connected to transportation, meant that an expanded array of goods began to enter the market, starting in Italy around the twelfth century. Expanded markets meant the growth of urban centres, in opposition to the rural-based feudal mode of production. As markets grew, demand for products grew, leading to increased production of goods. Pressure increased to further extend trade routes to bring an expanding supply of luxury goods into the marketplace.

If most of us were asked how feudal societies became capitalist ones, we would probably guess that it was simply a case of markets growing bigger and bigger, until feudal markets became capitalist ones. However, markets alone cannot explain the rise of capitalism and the decline of feudalism. Many parts of the world—including various parts of Europe—had large urban areas and extensive trade, but retained feudal class relations. Capitalism was an outgrowth of feudalism, but distinct from it. The growth of capitalism—a socioeconomic formation that had at its core the need to intensify labour and improve productivity to increase profitability—seems to have been most clearly rooted in England (E. Wood 1999).

The Decline of Feudalism

Suppose you could enter a time capsule and be transported back to fourteenth-century England. After a pleasant lunch with the Baron of Byng, you inform him that the system in which he lives, from which he so grandly benefits, is on its way out and will shortly be replaced by a totally new form of social organization. You also inform him that he, in part, is contributing to this process. Needless to say, he doesn't believe a word you're saying.

Of course, it is far easier to analyze the past than predict the future. In this case we know what the baron could not, that capitalist societies arose out of—and eventually replaced—the feudal forms of central Europe and England. For approximately 400 years, starting in about the fourteenth century, feudalism decayed from within, until its last remnants finally disappeared and it was replaced by a capitalist mode of production.

The question of what led to the decline of feudalism has been hotly debated in the social sciences, and there is not full agreement regarding the exact processes of change. If we think dialectically, we will recall that change is the result of a complex interplay of connected elements, each feeding back on and reinforcing the other. As a result, the process of social transformation is neither linear nor uniform in all places. Thus, while it is impossible to give a simple explanation of what led to the development of capitalism, it is possible to examine some of the key changes—most reaching their full development after 1500—that eventually altered feudalism forever.

New Class Relations: The Rise of Agrarian Capitalism and Growth of Capitalist Markets

For thousands of years prior to capitalism, classes existed. The dominant class was able to take the surplus from the producing class through force. Slavery was the most extreme form in which extra-economic coercion was used; feudal forms were somewhat more moderate. In both slave and feudal formations, the producing classes gave up most of what they produced because the alternative was some form of severe punishment. In these societies there was no incentive for either the slave or the peasant to increase their labour productivity. In most instances no matter how hard they worked, their lives remained more or less the same.

The first major change to feudal class relations occurred in England, where a variable rent system began to replace a system of fixed rents; in other words—as in today's world—a landlord could independently set the amount that the peasant had to pay in rent to work the land. If one peasant family was less productive than another, nobody would beat them or put them in jail. However, they might not be able to pay the going rent when someone else could; consequently, they might lose their livelihood. Thus for the first time, *economic* coercion—in contrast to the earlier non-economic forms of coercion—began to play a role in the production of surplus. As a result of the shift to a variable rent system, both feudal landlord and tenant farmer became interested in "improvement," or increasing productivity for profit (E. Wood 1999, 80). In other words, an idea we take for granted today—working harder and harder to

> It was [in Europe at the beginning of the sixteenth century] that capitalism introduced the idea of using scarcity as a deliberate tool of economic organization. By intentionally creating scarcity (for the many), capitalism used scarcity to generate wealth (mostly for the few).
> —Linda McQuaig, *All You Can Eat*

create more and more in competition with others—can be seen as a relatively recent development.

Urban centres, meanwhile, saw an expansion in the number of merchants and craftspeople. In the pre-capitalist marketplace, merchants were nothing more than traders who made profits through the difference in the buying and selling price of the product. But gradually some merchants, rather than simply buying and selling goods, realized that they could improve profits via greater control over the productive process. Thus, they began to provide the raw materials and, later, the tools to those who made products for them. In this way they were becoming a class of owners, which Marx referred to as the **bourgeoisie**. Nowhere did this group develop more clearly than in England.

The driving force for the growing bourgeoisie, or capitalist class, was the need for ever-expanding profits. Each capitalist enterprise is in competition with others, and if capitalists hope to maintain a place in the market their enterprises must continue to expand. From the outset, the overarching theme of capitalist economic activity has been that "you grow or you die." Because of this reality, it is not simply profits that the capitalist seeks, but rather the *maximization* of profits.

Think About It

Suppose I am a caring factory owner. I don't want to make a lot of money, just enough to live modestly. I pay my workers higher than average wages, give them better benefits and longer holidays, and make lower profit than others in my industry. Why might I have trouble keeping my business going?

The capitalist owning class, of course, could not survive without a class of workers. Marx referred to these new wage workers as the **proletariat**. This class of workers was made up of the displaced peasants, artisans, and craftspeople who now could survive only by selling their labour power in exchange for a wage.

Accumulation of Capital

What did the feudal nobility do with their wealth? Most of us probably assume that they invested it. That is because in our world it seems an obvious thing for rich people to do with their money. But what exactly is meant by "investing" money? Put simply, it is a way of using money with the specific goal of obtaining more money. Money used this way is referred to as **capital**. Investing money is pre-eminently a capitalist notion and was far from the minds of the nobility until quite late in the feudal period. For most of the landed aristocracy, wealth either was held or was used to maintain an entourage of servants and retainers, to fight battles, and, with the growth of markets, to live in opulence. In the feudal era, the quest for money was generally considered beneath the nobility. Indeed, the Catholic Church viewed usury—lending money with interest—to be a mortal sin.

Think About It

When you hear about someone "investing" their money, what does it mean to you?

If most of the wealthy weren't investing, and the expansion of the market required a huge infusion of capital in order to grow, where did this money come from? Some of it came from the expansion of trade as well as from new technologies and increased rates of productivity. In addition, as markets grew, some nobles—particularly in England—did turn their wealth into capital and become part of the expanding market economy. There was also an influx of capital from the rapid rise and expansion of colonialism at the beginning of the sixteenth century.

In a short span of time, primarily between the late fifteenth and eighteenth centuries, European powers expanded around the globe in competition for valuable resources, new markets, and a cheap labour force. The earliest colonial adventures brought huge sums of money into both England and continental Europe, and it was not long before the looting and plundering of non-European peoples and their resources acquired global proportions. In England, much of the wealth was used to develop a capitalist market, while in most of continental Europe, the new wealth was retained by a powerful monarchy. As a result, England became the main centre for industrial production at this time.

Some enterprising capitalists realized there was great wealth to be made by turning human beings into commodities, and soon the modern slave trade—from Africa to the New World—began in earnest. Slaves were also a cheap source of labour for the colonial powers in the Americas when indigenous workers proved insufficient. At the cost of untold millions of lives, the total wealth of the European nations involved in colonization appreciated immeasurably. But we should not assume that only people in the colonies were forced to be part of the developing capitalist economy. Wherever capitalism has taken hold, whether in Europe or its colonies, it has had to first wrest people from their land, alter their traditional ways of life, destroy their social bonds, and leave most of them economically destitute.

> ...capital comes [into the world] dripping from head to foot, from every pore, with blood and dirt.
> —Karl Marx, *Capital*, Vol. 1, 1867

Advances in Technology and the Growth of the Labour Force

Early feudal society saw the development of many new technologies, including the use of water, wind, and horses as sources of power. The growth of iron mining and advances in the smelting of iron also became important both for agriculture and for industry. In an attempt to increase profits, some merchants gradually began to expand control over the small, largely home-based units of craft production. By around the sixteenth century, many workers came to be drawn into what was at first referred to as the "manufactory" system, in which all the operations involved in a specific type of production took place in particular locations under the direction of the owner.

The large influx of capital into England and continental Europe would have meant little unless production expanded with it. Expansion required a massive increase in the number of workers. As already noted, dispossessed peasants who couldn't pay their rent were driven into urban centres to find some means of survival. A crucial push was also provided by the feudal lords themselves. Many lords, looking for new ways to increase their wealth, began to "enclose" the public commons—land that was collectively farmed by all peasants—as well as the forests on or around their estates, and turned it into grazing land for their own sheep and cattle. This *enclosure movement*, as it came to be known, meant that peasants who had eked out a living no longer had access to the public lands on which they survived. Unable to subsist any longer on the land, large numbers were driven into the towns and cities.

As capitalism developed, workers needed to be disciplined to help increase productivity and profits. As a result, workers gradually came under the strict control of their employers. The shift away from small-scale "cottage" production only worsened the lives of the workers. Wages were so pitiful that whole families had to work to acquire enough simply for their survival. While classical feudalism had been a harsh system for peasants, they could at least be assured that, because of feudal obligations, they would be protected by their feudal lord and always be allowed to work their land. Now, freed from feudal bonds, they were also "free" to be potentially unemployed and without any means of subsistence.

The Industrial Revolution (as we now refer to this period in history) occurred, then, not simply because of the new technologies, but because there was a group of individuals with enough capital to purchase them, as well as an available labour force to work at them. With new technologies, and under pressure from the capitalists for expanding profits, labour productivity increased enormously. Most social scientists and historians agree that while capitalist elements begin to appear in the fifteenth century, it is only the period following the Industrial Revolution in the eighteenth century that can be definitively described as a capitalist mode of production.

Political Transformation in Europe and the Rise of Nation-States

If someone tells us they are Turkish, Finnish, or Nigerian, we readily understand that they come from the countries of Turkey, Finland, or Nigeria. However, people in feudal Europe did not think of themselves as belonging to a country. Most people lived in small villages attached to feudal estates, and their villages seldom had names. The language they spoke was often a local dialect that could not be understood even by neighbouring villagers. At most they saw themselves belonging to a tribe or clan. The notion that they belonged to some larger national group had little or no meaning for them.

The growth of the concept of nation-states is linked to several factors. As market economies began to grow and the traditional feudal relations began to decline, two groups began to expand their power: the monarch and the growing capitalist class. The former began to gain *political* power as that of the feudal lords began to weaken, while the capitalists gained *economic* power through their expanding wealth.

Both soon discovered their shared interests. The monarchs realized that their political power could be expanded via the wealth of the rapidly expanding capitalist class. Capitalists, frustrated with many constraints on trade and commerce, sought the protection of a strong leader who could make and enforce new laws limiting the power of the feudal lords and the local craft guilds. However, while the capitalist class and the monarchy formed temporary alliances of convenience, their basic goals differed. As we shall see in Chapter 8, absolutist states (that is, those under the control of an all-powerful monarch) were not well suited to developed market economies.

However, in the short term, the capitalists benefited from a powerful sovereign at the head of a united kingdom, or **nation**. A nation is not simply a political entity; it also embodies the notion of a group of people living within a geographical boundary who share a common language, culture, and history.[2] The growth of nation-states in Europe gave momentum to the further expansion of trade and commerce, and colonialism was largely fuelled by competition for power between the heads of European states. Thus nation-states developed concurrently with capitalist economic relations.

At the same time, however, the new capitalist owning class increasingly resented the political power that continued to be held by the feudal nobility and restrictions on their profits. As a result, political transformation gradually spread across Europe to fit with the new capitalist economic relations. By the late eighteenth century the capitalist class had consolidated its power, and the absolutist monarchies that had existed across Europe had largely been replaced by some form of republic or constitutional monarchy. (In a few places such as Eastern Europe, as well as in Spain, Portugal, and Italy, the transformations did not come until some time later.) Most importantly, once capitalist market relations developed, the whole world eventually came to be economically drawn into the ever-expanding system known as capitalism.

Changing World View

Up to this point, we have been focusing on the objective material changes that gave rise to the new economic order called capitalism. But if we think dialectically, we must also pay attention to changing subjective conditions, including major transformations in religious and philosophical thought that began to spread across parts of Europe. One of the key thinkers of the time was British philosopher John Locke (1632–1704). Among other things, Locke argued that people

---

2. The question of what actually constitutes a nation and how more than one national group can live within a single state is quite complex. Canada has never totally resolved these issues, either with the francophone population centred in Quebec or with what are now referred to as the First Nations people.

have inherent rights, such as the right to life, liberty, and property, which exist independent of the laws of any particular society. While we take these notions for granted today, they were very radical for a time when people were thought to be simply servants of God and their monarch. Locke's views on individual rights, as well as on democratic forms of government, were appealing to the new expanding bourgeois class. They became a core element of the United States constitution after its War of Independence in 1776.

German sociologist Max Weber (1864–1920) felt that the origins of capitalism were closely linked to a new form of Christianity that spread across northern Europe starting around the fifteenth century. In *The Protestant Ethic and the Spirit of Capitalism*, Weber suggested that Protestantism's new world view was appealing to the growing class of capitalist entrepreneurs. The medieval Catholic Church saw the market as crass and usury as a sin; monastic life and doing good deeds were the things most highly valued. In contrast, Protestant churches attributed moral value to the rational pursuit of economic gain and saw hard work in the real world as a sign of grace. The sayings of American Benjamin Franklin (1706–1790) such as "Early to bed and early to rise makes a man healthy, wealthy, and wise" and "A penny saved is a penny earned" could be considered examples of the Protestant ethic, which valued planning and self-denial to achieve individual wealth. Today we refer to Weber's notion of the Protestant ethic as the "work ethic," and it is used to describe individuals of any religion or ethnic background. It must be remembered that this human attribute, highly valued in today's society, is not universal, but rather is tied to the socioeconomic formation we call capitalism.

What the Transition to Capitalism Teaches Us

The transition from feudalism to capitalism is an interesting case study of the process of major societal change. One of the most important lessons to be learned from this transition is that even societies that are relatively stagnant for long periods of time do change eventually, even if it takes hundreds of years. We can also see that change proceeds from the quantitative to the qualitative; that is, change within feudal societies occurred in numerous small ways until, finally, the sum total of many gradual changes led to the radical transformation of whole societies.

The class that had controlled feudal economies, as well as their political and ideological spheres, began to rot from the inside. The old feudal nobility came increasingly to be seen as amoral and unable to rule. It is as if the disintegration of an entire society is reflected in the decay of its ruling class. In opposition to the nobility was a new, forward-thinking class of capitalists that not only advanced technology and know-how but also began to have increasing moral authority within the old rotting system.

As feudalism transformed itself, the only thing the capitalist class lacked was numbers. This was ultimately resolved by drawing other disaffected sectors of feudal societies into the struggle for change. Indeed, many oppressed groups

Table 4.1 Comparison between Two Different Class Societies

Feudalism	Capitalism
Slow social change	Constant and rapid social change
Simple commodity production: limited production for exchange	Capitalist commodity production: everything a potential commodity
Workers retain some ownership or control of some means of production	Workers separated from ownership or control of the means of production
Limits to the appropriation of surplus	No limits to the appropriation of surplus
Surplus appropriated primarily via extra-economic forms of coercion	Surplus appropriated primarily via economic forms of coercion
Property and class relations a matter of tradition	Property and class relations a matter of legal contracts
Economic and political power identical	Economic and political power theoretically separated (although intertwined)

were swept up in and at times even led the reforms and revolutions that eventually spread across Europe and later into the colonies. However, once the old feudal nobility was defeated, the capitalist class began to assert its dominance, eventually gaining control of all aspects of the new order. By the mid-nineteenth century capitalism had gained ascendancy, and the modern industrial era had begun with the capitalist class firmly in control.

Living in the twenty-first century, with a long span of capitalism behind us, the majority of us probably think of it as the most natural and inevitable form of human society. However, our brief examination of the roots of capitalism helps us see that our form of economic organization has not existed throughout history; indeed it is a socioeconomic formation that has relatively recent origins.

The Development of Capitalism in Canada

What do changing conditions in Europe have to do with Canada? Obviously, the founding of colonies, first French and later English, in what subsequently became Canada was a direct result of the economic and technological changes that were overtaking Europe. But the growth and development of capitalism in Canada was not identical to the patterns seen in late feudal Europe.

Canada, of course, was not "discovered" by the Europeans. At the time of the European invasion there were more than fifty tribes and eleven distinct language groupings among the indigenous peoples. However, for the European monarchs and the growing bourgeoisie, the North American continent was a place to secure their glory and their profits. It was not long before wealthy merchants and nobles began to combine their capital into joint stock-trading companies, particularly once colonial expansion occurred.

A land of abundant natural resources, from its beginnings, Canada was seen as little more than a source of raw material and a market for goods produced

Box 4.1 The Meaning of Progress

The transition from the medieval feudal period to the modern capitalist one was not simply about a changing economy. It was also a period in which radical new ways of understanding the world arose. We saw in Chapter 1 that a scientific world view about both the physical and social world advanced at this time. Earlier in this chapter the new philosophical and religious world views in this transition were addressed. Linked to all these various new ways of seeing the world is the notion of *progress*. Progress is the belief that the world moves forward via a series of inventions and discoveries that lead to perpetual improvement; in other words, society always advances from worse to better. As already noted, "improvement" is a defining concept of capitalism. It should not surprise us, then, that belief in progress went hand in hand with the growth of capitalism and new technologies of the industrial age.

Most of us accept the notion of progress without even thinking about it. We believe that new is better than old, and that the present is inevitably better than the past. Thus we see human history as an upward path from simple hunter-gatherer societies, through agrarianism, to supposedly superior modern industrial societies. And because our culture measures human progress primarily by technology, it just seems self-evident that we have progressed from our technologically deficient ancestors. The idea of progress is pervasive in the world today, especially in advertising, where everything is described as "revolutionary," "new," or "improved."

Was the shift from feudalism to capitalism in fact progress for humankind? In many obvious ways the answer is yes. Even Karl Marx—a product of his time and a believer in progress—thought capitalism was a great advance from the backward and narrow-minded societies that preceded it. And yet, if we think dialectically, things are not as straightforward as they seem. Improvements for some have been setbacks for others. The same twentieth century that gave us the polio vaccine and indoor plumbing also gave us weapons of mass destruction and industrial pollution. For all our advanced knowledge and technology—indeed at times as a result of it—we have created a world that now stands on the precipice, uncertain of its own future. We shall return to these complex questions in later chapters.

"back home." Canada has a history of subservience to two masters: at first it was France, but after the defeat of the French forces in 1760 Canada came under England's control. From its beginnings, Canada's economy was highly dependent on resource extraction, at the expense of the development of a manufacturing sector. Canadians have often been described as "hewers of wood and drawers of water."

Industry did eventually develop, although later than in Europe or the United States. At the time of Confederation, half of Canada's population was in agriculture; by the beginning of the twentieth century Canada ranked seventh in industrial output among manufacturing countries of the world (Krahn et al. 2007, 9). Capital, seeking ever-expanding profits, poured in mainly from England and the United States, while a massive influx of immigrants, mostly from Great Britain and continental Europe, provided the majority of the labour power.

Before Confederation, Halifax was a main centre of industrial production; after 1867, the areas around Montreal and Toronto became the industrial heartland of the country.

Of course, making sense of Canada as an economic, political, or social entity requires that we understand the peculiarities of its geography—most of our land is not easily habitable, and as a result, our relatively small population has spread out over vast distances not far from the U.S. border. Thus, although this book analyzes how Canadian society works, we must always keep in mind that we are a highly regionalized country. Issues that might seize one part of the country—for example, language legislation, the fishing rights of indigenous people, or government changes to the Canadian Wheat Board—might be of little interest to another. Moreover, because the Canadian economy did not develop evenly across the country, regional disparities in economic growth and overall wealth have given rise to perpetual tensions between provinces and between regions.

Capitalism Explained

Up to this point, you may have been thinking, "But what exactly *is* capitalism?" This abstract entity is often hard to pin down. **Capitalism**—the name given to the socio-economic formation in which we now live—is, at its core, an economic system in which all production is subordinated to the imperatives of the market: accumulation, labour productivity, competition, and profit maximization. In a world dominated by the marketplace all things are potential commodities, including, as we shall see, labour power itself.

Almost everyone today is dependent on the marketplace to acquire their means of life; as a result, the requirements of the capitalist market dominate our entire society and culture. It is therefore quite impossible to understand how our society works without first understanding how the capitalist economy works. However, this task is not as easy as we might think because capitalism differs in two key ways from previous socioeconomic formations. First, capitalism is an extremely complex and ever-changing system; second, unlike slave or feudal systems, the class structure of capitalism is thoroughly disguised.

A number of classical theorists wrote exten-

> Capitalism is neither a person nor an institution. It neither wills nor chooses. It is a logic at work through a mode of production: a blind, obstinate logic of accumulation.
> —Michel Beaud,
> *A History of Capitalism 1500–1980*

> ...the distinctive and dominant characteristic of the capitalist market is not opportunity or choice but, on the contrary, compulsion.
> —Ellen Mieksins Wood,
> *The Origin of Capitalism*

> The defining characteristic of capitalism is, first and foremost, the fact that most of the means of production are privately owned and controlled.
> —Paul Phillips,
> *Inside Capitalism*

sively about the nature of capitalist systems. One of the earliest was Scottish political economist and moral philosopher Adam Smith (1723–1790) in *The Wealth of Nations,* published in 1776. His most well-known argument was that a free market, while appearing to be chaotic and unpredictable, was actually guided by an "invisible hand" that made it work for the benefit of all. For Smith, the wealth and collective well-being of society was invariably produced in the marketplace as individuals pursued their own self-interest. Karl Marx, writing a century after Smith, disputed this argument. For Marx, the capitalist marketplace primarily benefited the owners of the largest productive units. Workers received only a small share of what they produced, and small business owners struggled hard to survive in the competitive marketplace.

Like feudalism before it, capitalism is a mode of production with private appropriation of surplus. As noted earlier in this chapter, there are two major classes. The appropriating class is generally referred to today as the capitalist class or simply the owning class; this class owns or controls the principal means of production, distribution, or exchange of goods and services. The producing class is generally referred to as the working class, or simply workers; they must work for a wage because they own no significant means of production. In economic terms, the owning class is often referred to as *capital*, while the working class is referred to as *labour*. Between these two major classes is another class, referred to as the **petite** (sometimes written as *petty*) **bourgeoisie**. This class is made up of small-business owners, independent farmers, craftspeople, and self-employed professionals—those who have a small amount of capital and may or may not employ a few workers, but who survive largely through their own labour.

Think About It

In Chapter 1 you were asked to think about which size of "fish" you thought you were. Now we can understand that the fish in the cartoon represent classes in capitalist societies. Which class do you now feel you are in? Has your answer changed from your answer to the question in Chapter 1?

It is important to note that classes in capitalist societies are not easy to see. In pre-capitalist societies, the appropriation of surplus by the owning class was direct and observable. Moreover, because the producing class handed over something to the appropriating class, either in the form of direct surplus, or through some form of rent or tribute, it was clear who had the power and who was benefiting from the relationship. There were also usually markers of class difference—for example, styles of clothing or required acts of obeisance such as bowing—that clearly differentiated the classes.

In capitalist societies, class markers largely disappear and the power relationship becomes hidden. In contrast to earlier socioeconomic forms, it now appears as if employers are actually giving something to workers (both the job and the wage) rather than taking something from them. The workers, in turn, appear to be freely entering into a fair exchange with employers. Indeed, the entire basis of employer-employee relationships in our society is built on the assumption that both parties to an employment contract are equal, sovereign people (Glasbeek 1993, 285).

However, capital and labour are not equal: between them there is a relationship of dominance in which the class that owns and controls the means of production has the upper hand. In this way, capitalism is similar to all previous class societies. Certainly, most workers in capitalist societies are not in a relationship of servitude as in slave or feudal societies. Because workers in capitalist societies are not forced to work for any particular employer, the relationship appears to be a voluntary one. However, workers *are* forced to enter into a relationship with some employer; now, however, the coercive aspect takes on a primarily *economic* form. In other words, if workers don't sell their labour power for a wage, they won't normally be beaten or killed (although this does happen under certain circumstances). Rather, without work they will have no means of subsistence and will at best live a life of destitution. People can, in theory, start their own business if they don't want to work for someone else, but only a small proportion can do so.

Think About It

Why don't all dissatisfied and unemployed workers simply start their own businesses? What would happen if they all did?

Profit: The Driving Force of Capitalism

As we saw earlier in this chapter, the true capitalist is someone who moves beyond being a merchant. No longer interested in the simple buying and selling of commodities, capitalists are concerned with "investment," or what is also referred to as the *circulation of capital*. Capital is said to "circulate" because it enters the market with the sole purpose of coming back as an increased amount, which is realized as profits. Capitalists are concerned less with the absolute amount of profits than the *rate* of profit—that is, the amount of return they get on their initial investment. Capital must always keep circulating, and the faster this circulation occurs, the more can be reinvested. The larger the reinvestment, the greater the chances that even more profit will generated, in a never-ending process.

> The circulation of capital has no limits.
> —Karl Marx,
> *Capital, Vol. 1, 1867*

Because of the competitiveness within capitalist markets, the owners of businesses cannot just sit around waiting for commodities to be produced, sold in the marketplace, and later converted to profits. As a result, they try to speed up the cycle by borrowing money from banks or by selling shares in their companies to quickly raise new capital. This money may be used to expand production, hire new workers, or buy new machinery. It has become increasingly common for companies to seek to purchase all or part of other companies to get a higher and faster return on their original investment. More and more companies are being sold to other companies that actually produce nothing at all, but, rather, are simply holders of large amounts of capital. Their sole purpose is to buy companies and later sell them at a profit. Thus, although it appears that the largest businesses are producers of goods and services, this production is actually just a means to an end, which is the enlargement of profits.

The *short-term goal* of every capitalist is not simply profits, but the maximization of profits. Capitalists seek to maximize profits not because of personal greed (although any individual capitalist may indeed be very greedy), but because of the competitive nature of capitalist economies. However, despite the never-ending tension between capitalists competing against each other in the marketplace, they do share a common interest. All have a similar *long-term goal*, which is the maintenance of the capitalist system itself. At certain moments in history, capital may decide to forgo short-term profits in order to ensure that the capitalist system does not come crumbling down. But most often, profit maximization takes priority.

The Hidden Source of Capitalist Profits

When I was younger, my father gave me this advice: "You can put yourself to work or your money to work. The trick in life is to put your money to work so that you don't have to put yourself to work." The notion that money is animate, that it "works" and "grows," is not new. In capitalist systems, it does seem that money has some magic quality. In reality, however, most wealth is not created in the marketplace, where it simply moves about, but rather it is produced in the sphere of production. The key producer of wealth is the worker.

Labour power—the sum total of all a worker's physical and mental capacities that go into a particular work task—is a commodity that is purchased by the employer for one reason: workers add value to the business. They may add value by extracting raw materials from the ground, by converting them into new products that become commodities in the marketplace, or by some other contribution to the company such as design, marketing, or sales of a good or service. A Florida Chamber of Commerce advertisement (June 1978) urged businesses to come to a city in their state: "In Lakeland, Florida, your company could receive a yearly bonus of $12,769 in value added by manufacture per production worker. Workers give back $5.25 in value added for every dollar they're paid. That's a whopping 44.2% above the American average." This ad helps us see that the new value added by workers in production can sometimes actually be calculated. In this example, workers take home in wages only about one-sixth of the value they add to the commodities produced.

For employers, the lower the purchase price of labour, the better able they are to secure profits. The price of labour power is, of course, referred to as a wage, although worker benefits must also be included. Thus we can see the structural basis for class struggle in capitalist societies. In order to maximize profits in a competitive marketplace, employers generally try to keep wages low, keep the number of workers down, and get employees to work as hard as possible. Workers, if able, will try to improve their wages and working conditions.

The process of private appropriation of surplus, then, occurs in capitalism just as it did in earlier class formations. However, in capitalist systems the process becomes indirect. The shareholders of the major corporations don't take home the products produced by the employees. Rather, the commodities produced are first sold in the marketplace for money that, after all expenses are paid, finds its way into the hands of the company's shareholders. In Marxist terms this new wealth that is acquired indirectly through the marketplace is referred to as **surplus value**. As in all class societies, in capitalism it is a producing class that creates wealth for the owning class.

Of course, most workers today are no longer direct surplus producers. Because of rapid advances in technology, fewer and fewer workers are producers of actual objects. More and more of us are providers of knowledge or services that allow, in one way or another, for the surplus to be realized. Others of us are involved in the financial side of the economy. In the end, however, the principle remains the same: capitalists secure profits by paying out far less in wages than they secure, directly or indirectly, through the labour of workers.

The centrality of labour for the production of profit comes into high relief when workers go on strike. If the workers in a widget factory stop working, no widgets get produced. If no widgets get produced for some time, then no profits can be secured. Likewise, if professional basketball, hockey, or football players stop playing, little in the way of profits is made by the team owners. Whatever one might think of the high salaries of the players, it has to be acknowledged that it is the athletes, like the widget makers, who make money for the owners, not vice versa.

In order for class relations to be sustained, it is necessary for most people to believe that such relations are both natural and inevitable. For this reason, most of us have a hard time accepting that in capitalist societies workers may ultimately be more important than owners. This is because in a society where money determines value, those with the most money *appear* to be the most valuable. That the capitalist owning class is both deserving of its wealth and essential to our well-being are such strongly held notions that it is hard to think otherwise. Moreover, if so much wealth is—as Marx argued—created by workers, then questions arise as to why the majority of it seems to end up in the hands of the owners, not the workers.

The Rise of Monopoly Capitalism

Most of us have heard our economy described as a "free enterprise" system. **Free enterprise** occurs when no single buyer or seller can affect the price of a commodity by withdrawing their purchasing power or their product from the marketplace. This was the type of economic system lauded by Adam Smith, and much of the capitalist marketplace could be defined as free enterprise until well into the twentieth century. However, in the past half-century most of the dominant sectors of the world economy have undergone a process of **monopolization**, with the result that there are now so few companies that free-enterprise competition no longer exists. Monopolization does not require that only one company controls an industry. If a small number of companies controls a sector, then the free market effectively ceases to exist. In classical economic terms, this control is sometimes referred to as an *oligopoly*.

Reprinted by permission of United Electrical, Radio and Machine Workers of America (UE) from *UE News.*

Both in Canada and internationally, the growing concentration and centralization of capital in the major economic sectors as a result of mergers and acquisitions are increasing rapidly, and the size of mergers is enormous. In 2006 takeovers of Canadian companies were valued at an unprecedented $270 billion, nearly double the previous year (McNish 2007), while the total value of mergers worldwide was US$4 trillion. Many of the takeovers were by what are referred to as *hedge funds* or *private-equity funds*, which have been created by individuals with large amounts of surplus capital. The managers of these funds buy firms traded on public stock exchanges, control them privately for a time (where they are out of public view), and then attempt to re-sell them at a large profit. Often the profits are generated by firing many of the employees (Gwyn 2007). Such groups were involved in sixteen of the fifty-one so-called mega-deals of over $1 billion in 2006 (Erman 2007). In other words, more and more of the major corporations are owned and controlled by other companies that are not interested in the productive process whatsoever.

Think About It
Can you name some sectors of the Canadian economy that are highly monopolized?

The process of monopolization is part of a more generalized process referred to as the **concentration and centralization of capital**. *Concentration* refers to the fact that capital comes to be in fewer and fewer hands as a result of monopolization. *Centralization* means that capital is centred in a few core geographic areas both within countries and on a global scale. Within this loose structure, some regions and nation-states can be considered to be the *core*, while others are in the *periphery*. The core is made up of a small number of regions and nation-states that appropriate the majority of the world's wealth. The periphery is made up of the least economically developed countries or regions.

As a result of the concentration of capital, the owning class has become increasingly difficult to identify. The comic strip on the previous page visually represents the owning class as a man dressed in fancy clothes and smoking a cigar while walking around the factory floor. Ownership of the major companies today rarely involves a single individual, and the owners no longer direct their workers. Most ownership in Canada today is masked by the legal fiction known as the corporation, with many levels of management between the owner and the employee. But behind the corporation are real people. And despite the fact that most corporations are "public" (because they trade shares in public exchanges), there continue to be a few key individuals or families that control the major corporations, as we shall see in Chapter 5.

Think About It
Ask a number of working people if they know who owns the company they work for.

Table 4.2 Fortune 500 Top Ten Corporations, 2006

Company	Revenue (millions)*	Profits (millions)*	Home Country	Industry
1 Exxon Mobil	339,938.0	36,130.0	U.S.	petroleum refining
2 Wal-Mart Stores	315,654.0	11,231.0	U.S.	retail sales
3 Royal Dutch Shell	306,731.0	25,311.0	Holland	petroleum refining
4 BP	267,600.0	22,341.0	England	petroleum refining
5 General Motors	192,604.0	-10,567.0	U.S.	motor vehicles & parts
6 Chevron	189,481.0	14,099.0	U.S.	petroleum refining
7 DaimlerChrysler	186,106.3	3,536.3	Germany	motor vehicles & parts
8 Toyota Motor	185,805.0	12,119.6	Japan	motor vehicles & parts
9 Ford Motor	177,210.0	2,024.0	U.S.	motor vehicles & parts
10 ConocoPhillips	166,683.0	13,529.0	U.S.	petroleum refining

*U.S. Dollars
Source: <http://money.cnn.com/magazines/fortune/global500/2006/full_list/>

The Crisis of Overproduction

One of the strangest elements of capitalist economies—yet central to understanding how it works—is the irresolvable problem of overproduction. This occurs because almost all production is directed to the profit maximization of each individual enterprise, and it is not coordinated. This is referred to as the **anarchy of production**.

Let us imagine what happens in the widget industry every year. Each company assesses the maximum number of widgets it thinks it might be able to sell to maximize profits. This year company A will try to secure a slightly bigger share of the market than last year (perhaps with a new upscale widget or an advertising campaign to convince Canadians to buy their latest widget), and so they raise production somewhat. Companies B, C, D, and E all do the same. The final outcome is obvious. While some widget companies may indeed increase their market share, the sum total of widgets on the market far exceeds the total number of possible sales. Capitalist production thus leads inevitably to what is called the **crisis of overproduction**.

The first thing that is overproduced in capitalism, then, is goods. In some sectors, such as the clothing and shoe industries where fashions change rapidly, the unsold products will usually be discounted for quick sale and may even be sold at a loss. In other industries, such as the auto industry, other incentives such as low financing rates, free upgrades, or extended warranties may be offered. Why don't all companies simply lower the prices of their commodities to sell more? The problem is that lower prices can mean lower profits. Corporations can often make more profits by either destroying the excess or cutting back on production until surpluses are depleted.

This overproduction can clearly be seen in the automobile industry in North

America, where the "big three" corporations—General Motors, Ford, and Chrysler—have been forced to deal with weak profits. In 2006, both General Motors and Ford offered generous buyouts and early retirement packages to their employees. GM hoped to reduce its workforce from 24,000 to 13,000 in the United States, Ford planned to close sixteen plants, and Chrysler planned to lay off at least 11,000 workers, including 2,000 in Canada. All three offered special incentives and prizes to purchasers of unsold 2006 models as the 2007 models appeared. Each is going through major restructuring to try to reduce costs (Runk 2006). It should be noted that these companies remain very profitable (see Table 4.2). The problem is the decline in their rate of profit compared to others in their industry.

Capitalists are well aware of the crisis of overproduction, and as far back as the nineteenth century they formed trusts, cartels, and syndicates in an attempt to coordinate production and avoid such crises. Another way capitalists have attempted to deal with the overproduction of products is to convince working people to buy more and more of them. While this seems self-evident today, it was a radical notion less than a century ago when workers earned such low wages that they barely had enough to buy basic necessities. However, Henry Ford had a radical idea for his time. After developing the assembly line, he *raised* the wages of his workers. Ford was no friend of working people. Rather, he did this to raise his own profits, for not only did higher wages make them more reliable employees, it also allowed them to be future purchasers of his mass-produced products. We will look at the issue of mass consumerism in more detail in Chapter 6.

Think About It

Have you ever had a job where your employer allowed you to purchase their product at discounted prices? How can you connect this pattern to the crisis of overproduction?

In addition to an excess of goods, capitalism inevitably has too many workers, which helps drive down the cost of purchasing labour power. Of course, the anarchy of production means that there may sometimes be worker shortages in some fields or in certain geographical locations, but overall there is always a surplus of workers. In 2006, at least 200 million people around the world lacked employment.

At the same time that the drive for ever-increasing profits creates an excess, or glut, of goods and a glut of workers, we also see a glut of capital. This is a particularly strange phenomenon. On the surface, it seems absurd that capitalism could actually produce "too much" in the way of profits. However, with many investors looking for a rapid and high rate of return all over the globe, there are simply not enough places for all the capital to be reinvested. One analyst (Trumbull 2007) explained the large

> The world is awash in capital.
> —Jacques Gordon, LaSalle Investment Management, 2006

merger and acquisition activity of 2006 this way. "Perhaps the biggest force behind the merger wave is the simplest: piles of money."

The crisis of overproduction is one of the main factors that give rise to the economic cycles that occur within capitalist systems. These recurrent cycles of crisis, depression, recovery, and boom have occurred throughout the history of capitalist societies. During the crisis phase, as overproduction of goods occurs, enterprises cut back on production, and a portion of workers are laid off, thus adding to the excess of workers. These workers are then less able to buy products, which can lead to even greater surpluses, more cutbacks, more layoffs, and so on. It also leads to a horrible waste of a country's productive forces, as both machines and workers sit idle. However, while some crises in some countries may be relatively short-lived and not too severe, there are times in history when capitalism as a whole has gone into a major and prolonged crisis on a global scale. Later in the book we will see how governments and international organizations have played a key role since World War II in attempting to moderate economic crises.

The Growth of the Paper Economy

Money, of necessity, plays a major role in the marketplace. Not surprisingly, then, we find that money, now converted to capital in a capitalist marketplace, became increasingly important over the course of the twentieth century. Likewise, those who control and manipulate money—such as banks, insurance companies, brokerage houses, bond dealers, and investment companies—have taken on increasing importance. Because of the glut of capital, and the increased competition that such a glut creates, investors search the globe for an ever larger and faster return. Large profits can often be made quickly in highly speculative areas, such as the stock market, currency exchanges, or commodity markets.

> Increasingly, our economy is becoming divorced from reality. The activities which generate the highest monetary returns often have little or no real value.
> —John Dillon, *Turning the Tide: Confronting the Money Traders*

Corporations involved in the real economy have traditionally sought economic stability, which allowed them to plan production for profit over extended periods of time. Speculators in the paper economy, in contrast, thrive on instability. Their goal is to invest capital for the short term and extract maximum profit through slight changes in the stock market, commodity values, or interest rates. For these capitalists, the greater the instability of the financial markets the greater their opportunity to extract profits (Korten 1996, 199). Private equity and hedge funds, a new development in capitalist economies, now buy and then quickly sell major corporations not for what they produce but for how much profit can be generated in a short amount of time.

Of course, this need for volatility is contradictory, as too much instability could eventually bring the entire international financial system crashing down, a long-term consequence not desired by capital. Thus the shift to the paper economy imposes negative consequences not only on workers and their communities, but also on capital itself.

Social Production versus Private Ownership

We currently live in a society that emphasizes the individual. If we hear about a wealthy person, we usually look for what they *individually* did to acquire their wealth (i.e., they worked hard to build up their company; they got a great deal of education; they had a brilliant idea; they speculated cleverly in the stock market; they robbed a bank). Such a notion is a particularly capitalist one. In the feudal period, no one assumed that the feudal aristocracy had acquired their wealth as a result of some personal characteristic; it was simply accepted that wealth was unequally allocated, primarily on the basis of birth.

Because our society focuses on individuals, it is often forgotten that the production of wealth in capitalism is ultimately a social activity: it is produced by large groups of people working together in a highly complex division of labour. Indeed, capitalist production, when compared to the relatively small-scale peasant or craft production of agrarian societies, is the most complex production in history. Capitalist production continually expands to include more and more people in a worldwide network. Hundreds of thousands of people around the world are employed by the major corporations, and these corporations are increasingly interconnected.

And yet in capitalism as in all class societies, the surplus is *privately* appropriated. In fact, we shall see in later chapters that an ever-decreasing portion of the population is acquiring an ever-larger share of the surplus. Thus the product of social production is not placed at the disposal of all, but rather is appropriated by a small class of owners. Marx saw this as the basic contradiction of capitalism: the tension between the increasingly social nature of production and the increasingly private appropriation of the fruits of such production.

Moreover, capital must use a large portion of the surplus value in a very particular way: to further expand itself. In expanding, capital must search the globe for places to make ever-higher profits at an ever-faster pace. In this process, whether such self-expansion destroys human lives or the environment can never be the primary concern.

In Whose Interests?

If you take an economics course, or read the business section of any newspaper, you will hear about "the economy," "the markets," "productivity," and so on. All these terms are presumed to be neutral. If stock markets rise, we are led to believe this is a good thing, or if inflation increases as a result of higher wages, it is a bad thing. But what we are actually hearing about are *capitalist* markets, a *capitalist* economy, and *capitalist* needs. Within a single economy, some might be doing extremely well while others are suffering, and for exactly the same reasons.

It is commonly taken for granted that if big business is doing well, this must be good for everybody. On the surface, such a position seems self-evident. If corporations can secure ever-greater profits, so the argument goes, they will invest in economic expansion, the market will grow, jobs will be created, wages will rise, prices will drop, and so on. This tendency seemed to be a reality in the period between 1946 and the early 1970s. Even into the 1990s, a period in which these tendencies did not present themselves, arguments continued to be promoted that things had never been better, and that "the market" was helping create a better life for everyone.

> Rise in joblessness delights U.S. markets
> —headline on the front page of the International Herald Tribune, 3–4 June 2000
>
> Arms makers see opportunity in Gulf tension
> —headline in the business section of the Globe and Mail, 20 February 2007

However, recent trends in Canada and the rest of the capitalist world increasingly cast doubts on the legitimacy of such arguments. Between 1987 and 2004, the share of total gross domestic product (GDP) that went to corporate profits in Canada rose from 4 percent to 14 percent, while labour's share of national income fell from 56 percent to 49 percent (Fudge 2005). Moreover, it seems that jobs have been cut specifically to increase corporate profits. Not only do companies no longer try to disguise this fact, but they also are often directly rewarded for doing so. For example, in 2007 Nortel Networks saw the price of its shares rise 10 percent after announcing it was eliminating 2,900 jobs (*National Post* 10 February 2007, FP4). RadioShack Corp., the third-largest electronics chain in the United States, saw its profit rise five-fold after it closed 506 stores and eliminated 7000 jobs (*Globe and Mail* 30 April 2007, B15).

Such examples are clues that the interests of corporate owners do not seem to mesh with—and, indeed, often directly conflict with—the needs of workers. But this lack of commonality between big business and the average Canadian goes far beyond the workplace. The most extreme example would be in relation to war, which has been very profitable for many businesses over the last century. For example, while thousands of American soldiers and hundreds of thousands of civilians have died in the Iraq war that began in 2003, for many industries—such as petroleum producers and defence contractors—business is better than ever.

In the area of public health, research agendas are commonly linked to the interests of private companies seeking to increase profits. Put simply, sickness is more profitable than good health. While profits in the drug industry have soared in recent years, many diseases continue to kill millions of people because drugs to combat them make no money for the drug industry. Such diseases primarily affect people in the developing world who are too poor to pay for treatment (*Toronto Star* 4 July 2003, D2). Of course, preventing diseases in the first place—via public health education, the elimination of pollutants, and improved standards of living—would be the best direction, but there's little profit to be made in that at all.

The Changing Face of Capitalism

Earlier in this chapter we saw that feudalism was a relatively rigid and inflexible socioeconomic formation. In contrast, capitalism over the last two centuries has proven to be an extremely flexible and adaptable system. Some capitalist countries are quite wealthy overall while others are very poor; some have democratic political forms while others are totally undemocratic; some are closely tied to traditional religions while others are secular (that is, not affiliated with a religion). But whatever the superficial appearance, almost all countries, in one way or another, are now tied to a single global capitalist economy.

Moreover, the dominant form of capitalism has changed over time. The period of the mid-nineteenth to the early twentieth century is often referred to as the stage of **laissez-faire capitalism**, when free enterprise still dominated, there were many small or medium-sized productive units, and there was only moderate state intervention to control the worst excesses of capital. However, the inevitable instability of the capitalist system led to a number of serious economic downturns, the most serious of which was the time from the Great Depression, which began after 1929, until World War II. Following the war, there were dramatic alterations to the developed capitalist economies. Governments played an increasing role in economic affairs, while the public sector and social safety net expanded. This form of capitalism is commonly referred to as the **welfare state**, because governments developed policies that enhanced the welfare of most citizens rather than just the dominant class.

By the mid-1970s, however, the capitalist class found itself facing a number of serious difficulties. Extremely large corporate units had developed, and the competition was intense as they sought to increase their rate of profit. The welfare state gradually diminished in all capitalist societies and was replaced by a set of policies collectively referred to as *neoliberalism*, which shall be explained in detail in Chapter 9. In this period, more and more wealth has been transferred to the largest corporations and the wealthiest individuals, while social spending by most governments has been drastically reduced.

Capitalism as a Global System

Many of us think that globalization is a recent trend. However, the quote from Marx and Engels gives us a clue that capital has always looked beyond its own national borders for new sources of profit. In the expanding global economy of the late nineteenth century, it was the European nations that competed for territories in Africa, Asia, Australia, and North and South America. Many of these colonies had already been utilized as military outposts, as trading centres, for the seizure of slaves, for the looting of gold and silver, and for European settlement.

> The need of a constantly expanding market for its products chases the bourgeoisie over the whole surface of the globe. It must nestle everywhere, settle everywhere, establish connections everywhere.
>
> —Karl Marx and Friedrich Engels, *The Communist Manifesto, 1848*

However, with the advance of industrial capitalism, the world powers began to use their colonies in a different way. While Marx addressed the global nature of capitalism, it was several later analysts, including V. I. Lenin, who drew attention to the process of **imperialism**. In this advanced stage of capitalism large monopolies came to control the economy. For Lenin and other change theorists, imperialism has always been part of developed capitalism because capital must continually expand, something that eventually reaches its limits when capital is confined to its own soil. Capitalism, therefore, has always had an element of force that has required both financial and military support from governments.

The imperialist stage of capitalist development began at the end of the nineteenth century. Following the Treaty of Berlin in 1885, signed by the major European powers and the United States, the whole African continent was divided up; by the start of the twentieth century only Ethiopia and Liberia remained as sovereign African states. The same process occurred in the Far East and Southeast Asia. In this way the European states established absolute power over their colonies around the world. Some of the countries that are today considered minor powers—such as Belgium or Spain—were once major players in the growing global economy.

As part of this process, industrialization was actively discouraged in the colonies. Instead they became exporters of natural resources, which were processed abroad and sold back to them as finished products at exorbitant prices. In most colonies, impoverished peasants were forced to work under the most horrific conditions, living lives marked by chronic hunger, bad housing, ill health, illiteracy, and political tyranny. The skills and knowledge of the small stratum of educated workers were constantly underutilized, and persistent racism kept many from obtaining jobs for which they were qualified.

Direct colonial rule gradually came to an end in the era following World War II. However, although the colonies became independent in theory, their economies were so grossly distorted and dependent on the imperialist powers that the majority could not come out from under their conditions of underdevelopment. Moreover, internal political instabilities, an impoverished or underpaid workforce susceptible to graft and corruption, as well as continued alliances between the imperialist powers and the local elites, meant little true independence or advancement for the majority of people in the developing world. In this way, the imperialist powers, led by the United States since the end of World War II, have retained effective domination over the poorest nations of the world.

Thus, although the term *globalization* has become popular in recent years, it is in reality nothing new. Most of us think that globalization today is about trade. However, the recent era of global expansion has taken on a number of distinctive characteristics, the most important of which is the rapid expansion of foreign direct investment (FDI), which went from $216 billion in 1990 to more than $1.3 trillion by 2000 (Toussaint 2005, 60). After a subsequent four-year slump, it rose to $969 billion in 2005.

It is also important to note that the capitalist goal of maximizing profit has not led to the expansion of such investment equally around the globe. Instead, there has been a relocation of factories and businesses *within* the developed capitalist world, as well as an expansion of global capital to a select few areas such as China, India, some parts of Latin America, and parts of Eastern Europe. Nonetheless, all economies, whether big or small, are linked to a single global structure dominated by global capital. We will return to the issue of globalization in future chapters.

Think About It

Why do you think capitalist expansion has not developed equally around the world? What are capitalist enterprises looking for when they invest abroad?

The Transnational Corporation

Although capital has always sought profits beyond the narrow confines of any particular nation-state, a dramatic change occurred with the development of what are referred to as multinational enterprises (MNEs), or **transnational corporations** (TNCs).[3] With the pressing need to always search out new sources of greater profits, major corporations are driven to look beyond their national boundaries for new markets, cheap labour, cheap raw materials, and governments sympathetic to the goals of capital. It is mainly since the 1960s that TNCs have become a major force on the world scene.

TNCs are the largest and most powerful of the conglomerates and are assuming an ever-increasing share of the world gross domestic product. By the beginning of this century, over half of the largest economies in the world were corporations; in other words, the major TNCs were larger than many nation-states. The majority of these conglomerates are based in what is often referred to as "the Triad"—the United States, Western Europe, and Japan. The combination of size and international networks gives transnational corporations tremendous power, and they are increasingly able to move capital to wherever return on investments can be maximized. Recent rapid advances in information and communication technologies make such moves both possible and necessary for the major players in the competitive global marketplace. Even the threat of such moves is often enough to allow the TNCs to put pressure on governments or trade unions to accede to their demands.

Power in Capitalist Societies

Capitalism is unique in giving dominance to those who hold power strictly in the economic sphere. As we will see in later chapters, however, the power of those who own or control the means of production can also be linked to power in two

---

3. MNEs are technically somewhat distinct from TNCs. The former tend to be described in the economic literature as enterprises that are nation-based, whereas TNCs are truly stateless. In practice, however, the two terms are often used interchangeably.

other societal spheres: the sphere of ideas and the political sphere. Indeed, it will be argued that the owning class could not maintain its position for long if it did not effectively control all three spheres within society.

We have seen in this chapter that when we speak today about the owning class, we are referring not to the owner of a small neighbourhood store, but rather to the select few who own and control enormous amounts of capital worldwide via the entity of the corporation. Why should any of us care about this development? If we recall that ownership of the productive process gives societal power, then the concentration of ownership also means the growing concentration of power.

In a sense, the power of each class is a potential, and the degree to which each class uses its potential constitutes what was referred to earlier as the class struggle. This struggle can be envisaged as a game of tug of war: the more one class asserts its power to get its interests met, the less the other class gets its interests met. Hence the struggle between classes is structural, rather than personal.

Of course, class is not the only determinant of power within societies. In societies as large and complex as ours, many inequalities of power exist. Certain occupational categories—for example, doctors or lawyers—have more power than others. Men have more power than women. Certain ethnic or racial groups, for historical reasons, have more power than others. Parents have more power than children. The list is endless.

Many sociologists have given primary attention to such inequalities of power, which we can say exist mainly at the proximal level. In our everyday lives it is certainly these power inequalities that we experience most directly. Women are beaten by men, children are abused by adults, workers are humiliated by managers, patients are mistreated by doctors, and so on. However, as the rest of this book demonstrates, the power of the dominant class, while much more invisible and distal than these other, more localized, forms of power, is also all-encompassing and much more consequential for the totality of our life experiences. From the minute we wake up until the minute we go to sleep, all of us, whether we know it or not, are under the sway of capital.

Key Points

1. Capitalism developed out of the feudal system, beginning in England and gradually spreading to parts of Europe. The decline of feudalism is linked to many variables, which fed on and reinforced the others.

2. Capitalism has always been a world system to some extent, and Canada from the outset was economically and politically tied to a European power (first France, then England).

3. The transition from feudalism to capitalism teaches us that even the most rigid of socioeconomic formations can eventually decay and disappear. A clue that a social system is on the decline is the increasing inability of the dominant class to maintain its political and moral authority.

4. Capitalism is a mode of production with private ownership of the means of production. In capitalist societies, as compared to earlier class formations, all production is subordinated to the imperatives of the market, and all things become potential commodities.

5. In pre-capitalist societies, the surplus was extracted through various forms of political, legal, or military coercion. In capitalism, the coercion takes on a mainly economic form.

6. The insatiable drive for profits on the part of the capitalist is a necessary condition of the capitalist system itself. Because of the competitive nature of capitalism, the goal of every capitalist must be not simply profits, but the maximization of profits.

7. The cost of purchasing labour power is always far less than the new value that the worker produces. From the Marxist perspective, this is the ultimate source of profits for the capitalist and of wealth for society as a whole. This source of wealth becomes totally obscured in capitalist societies.

8. The anarchy of production in capitalist societies leads inevitably to the crisis of overproduction, which produces a glut of goods, workers, and capital itself.

9. The paper economy has been growing faster than the real economy. One of the many consequences of this development is growing economic instability.

10. There has been a growing contradiction between the increasingly social nature of production and the increasingly private appropriation of the fruits of such production. Those who own and control the productive process in capitalism have a particular set of interests that may not match the needs or goals of the rest of us.

11. Capitalism is a very flexible and adaptable system and can take many different forms.

12. Capitalism has, to some extent, always been a global system, looking beyond national borders for new sources of profit. In the last fifty years, transnational corporations have expanded in size and grown more powerful. The largest TNCs are bigger than many nation-states.

13. In capitalist societies, the power of those who own or control the means of production can also be linked to power in two other societal spheres: the sphere of ideas and the political sphere.

Further Reading

Beaud, Michel. 1983. *A History of Capitalism, 1500–1800*. New York: Monthly Review.
A useful overview of the historical development of capitalism, written by a French economist.

Marx, Karl and Friedrich Engels. [1848] 2005. *The Communist Manifesto*. Edited by Phil Gasper. Chicago: Haymarket Books.
This edition includes the full text, commentaries, annotations with historical references, additional texts, and a glossary. .

Rosenwein, Barbara H. 2002. *A Short History of the Middle Ages*. Peterborough, ON: Broadview.

An up-to-date and thorough overview of the period of medieval history from around 300 to 1500. Full of maps and photographs.

Frieden, Jeffry. 2006. *Global Capitalism: Its Fall and Rise in the Twentieth Century*. New York: W.W. Norton.
A comprehensive economic history of globalization from 1870 to the present.

Wood, Ellen Meiksins. 1999. *The Origin of Capitalism*. New York: Monthly Review.
A relatively recent addition to the debate on the roots of capitalist economic systems.

Wright, Ronald. 2004. *A Short History of Progress*. Toronto: Anansi.
Based on the CBC Massey Lecture series of the same name, Wright traces the history of our species from our beginnings to the present day. Will our arrogance soon lead to our extinction? This is the question Wright contemplates.

Yates, Michael. 2003. *Naming the System*. New York: Monthly Review Press.
An easy-to-read explanation of capitalism by an American economist.

5 Analyzing Social Class

In This Chapter

- How is class different from socioeconomic status?
- Aren't most of us middle class?
- How are classes structured in capitalist societies?
- What is class consciousness?

If you were asked to make a list of ten words that you would use to describe yourself, do you think that you would include your class affiliation in your description? In earlier chapters we defined social class as a person's relationship to the means of production. However, such economic divisions between people are not easy for us to identify in our society. As a result we seldom identify others, or even ourselves, in terms of our class.

Most often we think of ourselves with respect to our gender, religion, sexual preference, race, ethnic group, occupational category, and so on. In other words, we focus on *status* categories rather than class categories. **Status** refers to any position held by people in society. It is normal to have many statuses concurrently—for example, woman, sister, daughter, student, employee, and so on. A status can either be *ascribed*, as in the case of sex or race, or *acquired*, such as level of education, occupation, or marital status. Status positions can be ranked in relation to each other by their privileges and obligations.

Prior to the rise of capitalism, class relations were highly visible. With the rise of economic inequalities—that is, when private appropriation of surplus first appeared and the division of labour expanded—class categories were commonly defined in law and supported by religious beliefs and traditions. These categories were referred to as ranks, orders, stations, castes, or estates. In societies with such divisions, everyone knew their place and the place of others within these relatively rigid structures of inequality, which were noted through such symbols as official titles and different styles of dress. Positions were largely hereditary, although a small number were able to alter their position. Here is something to ponder: this whole book is an attempt to demonstrate that classes exist and that they have a major determining effect on your life. Although you are far more educated than any slave or feudal peasant, no one had to convince most of them of such an obvious fact. This is one of the many contradictions of the society in which we live.

Although at an experiential level we tend not to "see" class in our society, it is nonetheless a key tool to help us make sense of society and our place in it. The concept of class helps us understand both the dynamics of power and some of the tensions that lead to social change. As sociologist Wallace Clement (1983, 71) notes, "Class cleavages can, better than any other distinction, explain the dynamics of Canadian society."

The three major classes in capitalist societies—the *capitalists*, the *workers*, and the *petite bourgeoisie*—have been introduced in earlier chapters. However, the existence of another group, which Marx referred to as the **lumpenproletariat**, should also be noted. Because of the unplanned nature of capitalist economies, there is never full employment. As a result, there is an underclass that consists of the long-term unemployed, or those engaged in illegal activities, who are completely outside of production. For Marx, these were the individuals on the margins of every capitalist economy who have been used by the ruling class to oppose the working class. The lumpenproletariat should be distinguished from others—such as students, housewives, or the retired—who are outside of production, but who have not played this historical role. In some capitalist societies, although not in Canada, one may also find residual classes from the previous socioeconomic formation, such as an aristocracy or a peasant class.

Class and Socioeconomic Status: What's the Difference?

If you asked the average Canadian to describe social classes in Canada, it is likely that very few would speak in terms of the divisions noted above. Most often, people speak of an upper, middle, and lower class, with each class being thought of as linked either to income or to some combination of income, occupation, and education. Such differences between people are real, but are more accurately referred to as **socioeconomic status** (SES) rather than social class. Unfortunately, in much of the social sciences, as in our everyday understanding of social inequality, the concepts of social class and socioeconomic status are used interchangeably. This looseness has led to a rather muddied vision of the nature of structured inequality in capitalist societies and has diverted attention away from the true nature of power allocation within such societies.

In the late nineteenth century, the traditional conception of class was still a part of European social thought. The shift of emphasis away from a Marxist analysis of class in the social sciences more or less began with the work of German sociologist Max Weber. While Weber agreed with Marx that class was tied to the ownership or control of property, he felt that social inequality was multi-dimensional and not sufficiently explained by property relationships alone. For Weber, there were three dimensions of inequality: *class*, which in Weber's analysis meant socioeconomic status or individual life-chances; *status*, meaning the level of social prestige; and *party* (or power), which meant the degree of political influence. For Weber, then, social inequality had to be linked to these three dimensions. Following Weber, the ranking of individuals via status hierarchies, rather than historical class analysis, gained ascendancy in social theory.

This tendency was particularly evident in North America. In the twentieth century, the social sciences grew in the United States, which was idealized as a classless society, or at least one where classes were minimized and equality was an achievable goal. In this context, American social science, including sociology after World War II, increasingly moved away from a focus on structured inequality as linked primarily to property relations; instead, it focused on status categories, most notably occupational status, or on levels of prestige (see, for example, Warner 1949; Barber 1957; Nisbet 1959; Blau and Duncan 1967; Clark and Lipset 1991; Grusky 1994).

This distinction is reflected in the fact that American sociologists commonly use the term *social stratification* when referring to social inequality. Strata are layers, and the term *social stratification* leads us to conceive of inequalities in social positions, or statuses, as ranked from top to bottom. To some extent, the concept of stratification and the theories connected with it serve as a direct counterpoint to Marxist class analysis, which sees inequality as tied to a struggle between opposing interests. There are no struggles between layers, just differences.

Think About It

What do you think most people mean when they talk about someone's "class background"?

There is no single order theory regarding social inequality; however, the order theorists, or what—in this context—we might call *stratification theorists*, do share some common elements. Stratification theorists tend to focus on the complex division of labour in advanced industrial societies that leads to an inequality of power and income because of occupational status differences. Since in every society individuals and groups perform different tasks, stratification theorists see structured social inequality as inevitable. For the stratification theorists, classes are groups of people who have similar rankings, usually on the basis of some combination of occupational status, income, and education (see Box 5.1).

In contrast, the Marxist approach sees class being determined by a person's relation to production, that is, either through the selling of labour power or ownership of capital assets. Put more simply, Marxists ask whether a person makes his or her living through work or through ownership. In contrast to stratification theories, these definitions can remain constant over time and place and are more than simply constructs of a particular investigator. For example, a sociologist could use the identical Marxist definition of class to compare social class in Canada, Pakistan, Viet Nam, or Bulgaria. The same class categorization could also be used to compare classes in Canada today to the Canadian class structure in the eighteenth century. Only at the very margins of each class—for example,

Box 5.1 Limitations to the Traditonal Conception of Class

There is no agreed-upon non-Marxist explanation of social class. Kendall, Murray, and Linden's textbook *Sociology in Our Times* (2007, 239–42) offers a model, summarized below, of the Canadian class structure—using socio-economic status—that draws on the work of numerous sociologists:

The Upper Class (sometimes referred to as the *elite class*) The wealthiest and most powerful class in Canada:
a. upper-upper class
"Old money"—inherited wealth;
b. lower-upper class
"New money"—recently acquired wealth.

The Middle Class (about 40 to 50 percent of the population):
a. upper-middle class
People with a university education, authority and independence on the job, and high income;
b. lower-middle class
People with some postsecondary education, with jobs such as secretaries, semi-professionals, lower-level managers, or non-retail salespersons.

The Working Class (about 30 percent of the population):
People with relatively unskilled low-paying jobs.

The Working Poor (about 20 percent of the population):
People living just above the poverty line, including those holding seasonal jobs, lower-paid factory jobs, and service jobs.

The Underclass
People with low levels of education and income and high rates of unemployment; the poor.

We can see from this model that non-Marxist determinations of class can be very unclear, with categories often overlapping. For example, some individuals defined here as "lower-middle class" might just as easily be defined as "working class"; likewise, many "working class" individuals might also be "working poor," while the difference between "the working poor" and "the poor" is unclear. The categories provided here are descriptive and are not very useful for social analysis. In the end, constructing classes this way adds little to our understanding of how societies work.

whether an individual is haute (big) bourgeois or petit (small) bourgeois—might the social scientist be required to make a subjective determination.

While there is by no means a shared Canadian perspective on social inequality, most sociologists in English-speaking Canada have traditionally fallen somewhere between the Marxist class model, which focuses on economic ownership, and the American stratification model, which focuses on occupational ranking. This duality is seen clearly in the writings of John Porter, whose classic work *The Vertical Mosaic* (1965) became the basis for much subsequent Canadian sociology. On the one hand, Porter, like the stratification theorists, argues that "because there are no clear dividing lines, no one can be sure how many classes there are," and that "the... objective criteria of class are income, occupation, property

Table 5.1 A Comparison of Social Class and Socioeconomic Status

Social Class	Socioeconomic Status
Emphasized by change theories	Emphasized by order theories
Based on one's relation to the means of production	Based on occupation, income, education, or some combination of these variables
Linked to ownership/non-ownership of property	Linked to the division of labour
A relationship to another class	A position on a hierarchy of inequality
Always linked to power/lack of power in distal sphere	No necessary link to power/lack of power in distal sphere
Categories remain constant over time and place	Categories vary over time and place
Not readily visible in capitalist societies; highly visible in slave and feudal societies	Can often be visible because of status markers

ownership, and education" (1965, 9–10). On the other hand, in line with class analysis, one of the central themes of Porter's work is the concentration of power held by a relatively small, socially homogeneous group of individuals who sit on the boards of directors of major corporations.

It is important to note that *both* class and status differences exist within capitalist societies, and both must be taken into account in any social analysis. Some key statuses, such as race and gender, may even predominate in understanding certain social phenomena at particular moments in history. (We shall examine these two key statuses in depth in Chapters 11 and 12.) Moreover, there is an interrelationship between class and socioeconomic status. For example, the ability to acquire a high-status occupation or a high-level education is, to a fair extent, correlated to one's class position. Thus, we cannot ignore socioeconomic status but must appreciate that it is different from social class.

Canada: A Middle-class Society?

When asked what class they are in, most Canadians will say they are "middle class," even if they might not be clear about what that means. For most people, middle class means "neither really poor nor really rich." In other words, most people—like the sociological construction in Box 5.1—connect the term *middle class* with a reasonable income and a particular lifestyle. A number of social analysts have argued that despite its many failings, capitalism has allowed many people to improve the conditions of their lives and become middle class.

Marx and Engels argued that with the advancement of capitalism society would split into two opposing classes. However, following World War II, particularly in North America, it seemed as if their predictions were completely wrong. Wages rose, and expanding numbers of families were able to achieve standards of living formerly thought to be unattainable. Many could buy their own home and a car; even a summer home, annual vacation, and what were previously considered luxury items became possible for an expanding number of families. More and more people were able to send their children to college or university.

Those who critiqued Marxist arguments thought that Marx and Engels had failed to see the possibilities that capitalism provided for the attainment of a middle-class society.

How do we explain the expansion of the middle strata that occurred in the postwar period? While such a group is regularly referred to as the "middle class," it is, in fact, not a class at all. Rather, the term reflects a reality that a number of people—including well-educated, well-paid workers and some small-business people—were able to achieve improved life chances and lifestyles distinct from those of workers in the early twentieth century. The term *middle class* is, in reality, a *status* category, connoting differences in education, occupation, income, and consumption patterns. Without a doubt, these middle strata did expand in the postwar period in Canada and most of the developed capitalist world.

There are a number of factors that explain this phenomenon (Teeple 2000, 26). First, following World War II, the economies of the capitalist world expanded rapidly. New technologies meant a decline in the proportion of manual workers (in the developed capitalist world, at least), with a corresponding increase in the number of scientists, technicians, and engineers, in addition to managerial, clerical, and administrative personnel. There was also a large expansion of the non-productive sectors, such as those involving the exchange and distribution of commodities, as well as an expansion of the public sector.

The changes in the composition of the working class were accompanied by overall improvements in wages and working conditions. More and more people worked in comfortable offices rather than in the sweatshops that had dominated early capitalism. More people worked with their heads than their hands. The material conditions of life improved for a fair proportion of the population as rising wages, buying on credit, and an expansion of mass production—and consequently lowered cost—made a large number of what were formerly luxury items available to the average worker. Many small-business people made millions in the rapidly expanding postwar economy. All of these developments gave the impression that the predictions of Marx and Engels were wrong.

Changes to the middle class began to occur by the mid-1970s. As a result of a number of altered economic conditions, capital sought new sources of investment to increase its profits. As more and more countries in the developing world—and later the formerly socialist states—came to be integrated into the capitalist sphere, there was an ever-increasing pool of cheap labour. In simple supply-and-demand terms, this tended to lower the wages of North American workers. As well, many industries relocated into countries or regions with cheaper wages, putting many well-paid workers out of work. Rates of unemployment in Canada rose, while wages stagnated or fell. For small business there was also an ever-smaller share of the pie, and many people who farmed or fished for a living lost their livelihood altogether. At the same time, housing prices in many cities in Canada skyrocketed. The middle-class society—where large numbers of Canadians could achieve the "good life"—that many social analysts thought was an inevitable aspect of developed capitalist economies is now being called into question. Social scientists have noted increasing polarization in both wealth and income in many countries, including Canada, as we shall see in Chapter 10.

Are these recent changes a temporary phenomenon or a general trend? There is every indication that inequality in Canada is not declining, as processes such as the introduction of new technologies, the growing disparity in wages and hours worked, and the oversupply of capital continue. While the "middle class" is by no means disappearing, the predictions of Marx and Engels no longer seem as outrageous as they did forty years ago. Indeed, the usefulness of their concept of social class has grown, rather than diminished.

The Structure of Classes

In the last few chapters you have been introduced to the traditional Marxist concept of social class. To this point, this concept of class may have seemed fairly straightforward—one's class position is the result of one's relation to the means of production. However, class analysis is actually more complex than this, and therefore more detail is required at this point. It is important not to be overly simplistic or mechanical in our approach to social class. The following will help expand our understanding of social class:

Class categories are relational.

A class exists only insofar as another corresponding class exists. Within capitalist societies, there can be no bourgeoisie unless there is simultaneously a working class. That is because the existence of the owning class is dependent on its ability to appropriate the surplus value produced by the workers. Conversely, the working class exists because, under current economic relations, it must sell its labour power to the capitalists who "own" the jobs. Even the petite bourgeoisie can exist only insofar as they are connected to a market controlled by another class.

Classes are structurally in conflict.

As we have seen in earlier chapters, this conflict occurs because of the relationship of power wherever private appropriation of surplus exists. The more surplus that goes to one class, the less that goes to the other; the more one class has its needs met, the less the other class has its needs met. The problem is built into the structure of the private appropriation of surplus value and has nothing to do with personal feelings between people. The ongoing tension between the appropriating and producing class is referred to as *class conflict.*

Classes are not monolithic.

There are segments within particular classes (sometimes referred to as class fractions or class strata), and tensions can develop between the various sectors within a class. For example, in the working class, those who work in private industry may initially give more support to government cutbacks, while public-sector workers may show more opposition to them. Or perhaps white male workers oppose equity programs that would assist women or workers of colour, fearing possible loss of their own jobs. An understanding of such segmentation in all advanced capitalist societies is necessary if we are to make sense of our social world. However, while we must always note the distinctions between various strata, we must also keep in mind that all members of a particular class do share a common bond: those who appropriate surplus have a set of interests that is different from those who sell their labour power.

Classes change over time.

Classes can expand or contract in size, or their internal composition can change. For example, the small-business class has declined in the face of competition from large corporations. When studying the working class in Canada, it is important to note certain dramatic shifts that have occurred since World War II. These changes include the rapid increase in the percentage of women in the workforce, the shift from blue-collar to white-collar forms of employment, the recent expansion of the service sector, and the increase in the number of workers who have one or more part-time jobs. Thus, we must always study classes within a historical framework.

Class is linked to the allocation of power as well as the allocation of material resources within a society.

As has already been noted, ownership or control of the means of production in any society gives one enormous control over one's own life and the lives of others, because productive activity is so central to human existence. The power of ownership, however, extends far beyond the productive sphere in any society, to power within the political and ideological spheres as well. This point will be demonstrated in later chapters.

Classes must be seen in a global context.

We saw in the last chapter that capitalism in the twentieth century became global in structure, linking all nation-states to some degree in a single economy. While all countries, including Canada, retain their own distinct capitalist and working classes, no class system can be fully understood without linking it to broader global structures of inequality and power.

Class has both an objective and a subjective component.

One's class membership is determined by real attributes—that is, whether one survives through ownership (bourgeoisie), through work (working class), or through a combination of the two (petty bourgeoisie). Put differently, class is a material reality. However, while classes are objectively determined categories that are linked to productive relations, they have a subjective component as well. We humans are thinking social animals who try to make sense of the world in which we live. The term **class consciousness** refers to the understanding one has of one's place in the class structure and of the shared interests one has with others in the same place. Of course, not everyone in a class society has a high degree of class consciousness. Generally speaking, in any society where classes exist, it makes sense that class consciousness will be relatively high for the owning class, but low for the others. Otherwise, no class society would last for very long!

The Owning Class

Although most of us appreciate that there is inequality in Canada, our image of those "at the top" comes primarily from the mass media. Thus, when we think of such individuals, we tend to think of movie stars or professional athletes with large incomes rather than considering the ownership of property or corporate control. As a result, we usually think of the rich with regard to what they can purchase, rather than the power some of them may hold over our lives. It was noted earlier in this chapter that, although classes continue to exist in capitalist societies as in earlier socioeconomic formations, they have become increasingly invisible.

In Chapter 4 we saw that capitalism is a global economic system and that corporations became increasingly large and powerful in the last half of the twentieth century. But corporations are just legal fictions. Behind every corporation are real human beings who own and control them (as well as, of course, real people who work in them). Thus, although the term *corporate rule* is often used to describe the power of the major corporations, it must always be remembered that there is a small number of powerful individuals who are actually in control. Whether we are speaking of Canadian capital or global capital, those who control the economy tend to share a common set of interests and values.

Think About It

Can you name five of the most powerful members of the owning class in Canada? If not, why do you think you might be having such difficulty answering this question?

Many books have been written about the wealthiest and most powerful Canadians. Some are of an academic nature, but a number were written by journalists. Few of these authors could be considered Marxists, and, indeed, the journalists in particular take great pains to distance themselves from a Marxist analysis. Rather than speaking of a bourgeoisie or owning class, these authors use terms such as "the elite" or "the establishment" to describe those at the top. And yet over the years there has been unanimous agreement among many writers that a small core of individuals wields an enormous amount of power in Canada (Porter 1965; Johnson 1972; Clement 1975; Newman 1975; Niosi 1981; Francis 1986; Fleming 1991; Newman 1998; Carroll, 2004; Brownlee, 2005). This is true at the international level as well (Sklar 1980; Korten 1996; Carroll 2007).

> In Canada today, there exists an economic elite that controls the country's major industrial, financial, and commercial companies and utilities.
> —Jamie Brownlee, *Ruling Canada, 2005*

Because it is hard to get detailed and accurate information about those with great power and wealth, it is impossible to be precise about the exact size and composition of this class. The size is also dependent on how broadly or narrowly social scientists wish to cast their net. While classes are objectively real, there is always a grey area at the boundaries of each class that makes exact numerical precision difficult. One American author (Zweig 2004, 5) asserts that the capitalist class as a whole constitutes 2 percent of the population of the United States; it is reasonable to assume that the Canadian figure would be similar. Certainly, there is a "core" controlling bourgeoisie that is very small. Porter's classic study (1965, 579) noted 907 individuals who together controlled, at the time of his study, the major corporations in Canada. Newman (1975, 186) spoke of under a thousand people, while Francis (1986) dealt with thirty-two families. Veltmeyer (1986, 30), drawing on a number of authors, maintained that the number was under 2000.

Connected to but somewhat distinct from the owning class is the stratum of extremely highly paid executives. These are people who hold key positions of authority, who are chief executive officers (CEOs), or who sit on the boards of major corporations. Although most of these individuals are technically employees, their wages, bonuses, and stock options have become so high in recent years that they have become part of the owning class rather than the working class. The pay of CEOs in Canada pales in comparison to that in the United States. In particular, managers of hedge funds and private equity funds—groupings of capital largely hidden from public view—have amassed enormous wealth. In 2007, the manager and main shareholder of one such entity in the United States made *billions* of dollars overnight when his company issued public shares (Gwyn 2007). Beside huge incomes, most top executives also negotiate large "golden parachutes" to be received when they leave their jobs. For example, Robert L. Nardelli received a $210 million parachute when he left Home Depot in 2006 after an investor uproar about falling share prices.

The 1990s saw a transformation of the owning class in Canada. Prior to this decade, this class consisted primarily of what has been referred to as the "dynasties," the "old guard," or the Old Establishment—with family names such as Weston, Thomson, Bronfman, Black, Eaton, Irving, Desmarais, McCain, and Webster. These men (and they were almost all men) shared not only the commonality of wealth, but also a convergence of interests, histories, and lifestyles. Most of these individuals were also linked through common backgrounds at private schools and summer camps, through shared social activities, through membership in private clubs, through intercorporate ownership, through interlocking directorships on corporate boards, and so on (Brownlee 2005).

In recent years, however, some new faces have been added to the list of the wealthiest Canadians. This group constitutes what Peter C. Newman refers to as the "Titans," or the "New Establishment." The appearance of this new group is largely the result of the rapidly growing global economy as well as the sudden expansion of new technology sectors of the economy. However, as Table 5.2 indicates, the "old guard" continues to hold the top five spots in Canada with regard to wealth. Moreover, while this new establishment may not have quite the uniformity of shared family backgrounds, most of these corporate leaders were born into some wealth. Whatever their origins, the members of the owning

Table 5.2 The Wealthiest People in Canada, 2006

Name	Main business	Wealth/$billions
1. Thomson family	media	24.41
2. Galen Weston	groceries	7.1
3. Irving family	oil	5.45
4. Ted Rogers Jr.	media	4.54
5. Paul Desmarais Sr.	Power Corp.	4.41
6. Jimmy Pattison	entrepreneur	4.35
7. Jeff Skoll	eBay	3.93
8. Barry Sherman	Apotex drugs	3.23
9. David Azrieli	real estate	2.44
10. Fred & Ron Mannix	mining	2.38

Source: <www.canadianbusiness.com/>.

class continue to be linked to each other through various corporate networks, sharing a set of common interests and values.

On the other hand, there remain distinctions within the bourgeoisie, and sometimes tensions can arise between what are referred to as fractions—or sub-groupings—within this class. Such differences relate, in part, to the major source of capital acquisition—banking and finance, resource extraction, retailing, and so on—the size of capital controlled, or the nation-state in which the corporation is based. Nonetheless, although occasional disagreements do break out between individuals, families, or sectors within the bourgeoisie, the people at the top in terms of wealth and power continue to share a common perspective and a common interest. Their overarching goals are always the same: in the short term to maximize the rate of profit of the corporations they own or control, and in the long term to guarantee the maintenance of the system that allows them to privately appropriate wealth. Because their economic power allows them to exert pressure in the political sphere, as we shall see in Chapter 8, they can be described as a *ruling class* (see Mills 1956; Miliband 1969; Domhoff 1983; Panitch 1977; Sklar 1980; Teeple 2000).

It is sometimes argued that the notion of an owning class has become outmoded in an era when anyone can become an "owner" simply by purchasing stocks or mutual funds. However, despite the growth of mutual funds and other forms of stock ownership, the vast majority of shares of major companies remain in the hands of a small number of players. In 1999, the richest 20 percent of Canadians owned 94 percent of the $92 billion in stocks outside of registered retirement savings plans (RRSPs), 81 percent of the $80 billion in mutual and investment funds outside of RRSPs, and 72 percent of the $420 billion in RRSPs and other registered savings plans (Kerstetter 2003, 5). Even within this select group of individuals, the main means of subsistence for the majority continues to be through their work. Few individuals can survive on dividends alone.

Box 5.2 Class Has Its Privileges: Three Stories

Story 1: In early 2007, three female farm workers in British Columbia were killed and nine others seriously injured when a van transporting them to a greenhouse flipped. Evidence indicated that the van carried seventeen people, two more than it was legally registered to carry, and that the seatbelts had been removed. The firm that owned the van had previously committed multiple violations of the provincial Employment Standards Act and in 2005 was fined $500 for each violation.

Story 2: Three days before the accident in Story 1, Betty Krawczyk, a seventy-eight-year-old great-grandmother, also known as the Green Granny, was sentenced to ten months in prison in British Columbia. Her crime? She ignored a court order not to return to a construction site at Eagle Ridge Bluffs in North Vancouver where she and other protesters had been demonstrating opposition to a road being built for the 2010 Olympics. Betty had already spent two years in prison for anti-logging protesting.

Story 3: In 2005, a Canadian National Railway train derailed along the north shore of Lake Wabamun, west of Edmonton, spilling about 730,000 litres of bunker C fuel oil and a potentially hazardous chemical along the shore and into the lake. Three days after this accident, another CN train derailed on a track north of Vancouver, causing 45,000 litres of highly toxic sodium hydroxide to spill into the pristine Cheakamus River, killing all the fish in the river. In the same year, two CN freight trains collided in Mississippi, killing four employees.

Hunter Harrison became CN Rail's president and CEO in 2003. His job was to raise corporate profits. One way to do this was to have locomotives run faster and with longer trains, which may explain why CN Rail had 103 main-track derailments in 2005, compared to 76 in 2004, and 56 in 1999. While CN Rail accepted liability for the two major spills in Canada, Mr. Harrison was not considered personally responsible because CEOs are rarely charged in such cases. Mr. Harrison's total compensation in 2005 was over $46 million, including a bonus of approximately $4.5 million.

Sources: Camille Bains, "Elderly Anti-logging Protester to Check into the Crowbar Hotel—Again," <http://www.metronews.ca/storyCP.aspx?pg=./n030550A.xml> (accessed March 7, 2007); Brent Jang, "The Bottom Line: Did CN push too hard?" *Globe and Mail*, 23 Feb., 2007: B3; Larry Pynn, "Owner of Van Involved in Deadly Crash Violated Labour Standards," *Vancouver Sun*, 9 March, 2007: A1; Neil Waugh, "Heat's on Hunter," *Edmonton Sun*. 13 Feb., 2007. <http://www.edmontonsun.com/Business/Columnists/Waugh_Neil/2007/02/13/3605762.html> (accessed March 7, 2007).

Some people also argue that the large amount of wealth transferred to the owning class is a result of their hard work. Some members of this class may indeed work hard; however, what differentiates this class from the rest of us is that it is their ownership or control of corporate assets, not their labour, that provides their wealth. If some of them suddenly decide to give up working, their way of life will not substantially decline.

We should also remember that wealth is actually created socially. It is the work of many thousands of people, drawn together in collective activity, which creates the surplus value in advanced capitalism that is then dispersed throughout the economy. Each one contributes a small share to the whole. Certainly it can be said that some, because of special skills or knowledge, contribute more than others. However, the huge amount of wealth that is transferred to the appropriating class is not the result of any particular individual attribute, but—as in the feudal era—simply a right that accrues to the dominant class.

Class Consciousness in the Owning Class

As was noted earlier in this chapter, class has both an objective and a subjective component. Getting at the latter, which is referred to as *class consciousness*, is no easy matter. This is particularly true of the owning class, which values its privacy and has the power to maintain it. It is therefore not easy to provide extensive empirical data that indicate the degree of class consciousness among this class. More indirect sources must therefore be drawn upon.

One indicator of the degree of class consciousness of a particular class is the organizations it forms to protect its own class interests. In this regard, it seems that the owning class has a fairly high degree of class consciousness. From the earliest period of capitalism in Canada, business owners formed their own organizations, although they tended to be strictly regional or industry based. However, there are now a number of organizations in Canada that attempt to represent broader business interests: the Canadian Chamber of Commerce, the Alliance of Manufacturers and Exporters of Canada, the Canadian Federation of Independent Business, the Canadian Council of Chief Executives, and le Conseil du patronat in Quebec.

The Canadian Council of Chief Executives constitutes the most powerful voice of big business in Canada. It began in 1976 as the Business Council on National Issues. The Business Council on National Issues (BCNI) was originally modelled on the Business Roundtable in the United States, a lobby group of about 200 corporate executives, although the BCNI eventually decided to become more public than the American group. Its aim, as stated by its original co-chair, was to "strengthen the voice of business on issues of national importance" (*Globe and Mail*, 6 April 1979). In January 2002, the BCNI changed its name to the Canadian Council of Chief Executives (CCCE) to reflect its increasing global orientation. Its aim is to promote the common interests of Canadian big business, both within Canada and internationally. This includes achieving a consensus within the corporate sector on major policy issues, influencing various levels of government, and swaying public opinion (Dobbin 1998, 165–78).

At the international level, there are also organizations of the most powerful circles of capital, where corporate leaders come together to discuss common concerns and plan future strategies. In the United States, the Council on Foreign Relations has long been a meeting ground where the corporate elite and foreign-policy experts can formulate strategies that their government might undertake. Another influential organization is the extremely secretive Bilderberg Group, named after the hotel in Holland where a number of North American and

European corporate and government leaders first met in May 1954. One of the founders of this group stated that its aim was "to reduce differences of opinion and resolve conflicting trends and to further understanding... by... trying to find a common approach to major problems" (quoted in Korten 1996, 137).

Other key international organizations that bring together corporate leaders are the International Chamber of Commerce, the World Economic Forum—held once a year in Davos, Switzerland—the Trilateral Commission, and the World Business Council for Sustainable Development. All of these organizations are made up of prominent individuals from the developed capitalist nations, including Canada. The purpose of these organizations is similar to that of the CCCE, but on a global scale: to formulate coordinated economic policies, influence governments, and affect public opinion, with the goal of advancing the interests of the TNCs. There are many interconnections between the key members of these various international organizations (Carroll 2007).

The existence of such groups is a clear indicator that those at the top—or at least those who represent them—are aware of their shared interests, understand the collective with whom they share these interests, and appreciate what positions or actions must be taken to protect their interests. These groups play a key role in allowing the various fractions of capital to express their differences within a relatively private setting, and to come to a consensus on the best way to advance their common class interests.

Think About It
Have you ever heard of the Council on Foreign Relations, the Trilateral Commission, the Bilderberg Group, or the Canadian Council of Chief Executives? Why do you think we so seldom hear or read about these powerful organizations? (To learn more, check them out on the Internet.)

Such groups are also important to note since they give us a clue as to how the owning class is able to convert its economic power into political and ideological power. Supported by vast sums provided by member organizations, these groups are able to lobby governments, as well as carry out independent advertising campaigns concerning important issues. The BCNI, for example, spent substantial sums to promote the North American Free Trade Agreement (NAFTA). The major Canadian corporations also fund several "think tanks" that publish supposedly "impartial" reports endorsing the views of the business elite. The two best known of in Canada are the C.D. Howe Institute and the Fraser Institute. It should also be noted that the major international organizations, such as Bilderberg and the Trilateral Commission, actually include government leaders, top intellectuals, and key members of the media.

It is not the existence of such organizations alone that indicates a high level of class consciousness among the owning class. Another indicator is the actual positions taken by these groups, as well as by individuals belonging to the capitalist class. For example, one author (Ornstein 1985, 142–51) concluded that the responses of the Canadian capitalist class to a questionnaire revealed opinions that were generally consistent with their class positions. A cursory examination of comments by business people in the mass media, while not statistically valid, confirms this consistency of opinion. Thus, it can be argued that a relatively high degree of class consciousness exists in the bourgeoisie. Certainly there are ongoing disputes among different fractions of the class. Nonetheless, capital clearly displays a fair degree of understanding of its class interests, and what positions and actions must be taken to protect those interests.

What Is the Working Class?

While most social scientists generally agree that there is a small and identifiable owning class in capitalist societies (even if they use different terms to describe this powerful group), there is much more disagreement about the nature and composition of the working class. The traditional Marxist view is that the working class is made up of all those who survive by earning a wage. However, among social scientists, even those who identify with the Marxist tradition, there has been a prolonged debate regarding the validity and utility of such a broad definition.

The reason for the split among analysts is rooted in the many real differences that exist among workers in advanced capitalist societies—differences in wages and working conditions, educational backgrounds, job autonomy, social status, control over the productive process and over other workers, and degree of class consciousness. There are also distinctions between those who work in the private sector and those who work for government, as well as between those whose work it is to produce ideas and those who produce products.

Most social scientists agree that the productive sector—that is, the industrial and rural proletariat—constitutes part of the working class. This sector includes "wage-workers who are engaged in the production of commodities, the extraction of natural resources, the production of food, the operation of the transportation network required for production and distribution, the construction industry, and the maintenance of energy and communication networks" (Veltmeyer 1986, 83). As a result of new technologies and increased productivity, the proportion of workers in this sector has been declining both in Canada and globally. Wage workers in the service sector, clerical workers, and low- to mid-level government employees are also generally included as members of the working class. This latter group of workers, although not directly producing surplus value, certainly helps maintain a system in which such surplus value can continue to be produced and realized in the marketplace.

It is over the issue of whether a number of other categories of workers actually constitute part of the working class that the greatest debate occurs. The different lines of thought and the nature of the debates regarding what constitutes the working class need not concern us here. We may summarize by stating that some authors feel that the higher strata of working people constitute a distinct class, some argue that they should be considered as part of the petite bourgeoisie, and others argue that they cannot be defined in class terms at all.

One of the best-known arguments is that of Erik Olin Wright (1980), who asserted there was a distinct category, the "new middle class," consisting of certain occupational categories, such as managers and supervisors, small employers, and semi-autonomous employees who had some control over their work. Wright saw these people as having contradictory class locations, in that they shared characteristics of more than one class. In a similar typology proposed by Clement and Myles (1994, 16), the new middle class (or modern petite bourgeoisie) consists of those who exercise control over the labour power of others but do not have real economic ownership of the means of production and, as a result of the latter, must still sell their labour power, skills, or knowledge for a wage.

However, the separating out of groups of workers on the basis of what are essentially *status* differences diverts our attention from class relationships and structures of power. Like other stratification approaches, it also draws our attention to distinctions *between* groups of workers—such as their occupational categories, income, or degree of control over the working conditions of themselves or others—and away from their overarching shared relationship to capital. It is therefore more analytically precise to describe the new middle class (with the exception of small employers, who remain the petite bourgeoisie) as a distinct fraction (or group) within a single class. This allows us to acknowledge the real status differences that exist between groups of workers, while simultaneously recognizing their common place in the relationship between classes.

For example, at first glance it appears that university professors are not at all connected to factory workers. The former are generally well paid, are well educated, have traditionally had high levels of autonomy in their jobs, and are in a high-status occupation that is usually regarded as a profession. They work with ideas rather than objects and generally work in the public rather than the private sector. The low degree of class consciousness of this sector is reflected in the fact that the campus organizations of university professors are usually referred to as faculty associations rather than unions, and, indeed, many are still not certified bargaining units. Certainly, at the level of self-perception, few professors like to think of themselves as workers.

Yet something has happened to many university professors over the last thirty years. As a result of massive cutbacks in funding to postsecondary education across Canada that began in the 1970s, wages and research funds have, with some exceptions, not been keeping up with increasing workloads. Faculty have had to deal with expanding class sizes, cutbacks in support services, breakdowns in basic equipment, deteriorating physical plants, and growing administrative control over their work. All of these developments have led to a general decline in faculty morale. Moreover, increasing use is being made of part-time and contract teachers who earn low wages, have heavy workloads, and have little or no job security. In other words, the university professor's job has come to have more and more similarity to that of a factory worker. In some cases, factory workers may even earn higher wages. This trend is sometimes referred to as the process of **proletarianization**.

University professors are far from being the only sector to experience such changes. More and more of the formerly privileged sectors of the working class are discovering that, in the end, workers of all strata neither own nor control their jobs. Indeed, many formerly privileged workers were hit particularly hard as corporations in the 1990s massively reduced many layers of middle management or outsourced some of their activities. For those who held on to their jobs, many experienced increased workloads, lower wages, and high levels of stress. Thus, regardless of the privileges acquired by some workers at particular times, they all—except for top executives and the highest-paid stratum of workers—share an overarching set of material interests that distinguish them from the owning class.

For this reason, it is important to define all workers who survive by means of a wage as members of the working class, as long as we do not do so in a rigid, over-simplified, and non-historical fashion. Using this broad definition, working people constitute the vast majority of Canadians. Since the term *working class* is so strongly identified in our country with only those who wear hard hats and carry lunch pails, it is often easier to refer to this class as working people, wage workers, or simply workers. For the purposes of this book, we shall use these terms interchangeably.

Having said that all wage workers share a common interest, it is important to remember that there are many ongoing stresses and strains between groups within this class. These are partly the result of real differences within the working class, partly the result of the forced competition between workers created by capitalism, and partly the result of the divide-and-rule tactics utilized by capital. These tensions within the working class are one of the major factors that have limited the ability of working people to unite and organize in their own interests. Thus, despite the fact that working people constitute a numerical majority in Canada and globally, they have been unable to attain the power that one might expect from their sheer numbers.

Class Consciousness in the Working Class

As noted earlier in the chapter, we would predict class consciousness in any class-based society to be relatively high within the owning class, and relatively low in the producing class. We saw that, indeed, there is every indication of a relatively high degree of class consciousness among the owning class. What is the case for working people? At the present moment, the evidence seems to indicate that class consciousness among working people in Canada is very low. Few individuals even identify their interests with a collective of working people, let alone understand what those interests are or how to act in such a way as to protect those interests.

Think About It

Ask a number of working people you know—such as your parents, other relatives, or friends—what social class they think they are in. What do your answers tell you about class consciousness among working people today?

If class consciousness is, in part, connected to membership in organizations designed to protect the interests of the class, we should begin with a brief examination of the union movement, which is both a cause and a result of class consciousness. Few Canadians are aware of the history of this movement or of the many battles of workers to obtain the right to organize and bargain freely with their employers. Until 1872, unions were illegal in Canada. After that time, unionization was still extremely difficult, with many constraints from both employers and various levels of government.

A **labour union** is a group of workers who join together to bargain with an employer or group of employers with regard to wages, benefits, and working conditions. While we often assume that the primary reason workers join unions is to obtain higher wages, this is not always the case. Certainly, most workers would like to feel that they are earning a fair wage for their work and want to obtain a "living wage" that provides a decent life for themselves and their families. However, many workers turn to unions because they are looking for a measure of respect at work and want better treatment in the workplace. Workers may also be seeking protection from arbitrary, discriminatory, or unfair work environments by creating seniority provisions, grievance procedures, and work rules (Zweig 2004, 9).

The first workers to organize were those engaged in crafts, such as weavers, printers, bakers, and so on. Workers in the resource and agricultural sectors fought a much harder battle to organize, particularly since the crafts workers generally saw unskilled workers as a threat and did not welcome them into their unions. Thus, at the turn of the century, it was the industrial unions, at least those in English Canada, that were the most class conscious. At this time unions with clearly militant, socialist, and internationalist leanings—such as the Industrial Workers of the World (IWW) and the One Big Union (OBU)—were formed, and during the Great Depression workers and their unions became increasingly radical. However, union consciousness (fighting the employer in the workplace) did not necessarily translate into a broader understanding of class relations.

> They have taken untold millions that they never toiled to earn,
> But without our brain and muscle not a single wheel could turn.
> We can break their haughty power, gain our freedom when we learn
> That the union makes us strong.
> —From the song "Solidarity Forever," written by American Ralph Chaplin in 1915 and usually considered the anthem of the North American labour movement

A decline in labour radicalism occurred following World War II. To a fair extent, this decline can be linked to the same conditions that saw the growth of the middle strata of workers with their improved living and working conditions, as well as to growing anti-communism, which resulted in the isolation of the most class-conscious workers and unions. It was not until the late 1960s that the union

---

Box 5.3 Ten Ways Employers Try to Stop Workers from Organizing

Canadian laws say that workers have the right to join a union, free from interference by their employers. But that is not the way it always works: employers regularly cross the line. Here are ten common ways that employers break the law during organizing drives:

1. They unfairly discipline union activists.
2. They threaten closure or layoffs if the union gets in.
3. They force meetings with the workforce to talk down the union.
4. They unfairly ban union insignia (hats, buttons, T-shirts).
5. They change working conditions (e.g., give workers a sudden pay increase).
6. They fire union activists.
7. They voluntarily recognize an in-house "employee association."
8. They unfairly communicate with workers (e.g., send letters or videos to workers' homes).
9. They intimidate or threaten workers.
10. They force one-on-one meetings with workers and ask them if they support the union.

Source: *Our Times* magazine, July 2003, 33. Compiled by Bill Murnighan.

---

movement began to grow again—largely as a result of the expansion of the public sector. However, the degree of class consciousness within the movement has remained low. In part, the low degree of class consciousness is connected to continued fragmentation and divisions within the labour movement.

Due to real structural differences among strata, the working class has frequently been divided within itself, weakening class consciousness. It should also be noted that union membership has stagnated, with just under a third of Canadian non-agricultural workers now belonging to unions (Human Resources Development Canada 2007). It is not simply problems within the working class that have caused this decline to occur. Rather, intensified globalization and the push of the corporate sector to create more "flexible" work arrangements have led to the decline of unions around the world. The increase in outsourcing, the decline of the manufacturing sector, and the use of contingent labour—all of which will be discussed in Chapter 6—are likely to further erode workers' ability to organize themselves into collectives that can protect their interests.

Voting behaviour, public opinion polls, and the low degree of worker activism also indicate that there is little class consciousness among workers. This is perfectly logical in a society where classes exist. The maintenance of any class society requires that the class with economic power also exert its power in the ideological sphere—the sphere of ideas. Of course, we must also recall that all things change over time. In spite of the ideological power of the owning class, the degree of class consciousness of working people will ultimately be connected to the material conditions of their lives. Given the rapid erosion of conditions for many working people, it is possible that class consciousness among workers could increase in Canada at some point in the future.

How Important Is the Variable of Social Class?

After the Russian Revolution in 1917, Marxist thought began to have an increasing appeal to many workers and intellectuals who saw in it a means to struggle against the negative consequences of capitalism. In the period between the two world wars, communist parties around the world grew both in size and activism despite ongoing anti-communism, or "red-baiting" as it is sometimes called. In addition, their consistent anti-fascism during World War II won communists many supporters, particularly in Western Europe. At the end of the war, the major capitalist world powers—dominated by the United States—quickly shifted their hostility away from their wartime enemies, Germany and Japan, to the Soviet Union. Following 1946, what came to be known as the Cold War began in earnest. Although the United States is better known for its period of vicious anti-communism, the "red scare" occurred in Canada as well. Many people in government and universities lost their jobs for appearing to have "communist sympathies." In this context, it is not surprising that Marxist ideas more or less disappeared from the mainstream.

We should also be reminded that the 1950s and '60s was a time of tremendous economic growth in North America. Many of the predictions made by Marx were considered to be outmoded or even absurd. Moreover, after the horrors of Stalinism were revealed, many became disillusioned with the Marxist cause. At the same time, the period saw the rapid growth of the middle strata, whose children began to enter the expanding university sector by the mid-1960s. Many of these students had a conflicting attachment to capitalism: on the one hand, they read about (and, in some cases, experienced) forms of oppression (particularly sexism and racism); on the other hand, their socioeconomic status made them relatively privileged within the capitalist order. While many writers continued to be influenced by Marxism—particularly outside North America—critical theory shifted from the traditional premises of Marx to new orientations. Two major interconnected transformations of traditional Marxism should be noted: the shift away from materialist analysis—that is, the focus on the real, material conditions of people's lives—to idealist analyses, which focused on subjective feelings and ideas; and the shift away from class analysis to the study of status variables, oppression, and personal identity.

Traditional Marxism saw the working class at the centre of social transformations, primarily as a result of its potential economic power as the producer of surplus value, as well as its sheer numbers and organizational capacity. However, many critics of this approach felt that traditional Marxists were unfairly "privileging" the working class with regard to its central role in changing society. We should also recall that class has become increasingly invisible in developed capitalist societies. In its place, people have come to identify more strongly with those who share membership in various status groupings, such as gender, ethnicity, race, sexual preference, and even age.

However, a number of new social developments—most specifically, recent economic transformations and the gradual erosion of Canada's social safety net—are changing the dynamic between class and non-class analysis. Both workers and status groups such as women, gays and lesbians, the poor, the disabled, and racial minorities are finding that many previous gains have been disappearing. At the same time, the working class in Canada has itself been changing dramatically, particularly in its gender balance. These changes have been reflected within the labour movement, which has, in general, begun to recognize diversity and oppose broad forms of social injustice. Moreover, many struggles have begun to overlap. For example, when nurses go on strike it is simultaneously a gender issue, a labour issue, and a health care issue.

Thus, ordinary working people of all backgrounds find themselves having to join together to protect their collective interests. Nonetheless, class consciousness remains low in the working class, and at the present time structures of power, both in Canada and globally, appear to most of us to be eternal and unchangeable. However, as we shall see in the final chapter, the future direction of class struggle is unclear at the moment.

Key Points

1. Although we tend to notice status differences rather than class differences, class is a central tool for understanding society and our place in it.

2. The class structure in Canada is made up of the two dominant classes, the owning class and the working class, plus two smaller classes, the petite bourgeoisie and the lumpenproletariat.

3. Class is often confused with socioeconomic status. The latter is a position in the hierarchy of inequality based on a combination of income, occupation, and education. Socioeconomic status is connected to, but distinct from, the traditional concept of class.

4. What is often termed the middle class is not a class at all; rather, it is a group of people with improved life chances and lifestyles distinct from traditional blue-collar workers.

5. We must always be careful not to be overly simplistic or mechanical in our approach to social class. We must therefore always recall that classes are relational, classes are structurally in conflict, classes are not monolithic, classes change over time, class is linked to the allocation of both power and material resources, and class has both an objective and a subjective component.

6. There has been a split in sociology between stratification theorists, who put an emphasis on socioeconomic status, and Marxist-oriented theorists, who put an emphasis on inequality of ownership of productive property.

7. Substantial evidence supports the notion that there is a relatively small and powerful owning class in Canada. This class shares a common set of values, beliefs, and interests. The degree of class consciousness among the owning class appears to be fairly high.

8. There is a great deal of controversy in the social sciences regarding what constitutes

the working class. In order to understand the shared interests of all workers, it is most useful to define the working class as all those people who survive by means of a wage.

9. It must always be noted that there are ongoing stresses and strains between strata or fractions within the working class as a result of the many status differences between them. These divisions have limited the ability of working people to unite and organize in their interests.

10. There was a rapid expansion of the middle strata following World War II, giving the impression that Marx had erred in his predictions about capitalism. However, since the mid-1970s, the middle strata have been under attack across the developed capitalist world.

11. Class consciousness among the working class is relatively low.

Further Reading

Brownlee, Jamie. 2005. *Ruling Canada: Corporate Cohesion and Democracy*. Halifax: Fernwood.
This is a detailed examination of the nature of the Canadian ruling class and the ways they are integrated.

Carroll, William. 2004. *Corporate Power in a Globalizing World: A Study in Elite Social Organization*. Toronto: Oxford University Press.
Carroll, who is one of the foremost writers on the Canadian ruling class, here examines the links of power in a global setting.

Dobbin, Murray. 2003. *The Myth of the Good Corporate Citizen: Democracy Under the Rule of Big Business*. 2nd ed. Toronto: Lorimer.
The author explains the expansion of corporate power in a non-academic manner, linking economic power to ideological and political power as well.

Kealey, Gregory S. 1995. *Workers and Canadian History*. Montreal/Kingston: McGill-Queen's Press.
An analysis of working class history in Canada that covers both theoretical debates and actual events.

Porter, John. 1965. *The Vertical Mosaic: An Analysis of Social Class and Power in Canada*. Toronto: University of Toronto Press.
This book remains a central work in Canadian sociology. The range of material is vast and the methodology thorough. If nothing else, it must be recognized for its influence on the discipline.

Seabrook, Jeremy. 2002. *The No-Nonsense Guide to Caste, Class, and Social Hierarchy*. Toronto: Between the Lines.
There are many easy-to-read books in the No-Nonsense series. This one looks at social rankings, past and present.

6 Living in Capitalist Societies

In This Chapter

- What effect do transnational corporations have on our lives?
- How has the way we work been changing?
- How does capitalism in the twenty-first century affect small business?
- What is the culture of capitalism?

When was the last time you shopped at Wal-Mart? Chances are it was not long ago. Wal-Mart is the largest retail corporation in the world, with annual sales of over $300 billion. If it were a sovereign nation, its Gross Domestic Product (GDP) would be larger than 80 percent of the world's countries. It sells more DVDs, magazines, books, CDs, dog food, diapers, bicycles, toys, jewellery, and toothpaste than any other retailer. It is the largest private employer in the United States, Mexico, and Canada, and more people are employed by Wal-Mart than any other private company in the world. It buys more than one *billion* dollars worth of land every month (Dicker 2005, 2–3).

This chapter expands on the nature of capitalism and its transformation in the twentieth century. Its goal is to help you understand that the distal sources of power—those individuals who own and control giant corporations like Wal-Mart—are becoming fewer in number yet more powerful on a global scale. The power of those who control capital—a force that so few of us see—goes far beyond the workplace, affecting everything we do, see, hear, or consume; everything we believe; and, indeed, everything we are.

In Chapter 4 we saw that capitalist economies changed in two very important ways in the twentieth century. First, an economy made up mainly of small, competing businesses was gradually replaced by one dominated by a few extremely large and powerful corporations. The second important development involved the globalization of capital. In order to maximize profits, the capitalist owning class had to seek new sources of profit throughout the world. The globe was essentially divided in two. In one part, there was now a small core of highly developed industrial nations where most of the ever-expanding corporations were located; in the other part, there was a much larger, less economically developed periphery.

While most of us are quite sensitive to power exerted in the proximal sphere—such as that of our parents, teachers, or landlords—the power wielded by large transnational corporations is often too intangible or invisible for us to notice. Yet the size and power of these corporations means they will have a major effect on many aspects of our lives. Let us return to Wal-Mart. This company employs millions of people and subcontracts to a large number of other businesses that employ many people as well. It thus has a major determining effect on such things as wages, working conditions, and worker health and safety. Its large purchasing power affects farmers and food distributors, producers of plastics and paper products, and the transportation industry, among others. And the expansion of its suburban big-box stores not only affects competing retail stores but also has a dramatic impact on urban environments.

Isn't Bigger Better?

Most of us are aware that giant corporations exist. After all, we eat at their restaurants, use their products, wear their clothes, and work for their companies. However, few of us are concerned about the size and power of the transnational corporations, because—if we think of them at all—we tend to assume they are generally benefiting society as a whole. Surely, some of us might argue, if Wal-Mart can offer equal or better products at a cheaper price, this is a good thing. Indeed, that's why so many of us shop at Wal-Mart. Moreover, on all accounts—wages, supplementary benefits, and rates of unionization—workers in the past, on average, have generally done better as the size of the company they worked for increased (Stanford 1999, 131–2).

However, if we think dialectically, we can also see the dangers inherent in the growth of transnational corporations. The creation of large global economic units means that the entire economy can be put at risk if one major company or country finds itself in crisis. As capital becomes increasingly international and the economy becomes a more integrated global entity, then the collapse of a major corporation can be a serious concern, even for the corporate sector itself. The sudden and unexpected bankruptcy in late 2001 of Enron—the seventh-largest company in the United States at that time, with a book value of at least US$65 billion—sent shock waves around the world as major banks, stock brokerages, and pension funds watched their investments disappear.

However, the biggest concern regarding large transnational corporations is their sheer global power. This power, as we shall see in future chapters, allows them to assert dominance not simply in the economic sphere, but in the ideological and political spheres as well. No aspect of Canadian society or culture can now escape their influence. Corporations are, of necessity, interested in primarily one thing, which is maximizing shareholder return on investments. The disappearance of free enterprise in whole sectors of the economy may actually lead to higher prices, as a few companies effectively control the market. There are also concerns about ways one or two enterprises may come to dominate a whole geographic area. With a lack of economic diversity, the closing of one or two plants or businesses can set in motion the collapse of whole sectors or whole regions. Another concern about the growth of transnational corporations is with regard to how such growth affects the way we work in the twenty-first century.

The Restructuring of Work

Back in the late 1960s, when I was in university, it was pretty much expected that if you were fortunate enough to get a university education, all doors were open to you. Most of us in that lucky position settled on a career choice and made our way into the work world. The assumption then was that we would stay in those careers for life, "settle down," and work our way up the ladder of success (perhaps with different employers, but in the same general field). For those who didn't go to university, prospects were still very good, and most people who worked hard at their jobs could expect to earn good pay and stay at their jobs for a long time. They could also look forward to buying a house, raising a family, having a reasonably good quality of life, and retiring with a good pension. While it may all sound a bit boring, it did guarantee income security and a sense of purpose. Certainly not everyone followed this career trajectory, but it was a rather typical pattern until the 1980s.

> High levels of unemployment and underemployment throughout the 1990s have conspired to reshape the wage structure and quality of working life in Canada.
> —Andrew Jackson, *Falling Behind*

Today's students are being prepared for quite a different future, a world dominated by various forms of **precarious employment**. The world of work they are entering expects them to be "flexible" and "adaptable," and they are being advised to prepare to make five or six different occupational changes in their lives. Precarious employment includes those forms of work characterized by "limited social benefits and statutory entitlements, job insecurity, low wages, and high risks of ill health" (Vosko 2006, 11). Not all groups are equally affected by the shift to precarious forms of employment. Women in particular, as well as young people and immigrants, are disproportionately finding themselves in this type of work. Those with a combination of these variables are even more likely to find themselves in forms of precarious employment. In addition, such forms of employment are found more frequently in certain sectors of the economy. For example, part-time employees are concentrated in areas such as social services (including the health care industry), retail trade, and other consumer services industries (ibid., 21–29).

Employers are increasingly replacing career employees with contingent workers, and whole sections of companies are being outsourced to other companies, often in other regions or countries. Outsourcing helps employers cut costs and have a fluid workforce to which they have few responsibilities. It should not be surprising that employment agencies are now the largest employers in North America. One company alone, Milwaukee-based Manpower Inc., placed more than four million workers worldwide in 2006. Outsourcing is a new element in the development of a global capitalist economy and now includes both unskilled and knowledge-based workers. For example, nearly two-thirds of all Wal-Mart products come from China. Most of the rest comes from seventy other countries, including Pakistan, the Philippines, and Indonesia, countries noted for workers' rights abuses, official corruption, and active terrorist organizations (Sweeney 2006). Many companies are now shifting their entire accounting, engineering, research and development, or human resources departments to various countries around the world where labour costs are lower.

Precarious employment means not only lower wages and less certain employment but also greater flexibility for the employer in hiring and work schedules. One study of contingent workers in Toronto (de Wolff 2000) also found a disturbing reality of discrimination on the basis of race, gender, and age. Temporary-agency employers in particular can be selective about whom they hire and whom they place in assignments. Many workers do not know their schedules in advance, must work split shifts, or are perpetually "on call." The reality for many people is juggling several jobs while trying to combine work and home life.

Because capitalist economies are unplanned and inevitably go through economic cycles, employers have always required some worker flexibility. In a boom period more workers may be needed to expand profits, while in the depression phase fewer workers are needed as production slows down. There is always a body of workers who move in and out of the labour force; these workers were referred to by Marx as the **reserve army of the unemployed**. The existence of unemployed people also helps increase the productivity of remaining workers, who are likely to work harder and moderate their wage demands for fear of layoffs. Thus the potential threat of unemployment is a way in which the owning class disciplines the working class.

While capital always needs a certain level of unemployment, in recent years the rate of unemployment and underemployment has increased across the capitalist world. In Canada the official unemployment rate has fallen in recent years, mainly due to the growth of a few resource sectors of the economy in western Canada. However, researchers have noted that unemployment figures would be much greater if we included all those who reported being unemployed for some part of the year (Shields et al. 2006). Including the underemployed—that is, people working in a job below their level of training and experience—would expand the figures even further.

The first major transformation of work occurred during the period we now refer to as the Industrial Revolution. Prior to the growth of the factory system, work (whether agricultural or craft production) was centred on the family unit and was under the control of the individual worker. New technologies and factories changed the way workers produced, as they were brought together into large productive units that were non-kin-based. At first the workers retained a fair degree of control over the productive process, but in an effort to discipline the worker and increase profits the employer increasingly gained control. This created tremendous social dislocation for new factory workers, and many fought to retain some control over their work.

In the early twentieth century, American engineer Frederick Winslow Taylor developed a new concept of worker control known as **scientific management**. Taylorism, as it was also known, spread rapidly across North America. It is epitomized by the image of a "time-study expert," stopwatch in hand, wandering around the shop floor to improve worker efficiency. Its aim was increased managerial control over the worker with the goal of maximizing worker output. At around the same time, Henry Ford developed the first automated production line, which advanced, via technology, the control over workers that was inherent in scientific management. The term **Fordism** is now used to refer to that period of capitalist development marked by intensive production, maximum use of machinery, and complex divisions of labour. Ford, as noted in Chapter 4, also introduced the notion of improving wages, which allowed his employees to buy the goods coming off the new assembly lines.

In the period following World War II, the North American economy expanded rapidly. This led to the availability of many jobs in such growth areas as manufacturing, construction, and transportation. At most, these jobs necessitated a high school education. As the economy expanded, office jobs in both the private and the public sectors also increased dramatically during this period. Increasing numbers of these jobs were unionized, providing good wages and reasonable job security. Although, of course, not everyone benefited from this booming economy, many workers at this time were able to buy a house, a car, and the other trappings of material comfort only dreamed about by their parents.

By the early 1970s major changes began to occur in the global economy. Competition between transnational corporations increased, as did the pressure to up their rate of profit. One major expense for employers is the cost of labour. Employers can try to save money in this area in a number of ways, including reducing the number of workers, lowering the wages or benefits of workers, making employees work longer for the same or lower wages, or making them more productive during their hours of work.

The evidence indicates that all these techniques are now widespread in the workplace; as a result, the way in which Canadians work has changed dramatically. Many analysts argue that these changes are linked to a shift from the Fordist model of production to what is referred to as **post-Fordism**. The post-Fordist stage involves new social and technical forms of work organization, with production linked to new information-based technologies. As a result of these new technologies, the owning class now has both the need and the capacity for a much more flexible and productive labour force, as well as expanded global production and sales. As a result it is no longer concerned with the Fordist notion of paying high wages to workers so they can buy the products they are creating. Some analysts argue that Wal-Mart—with many non-union part-time workers receiving low pay and few benefits—is the new model for twenty-first-century capitalism (Lichtenstein 2006).

The shift to a post-Fordist model can be connected to a set of new management policies needed to improve profitability, which has been termed *lean production*. The shift to lean production has three aspects. First, there is an attempt to eliminate "waste" by moving to just-in-time production, minimal staffing levels, and greater worker productivity. Second, the workplace is restructured around a more differentiated workforce, with precarious forms of employment replacing many permanent jobs. Third, there is increased "management by stress," as a result of a declining workforce and threat of layoffs, in order to discipline the employees and get them to work harder (Sears 2000, 146).

In this context, employment is increasingly becoming polarized between "good jobs" and "bad jobs." A minority of the jobs are of the former type: they provide high income, non-wage benefits such as pension plans and employee-sponsored health insurance, relative security, and high levels of job satisfaction, flexibility, and autonomy. More jobs can be defined as "bad": they offer low income and few or no non-wage benefits, are not secure, are often part-time or seasonal, and provide relatively low levels of job satisfaction, flexibility, and autonomy. Even in the boom cycle of the economy, it now seems that there are not a sufficient number of "good" jobs being created for Canadians. According to one study of adult employment in May 2001, more than half of all Canadian workers were then in a precarious employment status (Burke and Shields 2002).

Think About It

Do you have friends or family whose jobs have changed from "good" to "bad" in recent years? What effect does it have on the individual? When you think about employment after graduation, what job characteristics will you look for?

It is not hard to see how employers benefit from this process. Not only do they get workers who, in a highly competitive market, must sell their talents for the lowest possible price, but they also get to save on costs, such as pensions, medical and dental benefits, office equipment, and so on. In addition, new technologies and the shift to precarious employment have meant that workers are increasingly isolated from each other, making it more difficult for them to organize any collective response to their predicament. All these changes have meant lower real wages, fewer benefits, and less job security for increasing numbers of workers.

Decline in Real Wages

Connected to changes in labour-market participation is the decline of workers' real wages (that is, wages after inflation is taken into account). The economic boom in Canada that followed World War II gave the impression that the standard of living for the majority of Canadians was on the rise. Certainly, the expansion of the economy, in conjunction with new social programs, did improve the lives of many Canadians. However, the entry of increasing numbers of women into the paid labour market made gains seem higher than they actually were, as two incomes gave many families a substantially increased family wage packet.

In the decade between 1990 and 2000, average real earnings of Canadians did rise 7.3 percent. However, when the data are examined more carefully, it is clear that not all Canadians benefited from this increase. Census data for 2000 indicate that wages of Canadians reflect the growing split between "good" and "bad" jobs. Thus, the number of earners in higher income brackets—those who earned more than $80,000 a year, and especially those who made $100,000 or more—soared during the 1990s. At the same time, four out of every ten people with employment income in Canada earned $20,000 or less, essentially the same proportion as in 1990. More than one-fifth (22 percent) of this total, or 1,482,000 Canadians, were working on a full-year, full-time basis (Statistics Canada 2003a, 7–8). Not surprisingly, the low-income earners were more likely to be the same groups frequently found in precarious forms of employment—women, immigrants, and younger workers. With regard to the latter, a Statistics Canada study of 2000 Census data (ibid., 5) noted that "a clear generational divide has opened up in the labour market with younger groups on a lower earnings track than older, more experienced groups."

Think About It
Do you think young people today are concerned about the growing generational divide in wages? Why or why not?

A persistent problem for the capitalist owning class is that excessively low wages or high rates of unemployment may lead to social unrest. While the main goal of this class is to maximize profits, social instability could put the entire capitalist system at risk. Moreover, workers are also consumers, and wages must be kept high enough for workers to continue purchasing goods for sale in the capitalist marketplace. For these reasons, the owning class must search for additional ways to maximize the rate of profit besides simply keeping wages low.

The Growing Intensity of Labour

In 2007, a Canadian Imperial Bank of Commerce teller launched a $600-million class-action lawsuit against her employer, alleging thousands of hours that went unpaid to her and her colleagues. This case reflects a growing trend by employers, because a major way to increase profits is to extend the working day without increasing wages. While many Canadians are working too few hours, others are working too many. Statistics Canada found that 23 percent of the workforce now puts in more than an eight-hour day, but only 10 percent of workers are getting paid for it. For example, more than half of all nurses regularly work overtime without any compensation (White and Trevisan 2007).

Whatever the hours, for all those who work there is a growing intensity of labour, for profits can be improved if workers can be made to work harder within the same period of time. Even in the public sector, workers are made to do more because of cuts to the number of workers. On the assembly line this was originally referred to as "speed-up," because if the line were made to move faster, workers would have to work faster to keep up with the machinery. Today, the workers being subjected to speed-up are not primarily those on the assembly line. Computer technology allows workers of many types to be monitored and told to work faster. Even among the middle and upper echelons of management, there is an increase in the amount of work. Almost everyone is afraid of losing their jobs, and more and more employees are taking work home.

It should not be surprising, then, that in both 1994 and 2000 more than one-third of working Canadians cited too many demands or hours as the most common source of workplace stress (Williams 2003). Stress is also increasing because longer hours at the workplace lead to shorter hours with one's family. One study (Turcotte 2007) found that the average Canadian worker spent forty-five minutes less each workday with his or her family in 2005 than in 1986. This totals 195 hours a year—almost five forty-hour work weeks.

It is also worth noting that the deterioration of job quality is not bad for just individuals; it also has negative consequences for the broader community. If workers earn lower wages, have less job stability, work longer hours, or have to work at several jobs, this will inevitably have an impact on families, the health care system, the care of children and the elderly, and, as we shall see below, overall social participation. Overwork can also lead to various forms of addiction, including, ironically, addiction to work itself (Menzies 2005, 79).

Are New Technologies the Problem?

For those of us who grew up in the 1950s and 1960s, technology represented a utopian future. Automation and computers were—we were told—going to make jobs easier and create an abundance of wealth for all. The main problem by the end of the twentieth century, or so we believed, would be what to do with all our leisure time. Of course, reality has turned out quite differently. The data indicate that many of us are working harder and longer than ever before, while others of us are unemployed or underemployed. Why didn't technology prove to be the liberating force we all believed it would be? The answer lies in understanding who controls the technology, and the purposes for which it is introduced.

As part of its drive to maximize profits, capital is compelled to constantly introduce new technologies into the workplace. If a company can be the first to introduce a new method of production or a new machine that will raise productivity, it will then have the competitive edge in the marketplace, at least for a time. This fact helps us understand how capitalism, more than any other socioeconomic formation that preceded it, has revolutionized the forces of production. Undeniably, innovations in technology and knowledge have raised living standards, extended life expectancies, improved health, and so on. However, for capital, new technologies are introduced not to better the lives of workers, but rather to increase profitability and control over them.

From the viewpoint of the employer, machines have a number of advantages over workers. For one thing, the productivity one can get from a worker is finite, since there are limits to human physical and mental capabilities. In contrast, there are no similar limits to the productivity that can be generated from machines or computers. Moreover, technology doesn't complain, doesn't need washroom breaks, doesn't form unions, and doesn't go out on strike.

For workers, new technologies have quite a different meaning than they do for employers. This is because workers do not own or control the technology and therefore have little or no say over how it is used. Certainly, technology has eliminated or vastly improved some of the most horrific jobs formerly done by human labour power. It also allows for the possibility of shorter working time as productivity soars. Indeed, we often speak of machines as "labour-saving devices." But none of these realities are of much concern to employers. The main reason that employers introduce new technologies is to increase profit. This often means that, instead of having a better job, many workers have no job at all. It is for this reason that workers have often fought the introduction of new technologies.

Jobs that involve working primarily with one's hands are referred to as *blue-collar jobs*, because traditionally such labourers, predominantly males, wore darker shirts while they worked. Such jobs have been declining overall in Canada, particularly in manufacturing. Barely two million workers, or 12 percent of the workforce, now work in this sector, the lowest number since World War II (Stanford 2007). Most of these lost jobs were "good" jobs in the sense that they provided workers with reasonable pay, benefits, and employment security.

White-collar jobs—that is, jobs where workers (again, originally male) traditionally wore suits, white shirts, and ties to work, and where mental labour dominates—have also been affected by the introduction of new technologies. Once-secure jobs in accounting, sales, and management have been declining as computer technologies expand globally. Moreover, for those in professions such as medicine, law, education, or architecture, computer technology has meant that the individual's control over knowledge (and therefore their influence and power) has been declining (Teeple 2000, 70) while various on-the-job stresses have been increasing.

It must be made clear that new technologies can create jobs as well as eliminate them. But the new jobs that are created do not necessarily match the skills of the workers who lose their jobs, nor are they necessarily in the same geographic location. Digital technologies now allow for "virtual" workplaces, where the physical location of the worker becomes irrelevant and the worker is competing in a global labour market for a job. Moreover, as already noted, there are simply not enough good jobs being created to match the number of people in Canada who need or want to work.

The problem with blaming technology for the changing nature of work is that it leaves us with the notion that the transformations we see today are inevitable as societies progress. It is important, therefore, to repeat the point that technology could, in theory, allow for shorter working time, more leisure, and an improved quality of life for most workers. A shorter work day would also lead to

---

Box 6.1 Prescription for Stress

A Statistics Canada study on job stress ought to rivet the attention of Canadian economic and political leaders. Work-related stress takes a high toll on the emotional well-being of millions of employees, undermines the health of many and incurs a forbidding financial penalty. Stress-induced absences have been calculated to cost employers about $3.5 billion annually, and that figure does not include the medical expenses of treating stress-induced illness.

Job stress has been implicated in many conditions, from infections and pain in muscles and joints to multiple sclerosis, high blood pressure and heart disease, and mental conditions such as depression and anxiety. "Even among workers with only short-term psychological distress and adverse work-related psychosocial factors, the risk of musculoskeletal pain is increased," one British study concluded. Were the research net to be cast wider, job stress would likely be found to play a role in numerous other conditions as well, including autoimmune disease and cancer.

The StatsCan findings are in line with the extensive scientific literature on stress. The major psychological triggers for physiological stress are loss of control, uncertainty, and conflict. These irritants can all be exacerbated by poor social relationships and ameliorated by strong emotional bonds with others—the more genuinely we are connected with each other, the safer we are physiologically.

What could political and business leaders do to reduce job stress for working people? The first step would be to re-examine the wisdom of shortsighted bottom-line economics as a primary goal. While cutting public services and down-sizing businesses may save money in the short term, the long-term consequences of increased stress are increased social costs and reduced productivity.

Source: Adapted from Gabor Maté, the *Globe and Mail*, 17 September 2003.

---

the employment of more workers. It should be noted as well that laws regarding acceptable hours of work vary within the developed capitalist world, and some countries have not moved in the same direction as Canada. The government of France, for example, legislated a thirty-five-hour work week in 2000, and workers are entitled to a minimum five-week vacation. Thus, the nature of work—its quality and its quantity—is both an economic and a political issue.

Worker Alienation

That work holds a special place in the lives of humans is reflected in the fact that we speak of it as "making a living." Work is the means by which humans live. But it serves not only to keep us alive; at a very deep psychological level, it also defines who we are, both to ourselves and to others. Moreover, work is not just something we do for a fixed number of hours a day. We think about our work, we bring it home with us, we even dream about it. Work is the central defining characteristic of human existence.

For most of human history, "work" and "life" were inseparable. Without electricity and timepieces, people of necessity lived by the rhythms of nature, and work was seen as tasks to be undertaken—for example, to build a hut, weave a mat, or gather nuts and berries. With the beginnings of social classes, work began to change, as an appropriating class began to control the surplus produced by others. Nonetheless, in the pre-capitalist period, most people still controlled their means of production and managed to retain a fair degree of control over the work process, however onerous the process may have been.

Capitalism, however, brought about a dramatic change in the relationship between humans and the work that they did. This is because—for the first time in history—in capitalist societies most people who work are completely separated from the means of production, which is now under total control of the appropriating class. As a result our capacity to labour (for the majority of us the defining characteristic of human existence) has been reduced to an object that can be bought and sold—a commodity.

Marx referred to the separation of workers from their labour, and all that this entails, as **alienation**. By alienation, Marx meant that workers in capitalism lose control over the work process, the product, and the surplus value that they create. In capitalist societies another class decides what is to be produced and how it is to be produced, and decisions are made not to satisfy the needs of workers but to satisfy the needs of the capitalist owning class. Profit maximization is always the primary determining variable in the work process. Moreover, the majority of surplus value that is created by workers is not controlled by them. Most of it is converted into profits for the owning class. Thus the act of working, according to Marx, actually reproduces the very class relations that oppress workers. This process dehumanizes work. Rather than having a purpose in its own right, work comes to be seen primarily as something that allows us to consume.

Think About It

The Marxist concept of alienation embodies the notion that the very things workers produce end up being used against them. Can you think of some examples that affirm this idea? Keep in mind that workers produce not only goods and services but also the surplus value that is converted into capitalist profits.

Utilizing this analysis, we can also see why for so many of us work is not only unsatisfying but also unsafe. According to data collected by the Association of Workers' Compensation Boards of Canada, 976 workplace fatalities were recorded in Canada in 2006. Moreover, it is estimated that close to 900,000 work-related injuries and illnesses occur in Canada each year (Human Resources Development Canada 2003). This is not the result of a cruel and heartless owning class but rather of the need of capitalists to maintain their competitive edge. Safety costs money, and few capitalists are going to pursue it unless required to, usually by governments. Many countries in the developing world have become appealing places for capital investment, not only because of cheap labour, but also because of their governments' weak laws regarding worker safety and environmental standards.

It is not only unsafe workplaces but also the work itself that is killing many of us. Studies from Britain and Sweden on worker health found that job stress and lack of control seem to affect mortality rates and general health (Taylor 1993). Although many of us assume that it is those in positions of power who suffer most from stress and heavy workloads, the data seems to indicate otherwise. For example, a study of 10,000 British government employees found a gradual but clear increase in mortality from the top to the bottom of the job hierarchy. The Swedish study found heart disease most prevalent among those who saw their work as psychologically demanding but lacking in decision-making power.

At the same time, the lack of work is also destructive to our health. Unemployment can be linked to increased suicide rates, general physical or mental health problems, and greater use of health care services (Jin et al. 1995). Even job insecurity can be correlated with declining health. A longitudinal study of government workers in Britain noted a relative decline in health standards in employees anticipating privatization and subsequent job insecurity (Ferrie et al. 1995). Thus Marx's theory of alienated labour seems to be borne out by empirical data. Humans suffer in a real material way as a result of powerlessness in the workplace.

Although few of us have actually read Marx's work on alienation, most of us understand it at a gut level, and most of us sense that somehow it is preferable to be our own boss than to have someone else in charge of our work lives. Most of us want to be in control of our labour, and, not surprisingly, small-business owners do indeed feel that the best thing about ownership is independence and control (*Globe and Mail*, 17 July 1995, B5). However, life for most self-employed people in Canada today is not much rosier than for workers.

The Decline of Small Business and the Family Farm

Workers are not the only sector to be negatively affected by the capitalist accumulation of profits. Another major consequence of the process of monopolization has been the decline of the small-business sector in Canada. It is a popular myth in Canada that small business is the engine that drives the economy. However, the statistics indicate otherwise. In the dominant economic sectors in Canada and around the world (banking, insurance, automobile production, oil and gas), a small number of major corporations now control almost the entire sector.

The biggest of the corporations can afford to take losses for long periods of time until their competition is driven out of business. This is partially a result of ownership in diverse sectors, so that losses in one can be offset by gains in another. Losses can then be recouped after the competition has disappeared and prices are raised. Moreover, most small businesses in Canada cannot compete with bigger corporations as a result of the fundamental nature of the goods and services they produce (Stanford 1999, 136):

> Most smaller firms depend on sales to one of two markets: either the consumer purchases of individuals who already have jobs with other companies, or else purchases by those other companies of supplies and

services used in their own operations. Most small businesses need some *other* employer to do something *first*, therefore, before they can sell their own product and create their own jobs. In this sense, most small businesses cannot "lead" the development of the broader economy. They can only follow it.

Most small businesses have little in the way of independence. They exist solely at the behest of larger companies, who may cast them aside at any time for another company that offers a cheaper price or newer service. This is not to say that small business is irrelevant to the Canadian economy. While their aggregate volume may be low, small business continues to fill the nooks and crannies of the capitalist marketplace, largely in market niches that are low profit or high risk. The number of self-employed nearly doubled between 1978 and 2006 (Statistics Canada 2007c) to just under two and a half million individuals. Many of the newly self-employed are former wage workers who have been laid off, while others have started their own businesses after failing to find suitable work.

However, small business is very small indeed. Most of the recent growth of small businesses has involved individuals with no employees (Krahn et al. 2007, 71). The self-employed have a wide variation of income and other rewards. Although 6 percent of the self-employed earned more than $100,000 in 2002, 57 percent earned less than $20,000 (Statistics Canada 2004, 70). The self-employed generally have to pay for their own health, disability, dental, and pension plans and are not entitled to unemployment insurance. In addition, self-employed individuals work longer hours than paid employees, with more than one-third of all self-employed individuals working more than fifty hours per week in their main job (Lowe 2001).

While the number of self-employed entrepreneurs has been growing, small commodity producers of food—Canada's farmers and small-boat fishers—have become a rapidly disappearing breed. The number of family farms shrank dramatically in the twentieth century. It is not hard to understand why. In 2004, profits for the huge agribusiness monopolies soared, with some having their best year ever; in contrast, farmers had one of their worst years ever, with many barely getting by (National Farmers Union 2005). As a result, many farmers and their children are being forced off the land and face uncertain futures. The stress of losing their farms has led to increased rates of alcoholism, broken marriages, and even suicide.

> Today, farmers are paying to produce. Were it not for taxpayer-funded support, off-farm income, depletion of savings, and access to debt, farming in Canada would have to cease.
> —National Farmers' Union, 2005

The number of Canadians who fish for a living has also declined drastically. Fishing industries on both the west and east coasts have been in crisis, with many fish-processing firms closing as a result of low fish prices, declining fish stocks, and overcapacity in the harvesting and processing sectors. Recent federal government regulations have also prohibited a number of fishing activities. The crisis has meant that many families—particularly in the Atlantic provinces, where fishing has a long tradition and is often the only means of survival in small coastal communities—have been left totally dependent on inadequate government payments. More than 40,000 jobs were lost in Newfoundland alone as a result of the moratorium on cod fishing (Anderson 2003). What fishing remains (particularly on the west coast) is increasingly controlled by large foreign-owned TNCs, and fish farming (rather than catching fish in the wild) has become more common. Formerly self-employed individuals often find that the only work available is as low-skilled, low-paid workers at these farms.

The decline of farming and fishing is obviously not spread randomly across the country and has had devastating effects for particular regions. Coastal communities, particularly in Newfoundland and Nova Scotia as well as some in British Columbia, have been seriously affected; rural areas of Saskatchewan have also been very hard hit. The loss of the family business has meant not just a change of employment for those who farmed or fished going back many generations; it has in many cases also meant the decline of communities and whole regions as young people no longer have a future near their families and must move to other parts of Canada to find work. In addition, increased dependence on food grown in other countries, or even regions, diminishes communities' food security.

Think About It

Do you know where your food comes from? Much of what we eat today is grown thousands of kilometres away in other countries. Why do so few of us ever think about this?

To this point, we have examined how those who work or those who own small businesses have been affected by the growth of transnational corporations. But the power of capital is so great that it not only affects particular groups or individuals in Canada, it also sets the framework for our entire culture.

The Culture of Capitalism

Chapter 3 introduced the concept of culture, the ways that culture is linked to the economic arrangements of a society and the way humans are defined by the culture in which they live. Now that we understand the basics of how capitalism works, we can begin to examine how the culture we live in today is linked to the economic arrangements of our own society. People in capitalist societies, no less than in any other socioeconomic formation, have to eat, have a roof over their heads, and (in colder climates) have some clothing to keep them warm. They also need some love and affection, some sense of belonging to a community, and a reasonable degree of social stability. Within capitalist societies, however, all human needs come to be mediated by the market.

Almost all of us will eventually enter the capitalist marketplace, either as buyers or sellers of products or of labour power. However, we do not all enter this marketplace as equals. In the advanced capitalism of our era a small number of individuals have enormous amounts of wealth and power as a result of their control of immense amounts of capital. In turn, the interests and values of the capitalist owning class come to be the dominant ones within our society. In the process, everything is turned into a commodity, and everything is seen in terms of its marketability and profitability. What is defined as good in our society is increasingly linked to profit only.

In many ways, capitalism is a system in which the worst characteristics of our species—greed, individualism, crass materialism, selfishness—are encouraged and rewarded; in turn, such behaviours are defended as natural or inborn traits. For example, in recent years a whole school of thought about the economy—known as public choice theory—has argued that material greed is the single, natural, dominant motive underlying all human behaviour (Stretton and Orchard 1994). Not only is greed seen as inevitable in this argument, it is also seen as morally superior.

Regardless of our cultural background, most of us as children learn a common set of traditional values from our parents, our teachers, and our religious leaders: share your toys; do unto others as you would have them do unto you; honesty is the best policy; help those less fortunate than yourself. At the same time, however, it is clear that the society we live in frequently rewards the profiteers, the cheaters, and the greedy. How else do we explain that CEOs receive millions of dollars for increasing shareholder value by laying off workers, shutting down factories that have sustained local economies, or polluting the environment?

Capitalism is a system in which social value is determined by one's market value. Those who have great wealth or high-status jobs are seen as superior to those with lower incomes or low-status jobs. And some people—such as the elderly, the disabled, or the unemployed—are seen as having little or no value at all because they are either out of the market or peripheral to it. Indeed, where communities once collectively took responsibility for the care of their weakest members, now such individuals are considered to be a drain on societies.

The dominance of the corporate sector can be seen all around us. The largest buildings are those of the biggest corporations, and the tallest of those are the bank towers. Many new banks, office buildings, and shopping malls, extravagantly decorated in marble and other expensive materials, seem to be edifices constructed to honour the new god of money. Compare these buildings to our deteriorating public buildings. In addition, corporate branding has accelerated rapidly in the twenty-first century. Commercial advertising is everywhere in our lives, but few of us complain because most of us have never known anything different.

Think About It

For one day, walk around your city or town and count all the advertisements you see. Do these ads bother you?

The Culture of Consumerism

When you go out to shop for new clothes, what do you look for in a purchase? Price will probably be an important variable. But so will a thing called "fashion" or "style." Maybe you're more into technology than clothing. In today's world of electronics being new is even more important—when buying a cellphone, TV, or electronic game, everyone wants the latest item. This process of creating things that always need to be replaced, referred to as *planned obsolescence*, is an essential part of the capitalist need to sell us ever more products. Indeed, most new electronic technology is not built to last. But few of us mind, because a newer "must have" model has just appeared on the scene.

At the end of the nineteenth century, social scientist Thorstein Veblen (1857–1929) was probably the first to analyze growing consumerism in American society in *Theory of the Leisure Class* (1899). He is still remembered for coining the term *conspicuous consumption* to describe the tendency of an increasing number of people to buy things not out of need but rather to improve their social status. Since his time, consumerism has expanded exponentially. The twentieth century saw the creation of both societies of perpetual growth and an accompanying culture of consumer capitalism. In 1900, approximately $1.5 trillion was spent globally by public and private consumers. By 1975 it was estimated at $12 trillion. By 1998 it had reach $24 trillion, and it continues to grow (*CCPA Monitor*, March 2007, 3). Canada and the United States accounted for 31 percent of that amount although they only have 5 percent of the world's population (Anderssen 2007).

> The genius of contemporary capitalism is not simply that it gives consumers what they want, but that it makes them want what it has to give.
> —Timothy Garton Ash

> We're consuming more than the Earth can afford.
> —Lisa Mastny, Worldwatch Institute

With the never-ending glut of goods on the market, corporations must perpetually convince us to consume more and more. They spend billions of dollars a year persuading us that our lives will improve if we just buy their stuff. More and more of the people they target are children and youths (see Box 6.2). This is not surprising. Not only do young people today have a great deal of disposable income, but they also have a big effect on their parents' consumer choices. One American study found that 55 percent of young people will keep on asking for something they want, even if their parents' initial answer is no (Klaffke 2003, 38).

Because many of us feel at least some sense of insecurity, it is not surprising that we are highly susceptible to advertising, even though most of us like to think otherwise. Those who cannot afford to buy these things are made to feel less worthy for lack of them; conversely, those who are able to purchase the most expensive commodities are looked up to and envied. However, recent data seems to indicate that once people have moved beyond having their basic mate-

Box 6.2 Empowering Youth Through Consumption?

There are few places better than marketing conferences to find out what's really going on in the hearts and minds of corporate players. How they really feel about independence or critical thought... or, more accurately, how they deal with it. And this takes on a somewhat chilling edge when the topic of this marketing conference is youth.

Conferences of this sort really do present an alternate reality, one where criticism of consumer culture and the direct targeting of children is called "Commie-Pinko crap" (and I didn't realize that people still used that term seriously) from people who are "so behind the times."

After all, we're told, youth are cool. They're aware. They're savvy—"much smarter than I was at their age," lament the speakers with apparent envy and admiration. Kids know what they want. And it's the duty of advertisers to listen, and give kids what they want, what they will buy, what they will put their financial clout behind. This is a $1.8 billion a year market that affects the spending of ten times that amount. That's not small potatoes. Furthermore, this is a market that has a much greater longevity than one made up of older consumers—simply put, they will be around longer to spend more. That's why market research organizations prefer to call themselves "a youth market consultation and fulfill-ment house."

The message for marketers is clear. This is all about democracy. Give kids a platform to discuss issues important to them. Let them express themselves. It's not really about marketing to youth—it's all about empowering youth, giving them a sense of ownership and pride they can take in the media they create and the fashion they drive. The successful marketing campaigns that target youth are about respecting these young people, and recognizing that it's about fulfilling their needs—their need to feel important, to be treated as individuals, to be in con-trol—not simply selling a product.

Empowerment through commodifica-tion. It's an intriguing concept, really, and one that virtually guarantees lifelong support and consumption. The trick for marketers is to reinforce this message: "We know that you know that we want you to buy our product. Let's have a knowing giggle about this. You're past that. You're smarter than that. So buy our product because we acknowledge your superior market savvy." And to complete the illusion of respect, marketers must be creative—in their message, and in their advertising vehicle. The more interac-tive—sorry, empowering—the better.

Source: Adapted from Erika Shaker, *Our Schools/Our Selves*, July 2001, vol. 10, no. 4 (#64): 103–109.

rial needs met, increased amounts of money and material goods do not seem to buy happiness (Toynbee 2003).

How do corporations get individuals to buy more and more when most workers are earning less and less? In the post-Fordist era the answer is simple: the growth of personal debt. Increasing numbers of us are purchasing goods with money we haven't yet earned and paying interest for the "privilege" of doing so. In 2001 47 percent of all households in Canada were spending more than their pre-tax income, up from 39 percent in 1982 (Statistics Canada 2005). In 2006, Canadians rang up $94 billion in debt (excluding mortgages), double the amount in 1999. There are now twice as many credit cards in Canada as there are Canadians (Anderssen 2007).

If there is a single consumer item that is central to understanding capitalism, it is the automobile. The car is far more than just a utilitarian object to get us from one place to another. In some ways it embodies the mythology of capitalism itself—the individual (usually male), alone and free, speeding along on the open road, in total control of a sleek, brand-new piece of technology. This image is pervasive in the automobile advertisements we see. In reality, of course, the automobile provides few of us with the speed, freedom, and independence depicted in these commercials. Most of us who drive actually spend hours a week on clogged superhighways and overcrowded city streets. We also spend years paying off the bank loan we took out to buy the car and incur large costs for maintenance, insurance, and parking. Indeed, Statistics Canada (2005) found that the common variable in households that spent more than they earned was the thousands of dollars a year expended on car purchases. That the automobile is central to our economy can be evidenced by the number of car ads on TV, in magazines, and on the Internet, in addition to regular "auto sections" in newspapers and auto shows across the country.

Think About It

For one evening, watch television and monitor all the automobile ads. How many are there per hour? What images are they are selling you?

That there might be alternatives to growing consumerism is an issue that is rarely addressed. And since we are not taught to understand who has power within our society, we are led to believe that current cultural changes are inevitable in the face of global developments and technological change. Discussions of possible alternatives to our current social arrangements are simply not on the agenda.

"We" versus "Me"

We usually don't think much about how our society works. It just does. Yet making any society work is actually quite complex. Societies are made up of individuals, each with their own feelings, wishes, needs, and desires. In order to survive, each individual has to make a compact with others—I will live with you because I can't survive without you. But by making this compact we are of necessity giving up some of our individuality.

The complex question of the relationship between the individual and the social world, and between individuals within the social world is the core of what sociologists study. In earlier chapters we briefly examined foraging and agrarian societies. In such societies, where life was a struggle for most people and survival depended on support from others, the "we" generally took priority over the "me."

As far back as nineteenth century, social scientists and philosophers noticed

Box 6.3 Weddings Old and New

For most of human history, marriage has had little to do with the individuals concerned. In traditional societies, marriage was about the creation of a new family, the bonding of different clans, and—once classes had developed—the passing down of property. Marriages centred on the coming together of families more than of individuals, and were often arranged by parents. In a wedding in rural India in 2007, the groom arrived drunk at his wedding, so the bride married his younger brother instead (*Globe and Mail*, 3 May 2007, L1).

Clearly this would be unlikely to happen today in Canada, where weddings have taken on an entirely different meaning. In the advanced capitalism of the twenty-first century, weddings have become primarily extravagant shows of conspicuous consumption. The average Canadian couple now spends somewhere between $20,000 and $25,000 on a wedding, sometimes much more. Love has been commoditized into a diamond engagement ring, we "shower" the couple with expensive products (many of which they have pre-selected), and brides often spend thousands of dollars on a dress that will never be worn again. Weddings have become so large and complex that busy couples commonly hire a wedding planner to do the work for them. The goal for many—or at least according to wedding guides—is to make their wedding "unique." The bride often sees this event as her special day, with the engagement period seen as a time of self-perfection to prepare for the wedding. The tension of all this is so great that a new word has been coined for women whose stress makes them behave badly: "bridezillas."

We should not romanticize the traditional world of the "we." Too much "we" can mean a lack of individual rights and freedoms. For much of recent history, women have been forced into arranged marriages where they may be abused or even killed. But too much emphasis on the "me" is troubling as well, with some couples spending so much time planning the wedding that they forget to think about the impending marriage. Over one-third of all Canadian marriages eventually end in divorce; in Quebec almost one in two marriages fail (Statistics Canada 2005).

that the growth of industrial societies was changing social relationships. A key development was the movement of large populations from tightly knit rural communities to newly industrializing urban areas. New structures of work also changed family and social interaction. In addition, industrial society was one of constant change rather than a society centred on custom and tradition.

The movement of people into cities had a particularly strong effect on the way people connected with others. Cities had existed for centuries in many parts of the world, but for most of human history the majority of people lived far from cities or towns. In rural areas, human groups were connected to others primarily through kinship ties. Social rules were informal but adherence was expected; religious beliefs were a strong force binding people together. As people moved into cities, they were often separated from their extended families and forced to live physically close to total strangers. All these transformations were of interest to the growing field of sociology as it tried to create a science of society.

Marx noted that the growth of capitalist economies changed the way individuals were connected to each other and the larger social world. As workers were freed from their feudal bonds, they were also separated from their traditional connection to others and to a physical place. Their potential labour power became an atomized commodity for sale in the marketplace, now in competition with others who were also forced to sell their labour power to survive. Moreover, globalizing capitalism meant that people moved not only from rural areas to cities but also migrated to other regions or countries where their neighbours might have different cultural traditions and speak a different language.

Think About It

Are your parents immigrants from another country or did they move from one region to another in Canada? If so, how did they try to avoid social isolation?

In the late nineteenth century, French sociologist Émile Durkheim provided one of the early sociological analyses of modern societies. Durkheim thought there were two forms of social cohesion. In pre-industrial societies, groups were held together by what he called **mechanical solidarity**. Such societies had a simple division of labour and people were united by shared values and common social bonds. Industrialization and urbanization eroded such societies; their common consensus and moral integration were destroyed. How then, Durkheim wondered, was social order maintained? He felt that **organic solidarity** would develop in industrial societies and bind individuals together. With its complex division of labour and people performing highly specialized work tasks, he thought individuals would now be united by their interdependence (Durkheim [1893] 1933). Durkheim used the term "organic" to compare this interdependence to the ways organs in the human body are separate but connected.

Durkheim was an order theorist who thought that a newer form of social cohesion would simply replace an older form. Other social analysts were less optimistic. German sociologist Ferdinand Tönnies (1855–1936) also addressed the transformation of societies and loss of social solidarity as large industrial cities began to replace small rural villages in Europe. He used the term **Gemeinschaft** ("commune" or "community") to describe traditional societies, where social relationships were based on personal bonds of family or friendship that were held together by shared moral values usually tied to religion. In contrast, he used the term **Gesellschaft** ("association") to describe large urban societies where social bonds were eroded by the complex division of labour, individualism, and competitiveness. Tönnies was concerned about what the loss of traditional community meant to modern societies.

From the "Me Generation" to the "iGeneration"

Marx saw alienation as an inevitable aspect of living in capitalist societies. In the twentieth century, alienation—now taking on a broader meaning of an individual's loss of connection to community and other individuals—became a

---

Box 6.4 The Gym as Metaphor?

I have belonged to a gym for two years and attend three to four times a week. It is a popular gym, with people of all ages attending. It is a large facility, and it is not unusual for close to a hundred people to be there at any given time.

One day it occurred to me that the gym is an excellent representation of the isolation of individuals in today's society. Despite the large number of people coming together in one place—all sharing a common interest in exercise—only a very few people ever talk to each other. Many people are listening to a personal electronic device. Others are watching one of the many TV monitors placed around the gym. Not only do people not talk, they don't smile at each other or even make eye contact. Although I see certain people there regularly, none of us has ever acknowledged each other.

The only people who seem to frequently interact with others are the paid staff. Those at the front desk are almost artificially cheery. Every six months they phone to tell me it's time to schedule my personal assessment. There are always several personal trainers on the floor, chatting happily with clients.

The gym, then, is a microcosm of big city living. We are in close physical contact with others (in the case of the gym, often very intimate contact), and yet there is practically no social interaction occurring. The only friendly and caring people are those who—like the greeters that welcome you at many stores—are paid to be sociable in the hopes that you will buy more product.

Of course, the gym isn't the only place where we can observe large groups of people sharing space but not interacting. University classrooms, buses, movie theatres, airports, and even sidewalks all display this characteristic to a greater or lesser degree. We have shifted to an increasingly *Gesellschaft* world so aptly described by Tönnies over a century ago.

---

popular theme in fields as diverse as philosophy, psychoanalysis, and sociology. Social analysts were noticing that the growth of the "me" seemed to be having negative effects on both individuals and the society as a whole.

Following World War II, a number of American writers continued to focus on alienation, but its class component and connection to a capitalist economy were seldom discussed. Most authors now focused on what they saw as the increasing isolation of the individual from the broader social and political world. One author (Lasch 1991 [1979]) described modern society as having a "culture of narcissism." *Narcissism* is the excessive preoccupation with oneself and lack of empathy for others. The shift away from the collective was linked to the expansion of the middle strata, as well their movement to the suburbs of major American cities. Philip Slater (1970, 7) described the growing emphasis on the "me" over the "we":

> It is easy to produce examples of the many ways in which Americans attempt to minimize, circumvent, or deny the interdependence upon which all human societies are based. We seek a private house, a private means of transportation, a private garden, a private laundry, self-service

stores, and do-it-yourself skills of every kind.... Even within the family Americans are unique in their feeling that each member should have a separate room, and even a separate telephone, television, and car, when economically possible. We seek more and more privacy, and feel more and more alienated and lonely when we get it.

Slater was clearly referring to that sector of society with enough wealth to purchase the goods he describes. Nonetheless, his was a prescient description of what would expand to a wide cross-section of the North American population. Keep in mind that he wrote these words before the advent of personal computers, cellphones, MP3s, or home video players.

Social theorists have expressed concern over the decline of both social activism and general social engagement. Robert Putnam's book *Bowling Alone: The Collapse and Revival of American Community* examined the erosion of what social scientists call **social capital**, that is, the social networks connecting individuals to each other that are based on reciprocity, shared norms, and trust. Drawing on a vast amount of data, he concluded that Americans—regardless of gender, race, age, or social background—have increasingly become disconnected from community life. According to Putnam (2000, 403), a solitary quest for private goods has replaced the shared pursuit of the public good. Of particular concern for Putnam is a growing generational divide, with those born after 1970 showing the greatest decrease in commitment to the wider community.

The baby boom generation, born between 1946 and 1964 in North America, was referred to as the "Me Generation." These were the children who grew up in the increasingly privatized world described by Slater. While their parents' generation had lived through depression and war, the baby boomers were raised in an era of growing material comfort, increasing access to postsecondary education, and an ever-expanding marketplace. Despite the social consciousness and opposition to war, racism, and gender inequality that many showed in their youth, this cohort has shown itself to be more self-centred and more materialistic than its predecessors (Putnam 2000, 258).

Recent data indicate that the children of the baby boom generation, which one analyst has labelled "Generation Me" (Twenge 2006), are even more self-involved and detached from broader social networks. This group, born after 1970, still feels connected to family, friends, and co-workers. But the world they inhabit is more "me" oriented and less "we" oriented than ever. The popular culture of today glorifies the individual, embodied in the concept of "self." Young people are told to "be yourself," "respect yourself," "love yourself," "express yourself," "trust yourself," and "stand up for yourself." But according to Twenge, extensive U.S. data indicate that young people have higher rates of anxiety and depression than ever before.

On the one hand, young people are being told that if they only "believe in themselves" they can be anything they want. On the other hand, the changing world of work and the inherent nature of capitalism mean that many will not achieve their goals. Moreover, greater job insecurity, increasing debt, and less community involvement may leave young people feeling less and less committed to the broader society. As one author writes, "Those Canadians who not only feel economically insecure, but are insecure, are... displaying high levels of alienation and disengagement with mainstream institutions" (O'Connor 1997, 21). Overall, young people are less interested in politics today than the generations before them (Howe 2002).

The term "iGeneration" has also been used by some writers to describe young people today; it is a play on words, meant to reflect not only the perceived self-involvement of young people, but also their increasing connection to privatized technologies. Most young people now spend a good part of every day by themselves, hooked into DVD players, television, MP3 players, or electronic games; even when they connect to others, it is often via technologies such as cellphones or the Internet.

> The values of "looking out for No. 1" and "getting mine" are precisely what is needed [for an individual] to succeed in the capitalist marketplace. Yet these are the very values that teach our children to put material goods ahead of spiritual needs, to develop competitive rather than co-operative skills.... The marketplace fosters the development of a narcissistic personality structure adept at manipulating and controlling others.
> —Rabbi Michael Lerner

Putnam's book *Bowling Alone* was published shortly before the major expansion of social networking sites such as MySpace and Facebook, and social scientists are just beginning to analyze the implications of this new means of connecting with others. Those who use these sites often have a wide circle of people identified as their friends. However, while their networks may be broader than their parents' generation, they may also be shallower. Many of these "friends" may communicate only electronically from time to time, or they may occasionally organize to meet in small groups to go to a club or see a movie. What is not yet well-researched is whether the expansion of social networking sites has had any effect on overall social or political engagement. Clearly, some young people will use it as a way to connect with others in movements for social and environmental change. However, it has been suggested that the Internet in general is just another place for self-absorbed young people to document their every move and feeling (Smith 2006).

Think About It

Do you think that Slater's, Putnam's, and Twenge's analyses of American society apply to Canada? Do you think that new technologies and social networking sites have made young people more socially connected or less socially connected?

Consequences

Durkheim's work on suicide ([1897] 1951) was one of the first to link the lack of social connectedness to negative personal outcomes. Rates of suicide, he discovered, were lower among married people, those with more tightly knit religious communities, and those with children; suicides were more frequent in times of rapid social change. Studies since that time have confirmed what Durkheim first noted, that social connectedness is a strong determinant of individual well-being. Social connections make us healthier: data from more than a dozen large studies demonstrate that socially disconnected individuals are two to five times more likely to die from all causes than those with close ties to family, friends, and community (Putnam 2000, 327). We also feel better when we help others. A number of recent studies have concluded that everything from gratitude to generosity is good for our mental and physical health (Agrell 2007).

It should not surprise us that social connections make us happier. Being human means being social, and people will suffer a variety of mental stresses when they feel cut off from a supportive, cohesive community (Smail 1999). If, indeed, North Americans today are less socially engaged than in previous generations, it makes sense that we are seeing more and more instances of road rage, air rage, telephone rage, and even neighbour rage. Rates of depression in Canada almost doubled between 1999 and 2001 (Statistics Canada 2002).

Young people are responding to this sense of detachment in various ways. Many expand their social networks via the Internet. Others continue to look for a sense of community and meaning through religion or by getting involved in volunteer work or social activism. Yet many young people are looking inward rather than outward. Gradually losing a sense of connection to communities, more are seeking a regular emotional or sensual "high" by seeking gratification from alcohol, drugs, sex, gambling, or from the thrill of "extreme" sports. There is nothing wrong, of course, with feeling good or having fun. However, the potential addictiveness of such behaviours as well as the need to seek ever-increasing levels of excitement can be destructive to individuals, families, and communities. It also turns us away from any critical examination of our social world or formulating collective responses to changing social conditions.

The culture we live in today is a corporate culture, dominated by the values and needs of the transnational corporations. It is a culture of consumerism and narcissism, geared to getting us to buy more products while not challenging those with power. Some of us may be distressed by this state of affairs, while others may think that corporate expansion can only bring increasing prosperity and satisfaction. As already noted, humans act on the basis of their real material conditions. If people become disconnected from their economy, their political structures, or their social institutions, they will have little reason to sustain them and might actively oppose them. Society imposes itself on us, but at the same time we are the agents who both maintain and transform it. The rest of this book will expand on the various ways in which the power of capital imposes itself on our society, and the different ways in which ordinary people respond to it.

Key Points

1. Although few of us pay attention to the power held by large transnational corporations, they have a major effect on our lives.

2. There has been a major restructuring of the Canadian workplace, with an increasing number of individuals in precarious forms of employment. As part of this restructuring, there has been a polarization of work into "good jobs" and "bad jobs," with more of the latter being created than the former.

3. The wages of Canadian workers have reflected this polarization. Some workers in the upper-income brackets have seen their wages soar, while the real wages of most workers have either stagnated or fallen.

4. Many workers are putting in longer hours, and most people are finding themselves working harder and faster.

5. The conditions of workers in Canada have eroded because of the increasing pressure on the capitalist owning class to up its rate of profit, not because new technologies have changed the way we work.

6. Marx felt that workers in capitalism experienced alienation, in that the capacity to labour is turned into a commodity that is bought and sold in the marketplace.

7. The concentration of production and capital has led to the decline of small business and small commodity producers of food.

8. Canadian culture must be understood within the current arrangement of classes, with the interests and values of the capitalist owning class becoming the dominant ones within our society.

9. Our culture is increasingly one of consumerism and narcissism.

10. Some social theorists, particularly in the United States, are concerned about the decline of both social activism and general social engagement.

11. Despite increasing amounts of wealth, people in developed capitalist societies do not seem to be happier. Social connections make us happier. People will suffer a variety of mental stresses when they feel cut off from a supportive, cohesive community.

Further Reading

Alexander, Bruce K. 2001. *The Roots of Addiction in Free Market Society*. Ottawa and Vancouver: Canadian Centre for Policy Alternatives, April 30. Available online at <http://policyalternatives.ca/documents/BC_Office_Pubs/roots_addiction.pdf>.
The author argues that what appears as a personal condition is actually the result of the social dislocation that inevitably occurs within free market economies.

Heath, Joseph and Andrew Potter. 2005. *The Rebel Sell: Why the Culture Can't be Jammed*. Toronto: HarperCollins.
These authors argue that the countercultural opposition to capitalism has actually helped create the consumer society it opposes.

Krahn, Harvey J., Graham S. Lowe, and Karen D. Hughes. 2007. *Work, Industry and Canadian Society.* 5th ed. Scarborough, ON: Thomson Nelson.
A solid introduction to the basic issues pertaining to work and the workplace.

Marquardt, Richard. 1998. *Enter at Your Own Risk: Canadian Youth and the Labour Market.* Toronto: Between the Lines.
A careful examination of issues, both past and present, that face young people as they leave school and enter the workforce.

Menzies, Heather. 2005. *No Time: Stress and the Crisis of Modern Life.* Vancouver: Douglas & McIntyre.
A wide-ranging critique of how new technologies have made us "multi-taskers" who are overstressed and losing touch with our social world.

Mokhiber, Russell and Robert Weissman. 2005. *On the Rampage: Corporate Predators and the Destruction of Democracy.* Monroe ME.: Common Courage Press.
Short articles about corporate power and its negative effect on workers, the environment and consumers.

Vosko, Leah F., ed. 2006. *Precarious Employment: Understanding Labour Market Insecurity in Canada.* Montreal and Kingston: McGill-Queen's University Press.
This is an interdisciplinary work covering various aspects of the new forms of employment in Canada. Also explored are possible responses to changed working conditions.

7 The Social Construction of Ideas and Knowledge

In This Chapter

- What is meant by the concept of *ideology*?
- What is liberalism, and why is it the dominant ideology in capitalist societies?
- How do the mass media reinforce current class relations in our society?
- What is the place of public education in Canada today?

Have you ever thought about how you know what you know? Or why you believe what you believe? It was noted in Chapter 1 that most of us think we exist in a world with certain self-evident "truths" or "facts." However, we have begun to see in this book that many things that most of us take to be true are in fact false, while there are many essential truths that we know nothing about at all. The beliefs and ideas we have in our heads arise out of the particular conditions that individuals face at specific moments in history, and they arise out of a particular set of relations of power. In order to appreciate how certain ideas come to dominate others, we must place them within those power relationships.

> The power of global finance includes an extraordinary ability to create its own version of reality and persuade others to believe it.
> —William Greider, *One World, Ready or Not*

We refer to a body of assumptions, ideas, and values that combine into a coherent world view as an **ideology**. Few of us have actually sat down to consciously construct our own ideological framework; rather, it has been built up over our lifetime. We acquire this package of beliefs and values through the process of socialization. The package is a more or less integrated one, rather than a hodgepodge of unconnected ideas, beliefs, and values. At a certain point, some ideas may be accepted simply because they fit within our already-existing ideological framework; conversely, ideas may be rejected because they would be out of place in this package. Moreover, every ideology has as its underpinning an acceptance that our group's beliefs and behaviours are morally grounded and superior to others' beliefs and behaviours.

How do we come to accept ideas as true? Sometimes we accept them because everyone else believes them. Humans are social animals, and few of us feel comfortable being different. Sometimes we accept ideas because we hear them from some authority figure we believe to be truthful, such as our parents, teachers, religious leaders, or some "expert" in the media. Sometimes we come to believe ideas simply because they provide an easy explanation for the realities of our lives. Whatever the basis for our beliefs, once our ideological framework is in place it will seem so objective and so obvious that it may be hard to dislodge. Only the views of others appear to have a bias. Ours appear as eternal truths.

All societies have a set of core beliefs and values. In pre-class societies, everyone within a community would generally share this common set of beliefs and values. The rise of classes meant greater societal complexity and opposing class interests. Although a core set of beliefs and values remained, people began to see things within differing frames of reference. A simplified example of this is portrayed in the fish cartoon presented in the first chapter: there we see three fish, each with its own place in the fish hierarchy, each with a different view on the moral order of the world.

But there is a troubling aspect to this cartoon. If, like the small fish, those at the bottom of the social order feel that the world is unjust, why do they continue to put up with it? Marx and Engels provide insight into this question. They agree that ideas are social creations, but they argue that "[t]he ideas of the ruling class are in every epoch the ruling ideas; i.e., the class which is the ruling material force of society is at the same time its ruling intellectual force" ([1846] 1969, 47). If we apply this analysis to the fish cartoon, it is likely—for a time at least—that most small fish would come to believe that "the world is just."

In Canadian society this is exactly what happens. A few people appropriate the surplus produced by others, which leads to gross inequalities of wealth and power. While many of us do not benefit from such an economic arrangement, most of us come to support it. Indeed, the majority in our society come to see the entire social structure—with its particular institutions and values—as inevitable, probably even desirable. In this process, we also come to accept, without much questioning, many ideas that support the current social arrangements.

This chapter will analyze the dominant ideology of capitalism—liberalism—and two key agents of socialization that help sustain current class relations—the mass media and the schools. An important caveat needs to be added here. People may be willing to accept myths for a time, but social reality can be masked only for so long. Humans are not robots who passively accept received knowledge; as the contradictions within society become more and more evident, the demand for change increases and one or more counter-ideologies develops. In other words, at least some of the small fish will eventually notice that, indeed, "there is no justice in the world."

Liberalism: "We" versus "Me" Revisited

Understanding our own ideological framework is no easy feat, for it requires that we step out of our own brains, figuratively speaking, in order to look at our thoughts and values from the viewpoint of a detached observer. The problem here is that, in every society, the notions connected to the dominant ideology become so deeply embedded in our minds, and are so constantly reinforced, that it is hard to conceive of any alternative analysis.

It is important to note that something need not be true simply because most of us believe it. Throughout history, people have accepted and promoted ideas that have later proven to be false. If certain ideas or ways of seeing are widely accepted, there is little reason to challenge such assumptions. For example, if people are told by their parents, religious leaders, and teachers that the sun revolves around the Earth, and if everyone around them also believes this to be the case, would there be any reason to challenge this notion? Would it even be a point of debate? What would people think of someone who disputed this position? (Of course, the fact that we now know that it is the Earth that revolves around the sun is confirmation that reality cannot be masked forever.)

In class-based societies, it is inevitable that certain ideas will come to predominate over others. That is because the ruling class has a real interest in promoting and defending those ideas that best protect its interests and maintain the status quo. Given its economic power, this class also has the capacity to do so. The control that the ruling class has over a society's belief system is often referred to as **ideological hegemony**. This term, developed by Italian Antonio Gramsci (1891–1937), has embedded in it the notion that the dominant class maintains its power through a combination of coercion and persuasion. In other words, while force or the threat of it can be used to maintain the social order, class relations are more often sustained in the sphere of culture, or our everyday life. The ability of those with power to control the transmission of ideas means that the entire way we see the world, what we feel is "just natural" or "common sense," is socially constructed. The consequence of such notions is that we instantly dismiss alternative views and don't in any way question the basis for our own.

Within this framework for analysis, **liberalism** must be seen as the dominant ideology in all capitalist societies. Liberalism has many meanings—from the name of a Canadian political party to the notion of being open-minded on sexual matters. For this chapter we will be considering liberalism in its broadest philosophical sense. Put very simply, liberalism is a world view that gives prominence to the "me" over the "we" in society.

Most theorists agree that modern liberalism developed through the sixteenth and seventeenth centuries and can be linked to the disintegration of the feudal system in Europe and Great Britain. Some English writers closely identified with the early liberal tradition are John Locke, Adam Smith, Jeremy Bentham (1748–1832), Mary Wollstonecraft (1759–97), David Ricardo (1772–1823), and John Stuart Mill (1806–73). Early liberalism was a criticism of the dominance and control of the feudal aristocracy. Its advocates promoted a new form of society that increased freedom and the rights of the individual. However, freedom, liberty, democracy, and equality were all conceived of within the broader framework of capitalist class relations, and the privileges and rights of the owning class were never in question. In the twentieth century, liberalism went through various transformations, but its basic doctrines remain unchanged.

Sometimes students ask if one or another aspect of society is "good" or "bad." If we recall the concept of dialectics, we can see that there is rarely a simple answer to such a question. We saw in earlier chapters that capitalism itself was simultaneously a step forward and a step backward for humans. Likewise, its ideological underpinning, liberalism, is too complex to simply designate as good or bad.

For example, while liberal notions of freedom and equality were first promoted by the bourgeoisie to promote their own interests, these notions were taken up as rallying cries by others. Within capitalist societies, liberal argumentation has been used to advocate equal rights for women, racial minorities, gays and lesbians, the disabled, the poor, and so on. If people are told that freedom and equality are worthy goals, they will increasingly demand them.

Most of us feel strongly about individual freedom, choice, and equality. As a result, it may be hard to grasp how closely these concepts fit with modern capitalist economies. Our modern notions of freedom and choice become clearer if we contrast them with some traditional notions, carried over from earlier agrarian-based societies, which continue to the present day. For example, most of you reading this book have accepted the religion of your parents without question; it is unlikely that you were allowed to freely choose your religion. In this example, individual freedom of choice (where the "me" comes first) is seen as less important than traditions or obligations to family and community (where the "we" comes first).

In traditional societies, the interests of the group (family, clan, tribe) generally took priority over the individual; in industrial capitalist societies, the interests of the individual, in theory at least, predominate over those of the collective. Some of you may be frustrated or angered by your family's persistent desire to match you up with a prospective mate or to require you to practise their religious precepts; your parents, on the other hand, may be horrified by your unwillingness to follow centuries-old traditions and bend to parental authority. While these struggles appear to be in the proximal realm, reflected mainly as relations between parents and children, they are actually aspects of the conflict between traditional ideologies tied to agrarian-based systems and liberal ideologies more suited to capitalist market economies. They are a struggle of values, one that emphasizes the "we" and the other that emphasizes the "me" of human societies. Indeed, some of the backlash against liberal values—as most clearly observed in the current global expansion of fundamentalist religions and of social conservatism—are a visible expression of people's unease with a world they see as having too much "me" and not enough "we."

Box 7.1 Competing with a Corporation

Canadian law has increasingly come to treat the legal fictions known as corporations as individuals, now given most of the rights and freedoms once thought to belong only to real human beings. Thus the recognition of corporations in law as "fictitious persons" gives corporations rights to own property, borrow money, sign contracts, hire or fire, and accumulate assets and debts. But these rights go beyond the marketplace and also include the right to free speech (via advertising), as well as the right to sue for injuries, slander, and libel. Corporations in Canada have actually invoked the Charter of Rights and Freedoms to enhance their rights and privileges under the law.

However, corporations have certain characteristics that the rest of us lack. Corporations, unlike human beings, can potentially live forever. They can exist in a number of places at the same time. They can change their identities and become different "persons." They can sell themselves to new owners. They also are protected by limited liability, making it difficult to charge individuals for deaths or injuries caused by their companies. Most importantly, corporations have access to vast amounts of economic resources as well as political influence, which gives them a grossly unfair advantage in the marketplace. Thus although all individuals are theoretically given equal rights and freedoms under the law, some are more equal than others. In this way, the equality of our rights is separated from our economic reality, and the structural inequalities of our society are maintained.

Sources: Tony Clarke, *Silent Coup: Confronting the Big Business Takeover of Canada*, Toronto and Ottawa: Lorimer and CCPA, 1997; Harry Glasbeek, *Wealth by Stealth*, Toronto: Between the Lines Press, 2002.

Liberalism and the Market

The liberal tradition not only accepts a market economy, but also sees the market as the model for all things. Let's remind ourselves of what constitutes a market: in the market, a number of individual—and theoretically independent—units compete with each other. Freedom, then, is conceived of as the ability of these sellers to compete, along with the concurrent freedom of buyers to choose between these competing units. Freedom of choice in this model goes far beyond the actual marketplace. For example, most of us value the ability to choose our political leaders, our occupations, our partners, our neighbourhoods, our music, and so on. Such choices were possible for only a few in pre-capitalist societies.

However, in the real world, few of us can actually take advantage of our freedoms because structured inequality continues to exist in capitalist societies. With regard to equality, developed capitalism was an advance from dictatorial societies. But full equality did not occur. Although all of us have equality of *opportunity*, without equality of *condition* many of our rights and freedoms are absolutely meaningless. For example, we can all, theoretically, own a car; in reality, of course, we can own a car only if we have the financial capacity to do so. Moreover, all our choices can be made only from the items on offer, which means that we never have total freedom of choice. At the moment we cannot buy an electric car, even if we want one.

It should also be noted that there are many rights and freedoms that are not yet guaranteed in Canada because a capitalist economy *cannot* guarantee them: the right to a job; the right to decent housing; the right to sufficient food and clean drinking water; the right to an adequate standard of living; the right to a full education; the right to a healthy environment; the right to a safe workplace; the right to be free of racism, sexism, homophobia, and other forms of social intolerance. Thus rights and freedoms are not abstract; they exist within particular socioeconomic formations, and they can change over time. Liberalism promotes the notions of freedom and individual rights, a social advance from earlier socioeconomic formations. However, such rights and freedoms are selective, framed as they are within the already existing class relations of capitalism. Moreover, the rights we have won can be taken away under certain conditions

Liberalism and Ideas

Liberal notions of freedom and equality are also applied to the world of ideas. Within the liberal framework, competing ideas are seen as the equivalent of goods competing in a marketplace, with individuals having the freedom to choose from the marketplace of ideas. Just as liberals believe that a free market will produce the best goods, they also believe that a "market of ideas" will lead to the most rational and useful ideas. Of course, we have seen in previous chapters that only a few producers or consumers control the market of goods or services; the same is true in the marketplace of ideas. Our freedom of choice with regard to ideas is largely illusory because not all ideas are presented equally or fairly. In the midst of a so-called information explosion, Canadians are facing a world in which the control over information is in fewer and fewer hands.

Whether it is the choice of shampoo, sociological theories, movies, or politicians, capitalism requires that we *believe* that we have true freedom of choice. However, in all developed capitalist societies the choices we are offered are actually very narrow. For example, at any large grocery store across the country one can find a countless array of breakfast cereals on the shelves. But they are all produced by a few transnational corporations, and the variation in taste, nutrition, and cost is small. The situation is similar in the world of ideas. The Internet, hundreds of television channels, and huge bookstores full of a variety of books, magazines, and newspapers give us the impression that we have more ideas to choose from than ever before. Yet the variation in ideas, as with breakfast cereal, is, in fact, becoming smaller and smaller.

Think About It
Do you think the Internet has actually given us greater freedom of expression? Do you think it is a place that can really challenge those with power, or is it simply a place where social activism is diverted?

In agrarian societies, religious institutions or an all-powerful state controlled the dissemination of most knowledge. Industrial societies, in contrast, do offer more than one narrow point of view to an increasingly educated working class. A particular newspaper article, TV show, or sociology textbook such as this one may challenge the dominant beliefs and values or the legitimacy of the ruling class. Such exceptional cases can actually reinforce our belief that there is, indeed, a true marketplace of ideas.

However, while there is an apparent free "market" of ideas in capitalist societies, those with power have the ability to censor with few of us even knowing it. For example, in 2007 a dance-punk band received a notice from MySpace, a communication website owned by Rupert Murdoch's News Corp., that its account had been deleted, with no explanation offered. The band set up a new page that encouraged others to come forward with similar tales of website deletions and discovered that those with deleted accounts were primarily gay or sexually liberated arts groups and that most of them were non-profit activists (Xing 2007).

Ideology, Culture, and Socialization

For sociologists, socialization is considered a central concept. This should not be surprising if we recall from Chapter 2 that sociology rejects the notion that human behaviour is biologically determined. Rather, sociologists argue that every member of our species—required to live in a social group—must learn (and relearn throughout life) the many complex components of culture from other human beings. It is important to note, however, that what we learn, primarily as children, is more than simply a body of information. The process of socialization affects not only what we know, but also who we are.

In Chapter 6 we saw that our culture cannot be separated from structures of power and economic relationships. The culture in which we live is a *capitalist* culture, with a set of beliefs, values, and material elements that can be understood only within a capitalist economy. Hence, when we speak of the process of socialization, we must also understand that it is occurring within a particular socioeconomic formation.

There are a number of important agents of socialization in all societies. These include the family, schools, religious institutions, peer groups, and the mass media. No one sat down with our parents or teachers to instruct them on the key norms, beliefs, and values of a capitalist society that they are required to transmit to the next generation. As in all societies, the dominant beliefs and behaviours are so prevalent that most people simply accept them without question.

In the not too distant past, people understood little about their existence and looked to the supernatural for hope in a world that could often be unpredictable and cruel. Religious values framed the imagery of language, dance, music, art, and physical place. If we look around us today, what do we see? Everywhere we look—including educational institutions once thought to be outside of market relationships—we can see the logos of major corporations. Public buildings, cultural institutions, and even social and charitable events are named after corporations that in many cases have bought—with a tax-deductible donation—the

154

right to promote their companies.

Billboards and outdoor advertisements are everywhere. Sports arenas and the athletes themselves are increasingly covered with corporate brands. Ads have become so commonplace that students don't even complain anymore that commercial advertising has expanded into their colleges and universities. And people, particularly the young, actually pay for the "privilege" of being able to wear (and advertise) a corporate name. Apparently, some people have become so fond of corporate brands that they are even naming their offspring after them. Records show that, in 2000, children in the United States were named Canon, Jaguar, Bentley, Timberland, Chanel, and Camry. One child was actually named Xerox (*Globe and Mail*, 3 October 2003, A16).

There is every indication that corporate branding is continuing to accelerate. As governments increasingly cut back their spending, more and more public institutions are either turning to the corporate sector for funds or becoming completely privatized. Everywhere we look we are being told that our entire culture "is brought to us" by the major corporations. Lost in this imagery is the reality that much of the massive wealth in the hands of the corporate sector has been privately appropriated from those who produced it.

As noted in the previous chapter, children are learning this corporate-controlled culture at an earlier and earlier age. On a daily basis, children and young adults are bombarded with commercials trying to mould their needs and desires. Young people are particularly appealing to companies that want to instill product loyalty at the earliest age possible. Advertising jingles become popular music. Childhood heroes are determined not by family cultural traditions, great people in history, or celebrated pieces of literature, but rather by the latest film or, for older children, the latest sports star or pop band. Children speak the language of advertisers and demand the brands seen on TV.

Everything is commoditized in capitalist societies, even rebellion, and young people who want to opt out of the dominant culture often do so through purchasing certain clothing styles or shoes. Much youthful rebellion has been co-opted by transnational corporations, repackaged, and sold back to young people looking for a collective with whom to identify. There is no clearer example in recent years than the hip-hop movement. Started in the Black ghettos of the United States by young people who felt marginalized economically, politically, and culturally, hip-hop soon transformed into a multi-million-dollar mainstream industry producing music, videos, and clothing. One newspaper article about Black teens in the Jane-Finch area of Toronto who liked to dress in the "gansta" style described a fifteen-year-old with thirteen pairs of sneakers, including Nike, Reebok, Adidas, and a pair of $180 Air Jordans; he was saving money to buy jewellery worth around $500 (Friesen 2006).

Think About It

Do you think it is possible to truly opt out of corporatized culture today?

Box 7.2 The Telling of Tales

Humans are story-tellers, and for most of human history we communicated without writing. Much of what we talked about throughout the ages is today embodied in the word "gossip." That is, we chatted informally with each other about what was happening in our immediate social world.

But there were also stories that transcended our everyday experiences. These stories were passed down orally from one generation to the other, and there was no distinction between "myths," "fairy-tales," "history," or "religion." Whether these stories had actually happened was irrelevant; they were often full of magic, but generally accepted as true, belonging to a people and transmitted mainly by elders. These stories answered life's big questions: Where did we come from? Why are we here? Why is there good and evil in the world? How do I become a better person? What happens when we die? It was these stories that bound people together, explained the unexplainable, and linked the past and the present to the future. These stories were also reflected in songs and dances, in various celebratory events, and various forms of material culture.

Where do the stories of today come from? Most of us still learn at least some traditional stories from our parents, our grandparents, or our religions. But more and more of our stories come from the popular media, that is, via music, movies, literature, and television. In most cases, these stories are mediated by the marketplace—their primary purpose is not to enlighten but rather to generate profits for the companies that produce them. And what makes the greatest profits is often that which is appealing to our basest emotions—violence, deviance, excessive sexual imagery, and so on. Sometimes films have little or nothing in the way of a story to tell. Often we go simply to be shocked by the special effects, excessive violence, swearing, or the breaking of sexual norms.

Corporations don't like to take excessive risks. If a film, television show, CD, or book is a hit, then companies want to make more of the same. And if young adults are the largest consumers of popular culture, then filmmakers, television producers, or those in the music industry will tend to go after that age group. Some of the highest paid Hollywood stars have made their fortunes by being permanent adolescents. While much media content might give us a laugh or a thrill, there is little offered today that helps us better understand the world or our place in it.

In Canada we face an additional dilemma. We are closely connected, physically and culturally, to the United States, and most of our popular culture is from there. These stories are not necessarily the same as ours. Minorities in Canada have a particularly hard time having their stories heard. There is a danger here. If we don't see ourselves and our lives reflected in our culture, then we may become less interested in protecting it.

Mass Communications in Canada

When you last got together with some friends, what did you talk about? Chances are good that you spent at least some of the time talking about a movie, TV show, CD, band, or the latest woes of a Hollywood celebrity. It is clear that the various forms of mass communication are pervasive and important in the lives of young adults in the twenty-first century. Social scientists have noted that, given the sheer amount of time we all spend in contact with the various forms of mass communication in our society, we are all affected by them in a major way.

It was in the twentieth century that the mass media came to be the most important means of transmitting and maintaining the dominant ideology. As C. Wright Mills observed (1956, 311), "The media not only give us information; they guide our very experiences. Our standards of credulity, our standards of reality, tend to be set by these media rather than by our own fragmentary experience." Functionalist theories see social institutions such as the mass media as a harmless means of maintaining social order and control in the interests of society as a whole. Change theories, on the other hand, view the mass media as playing a key role in the maintenance of class and status inequalities.

> A specter now haunts the world: a global commercial media system dominated by a small number of superpowerful, mostly U.S.-based transnational media corporations.
> —Robert McChesney

> The mass media are massive. They have the power and, most important, the capital to call the shots and the stories.
> —Antonia Zerbesias

The last century saw the creation of new technologies that allowed for the widespread dissemination of information, ideas, and values: new forms of communication, such as radio, television, and computers, reached a "mass," or a large number of unconnected individuals. At first, many intellectuals believed that the growth of the mass media would be beneficial to ordinary people, as it would expand their traditionally narrow world views by giving them increased access to knowledge and a wider variety of perspectives.

By the second half of the century, a number of authors were beginning to challenge these assumptions. C. Wright Mills in the United States and Ralph Miliband in Britain saw the mass media as the primary means of transmitting the dominant ideology. Miliband argued that the various agencies of mass communication play a key role in the legitimation of capitalist society. In this context, "freedom of expression" meant the expression of ideas that help maintain the system of power and privilege (1969, 197).

These notions were taken up more recently by Edward Herman and Noam Chomsky in their book *Manufacturing Consent: The Political Economy of the Mass Media* (1988). Herman and Chomsky argued that one of the main functions of the mass media is *propaganda*, or the promotion of the interests of those with economic and political power. Built into such arguments is the assumption that the mass media in capitalist societies are controlled by a small and integrated elite. This theme was first pursued in Canada by Harold Innis, who felt that varying forms of communication needed to be understood in terms of power relationships in societies (1964 [1951]). Sociologist John Porter further advanced this argument in *The Vertical Mosaic* (1965).

Box 7.3 The Global World of Rupert Murdoch

Print Properties
- *New York Post,* weekday circulation of 725,000
- *TV Guide* magazine (41 percent)
- *The Times,* London's premier newspaper group
- *The Sun,* Britain's biggest-selling daily paper
- *The Australian,* and more than 100 other Australian papers
- HarperCollins, international book publisher

2006 revenue: US$7.3 billion

Broadcasting and Entertainment
- Fox Television, three dozen local stations
- Fox cable networks, including National Geographic Channel
- BSkyB (38 percent), satellite broadcaster in Europe
- DirectTV (38 percent), U.S. satellite broadcaster
- More than a dozen television channels in Asia
- Fox Filmed Entertainment, film and television producer

2006 revenue: $17.4 billion

Dow Jones & Co. Inc.
- *The Wall Street Journal*
- Dow Jones newswire
- *Barron's* magazine
- Marketwatch.com
- Several leading market indicators including the Dow Jones industrial average
- 8 daily and 15 weekly newspapers

2006 print revenue: $1.8 billion
2006 profit: $386 million

Internet and More
- MySpace.com
- FoxSports.com
- RottenTomatoes.com
- News Outdoor Group, an outdoor advertising firm based in Eastern Europe
- National Rugby League (50 percent), Australia's top professional rugby league

2006 revenue: $1.4 billion

Source: *Globe and Mail,* 2 May 2007, B10.

Ownership and Control of the Media

John Porter's study was the first to undertake a comprehensive study of media ownership in Canada. Using 1961 data, Porter concluded that the mass media were controlled by a small, although by no means cohesive, group of men who shared certain common characteristics. Most of them came from well-established families already connected to the publishing industry; they had graduated from private schools and belonged to exclusive social clubs; almost all had attended university; and all (in English-speaking Canada) belonged to the British charter group of Canadian society (1965, 483). Subsequent research by Wallace Clement (1975) confirmed that media ownership was indeed highly concentrated.

Since that time, the concentration of media-based capital has escalated, with only a few key players remaining in a complex web of interlocking ownership. This process is not restricted to Canada, although Canada has one of the most concentrated media markets in the world (Reguly 2002). It is a global phenomenon that is linked to a process known as **convergence**. Convergence refers to the merging of the technology and content of the telecommunications, entertainment, publishing, and broadcasting industries.

The process of convergence is linked to the growing vertical integration of ownership, in which a few giant corporations now control huge chunks of these rapidly integrating industries. In Canada, the major players include Astral Media, CanWest Global Communications, CTVglobemedia, Shaw Communications, Rogers Communications, and Quebecor Media. CanWest Global alone owns fourteen English-language metropolitan daily newspapers and more than 120 community newspapers; eleven television stations across Canada and five independent stations; Prime TV; and Canada.com, an Internet news-content provider. A number of key acquisitions took place in 2007: CTV offered $1.4 billion to purchase CHUM Ltd.; CanWest offered $2.3 billion to acquire Alliance Atlantis Communications; Astral Media offered $1.1 billion to purchase Standard Communications; and Quebecor offered $414.4 million to purchase newspaper publisher Osprey Media (Brent 2007).

In the United States, five huge conglomerates—Time Warner, Disney, Rupert Murdoch's News Corporation, Bertelsmann of Germany, and Viacom, with General Electric's NBC a close sixth —now own most of the newspapers, magazines, book publishers, radio and TV stations, and movie studios in that country. That number has shrunk from fifty in 1983 (Bagdikian 2004). This enormous concentration of capital leads to obvious concerns about the true degree of choice that we actually have over media content.

Many of us may assume that it is individuals such as the managers of the TV stations or the editors of newspapers who actually determine the content of various forms of mass media. However, the reality is that the owners of the media do retain their powers of control over content. Sometimes the control can be quite direct. More often, it can be maintained simply because the various levels of management are ultimately beholden to those who employ them. As one author put it, "By controlling the journalist's job, the media boss can control the journalist" (Parenti 1995, 167).

Owners and managers are not alone in the power to control what we see, hear, and read. Advertisers also exert much influence on media content, since advertising is the media's primary source of funding (see Box 7.4). Sometimes this economic power can be used to directly influence the content of the media: advertisers who feel that they or their product are badly represented can threaten to withdraw their advertising. However, such actions are rarely necessary. While there may be variations in the opinions of specific journalists or TV news commentators, the overarching orientation of newspapers, television, radio, and mainstream magazines is in support of the status quo.

In fact, we cannot understand the mass media without understanding the key role played by advertisers. With growing affluence after World War II, corporations needed to find ever-growing markets for their new consumer goods. Advertisers played an important role in the shift from a "mass" market in the 1950s to a "segmented" one. Shows that brought families, friends, and neigh-

Box 7.4   Strangling Canadian TV

Most citizens don't understand how North American commercial television works. They think it's a little like a movie theatre. The owner of the theatre tries to get the best movies he can, to attract the most customers, and make his profit from selling tickets.

But that's not the economic model of commercial television at all. The product of commercial TV is not the program. The product—that which is being bought and sold—is you. The exchange of money is not between the viewer and the network, it is between the network and the advertiser. The advertiser is buying "eyeballs" by the hundreds of thousands, from a network.

Certain demographics are far more valuable to the advertiser than others. A woman, 18 to 35, for example, is worth at least 10 people over 50. That's because the people in the 18–35 demographic still have their major purchasing decisions to make—fridge, home, car. Commercial television is part of the marketing and distribution system of the manufacturing economy, not part of the cultural production system. It's arguably the very engine of consumer distributing.

We are bought and sold, in our hundreds of thousands, by companies that assemble viewers—networks, in other words—and sold to agencies representing auto and computer manufacturers, pharmaceutical companies, and toy manufacturers. None of this is inherently pernicious. But what has happened is that the commercial television industry has successfully hijacked the rhetoric of democracy, liberty and choice. In the cornucopia of choices, you have pure democracy at work, and the viewer ultimately decides what will be aired or not aired.

The question of freedom of choice has been defined, by the commercial industry, as the freedom to pick between 200 channels' worth of such programs. But freedom of choice—in radio, television or cinema—should be defined as the freedom to produce television, not just to consume.

Like any Canadian, I want my American programs. But how did we come to delude ourselves that everything that appears on our screens must be arbitrated totally by what is essentially a massive consumer distributing industry?

The experience of Canada: A People's History is painfully pertinent. For two years, not a single Canadian corporation would become a sponsor of the series. Not until the last minute when one, Sun Life, came on board. The truth is, the marketers felt there were more efficient ways to sell cellphones, Toyotas and Tylenol than in a Canadian history series.

They're probably right. We probably weren't the most cost efficient delivery vehicle of 18- to 25-year-olds, or the best platform for selling cosmetics. But the people wanted this programming. They set national viewing records. That series would never have seen the light of day if it had to meet the market consumer delivery test.

I understand and accept that if a Canadian program isn't popular and has not found a significant audience, it should probably die. But I resent that a Canadian program will not even be born, even if it reaches a large audience, if I can't prove it will sell shampoo.

Source: Excerpted with permission from Mark Starowicz, *Toronto Star*, 1 May 2003. Starowicz was the creator and Executive Producer of the TV series *Canada: A People's History*.

bours across North America together around the TV screen in the 1950s were gradually replaced by shows of interest to specific groups whose members shared their socioeconomic status, gender, age, race, lifestyle, and so on. These shows were then used to sell products specifically targeted to these particular groups. Connected to this trend was the growth of market research, which provided essential data to advertisers about the purchasing habits of each particular segment (Cohen 2003, 292–344).

Think About It

The segmentation of the market is not unique to television; rather it can be seen in various forms of mass media. Next time you go past a magazine store, check out how many different interest groups have their own magazines.

The main goal of the private media, like any other industry, is to maximize profits. Since the main source of profits in the print and television media is advertising revenue, the news and entertainment that accompany advertising serve as the means of getting people to read the ads or watch the commercials. Advertising does not simply try to sell us a product; it also tries to sell us a way of life. Put in the most general terms, advertising tries to convince us that material possessions will make us happy. This message begins early in life, and we are constantly bombarded by it.

Connected to this theme is that of improvement. In Chapter 4 we saw that the notion of improvement goes back to the very beginnings of capitalism. Today the media promote primarily self-improvement. Television and magazines are now full of people who get a "makeover." Fashion magazines have long had a section where a woman got a new look via a change of hairdo, make-up, and clothes. Today's men and women often have plastic surgery and dental work done as well. And it is no longer just physical appearances, apparently, that need to be improved. We have shows to improve relationships, diets, and a whole channel about home improvement. All these shows teach us that we are not good enough the way we are. The underlying message is that our problems are rooted not in the broader society but in ourselves, and in most cases if we just buy stuff we will be happier people. The weight-loss industry alone is valued at $40 billion a year (Ogilvie 2007).

Think About It

Are you satisfied with who you are and how you look? Could the capitalist economy survive if most of us answered yes to this question?

The Myth of Objectivity

It was noted in Chapter 1 that there is no such thing as true neutrality or objectivity; as humans, all of us process information through our own pre-existing ideas or biases. The media, controlled by human beings, are no more neutral or unbiased

Box 7.5 Two Sides to Every Story?

Whenever people enter into a debate, no matter what the topic, it is likely that someone will eventually say, "Well, you know, there are two sides to every story." We have heard this saying so often that it just seems to be correct. But is it? The world is round. Is it equally possible that the world is flat? Halifax is on the east coast of Canada. Could it be on the west coast instead? Clearly, not every idea or argument has an alternative point of view. Most of the time, we do not truly believe that there are two sides to every story.

The media like to project the image that the news we read or see is neutral, and to show they are fair, they supposedly offer us "both sides of the story." However, this is seldom the case. For example, it is extremely rare to find anyone contradicting a politician who speaks of Canada as a democracy, even though there are many who question to what extent we are a truly democratic country. In most instances where the alternative view would seriously critique the world as it is currently structured, we don't hear "the other side." In contrast, when people publicly take a position that opposes a corporate or government policy, the news media suddenly feel compelled to present a contrary view. For example, in 2007 thousands of people across Canada participated in a march to oppose the involvement of Canadian troops in Afghanistan. In Toronto, a few dissenters stood on the sidewalk and held up signs supporting the government's position. A number of media subsequently reported on the marchers and the opponents as if they represented "two sides of the story" in an equal way.

Corporations are well aware that the news media like to portray themselves as neutral by having two sides to a story that might be controversial, and they often exploit this tendency. The largest corporations regularly hire public relations firms whose job it is, among other things, to discredit their critics. We now know that tobacco firms such as Phillip Morris and RJ Reynolds paid large sums of money for many years to ensure that the link between smoking and lung cancer was discredited, or at least seen as unclear. This ensured that whenever the issue of the safety of smoking arose, there were two sides to the story.

The same thing is happening today in the debate about global warming. Even though the vast majority of scientists believe that climate change is real and will have catastrophic consequences for the planet, fossil fuel corporations have been making it appear—just as in the case of the effects of smoking on health—that there are two sides to this story. In 2007 the Intergovernmental Panel on Climate Change presented rigorous scientific evidence that climate change exists and is likely caused by human activity. Nonetheless, companies such as Exxon Mobil, working with top public relations firms, have found a small number of individuals and organizations willing to question the science behind climate change. It has provided funding for some of them, their organizations, and their articles (fifth estate 2006).

Are there two sides to every story?

than any other source of information. However, because media biases so often match our own and because these biases are so pervasive and constant, we seldom notice them. Nor are the biases of the media random. Despite supposed diversity, the media have consistently favoured management over labour, private enterprise over public ownership, white people over Blacks, males over females, officialdom over protesters, traditional politics over dissent, and so on (Parenti 1993, 8).

Newspapers have business sections but not labour sections, and business people—not union leaders—are considered experts on the economy. The invisibility of ordinary people is not limited to the news; television shows and movies seldom depict ordinary working people. Strangely, what is referred to as "reality" television is not about reality at all, but rather about the depths to which people will sink in order to achieve some momentary fame or money. Practically no television, films, or magazines today offer viewers a critical analysis of their society or a sensitive and in-depth vision of people whose struggles are similar to theirs and who, together with others, have fought to improve their life conditions.

Bias can be seen in the words or images used in a story. One survey of newspaper articles about unions (Finn 1983, 20) found that the same unfavourable words kept occurring: strike, picket, demands, helpless public, breakdown, inflationary, labour unrest, held to ransom, inconvenience, labour bosses, callous, irresponsible, violence, contempt, lawless agitators, greedy, blackmail, and abuse of power. Such biases are often reinforced by imagery, such as pictures of violence on a picket line or at a protest rally, even when these constitute only one small aspect of the event and may even, at times, have been initiated by outside agitators.

Much has also been written about gender stereotyping in the media. As far back as 1970, the Royal Commission on the Status of Women in Canada spoke out against the stereotyping of both sexes in the mass media. Since that time, the awareness of such issues has increased, and both women and men are certainly portrayed in a broader range of roles. However, all forms of the media continue to represent gender in ways that are often unrealistic or limited. Transgendered people in particular are almost invisible.

Both sexes continue to be portrayed by the media in stereotypical ways. Men are disproportionately shown as serious, confident, competent, powerful, and in high-status positions (except in comedies, where even adult males are often portrayed as infantilized sex-obsessed adolescents and become the butt of the humour). Rarely are men shown as nurturing and caring (unless they're gay), or interested primarily in family and home life. In contrast, women are frequently portrayed as passive, dependent on men, and wrapped up in relationships or housework (J. Wood 1999, 225). They are generally younger and thinner than women in the population as a whole. Rock videos commonly portray women in hypersexualized roles satisfying men's sexual fantasies. These women are the sex objects (frequently in scanty clothing), with men as the sexual predators.

Images of racial minorities in the media are also troubling. When racialized people appear in the media, the image is often either a stereotyped or a negative one, or both. Some ethno-racial groups such as South Asians, East Asians, and Arabs are almost invisible in film and television, except when portrayed as the evil "other" or the humorous bumbling outsider. Aboriginal Canadians have also not been well served by the media and have until recently been underrepresented—or represented in stereotypical ways—in Canadian television and films.

While most of us strongly oppose censorship, it is hard to oppose what you cannot see. With so few companies controlling the entire media industry, our choices become diminished. With regard to the news, much information that is essential to our understanding of the social world simply doesn't get revealed. One of the most glaring examples in recent years was the lead-up to the U.S. invasion of Iraq in 2003. Most American journalists got information solely from military or government sources that insisted Iraq had "weapons of mass destruction." The few that challenged the government line were barely heard from. Even in Canada, only one newspaper, the *Toronto Star*, opposed the U.S. invasion of Iraq (Zerbesias 2007).

Some media analysts feel that news and entertainment have merged into what is sometimes referred to as "infotainment." More and more of what we see and read is celebrity-dominated, shallow, and devoid of substance. One author (Schechter 2007) feels that Chomsky and Herman's notion that those with power are "manufacturing consent" needs to be changed to "manufacturing indifference." As Schechter notes, the media owners want eyeballs for advertisers, not activists to promote change.

Our ability to critically assess bias in the media is limited by the fact that we often lack the background information to adequately understand the issues. For example, our ability to fully understand the current debate about globalization requires that we understand both the corporate agenda and the particular economic framework in which it is taking place. Understanding current U.S. foreign policy requires a thorough comprehension of its hundred-year history of intervention in other countries around the world. However, such in-depth analyses are rarely provided. Rather, the electronic media in particular now rely on short sound bites, with instant analyses of issues provided by so-called experts. These commentators are often government spokespeople or, increasingly, other journalists. Moreover, since the media offer us information in highly disconnected form, we are often unable to put all the pieces together even when the information is available to us. Without an ability to really comprehend what is happening around the world, many of us simply tune out what appears to be nothing but bad news.

Think About It

Do you think the Internet has given us greater access to alternative views, or is it just so overloaded with information that we simply ignore most of it and cling to what we already believe to be true?

It is worth noting that those with dissenting viewpoints are not totally voiceless. There are many cultural workers who are critical of the status quo in one way or another, and who are able to promote their ideas via websites such as rabble.ca in Canada and commondreams.org in the United States, small presses, alternative journals, and so on. A few individuals in Canada and the United States, having achieved some legitimacy, can even be seen or heard via the mainstream media. Nonetheless, the ability of alternative views to be heard in the face of increased monopolization of media ownership is a troubling issue for the democratic process.

The Role of the Government

The government of Canada has always intervened more directly in the mass communications industry than has the United States. Such direct state involvement was seen as part of the nation-building process in this country (McBride and Shields 1997, 97). The Canadian Broadcasting Corporation (CBC) was created in 1936, with a mandate to help unite the country and provide an alternative to American radio. As a side benefit, public film and broadcasting organizations have also provided a public service by producing material that does not necessarily turn a profit in the media marketplace.

The government has also directly intervened in the regulation of the broadcast media. This role, originally assigned to the CBC, later passed into the hands of the CRTC (the Canadian Radio-television and Telecommunications Commission). The CRTC has the power to issue, renew, or revoke broadcasting licences, as well as to set out conditions for Canadian broadcasting as a whole. Its role, in the main, has been to protect and encourage the development of Canadian culture in both French and English. In reality, the CRTC has frequently turned out to be little more than a body that legitimates current arrangements, rather than an entity that has any real power over the media or their owners (Lorimer and McNulty 1996, 236–37). In particular, the growing convergence of media ownership in Canada—with very few giant corporations controlling whole sectors—has not been challenged by the CRTC.

Historically the CBC and the CRTC have been a restraining force against a total incursion by the much larger American mass media. However, it seems that the government is retreating from its protectionist role, as it has increasingly endorsed greater private-sector control of the media while gradually eroding support for public broadcasting. These trends can be seen in the massive cuts imposed on the CBC, the National Film Board, and Telefilm Canada, and in the government's inability to fully protect Canadian culture under the North American Free Trade Agreement (NAFTA). In 2007 the head of the CRTC announced a future review of the CRTC itself, stating that the government "has directed us to accept market forces as the default and regulation as the exception" (Robertson 2007). The decline of government protection will almost certainly guarantee that Canadian culture—our stories, our history, our actors, our writers, our dancers, our music, and so on—will gradually be swallowed up by the much larger and wealthier U.S. entertainment industry.

The Education System

Although most of us take public education for granted, it is actually a relatively recent phenomenon. Indeed, its development and expansion are a clear example of how social institutions can be understood only within the socioeconomic formations of which they are a part. For most of human history, the majority of people were taught the necessary skills in life by their parents or their communities. Whether foraging or farming, the skills required for survival did not require schooling. For the few who followed a trade, apprenticeship was the means of acquiring the requisite skills and knowledge. Wherever formalized learning did occur, it was accessible only to a small elite recruited almost totally from the upper strata.

The growth of mass compulsory education in the late nineteenth century must be connected to the development of capitalism. As industrialization advanced, people moved to cities to fill the factories hungry for workers. At first the whole family—men, women, and children—worked for pitiful wages out of economic necessity. In Europe most of these people came from outlying rural areas. In Canada the workforce was supplemented by many immigrants who had fled horrible conditions abroad.

The rapid advances in technology led to two important consequences. First, as technology advanced, a more educated and skilled workforce was required. Second, increased productivity meant that ever-expanding profits could be produced using fewer workers. A public education system developed to fit into these changing conditions. Some educational reformers feared that children, no longer needed in factories, would become troublemakers. Public schools were thus seen as a place to keep them busy. The new schools would also provide the next generation with the basic literacy and numeracy skills required by many employers. Even more importantly, schools could help the young develop certain characteristics—such as discipline, industriousness, docility, politeness, punctuality, and obedience to authority—that would make them good workers.

The school system was also seen as a primary agent of socialization that would teach young people the values and norms of the dominant culture. This was particularly important in Canada, where so many were foreign born. Moreover, following the rebellions of 1837, there was a fear of social instability and class tensions, and schools came to be seen as a means of maintaining social order. Thus, by the mid-nineteenth century, school promoters such as Egerton Ryerson in Upper Canada, Alexander Forrester in Nova Scotia, and John Jessop in British Columbia sought to establish a system of universal tax-supported elementary education, which guaranteed access to all children. Teachers would be trained and certified, and all pupils would receive standardized textbooks.

Since the late nineteenth century, there has been a gradual increase in the years of formal attendance at school. While an elementary-school education was once considered sufficient, students are now being told that postsecondary education is the minimum requirement to get a reasonably well-paid job. To some extent such a trend reflects the increasing complexity of technology, but it is also the result of the growing tendency toward **credentialism**. As the number of applicants expands, paper credentials are increasingly used as a means of limiting access into certain job categories, even if the particular credentials are of questionable utility in job performance. Many jobs that now require a university degree were formerly performed quite adequately by people out of high school; likewise, graduate degrees are often the minimum for jobs in which, only a short while ago, a B.A. was more than sufficient. It has also been argued that credentialism is primarily a means of justifying structured inequality, by linking social inequality to the individual's ability to attain a particular level of education (Bowles and Gintis 1976).

A growing problem is that of over-qualification. Young people are being urged to get postsecondary education, but upon graduation many in Canada are finding that they cannot get jobs suited to their qualifications. For example, nearly one out of every five people in the workforce who had a university education had worked in a job that required at most high school education at some point during 2001. The number of university-educated workers who were over-qualified for their job was nearly one-third higher in 2001 than in 1993 (Li et al. 2006).

Moreover, while there has been an extensive expansion of education in Canada in the last fifty years, particularly colleges and universities, not everyone has been able to take advantage of it. For example, in 2001 a little fewer than half of all Canadians over the age of twenty-five had some postsecondary education (Statistics Canada 2003b, 26). Moreover, educational attainment is not random, but rather is linked to a number of variables. For example, studies have repeatedly shown that levels of educational aspiration and attainment are strongly correlated with the socioeconomic status of one's parents (Guppy and Arai 1993; Cheng et al. 1993; Boyd et al. 1985; Porter et al. 1982; Anisef and Okihiro 1982) and, to a lesser extent, race and ethnicity. For biological determinists, such findings confirm the "natural" inferiority of certain groups. However, most sociologists argue that the cause of such inequalities lies within the social system rather than with the individual.

Education in the Twenty-first Century

The nature and functions of the education system have been explained by a variety of analytical frameworks. Of the order theories the best known is structural functionalism, most clearly exemplified by Talcott Parsons in an essay entitled "The School Class as a Social System: Some of Its Functions in American Society" (1961). For Parsons, the school performs two essential functions for the maintenance of an orderly and stable society: it socializes children, not only by teaching them a body of skills and knowledge, but also by transmitting the values and attitudes considered acceptable within society; and it sorts individuals through a grading system, preparing them for a differentiated labour market.

For functionalists, the school system is seen as neutral, with structural inequalities not considered relevant. Within this framework, both the individual and the society benefit in equal measure from the system of public education: society gets the various jobs filled by the most qualified personnel, while individuals get to achieve personal growth and development. In this sense, structural functionalism is an underpinning of liberal ideology, with public education the tool that gives everyone a chance to compete in the capitalist marketplace and succeed both occupationally and personally.

Such assumptions are part of much educational theory. A classic example is Hall and Dennis's *Living and Learning*, which became the basis for educational reform in Ontario in the 1970s:

> The underlying aim of education is to further man's unending search for truth. Once he possesses the means to truth, all else is within his grasp.... [Education] is the key to open all doors. It is the instrument which will break the shackles of ignorance, of doubt, of frustration, that will take all who respond to its call out of their poverty, their slums, and their despair. (1968, 9)

If we return to a point made earlier in this chapter, capitalism addresses inequality of opportunity, but not inequality of condition. In the above quote, Hall and Dennis see education as the core element that will provide every child an opportunity to succeed. However, since inequality of condition is ignored in this argument, any failure to succeed will be seen as the individual's own fault because that person did not "respond to the call" of education.

In contrast to the order theories—with their notion of a neutral education system that exists to benefit both society and the individual—are the change theories. The various change theories agree with the order theories that socialization and sorting are the two key functions of education; however, in contrast to the order theories they recognize that societies have an unequal allocation of power, wealth, and prestige. In this context, the education system is a social institution that, in the main, helps sustain existing class relations.

Bowles and Gintis's *Schooling in Capitalist America* (1976) presented a major theoretical challenge to the functionalist view of education by emphasizing the ways in which schools reproduce the social relations required for capitalist production. While there has been some subsequent criticism of their theory as too simplistic, it can be argued that their general analysis is valid: the present school system can be understood only as a part of broader capitalist class relations. Employers require workers, and workers of a specific type. At a more general level, the ruling class requires relative social stability and ideological acceptance of capitalist class relations. Given the power of this class, it should not be surprising that it will pressure governments to ensure that schools meet its needs. That is not to say that schools act *only* on behalf of the dominant class, but rather that this class does have a broadly shared set of interests pertaining to the public education system and that it does have the capacity to promote such interests.

This argument was expanded upon by Canadians Maude Barlow and Heather-jane Robertson in *Class Warfare* (1994). As capital globalizes, the needs of the corporate sector vis-à-vis the education system are rapidly changing. According to Barlow and Robertson, North American corporations have three goals as they increasingly intervene in public education:

> The first is to secure the ideological allegiance of young people to a free-market world view on issues of the environment, corporate rights

and the role of government. The second is to gain market access to the hearts and minds of young consumers and lucrative contracts in the education industry. The third is to transform schools into training centres producing a workforce suited to the needs of transnational corporations." (79)

The first goal is certainly not new to public education. Many analysts have discussed the ways that our education system ultimately reinforces the status quo. In part, this is the result of the very structure of education—a person in authority presents what will be learned, offers it to students in narrowly framed units of knowledge, and then tests the student on what is learned. Students, then, generally "succeed" not by questioning authority, but by learning what is required. The same, of course, is true for teachers. In this context of general conformity, students seldom learn about the fundamental structure of our society or the relations of power, let alone how to challenge them.

Think About It
Did you or any of your friends ever get in trouble in school for challenging some authority figure?

Given this reality, it is obvious that most of us will come to see the world around us as natural and inevitable, rather than as something to be questioned or challenged. What has changed dramatically in the last twenty or so years in Canada is the increasingly direct involvement of the corporate sector in education. In part this is a result of the capital glut discussed earlier in the book—as capital looks for new outlets for investment, corporations now see components of education (including food and janitorial services, electronic technologies, standardized testing, and building management) as possible sources of profit. Connected to this trend is increasing pressure to harmonize Canadian education with that in the United States. Under NAFTA, private American educational services can now bid on Canadian contracts.

There is also an increasing desire on the part of business, both in Canada and globally, to be more directly involved in determining the content of education. For example, a paper produced for APEC (Asia-Pacific Economic Cooperation, a group of Pacific Rim countries) in 1997 stated that "decisions must be taken by a school system for good business reasons with maximum business intervention" (cited in Kuehn 1998, 53). Built into this goal is the philosophical belief that schooling should be more about skills training for specific jobs than about education that might provide critical-thinking skills and broader social awareness.

Increasing corporate involvement in education can also be seen at the postsecondary level. With government underfunding to postsecondary education a reality in Canada since the 1970s, universities and colleges are increasingly turning to corporations for donations of money and technology, as well as for research grants. The fear of many is that the direction of research and education is shifting to fit corporate interests. The link between the corporations and higher education was formalized some time ago in the Corporate Higher Education Forum, a national coalition of university presidents and corporate CEOs. The aim of the group is to promote a merging of goals and activities of the two sectors. The group campaigns against government regulation of postsecondary fees and for closer business-education ties. The government is obviously listening. In May 1999, a government report was issued recommending that profit become the number-one priority of university research, and that the discoveries and inventions of students and professors be handed over to the private sector (*CAUT Bulletin* June 1999, 1).

As government spending on public education has been cut, a number of worrying trends have appeared. First, there has been a slow but clear movement toward a two-tiered system of education, one for the well-to-do and one for everyone else. While private schools for the rich have always existed, the erosion of the public system has led more middle-income earners to look for alternatives. Although some have chosen private education, it is obviously a costly option. As middle-income parents increasingly move their children to private schools, their social commitment to public education declines, and public schools deteriorate even more. As public funds decrease, more and more public schools are shifting aspects of public education to the private sector.

> Education reform is one aspect of a broad-ranging neo-liberal agenda that aims to push the market deeper into every aspect of our lives by eliminating or shrinking non-market alternatives.... Students are to be prepared for life without a net, or at least for a world with an Internet rather than a social safety net.
> —Alan Sears,
> *Retooling the Mind Factory*

At the postsecondary level, tuition fees for undergraduate students in Canada increased by 135.4 percent between 1990 and 2002, compared to a cost of living increase of 20.6 percent (CAUT 2002). Although tuition fee rises have since moderated, the costs of postsecondary education continue to grow. Many professional programs have seen their tuition fees skyrocket. Moreover, Canada is one of only three industrialized countries that do not have a national system of student grants. Given both the recent increase in tuition fees and the lack of government grants, it is not surprising that the average debt load for a student graduating from a four-year program has more than tripled since 1990, from $8,000 to $25,000. As tuition fees rise, accessibility to postsecondary education for lower-income students generally declines (Shaker 2003, 141).

Think About It

There is some controversy about whether higher tuition fees act as a deterrent to lower-income students. What do you think? How might higher tuition fees affect career choice?

The changes noted here are worrying because every democratic society must have at its core a viable, accessible public education system. As we shall see in the next few chapters, the growing power of large corporations has allowed them to increasingly determine the direction of public institutions. One consequence of this trend has been a growth in social inequality around the world, including the expansion of two-tiered systems of education. However, having noted the increasing control of big business over all levels of education, we must be reminded that such control is neither mechanical nor absolute. Rather, the various interested parties connected to public education—including businesses, parents, students, teachers, educational administrators, and government bureaucrats—are constantly engaged in a struggle to get their interests met. While big business has the advantage in this struggle, it by no means always achieves its goals.

Since the nineteenth century there has been debate over the purposes and goals of education, as well as over preferred curricula and teaching methods. Teachers across Canada have fought a long battle for better wages and working conditions and for increased autonomy in the classroom. Parents, students, and teachers in many communities have struggled with administrators over educational issues. It is certain that debates about the purpose, goals, and structure of the various levels of public education will continue in the future.

Ideas and Power

Culture defines us as a species. Unlike other animals, humans must live together in social groups and learn their means of survival. Culture is not created in a vacuum; rather, it must always be understood in terms of the relationships of power within a given society. As we have seen in earlier chapters, the majority of power in society is held by those who have ownership or control of societal resources.

Wherever social inequality exists, the dominant class needs to legitimate both itself and the social system that gives it power. Most of us internalize the dominant norms, beliefs, and values of our society. Thus in the process of becoming human, we come to internalize the existing structures of power as well. It is this power of ideology that allows the dominant class to maintain its rule. While force can always be used to repress those who wish to challenge the structures of power, such actions can lead to increased instability and resentment. Ideological hegemony—the ability to control or dominate the belief system within any society—is a more subtle and effective means of maintaining power.

Within all advanced capitalist societies the mass media and the education system are two of the main agents of socialization that help maintain and reinforce class relations. At the same time, these two social institutions are not simply the mouthpieces of the ruling class. As we have seen in this chapter, both continue to be contested domains within Canadian society. Nonetheless, the power of economic ownership gives the dominant class an advantage because of its ability to control the content of these institutions, particularly the media. Moreover, the pervasive ideology of liberalism reinforces the status quo without any necessary direct intervention by capital.

Neither the mass media nor the education system lacks critics. Yet much of the criticism is directed at these institutions as if they existed independently. As a result, we often fault them for failures of the broader society. This is particularly true of the education system, which we hope will give us true equality of opportunity by negating differences of birth, while at the same time providing the skills and knowledge necessary to find employment. When we (or our children) fail to get jobs, or when we see inequality persisting, it is easy to put the blame on our schools. However, in all capitalist societies, the anarchy of production makes both unemployment and lack of fit between training and jobs inevitable. The persistence of poverty and extremes of social inequality, as we shall see in Chapter 10, are rooted in the economic system, not the schools. While the education system may be able to moderate the worst tendencies of capitalist economies, it can never eliminate them without some more drastic form of social change.

Likewise, the mass media are often blamed for promoting values detrimental to society. For example, violence in the media is often discussed. However, like the schools, the media are part of a broader social world. While they may, indeed, play their part in promoting violence, they are not, in and of themselves, the problem. We live in a world where violence is a fact of life. Moreover, violence sells in the marketplace. As long as the media remain largely in private hands, as funding to public television and film is slashed, and as American media giants make increasing inroads in Canada, the ability of ordinary Canadians to affect media content will be limited.

The struggles about the education system and the mass media are ultimately struggles regarding democracy and power, for the bottom line in these debates is who should control our social institutions. The corporate agenda quite directly hands over increasing amounts of control to private enterprise. People who oppose this agenda dispute the argument that the marketplace can meet social needs. Such individuals and groups demand that the state fulfill its mandate of supporting public education as well as public broadcasting and film. It is likely that these struggles will continue in the near future.

Key Points

1. Ideas do not develop in a vacuum; rather, they arise out of particular conditions at specific moments in history. The body of assumptions, ideas, and values that come together into a coherent world view is referred to as an ideology.

2. Those who have economic power in a society are able to dominate the ideological sphere as well. This dominance is referred to as ideological hegemony.

3. Liberalism is the dominant ideology within capitalism. The liberal tradition sees the model for all things as the marketplace.

4. One of the main themes of liberalism is equality, conceived of as equality of opportunity. However, without equality of condition, equality of opportunity will be limited.

5.   Within the liberal framework, ideas are seen as goods competing in the marketplace. But ideas, like goods, are not equally represented in the marketplace. Thus there is the appearance of choice, when in reality there is little variation in the ideas most of us read or hear.

6.   The education system and mass media are two of the major agents of socialization that transmit the dominant ideology.

7.   In recent years there has been tremendous concentration of ownership of the mass media in Canada and around the globe. The content of the media is largely controlled by those who have economic power.

8.   The overall thrust of the mass media is in support of current social arrangements. Despite a variety of orientations, there is almost universal support for the private-enterprise system and the dominant ideology, liberalism.

9.   The direct intervention of the state into areas of culture has always been widely accepted in Canada as a means of protecting Canadian media. However, this intervention is now declining; as a result, U.S. media domination will likely increase.

10. Both the order theories and the change theories agree that schools perform two major functions: they socialize children and they help sort individuals for the labour market. However, the various change theories argue that these functions help sustain existing class relations.

11. As globalization advances, the corporate sector has had an increased desire to be directly linked to educational institutions. Big business is also gaining a foothold in the college and university sector.

12. Despite the power of capital, schools remain a contested terrain where the various interested parties struggle to get their needs met.

13. Current debates over education and the mass media must be understood as democratic struggles, in that they address the question of who should control various social institutions in Canada.

Further Reading

Eagleton, Terry. 2007. *Ideology: An Introduction*. London: Verso.
     This updated version of a classic work by a Marxist literary critic examines the many definitions of the term and traces the concept's complex history in contemporary society.

Grogan, Sarah. 1998. *Body Image: Understanding Body Dissatisfaction in Men, Women, and Children*. London: Routledge.
     We have become a society obsessed with appearance, yet few of us are happy with our bodies. This book examines how media presentation of the ideal body and other cultural influences affect how we see ourselves.

Hackett, Robert A., and William K. Carroll. 2006. *Remaking Media: The Struggle to Democratize Public Communication*. New York: Routledge.
     Two Canadian sociologists examine the "democratic deficit" in the mainstream media and assess the ways alternative forms of media and new forms of activism might counter this problem.

McChesney, Robert W. 2007. *Communication Revolution: Critical Junctures and the Future of Media*. NY: New Press.
One of the foremost analysts of media in the United States argues here that new forms of communication in the twenty-first century call for a new way of thinking about media.

Sears, Alan. 2003. *Retooling the Mind Factory: Education in a Lean State*. Aurora, ON: Garamond.
A detailed examination of the links between current education reform and the neoliberal agenda.

Slee, Tom. 2006. *No One Makes You Shop at Wal-Mart: The Surprising Deceptions of Individual Choice*. Toronto: Between the Lines.
Using game theory, the author undertakes a critical evaluation of the mythology of "choice" in capitalist societies.

Tudiver, Neil. 1999. *Universities for Sale: Resisting Corporate Control over Canadian Higher Education*. Toronto: Lorimer.
An examination of growing corporate control over our universities and colleges, and how faculty have been trying to resist.

8 The Role of the State

In This Chapter

- What exactly is the *state* and how does it differ from the concept of *government*?
- How does an understanding of social class help explain what states do?
- Do we live in a democracy?
- What is fascism?

Up to this point we have been talking about power that is rooted in the economic relationships of society, that is, in class relationships. But when most of us think of power in a society, we think of it in political terms rather than economic ones. For example, if we were asked to name the most powerful person in Canada, it is likely that the majority of us would choose the prime minister. At one level, this is not incorrect—those who hold high positions in government do indeed have a great deal of power. However, as this chapter demonstrates, the power of our elected representatives can only be understood within capitalist class relations.

> There is little doubt that the concentration of financial wealth in Canada is also leading to a concentration of political influence....
> —Jim Stanford, *Paper Boom*

All advanced class societies have had some kind of state formation, although most were small and centred on a strong leader such as a king or emperor. The **state** is an organized political structure that carries out tasks required by more complex societies as their population and geographic size increase, as warfare and trade expand, and as social inequalities become more extreme. However, the state is more than a simple organizing structure; it is also a major means of social control. As Max Weber noted, "The state is considered the sole source of the 'right' to use violence" ([1921] 1958, 78). In state societies, rules that have previously been informal become codified into law and enforced by a military/judicial apparatus. Although we often use the term *state* interchangeably with the term *government*, the government is only one aspect of the state. The concept of the state is more inclusive and allows us to appreciate the element of force that is a key part of this social institution.

The state has not always been a part of every human society. While all societies require some means of maintaining social control or of handling relations with external groups, for most of human history this was done informally. In foraging societies, political power tended to be loosely organized, with a pattern of shifting leadership. Leaders used personal influence to encourage others to undertake activities, but there was no structural means of coercing anyone into following directions. With an increase in surplus and the subsequent unequal allocation of resources, increasingly formalized leadership developed.

As agrarian societies with large surpluses and social classes developed, more formalized state structures arose. The important role of the family was reduced as the state became increasingly powerful. Along with the growth of the state apparatus, an ideology developed that supported and legitimized such a structure. In other words, most people came to see their state structure as inevitable and eternal.

The Separation of the Private and the Public Spheres

The capitalist state is different than earlier forms of the state. In agrarian societies, the owning class was in direct control of the state, which was used to appropriate surplus from the producers. For example an emperor could accumulate wealth directly via various forms of tribute or taxation. In capitalist societies, in contrast, the owning class is separated from the state. The economic sphere is "privatized"—it comes under full and direct control of the dominant class. At the same time, the *social* activities formerly carried out directly by the owning class—that is, military, administrative, or legal functions—become transferred to the state, which is in the public sphere.

It is important to note that the separation of the private and public spheres in capitalist societies is only partial. The capitalist class gets to privately own and have control over most economic activity. This gives this class enormous power over the productive process because it has the capacity to organize and intensify production for its own immediate interests. However, the negative consequences of its activities—pollution, poverty, unemployment, and so on—are expected to be dealt with by governments. In reality, then, it is only the *benefits* of productive activity that are privatized in capitalist societies, while the *costs* are transferred to the public sphere. Moreover, as we shall see throughout this chapter, the capitalist class would not be able to secure these benefits without the assistance of the state.

Understanding the Modern State: Two Views

In Canada today there are three levels of government. First there is the federal government, with its centre in Ottawa; second are the ten provincial and three territorial governments; third are the various municipal, or local, governments across the country. All of us connect to numerous components of all three levels on a daily level. For example, on any given day we might listen to CBC radio on waking (federal government), have a glass of tap water and put out the garbage (municipal government), take a bus (municipal and provincial governments), renew our driver's licence (provincial government), buy an item and pay sales tax (provincial and federal governments), take courses at a university (provincial and federal governments), or visit a relative in the hospital (provincial and federal governments).

Because of the huge amount of power that the various levels of government ultimately hold over our lives, it is important to take a closer look at exactly what the state is, how it functions, and on whose behalf it acts. A number of competing theoretical frameworks have tried to explain who controls the state and how it works. Two dominant analyses of the state—reflecting the order and the change frameworks, respectively—are the *pluralist approach* and the *class approach*.

Most of us don't think that we carry theoretical frameworks around in our head. And yet most of us, if asked to describe on whose behalf governments act, would likely respond with an approach known as **pluralism**. In the pluralist analysis, society consists of a variety of groups and associations with highly diverse and often conflicting interests. According to the pluralist analysis, no single group totally dominates political structures. A key function of the state, from this perspective, is *mediation* between the many different interest groups—workers, students, the disabled, Aboriginal peoples, big business, small business, women, to name but a few—trying to get their needs met within a given society. Indeed, by balancing out the various interest groups, the state supposedly helps guarantee that order is maintained, while ensuring that the overall best interests of society as a whole are met.

From this point of view, the state has a high degree of autonomy, that is, the ability to act independently of any single pressure group. Pluralists recognize the greater power of big business relative to other interest groups but do not see this as a problem because of its important role in the economy. For pluralists, the state is a body that acts on behalf of society as a whole. Because it does not emphasize the element of social control, the pluralist approach usually speaks of "government" rather than "the state."

The pluralist analysis of the state is the one most of us feel comfortable with, both because it fits with our already accepted notions of how societies work and because it does seem to match our own experience. On the surface, it appears that governments are, more or less, working on everyone's behalf. After all, while few of us may agree with everything our governments do, most of us feel we have benefited from the many services provided by the three levels of government, with our state-funded medical system[1] being the most popular. In addition, since all adult citizens get to vote in elections, we have the common-sense understanding that Canadians as a whole are choosing the individuals who

---

1. While most of us think of our medical system as being fully funded by the state, many aspects of health care—including drugs, dental care, physiotherapy, massage, eyeglasses, and so on—are not covered.

sit in positions of power, and, therefore, it does seem that those individuals must by and large be representing our collective interests. The pluralist approach fits with the order theories: "The world is just."

The change theories do not support this commonly held view of the social world. Unlike the pluralist approach, which sees the Canadian state as essentially neutral, the class approach sees the state as an institution that acts primarily in the interests of the dominant class. Thus, in contrast to the pluralist notion of the state, the class approach sees the Canadian state as only partially autonomous, because the economic power of capital also gives it political power. Moreover, given the goals of the dominant class, having the state accede to its interests will mean the interests of others are not necessarily met.

Although nineteenth- and early twentieth-century class analysis initiated by Marx, Engels, and Lenin provided a general theory of the capitalist state, the actual process was never clearly worked out. This issue was taken on in the second half of the twentieth century by a number of neo-Marxist social scientists, who were interested in the relationship between the state and the economy. Nicos Poulantzas, James O'Connor, and Ralph Miliband initiated a debate that has continued to the present. Despite differences between various authors, all share a critique of the pluralist approach and a belief in the connection between the state and the appropriating class.

From the point of view of class analysis, the state carries out three inter-connected functions on behalf of the dominant class, although the relative importance of each may vary in different socioeconomic formations and even at different historical moments within a specific society (O'Connor 1973, 6; Panitch 1977, 8):

1. *Accumulation function.* The state must try to create or maintain the conditions for profitable capital accumulation.
2. *Legitimation function.* The state must try to maintain social harmony, mostly by legitimating the current class structure and the right of the ruling class to rule.
3. *Coercion function.* The state, when necessary, must use force to repress subordinate individuals or classes on behalf of the dominant class.

The state is made up of a number of institutions, which can be classified into three categories: *repressive agencies*, which include the army and police, the judiciary, and the penal system; *government*, which includes the various administrative bodies, such as legislatures, parliaments, and councils, as well as the civil service; and *government-owned bodies*, which in Canada include such components as the education system, the health care system, the postal service, and such "publicly owned" services as the CBC.

Although most of us want to believe in the pluralist view of the state, there is ample evidence that the state in all capitalist societies acts primarily in the interests of the ruling class. However, each country must be analyzed in terms of its own historical specificity. Even within countries, the exact connection between the various levels of the state and the dominant class may change over time.

The rest of this chapter describes and analyzes the ways the Canadian state is linked to the capitalist owning class, and, in the process, refutes the pluralist notion of a neutral state apparatus. Indeed, it will be argued that the current activities of the various levels of the state in Canada—federal, provincial, and local—and their dramatic transformation in the last thirty or so years make no sense without understanding their class-based nature. The class perspective on the state immediately calls into question the strongly held notion that ours is a fully democratic society. Therefore, a preliminary discussion of the meaning of democracy is in order.

Think About It
What does the term *democracy* mean to you?

Democracy in Capitalist Societies

The argument that the various levels of the state act *primarily* in the interests of the appropriating class does not mean that it is the *only* group whose interests are being met. As shall be argued in the rest of this chapter, states act on behalf of the ruling class *in general*, but this does not mean that every individual activity of every level of state at every moment necessarily benefits the dominant class. First, we must be clear that the various individuals who are part of the state apparatuses are not under the total control of the ruling class. On a daily basis, they may make decisions for a wide variety of personal or political reasons. Thus human agency must always be taken into account when we analyze social institutions.

It must also be recalled that the capitalist owning class has two goals: its short-term interest is to maximize profits, while its long-term interest is to maintain the system that allows it to privately appropriate surplus value. If states only helped the owning class maximize its profits, the long-term stability of the entire capitalist system might be put at risk. Moreover, no political party would ever be voted back into office. Thus every state in capitalist societies must, to some degree, balance competing forces. One way of increasing stability has been the acceptance of democratic political forms.

The Meaning of Democracy

In its original Greek, *democracy* meant rule by the people. However, even within the Greek city-states that practised democratic forms, "the people" were a relatively small group, excluding women, slaves, and the foreign-born. Likewise, the *Magna Carta*, the great constitutional document of the feudal period, was a codification of the rights and privileges of the feudal lords, not the serfs. Democracy, then, is not an absolute; rather, it must be understood within particular social and historical conditions.

There are differing views about the relationship between the economic arrangement that we call capitalism and the political arrangement we call democracy. Some theorists feel that capitalism furthered the democratic process. In some senses this is true, as pre-capitalist societies have tended to be dominated by authoritarian states closely linked to a small and very powerful ruling class. Notions such as human rights, equal opportunity, or elections of government representatives do not normally exist in such societies.

However, while there is no question that capitalist economies have advanced the process of democracy, they have done so in only a limited way. In capitalist societies, democracy has a very specific meaning, limited to the political sphere rather than to the economic one. Since economic property is "privately" owned, it remains outside the framework of democratic principles. Most of us accept, for example, that in capitalist societies only company owners should have the right to decide whether a particular company should be able to close down, increase production, fire its workers, or move to another locale. While it is true that there are now many laws constraining corporations—for example, labour laws or environmental protection legislation—such laws were put in place only after a long struggle, and many of these constraints have actually deteriorated or disappeared in recent years.

Even within the political or "public" sphere of capitalist societies, democracy has a rather specific meaning. It pertains mainly to the electoral process whereby, at regular intervals, individuals get to select those who will represent them in some parliamentary-style body for a fixed period of time. Democracy is never connected to socioeconomic conditions. Thus countries with massive poverty, extremes of rich and poor, and mass powerlessness are nonetheless called "democratic" simply because they hold elections from time to time. Moreover, in many of the more developed countries—of which Canada is one—fewer and fewer people are actually voting in elections.

Unlike pre-capitalist societies, few members of the ruling class in Canada actually hold government positions. How, then, does the ruling class rule? In Chapter 6 we saw the important role played by lobbying groups for big business, such as the Canadian Council of Chief Executives, and think tanks, such as the Fraser Institute. Such groups not only directly influence the decisions of governments, they also play an extremely important role in influencing public opinion. Thus capitalist governments do not have full autonomy.

There are also a number of paid lobbying groups in Ottawa whose job it is to get the ear of the government on behalf of those who hire them. While they will certainly lobby on behalf of any interest group, it is obvious that only a small number of groups have enough money to pay for such lobbying activities. Moreover, a number of lobbying groups that represented non-business groups, such as women and the poor, saw their government funding cut in 2006. Much lobbying is also done on an informal basis. While it is true that few elected government officials and even fewer civil servants are actually members of the bourgeoisie, many travel in social circles where they will regularly come into contact with such individuals or their representatives. Corporate leaders and government officials mingle at social clubs, political fundraisers, charity fundraisers, and so on.

It should also be pointed out that those who have more powerful positions in the economy are always taken into consideration by the state simply because of such power. A key goal of the Canadian state is to advance the economy, and that economy is, by definition, a capitalist one. In this regard, Thorstein Veblen ([1904] 1932, 287) noted a century ago:

> Representative government means, chiefly, representation of business interests…. The government has, of course, much else to do besides administering the general affairs of the business community; but in most of this work, even in what is not ostensibly directed to business ends, it is under the surveillance of the business interests. It seldom happens, if at all, that the government of a civilized nation will persist in a course of action detrimental or not ostensibly subservient to the interests of the more conspicuous body of the community's businessmen.

In other words, true democracy is always limited by the economic power of the ruling class. Capital owns the productive units; capital owns the jobs. Businesses can threaten to move to other cities, provinces, or countries if their needs are not met. No political party that wishes to stay in office risks alienating the class with economic power in any major way.

Representative democracy in capitalist societies by no means guarantees accountability from political leadership; nor does it guarantee that political parties, once elected, will adhere to their own party policies. Indeed, it is becoming increasingly common for politicians to run on a specific platform and then either ignore or actually contradict their promises after they are elected. As a result, many Canadians have become cynical about politicians and the electoral process, and as already noted, many citizens—particularly the more powerless—do not even bother to vote. This, of course, gives increased power to the upper strata, which tends to vote in larger numbers, which further erodes democracy.

The Need for Democratic Forms

In any discussion of democracy in capitalist society, an obvious question arises. If class analysis is correct, why doesn't the ruling class in capitalist societies simply maintain their power in the manner of slave or feudal socioeconomic formations; that is, why is there democracy at all?

Unlike agrarian societies, which have fairly homogeneous ruling classes, the upper class in commercial societies is highly diverse and segmented. In capitalist societies there are, for example, small, medium, and large corporations; even within the latter we see finance capital, industrial capital, retail capital, and so on. Democratic forms, in which political parties compete within a narrow framework of electoral representation, allow differing sectors of the dominant class

Box 8.1 Power Corporation and Desmarais Power

Even though few Canadians have ever heard of the Desmarais family, they are one of the most influential families in the country. Paul Desmarais Sr. founded Power Corporation of Montreal, a multi-billion-dollar conglomerate. Desmarais Sr. had a stroke in 2005; his sons Paul Jr. and André are now co-CEOs of the company. The Desmarais family has long had extensive connections to key politicians in Canada and globally:

- Former prime minister Paul Martin was at one time an executive member of Power Corp. He was personally mentored by Paul Desmarais Sr. and bought Canadian Steamship Lines from him.
- Former prime minister Jean Chrétien sat on the board of the Power Corp. subsidiary Consolidated Bathurst before winning the leadership of the Liberal Party. Chrétien's daughter, France, is married to Paul Desmarais' son André.
- Desmarais Sr. backed Brian Mulroney's bid for the federal leadership of the Conservative Party of Canada in 1976, and Mulroney has done legal work for Desmarais Sr. since returning to the private sector.
- Pierre Trudeau sat on the international advisory council of Paul Desmarais Sr.
- John Rae (brother of former Ontario premier Bob Rae) was executive vice-president of Power Corp. He ran Chrétien's 1993 campaign and became a personal adviser.
- Former Quebec Liberal leader Daniel Johnson worked for Power Corp.
- Former Mulroney cabinet minister

Don Mazankowski is currently the director of Power Corp.
- Michael Pitfield, a top-level bureaucrat in the Trudeau government, was a vice-chairman of Power Corp. and is still listed as a director emeritus.
- Gilles Loiselle, finance minister under former prime minister Kim Campbell, has been an adviser to Paul Desmarais.
- Former head of Ontario Hydro, Maurice Strong, was at one time president of Power Corp.
- Former Ontario premiers William Davis and John Robarts have sat on the board of Power Corp.
- In 2006 Paul Desmarais Jr., along with nine other corporate leaders, was appointed by Prime Minister Stephen Harper to the North American Competitive Council, a group of business people overseeing the integration of the Canadian, U.S., and Mexican economies.
- The French connection: Power Corp. is one of the major owners of Groupe Bruxelle Lamber (GBL), which is the biggest shareholder of some of France's largest corporations, including Total (oil), Suez (gas and electricity), Lafarge (cement), and Imerys (building materials). Paul Desmarais is a personal friend of French president Nicolas Sarkozy.

Sources: Adapted and updated from *Saturday Night*, February 1996, 12; Konrad Yakabuski, "Desmarais' French Connection," *Globe and Mail*, 17 May 2007: B1.

to compete with each other without the risk of destabilizing the entire system. Democracy as we know it also allows working people to feel a commitment to the very system that structurally disempowers them. Thus the tensions both within and between classes are reduced within the framework of representative democracy.

The reduction of such tensions is important if the capitalist market is to function. Wage and price fluctuations, strikes and protests, arbitrary government decisions, constantly changing regulations, and so on make it difficult for businesses to secure their profits. The owning class likes stability, and parliamentary or representative democracies seem to work best at providing such stability.

Limits to Democracy

Although the dominant class in capitalist societies prefers a democratic political form, there is no automatic relationship between democracy, even in its limited meaning of the electoral process, and capitalism. The central component of democracy that we usually take for granted—one person, one vote—has not always existed in capitalist societies. For example, the right to vote in Canada was only gradually extended. Prior to 1918, this right was generally limited to white males who were British subjects, and several provinces required literacy tests for prospective voters. Women in Quebec did not receive the right to vote in provincial elections until 1940; in British Columbia persons of an "oriental or Hindu" background were disenfranchised until 1945, while Japanese in that province could not vote until 1948. Status Indians were first able to vote in federal elections in 1960.

Moreover, electoral democracy has not existed in a large number of developing countries around the world. Although the ruling class generally prefers some democratic form of capitalist rule, this is possible only under certain conditions. When economic conditions lead to a lack of social or political stability, a more repressive form of rule may be preferable to democracy. In such a situation, the capitalist class may willingly accept the removal of civil rights or may support the rule of an anti-democratic leader. This point will be addressed in more detail later in this chapter.

Thus the ruling class in capitalist societies maintains its power through what can be described as "carrot and stick" tactics.[2] In order to maintain social stability, ordinary people (in the developed world at least) are offered the "carrot" of representative democracy, civil rights, and some social welfare. When that fails, and people increasingly demand greater democracy or a larger share of the social surplus, then the "stick" of the repressive state apparatus is there to restrain them. This is the coercion function of the state, which we will examine in more detail later in this chapter. But first we should examine the key role the state plays in promoting the economic interests of capital.

---

2. The term "carrot and stick" means offering a reward (a carrot) while simultaneously threatening a punishment (being hit with a stick). This is how donkeys were traditionally made to pull carts.

The Accumulation Function of the State

It is often presumed that the state plays little or no role in capitalist economic matters. In fact, direct state intervention in economies is often thought of, incorrectly, as socialism. It therefore may come as a surprise to learn that governments in every capitalist society are actively involved in their economies. Indeed, the market economy of capitalism actually *requires* such involvement.

From the beginning, all capitalist states had to put in place the legal structures that permitted the private accumulation of capital to take place and allowed capitalist class relations to be maintained. The state continues to be the regulator of capitalism. It sets the rules regarding economic activities, and in the long run those rules always favour capital. Moreover, because capitalist economies are unplanned and therefore subject to instability and crises, most people—even those in the ruling class—count on the state to limit its worst excesses, particularly those that might lead to major economic downturns.

> ...it is beyond dispute that the development of capitalist enterprise has always been crucially dependent on significant state intervention.
> —Harry Shutt, *The Trouble with Capitalism*

Some might wonder why, in a capitalist economy, all economic activities aren't carried out by the private sector. Many activities have been undertaken by the state because, while they may have been necessary for industry, they simply are not profitable enough for the private sector to run on its own (for example, the post office). Other enterprises have traditionally been owned or controlled by the state because they were seen as part of the public good and were therefore expected to be outside the marketplace (for example, the public education system and hospitals). Often the reason for public ownership was a combination of both.

Money Coming In: The Tax System

If there's one thing everybody loves to hate these days, it's taxes. What are taxes? Taxes are the mandatory payments people and businesses make to the three levels of government. Since states generate little wealth on their own, they must appropriate a portion of the socially created surplus value to carry out various activities. One part of these revenues is used to sustain the various components of the state itself (the civil service, police and military, judiciary, and so on). The rest is used for a variety of purposes, ranging from road and bridge construction to education and support for the arts. While, in theory, the state both collects and distributes moneys for the benefit of all Canadians, various levels of the state in Canada have consistently favoured corporations and the wealthiest Canadians.

Think About It
Although money collected from our taxes helps pay for such important things as health care, education, roads, libraries, and so on, most people see taxation in a very negative light. Why do you think this is the case?

Governments take in money in a variety of ways, such as various direct forms of taxation, licensing fees, excise and customs duties, fines and penalties, and user fees, to name but a few. In Canada, different levels of government have access to different means of acquiring funds. Taxation can be described as either progressive or regressive. **Progressive taxation** occurs when citizens are taxed on the basis of their ability to pay. In a fully progressive taxation system, the more wealth or income one has, the more taxes one pays. With **regressive taxation** there is no connection between the amount of wealth or income one has and the tax one pays. Most people assume that Canada has a relatively progressive system of taxation. In reality, Canada's system of taxation has been, at best, only mildly progressive, and all levels of government have been moving to increasingly regressive forms of taxation.

The most progressive form of taxation in Canada, introduced in 1917, is that of taxation on corporate or personal income. Both federal and provincial governments use this form of taxation as a source of revenue. However, while it is certainly more progressive than other forms of taxation—because, in theory, the more you earn the more you pay—the income tax system is by no means fully progressive. While supposedly taxing people and corporations in proportion to their incomes, there are so many allowable deductions and tax credits that the degree to which income tax can be described as truly progressive is limited. Of course, all Canadians are legally entitled to such deductions and tax credits, and some specifically benefit low-income earners. However, most credits and deductions—such as those allowed for investments, retirement savings plans, charitable donations, childcare expenses, or political party contributions—require an initial outlay of money, which lower-income earners lack.

As a result, primarily higher-income earners are able to benefit from credits and deductions. In addition, in 1988 the government reduced ten tax brackets (with rates of taxation ranging from 6 percent to 34 percent) to three. In 2001, a fourth bracket was added, with rates at 16, 22, 26, and 29 percent, with the highest rates for those earning more than $100,000. This flattening of tax rates primarily benefits those at the top, whose tax rate declined, while the rate of those at the bottom increased. The proportion of income paid in income tax by the richest 20 percent of Canadians fell from 25 percent in 1995 to 22 percent in 2004 (MacKinnon 2007). Many countries and some U.S. states have recently moved to a flat-rate tax, in which everyone has the same tax rate; this system is not progressive at all.

It should also be noted that increasing numbers of Canadians are investing in countries with secrecy laws and may not be paying any taxes on the profits from such investments. Between 1990 and 2003, Canadian assets in what are now referred to as offshore financial centres (OFCs) increased from $11 billion to $88 billion. In 2003, these centres accounted for more than one-fifth of all Canadian direct investment abroad, double the proportion thirteen years earlier (Lavoie 2007). As a result of tax cuts, new tax laws, and increasing off-shore investments, the total amount of tax collected by the government has fallen. Tax revenue as a percentage of GDP dropped from 36.7 percent in 1998 to 33.5 percent by 2004, and was lowered even more by Prime Minister Stephen Harper (MacKinnon 2007).

Large corporations have available to them many tax deductions and complex accounting procedures that substantially reduce their tax rate—sometimes less than 5 percent. In fact, every year many extremely profitable companies pay no corporate income tax at all. Also worth noting is the size of corporate tax deferrals. While individuals are expected to pay their taxes in full at the end of each taxation year (or pay a substantial penalty), corporations are allowed to defer a large chunk of their taxes without interest. Although in theory these taxes have to be paid eventually, the reality is that when taxes are deferred, they are deferred indefinitely. As far back as 1980, the total amount of tax deferrals that had accumulated in corporate accounts was $24.5 billion, more than the entire federal deficit at that time (*Canadian Business*, January 1985).

There are many other ways that the various levels of government acquire revenue, all of them regressive. Various taxes at the point of consumption (that is, sales tax) are increasingly utilized by the federal and provincial levels of government. Since the tax is determined by the cost of the item rather than the ability of the individual to pay, sales taxes are clearly regressive. Likewise, property tax, the main tax employed by municipal governments, is not progressive for a variety of reasons—primarily, as with sales tax, because it is not linked to the income or wealth of the property owner. In recent years the federal and provincial levels of government have increasingly cut back on their **transfer payments** to municipalities, while at the same time downloading more functions onto them. This has meant that local governments, which carry an increasing burden for the cost of such necessities as education, welfare, policing, and public transportation, have been financially strapped and forced to cut back on social services.

Although not technically taxation, an increasingly popular way for governments to raise funds is via what can collectively be referred to as hidden taxes. For example, the fees one pays to use a government service is such a hidden tax. These include such things as public transportation fares, entrance fees to public museums or galleries, tuition fees, licence fees, and toll roads. Since this form of taxation appears as an optional fee for a service, it might be argued that one need not pay for the service if one so chooses. However, many user-pay services are essential to most citizens (public transportation being an obvious example). Such user-pay schemes are regressive because, once again, they are unrelated to the user's ability to pay. Hidden taxes are actually a double tax: having already paid taxes to support various government services, individuals are asked to pay

---

Box 8.2 Why Our Taxes Are Too Low

Governments at all levels are increasingly obsessed with tax cuts. They should stop cutting. Here's why.

Other countries, using different tax and public policy strategies than ours, have significantly lower poverty rates, more equal income distribution, higher pensions for seniors, greater economic security for workers, lower infant mortality rates, longer life expectancy, higher educational outcomes, less drug use, better environmental performance, greater levels of trust, higher productivity, and higher GDP per capita. In Canada we are moving ever further away from the policies that produce these desirable outcomes. Instead, we cut taxes.

Among high-income OECD countries, Canada's tax revenue as a percentage of GDP is already well below the average. High-tax countries have had greater success at achieving their social objectives—without economic penalty. Using fifty commonly used social indicators, it can be seen that outcomes in high-tax Nordic countries are better than in low-tax countries and in particular the U.S., the country that tax-cut proponents most often use as a model. Norway outperforms the U.S. with higher GDP per capita and higher productivity. The World Economic Forum ranks high-tax Nordic countries among the most competitive in the world.

Low-tax countries like the U.S. have higher rates of poverty, high mortality rates, lower life expectancy, and poorer life satisfaction than high-tax countries. Yet business groups continue to call for tax cuts. While the lure of tax cuts may seem tempting for Canadians feeling financially insecure, many are beginning to see the evidence that tax cuts provide benefit primarily to high-income earners and come with a high cost for the rest of us. The recent loss of billions of dollars from federal tax cuts has cost us a national childcare program and hopes for a national pharmacare program plus cuts to literacy programs and women's programs—programs essential to increasing equality of opportunity.

Cutting taxes will not correct these problems. Public investment will. While politicians try to reassure us that we can have it all—tax cuts and better services—it just doesn't add up. You simply cannot be a low-tax jurisdiction and have the level of services that provide us with the hard-earned security of knowing that we have access to health care, elderly and disabled Canadians have decent economic means, and our children will have access to childcare, education, and future economic opportunities.

Source: Adapted from Shauna MacKinnon, *Selling Our Soul for Lower Taxes*, 4 Jan. 2007. Canadian Centre for Policy Alternatives – Manitoba <http://policy-alternatives.ca/documents/Manitoba_Pubs/2007/FastFacts_Jan4_07_Selling_our_Soul.pdf >.

---

again when they use a particular service. Obviously, lower-income earners are hardest hit by such schemes, and many end up excluded from some of these services.

Lotteries, video lottery terminals, and gambling casinos constitute a rapidly increasing source of funds for the state. Overall revenues from gambling grew in Canada from $1.7 billion in 1992–93 to $6.3 billion in 2003–04, a 275 percent increase (Azmier 2005, 5). This is a particularly regressive way for governments to raise funds. While more high-income households are involved in gambling than poorer ones, those with low incomes spend a greater proportion of their incomes on gambling (Carey 2003). Although gambling is voluntary, this makes it no less regressive. Lotteries and other forms of gambling also serve the function of directing people to personal rather than collective solutions to structural problems.

Before leaving the issue of taxes, it is important to point out certain kinds of wealth in Canada that are not taxed at all. For example, Canada is one of only three advanced industrial nations to lack any inheritance taxes or taxes on net wealth. Even a modest inheritance or wealth transfer tax on estates of more than $1 million could add billions of dollars to government coffers.

Not surprisingly, as corporations and the very rich have seen their taxes decline relative to others, middle and lower income earners have had to absorb some of the losses. In other words, our entire system of taxation has become increasingly regressive. In the 1980s and onward, as middle- and lower-income Canadians faced a heavier tax burden—at the same time that wages stagnated—increasing numbers of them became sympathetic to the call for lower taxes. Once government funds shrank as a result of declining taxation, it was only a matter of time until governments claimed there was "just not enough money" to provide required public services. Indeed, some change theorists have argued that the main goal of tax cuts was primarily about justifying a dramatic shift in government priorities, as we will see in the next chapter.

Money Going Out: The Growth of Corporate Welfare

In recent years many Canadians have become hostile to people on social assistance because they mistakenly think that these individuals may be getting "something for nothing." In reality, social welfare is paid for by municipal governments and is only a very small part of their total budgets. However, in *Louder Voices: The Corporate Welfare Bums* (1972), David Lewis correctly pointed out that the real welfare recipients in Canada have not been those on various forms of social assistance, but rather the major corporations. Between 1982 and 2006, $18.4 *billion* in various forms of government assistance to corporations was authorized by the federal government. Of that amount, 39 percent ($7.1 billion) is classified as repayable. Less than 20 percent, or $1.3 billion, has actually been paid back (Canadian Taxpayers Federation 2007, 12).

In all capitalist societies, the state provides major financial support to its corporations. Therefore, support for "corporate welfare," or what is sometimes referred to as "wealthfare," is not limited to any one political party. If we examine policies at both the federal and provincial levels, all major political parties in Canada—including Lewis's own New Democratic Party—have allocated grants, loans, and tax concessions to those at the top. In theory, governments do this because these corporations will create jobs. However, the data demonstrate that many corporations have received substantial sums of money even as they were losing money or reducing the number of jobs. If the true aim of governments

Table 8.1 Top 10 Govt. Assistance Recipients, Fiscal Years 1982–2005

Company	Amount Authorized ($)
1. Pratt & Whitney Canada Corp.	1,495,509,079
2. Bombardier	745,282,654
3. General Motors of Canada Limited	360,829,000
4. Bell Helicopter Textron Canada Limited	338,747,004
5. CAE Inc.	321,022,296
6. Société Générale de Financement du QC	293,000,000
7. Groupe Mil Inc. (Le)	230,500,598
8. Honeywell Aerospatiale Inc.	207,922,914
9. CMC Electronics Inc.	158,798,133
10. Trentonworks Ltd.	127,753,226

Source: Canadian Taxpayers Federation 2007.

was about the creation of jobs, they would be pouring money into the public sector, where labour-intensive fields such as health care, education, or social services would create many more jobs than in, for example, the biotechnology or aerospace sectors.

According to one analyst, the main role of governments in relation to the economy is to provide a favourable fiscal and monetary climate for capital to secure and increase its profits (Panitch 1977, 14). This involves a number of tasks, including underwriting the private risks of production by providing companies with grants, loans, subsidies, tax breaks, and so on. Governments also provide technical infrastructure for capitalist development—including state ownership and state construction of railroads, harbours, canals, power-generating plants, airports, and highways—when the costs or risks for capital are too high to undertake themselves. As well, both provincial and federal levels of government in recent years have regularly funded global trade missions to directly sell Canadian products to foreign buyers. Less obvious are the ways that governments create capitalist labour markets via control of land policy and immigration policy, and the way governments absorb the social costs of capitalist production, via such activities as environmental clean-up, welfare services, or health care.

Think About It

Look at the list of corporations in Table 8.1. How many names do you recognize? Check them out on the Internet to find out what they actually do. Keep these figures in mind the next time a government official comments that there's just no money for education or social services.

Strangely, even the funding of certain social services—particularly health care and education—can be seen as a benefit to the ruling class. To understand this point, we need only look to the United States, one of the few developed capitalist countries that never developed a state-funded health-care system. As a result, most of the larger U.S. companies have been covering health insurance costs, at an average of $8,000 for each of their employees (McKenna 2007). In Canada, employers do not have to consider such expenses.

However, while the Canadian government continues to fund social programs, the proportion of the budget allocated to these expenses has been dropping. According to data from the Organization for Economic Co-operation and Development (OECD) Canada's social spending in 2003 was only 17.3 percent of its GDP. Only five OECD countries had a lower proportion: the United States, Ireland, Turkey, Mexico, and Korea. The countries with the largest proportion of social spending were Sweden at 31.3 percent, France at 28.7 percent, and Germany at 27.6 percent (www.oecd.org/statistics/).

Money to the Military

World War II saw the development of a symbiotic relationship between government and the arms industry, which has continued to the present day. Dwight D. Eisenhower, then president of the United States, coined the term *military-industrial complex* to describe this relationship. In essence, the interests of the top military—to obtain the latest technology and equipment—and the interests of the corporate sector—to maximize profits—were merged. In the centre was the state apparatus, which, in effect, wore two hats. Not only did it set policy for both budget allocation for military spending and political decisions with regard to military activity, it was also the direct purchaser of military-related goods and services from private corporations. Moreover, the state, as we have already discussed, was not a neutral body: it consistently favoured capital.

While industries in the aerospace, electronics, transportation, and armaments sectors (such as most of the companies listed in Table 8.1) may sell products for civilian use, they also do large-scale production for military purposes and sell primarily to governments, particularly their own governments. For example, more than half (58 percent) of CAE's $46 million in profits in 2003 came from the sale of weapons and other military equipment (*CCPA Monitor*, November 2005, 3). While Canada has long had the image of being a peacekeeper, in recent years the federal government has vastly increased military spending. In 2005–06 the Canadian government spent almost $14.7 billion on the military. After the Conservatives were elected in 2006, Stephen Harper announced that they were adding $5.3 billion to that amount (Staples 2006). Meanwhile Canada has reduced its commitment to peacekeeping efforts. Projected government funding for U.N. peacekeeping missions in 2006–07 was only $6.2 million, while the number of Canadian military personnel involved in U.N. peacekeeping dropped from 1,149 in 1991 to 56 in 2006 (ibid.).

Production for military use is big business, with global military spending in 2006 estimated to have reached over $12 billion, a 37 percent increase since 1997. The fifteen countries with the highest spending accounted for 83 percent of the world total (Koring 2007). It is also a highly monopolized sector of business, with very few corporations controlling the entire industry. One of the largest of these, U.S.-based United Technologies, owns Pratt & Whitney Canada, the number one recipient of government funding between 1982 and 2005.

Unlike products such as clothing or household appliances, which are produced before they are sold in the marketplace, military hardware is manufactured only after contracts have been secured. As a result, there are no unsold products, and no wastage occurs. Moreover, companies often don't even have to compete for government contracts. The percentage of all military contracts in Canada that were classified as "noncompetitive" (meaning that the government didn't solicit multiple bids) doubled over two years between 2004 and 2006, to 40 percent (Staples 2006). At the urging of military leaders, governments are often convinced to buy the latest technology, whether or not it is needed. Such technology is, of course, rapidly made obsolete and must constantly be replaced.

Because such industries bring immediate commercial benefits, governments often become promoters of trade in military goods with other countries. For example, the Canadian government has sponsored trade missions, engaged in direct-marketing efforts, and modified legislation that had limited some questionable overseas arms sales. Despite supposed restrictions, the federal government has allowed sales of military equipment to countries whose governments are engaged in internal conflicts, human rights abuses, or violation of other Canadian guidelines (Epps 2002).

Thus the Canadian government is tied to the global military-industrial complex in a number of ways. First, it sets government policy about participating in global conflicts, such as the war in Afghanistan, which increase our country's need for more military machinery; second, it purchases products produced by the major corporations for military use; third, the government gives large loans and grants to producers of military hardware and technology; fourth, money from the Canadian Pension Plan is now used for military purposes. In late 2003, the CPP had over $2.6 billion invested in military contractors. Almost a third of that was invested in sixty-five U.S. military corporations (Sanders 2004).

While the benefits of such policies to the owners of companies producing goods for military use are obvious, the costs to the rest of us are less evident. Of course, there is the clear moral concern that a substantial portion of our manufacturing base produces weapons of destruction that are increasingly being used in military conflicts around the world. It is also of some concern that governments, having spent large amounts on military expenditures, must continually look for uses to justify such expenses. But in straight economic terms, production for military use is also problematic. Although such production supposedly creates jobs, it is actually more capital-intensive than labour-intensive, which means that relatively few jobs are created. For example, Pratt & Whitney currently employs around 7,000 workers, down from 7,500 in the late 1990s (Reguly 2006). Moreover, because it is either largely produced for export or stockpiled by the Canadian government, military hardware does not generate much of a spin-off effect to other Canadian industries. Thus excessive military spending does not benefit the average Canadian; rather, it is a key way in which the accumulation function of the state acts in the interests of the corporate owning class.

Coercion: The Repressive State Apparatus

When we are small, we learn to go to a police officer if we are in trouble, since the police are there to "serve and protect." Certainly, most of us would want to be protected from those who might want to physically harm us or do damage to our personal property. However, while in theory the police as part of the entire repressive state apparatus exist to benefit every Canadian, the reality is that their primary role has always been to serve and protect those with wealth and power. This role is not the result of some insidious or evil plot on the part of police officers but rather is a necessary part of all class-based societies.

The state ultimately decides what is legal and what is a crime; determines, via the judiciary, who is innocent and who is guilty; and hands out the punishment for those found guilty. All advanced capitalist societies accept—at least in theory—the notion of the **rule of law**, a formally determined set of rules or principles that applies to all within its jurisdiction. In theory, then, the coercive component of the state is neutral and unconnected to class relationships. Whether you are rich or poor, unemployed or an employer, a corporation or a communist, all are supposedly equal under the law. In reality, however, class relationships impose themselves on the repressive apparatuses as they do in other spheres of the state. Indeed, the ruling class could not retain its rule without support from the coercive element of the state.

Although all societies have rules of behaviour and punishments for violations, it is only with the development of class societies that these rules come to be formalized as laws. Since agents of the state write the laws, it should not be surprising that most laws in any society will protect the interests of those in power. In all class societies, the majority of laws are linked to rights of property. In theory, the forms of property in law are not necessarily distinguished; that is, economic property and property for personal use are generally treated in the same way. In practice, however, those who own and control economic property are treated distinctively.

We saw in Chapter 7 that corporations are treated in law as if they are human beings in some ways, yet are privileged in other ways. For example, according to the Canadian Cancer Society, there are more than 45,000 smoking-related deaths in Canada each year. It goes without saying that any individual who killed that number of Canadians would be considered a mass murderer. Yet in 1995 the Supreme Court of Canada decided that the tobacco industry's constitutional rights of free expression had been denied when tobacco advertising was banned in Canada. Thus corporations are treated as individuals with regard to their so-called rights, but not with regard to the consequences of their activities. Moreover, the state must pay the bill for all smoking-related health costs, family benefits to survivors, and so on. This reality reinforces the point that in capitalist societies the benefits of private appropriation of surplus are generally privatized, while

---

Box 8.3 The Westray Mine Disaster:
Twenty-Six Dead and No One Found Guilty

On May 9, 1992, an explosion at the Westray coal mine in Pictou County, Nova Scotia, killed twenty-six coal miners. Fifteen bodies were recovered; those of the other eleven men will never be returned to their loved ones. They remain interred in the now-flooded mine. In the months and years after the explosion, the Westray saga attracted a huge amount of public attention. It did so not just because the outcome was a tragedy, but also because the behaviour of the central actors was sleazy beyond belief. What we find is that the enterprise involved used the corporate form to avoid legal and moral responsibilities.

The commission of inquiry set up afterwards to fathom what had happened found that the operators had been heedless of, and reckless in respect of, health and safety requirements. The finding did not surprise anyone, because by the time the commission began its hearings it had been revealed that, in its short period of operation, the mine had suffered a series of cave-ins and technicians had recorded a large number of above-acceptable levels of methane gas readings (methane

being a very explosive gas). As well, it was known that the coal-mine owners had been found to have committed fifty-two violations of the provincial safety regulations prior to the explosion. The government had dispatched inspectors, as its health and safety law required, but, while the Department of Labour had dutifully recorded the violations, it had not seen fit to bring any charges against the mine-owners and/or its managers. From this perspective, the explosion was a totally predictable event. It would be misleading to characterize such a predictable outcome as an "accident," yet that is how it is conventionally viewed. The obscenity of that characterization is exacerbated by another feature of the story: after public monies had been funnelled into private actors' pockets, those actors had drawn a corporate veil over their heads and simply disappeared from *legal* sight when authorities and others concerned sought to pin down responsibility for this predictable event.

Source: *Wealth by Stealth*, Copyright 2002 Harry Glasbeek. Published by Between the Lines. Used with permission.

---

the costs are socialized (see also Box 8.3).

Although in theory everyone is treated equally before the law, it is primarily those with money and influence who can get the best lawyers and present the strongest cases. Indeed, at all stages of the justice system—who gets arrested, who gets charged, who gets probation, who gets convicted, and how long the sentence is—socioeconomic status, in addition to the variables of race and gender, plays a role (Samuelson 1995; Brannigan 1984). An apt title of a popular book on the criminal justice system in the United States is *The Rich Get Richer and the Poor Get Prison* (Reiman 2006). We shall look at this issue in more detail in Chapter 10. It should also be noted that in every society, including Canada, the police and other members of the repressive state apparatus are almost immune from prosecution regarding criminal acts carried out in the course of their occupational activities.

The repressive state apparatus also keeps watch over the behaviour of the population. It may come as a surprise that Canada has a long history of spying on its citizens. While every country has some form of spy agency, the activities of Canada's secret police have always been more secretive than most (Kinsman et al. 2000, 2). In theory, the purpose of citizen surveillance is to protect the state and its citizens from any threat. In reality, the RCMP, and later CSIS (the Canadian Security and Intelligence Service), has deemed anyone who even mildly challenges the status quo—because of either political or personal activities—to be a potential threat to the state. In 2007 it was revealed that during the 1970s Canadians were also spied on by agents of a foreign country, the U.S. Central Intelligence Agency.

Over the last century national security surveillance in Canada has included spying on trade unions, left-wing political groups, Quebec sovereigntists, First Nations people, peace activists, gays and lesbians, feminists, consumer housewives' associations, high school students, university students and professors, black community activists, and immigrants. Files have been kept on hundreds of thousands of Canadians, very few of whom could actually be considered a threat to national security. The keeping of such records may make many of us wary of attending a rally, joining a political organization, or even signing a petition.

Think About It
Why do few of us seem to care about governments spying on us?

The issue of the state being able to spy on its citizens has become even more worrying in recent years as a result of new technologies. For example, many cities in Canada are currently expanding use of closed circuit television cameras (CCTC) on city streets. These cameras have been used extensively in Great Britain since 1994, and on a typical day, someone may be captured by cameras as many as 300 times. Many question their large cost, their invasion of privacy, and their limited ability to reduce crime (Contenta 2007). Others are concerned about the creation of a new "security-industrial complex," that is, the joining together of private data and technology companies with the repressive state apparatus, supposedly in the pursuit of terrorists. Few of us are aware that every time we use a cellphone, computer, and a debit or credit card, we leave a record; our profile can be purchased by anyone for a small price (O'Harrow Jr. 2005).

The law and the courts are another means of constraining dissent, and the judicial system in Canada has repeatedly been used to punish those who have opposed the ruling class or simply the status quo. Police have commonly been used to harass strikers, attack protesters, and—as undercover agents—undermine legitimate dissent. In 1970, the Liberal cabinet of Pierre Trudeau—without seeking the approval of Parliament or even its own party ranks—invoked the War Measures Act, a powerful piece of legislation that removed the civil rights of all Canadians, to deal with a supposed "apprehended insurrection" by the Front de Libération du Québec (FLQ). Evidence was later presented that the hardcore of the FLQ consisted of only a few dozen members, including a number of RCMP infiltrators. Of the more than 450 detained under the War Measures Act, few were ever charged with any offence (Finkel et al. 1993, 528).

A number of analysts have noted the recent advance of this process, referred to as the *criminalization of dissent*. While the repressive apparatus of the state has always been used to control those who oppose the existing power structure, the tendency to repress and criminalize dissenting voices has been increasing in Canada and around the world. This trend was first observed in Canada in 1997, when the RCMP used pepper spray to suppress a small group of peaceful protesters in Vancouver. The protesters, mostly students, were opposing the repressive policies of the then president of Indonesia, who was visiting Canada for an international meeting. Since that time, observers have noted that the RCMP, as well as provincial and municipal police forces, have all increased their repression of legitimate dissent.

The process of criminalizing dissent took a giant leap forward at the end of 2001, when the Canadian government, in line with many governments around the world, passed extremely repressive and anti-democratic legislation in the wake of the attacks on the World Trade Center and the Pentagon in September of that year. Although the new legislation was passed allegedly to protect Canadians from the risks of terrorism, most analysts agreed that pre-existing Canadian law would have been more than sufficient to deal with a real threat. The fear of many civil libertarians and lawyers specializing in criminal law has been that this legislation gave widely expanded powers to the repressive state apparatus, while restricting the civil rights of all Canadians (Daniels et al. 2001). One particular concern is that the definition of what constitutes terrorism is so vague and its sweep so broad, that it can potentially include certain forms of legitimate dissent.

Think About It

Did you know that one of the few people to ever be granted honorary citizenship in Canada, Nelson Mandela, spent twenty-eight years in a South African jail for terrorist activities as a member of the African National Congress? Have you considered that any Canadian today who actively supports liberation movements similar to the ANC in the 1970s could be charged under Canada's anti-terrorism legislation?

There are also serious concerns about the rights of people accused of terrorist activities. The government can now issue security certificates for individuals with a lower threshold for evidence than was previously required; legislation also allows for arbitrary arrest without the right of traditional legal defence and no right of appeal (Harding 2004, 60). These changes are all in violation of the traditional concepts of the rule of law.

For most of us, these fine points of law would seem to have little relevance to our lives. Indeed, most Canadians probably support strong anti-terrorist legislation, since few will ever be directly affected by it and since people want

Box 8.4 Everyone's Worst Nightmare: The Case of Maher Arar

Maher Arar, a wireless technology consultant, was born in Syria in 1970 and came to Canada with his family at the age of seventeen. He became a Canadian citizen in 1991. On September 26, 2002, while in transit in New York's JFK airport when returning home from a vacation, Arar was detained by U.S. officials and interrogated about alleged links to al-Qaeda. Unbeknownst to Arar, the man who had witnessed the signing of his apartment lease in 1997—the brother of Arar's friend—was under suspicion by U.S. security officials.

Twelve days later, Arar was chained, shackled, and flown to Syria, where he was held in a tiny grave-like cell for over ten months before he was moved to a better cell in a different prison. In Syria, he was beaten, tortured, and forced to make a false confession. Arar's wife campaigned tirelessly on his behalf until he was returned to Canada in October 2003. In early 2004, under pressure from individuals and groups, the government created a commission of inquiry to examine the Arar case.

In 2006, the inquiry cleared Arar of all terrorism allegations. It also concluded, among other things, that the RCMP gave the United States incorrect information about his terrorist leanings, that officials should have known Arar was being tortured, that the RCMP failed to inform the government properly, and that government officials leaked damaging information to the media. Subsequently, three other Muslim Canadian men claimed that they too were tortured in Syria with the help of Canadian security services.

Sources: Maherarar.ca, "We All Have a Right to the Truth," <http://www.maherarar.ca/>; CBCnews, "Maher Arar Timeline," <http://www.cbc.ca/news/background/arar/>; Jim Harding, *After Iraq: War, Imperialism and Democracy*. Halifax: Fernwood, 2004; Jeff Sallot, "How Canada Failed Citizen Maher Arar," *Globe and Mail*, 19 Sept. 2006: A1; Thomas Walkom, "Somebody Should Probe This Man's Case," *Toronto Star*, 7 April 2007 <http://www.thestar.com/News/article/200178>.

to feel assured that the government is protecting our security. But whenever expanded powers are given to the repressive state apparatus, all citizens should be concerned. Any one of us can be arrested unexpectedly or charged with a crime. Perhaps it is a case of mistaken identity, being in the wrong place at the wrong time, or having a friend or relative suspected of criminal activities. Such a possibility increases if we have physical characteristics or national origins that identify us with groups more often thought in these times to be "terrorists." The Maher Arar case (see Box 8.4) was a clear example of what can happen in a so-called civilized society when more power is given to the repressive state apparatus

Forcing governments to be transparent and accountable to their constituents is an essential part of the democratic process. Most people working in government agencies would rather go about their business without having to be accountable to citizens for everything they do or every dollar they spend. This is not necessarily because they are up to something evil, but simply because it takes more time and effort to be certain that every elected government official or public employee is acting within the law and according to accepted policies. It is therefore worrying that Canada has seen an erosion of access to information laws in recent years. In 2006 the Canadian Newspaper Association had sixty journalists from across the country visit various government offices, police forces, and hospitals to find out how public officials would respond to requests for information. Nearly one-third of their requests were denied despite the fact that the information was not controversial and should have been readily available. Some of the requests involved lengthy delays or large fees (Cribb 2006).

> Though we tend to take it for granted, privacy—the right to control access to ourselves and to personal information about us—is at the very core of our lives. It is a fundamental human right precisely because it is an innate human need, an essential condition of our freedom, our dignity and our sense of well-being.
> —George Radwanski, The Privacy Commission of Canada, *Annual Report to Parliament, 2001–02*

History has shown that governments—even those that may be relatively democratic—under certain conditions may arbitrarily move to more repressive forms of rule. Germany under the Third Reich was an extreme example of this process. As a result, any legislation that gives more power to the repressive state apparatus, even if that power isn't immediately evident, should be of concern to all. Dissent is an essential requirement of a democratic society, and without it any country will have moved toward becoming a police state.

What Is Fascism?

Fascism is one of those words that most of us have seen or heard on numerous occasions but could probably not define. At best, we might be able to link it historically to the governments of Germany, Italy, Spain, or Japan that came into power prior to World War II. Perhaps we might see it simply as some kind of dictatorship or autocratic rule. While both these points are partially correct, they are far from giving us the full picture of either the meaning or history of fascism. That is because most of us understand fascism as a political form but do not link it to a particular economic arrangement. However, fascism cannot be understood without linking it to capitalist economies. Stalin's regime in the Soviet Union may have been repressive but it was not fascist (Paxton 2004, 212). And although George W. Bush claimed to be fighting "Islamofascism" in the Middle East, groups such as al-Qaeda do not fit the classic definition.

Fascism is essentially capitalism in its most repressive, undemocratic, and militaristic form. Although the personal lives of ordinary citizens are strictly controlled and there is an obsession with crime and punishment, large corporations are able to operate in relative freedom and gain increasing control over the economy. Put simply, fascist societies are capitalist economies within a police state. As an ideology, fascism emphasizes a strong leader and a strong state, while opposing human rights, democracy, pacifism, and collectivism. It is

197

usually embedded with a notion of racial or ethnic superiority and is linked to some form of intense nationalism; it promotes fear—particularly of the "other"—in the general population. The term *fascism* derives from *i fasci di combattimento*, a movement led by Benito Mussolini that grew following World War I in Italy.

> Fascism should rightly be called corporatism as it is a merger of state and corporate power.
> —Benito Mussolini

We saw earlier in this chapter that the owning class in capitalist societies prefers to rule when possible via a liberal democratic state form. However, there are times in history when this class, for various reasons, has forged alliances with fascist movements that shifted the state from democratic forms of rule to direct repression. This was the case in Italy in the early 1920s, as it was at that time in many other countries, including Germany. When the fascists took state power in these countries—which they were able to do as a result of large-scale financial support from the wealthy and powerful—organized labour was crushed, opposition parties and independent publications were outlawed, and most civil liberties disappeared. Hundreds of thousands of opponents were imprisoned, tortured, or murdered, and in Nazi Germany millions of innocent people were sent to the gas chambers.

Charles Higham (1983) uncovered evidence that it was not simply German capital that supported Hitler, but capital from major American corporations as well. These included General Motors, General Electric, Ford, and Standard Oil, among others. These U.S. corporations continued to provide support to Hitler right through World War II, when Germany was ostensibly America's enemy.

Fascism, while most often connected to Italy and Germany, can actually occur in any capitalist society under certain conditions. Fascism does not develop overnight. Rather, there is a gradual shift from a democratic to an undemocratic form of governance, with the growth of fascist beliefs and values. Since the events of September 11, 2001, a number of analysts in the United States have argued that their country has been slowly shifting to a fascist form. Certainly, the rule of law in that country has increasingly been eroded; patriotism and militarism have escalated; more citizens are being spied on; and the repression of dissent has increased, among other things.

Although fascism is ultimately of benefit to the ruling class, fascist political movements cannot take power without support from a wide section of the middle strata. At certain moments in history, these people—the "middle fish"—feel squeezed economically and are frightened by rapid social change or groups they see as outsiders in their midst. Fascist movements give such people a sense of belonging, of moral certitude in uncertain times, and of protection against supposed "enemies" that have infiltrated their communities. These fascist movements develop long before actually taking state power. Often they remain on the fringes of legitimacy until such time as they win substantial financial and moral support from those with wealth and power.

This chapter has demonstrated that our common-sense understanding of the state—the pluralist view that our governments act in the interests of all citizens—is not borne out by a detailed examination of state activities. While the three levels of government in Canada certainly do many things that benefit the average citizen, the overarching role of the state is to protect the interests of the capitalist ruling class. In the next chapter we shall see how many of the benefits that Canadians have been able to win from their governments over the years are now being eroded. We shall see how this process—happening across the developed capitalist world—must be linked to the recent transformations of capitalist economies in the era of globalization.

Key Points

1. State structures arose with the growth of surplus and the consequent development of classes and exploitation.

2. In capitalist societies, the economic and political spheres come to be separated. The appropriating class gains enormous control over the productive process, while the state is assigned the social, or public, activities formerly carried out directly by the owning class.

3. A number of frameworks explain how states function. The main approach within the order theories is pluralism, while the change theories emphasize the class approach.

4. Pluralism sees the key function of the state as one of mediation, while class analysis sees the state carrying out the accumulation, coercion, and legitimation functions on behalf of the dominant class.

5. While capitalist societies, in general, have been more democratic than pre-capitalist societies, capitalist democracy is, at best, a limited form that must always be understood within the specific class relations of power.

6. Capitalist economies require active intervention from the state.

7. In recent years, there has been a dramatic shift by all levels of government in Canada to more regressive forms of taxation.

8. All levels of government in Canada, regardless of political affiliation, have provided a large degree of financial support—directly or indirectly—to major corporations.

9. The Canadian government supports the military-industrial complex more substantially than many people realize.

10. All capitalist states have a coercion function. No ruling class could retain its power without the ability to resort to the coercive component of the state when necessary.

11. Although all Canadians are, in theory, equal before the law, corporations are not held responsible for criminal activities in the same way as individuals. Moreover, those with money and influence are advantaged within the criminal justice system.

12. There has been a recent increase in the criminalization of dissent in Canada.

13. Capitalism in its most repressive, undemocratic, and militaristic form is referred to as fascism. Any capitalist society can shift to a fascist form if conditions are right.

Further Reading

Brown, Lorne, and Caroline Brown. 1973. *An Unauthorized History of the RCMP.* Toronto: James Lewis & Samuel.
A critical examination of the history of Canada's police, revealing the truth behind one of our most revered icons.

Glasbeek, Harry. 2002. *Wealth by Stealth: Corporate Crime, Corporate Law and the Perversion of Democracy.* Toronto: Between the Lines.
This work explains how owners and investors can legally hide behind corporations, enabling them to carry out heinous acts on the general population with impunity.

Kinsman, Gary, Dieter K. Buse, and Mercedes Steedman, eds. 2000. *Whose National Security? Canadian State Surveillance and the Creation of Enemies.* Toronto: Between the Lines.
This book provides a variety of articles detailing the long history of surveillance activities of the Canadian government, which has regularly and extensively spied on any citizen deemed to be a security threat.

Panitch, Leo, and Donald Swartz. 2003. *From Consent to Coercion: The Assault on Trade Union Freedoms*, 3rd ed. Aurora, ON: Garamond.
This book provides concrete examples of the ways various governments have shifted toward coercion of the labour movement in Canada. Proposals for change are offered.

Parenti, Christian. 1999. *Lockdown America: Police and Prisons in the Age of Crisis.* London: Verso.
The author does an excellent job of showing how penal and policing policies in the United States are used to maintain class societies.

Parenti, Michael. 2008. *Democracy for the Few*, 8th ed. Belmont, CA: Wadsworth.
Although the data are American, Parenti's book is a highly relevant and readable examination of the link between economic ownership and political power.

9 Neoliberalism and Globalization

In This Chapter
- What is meant by the term *welfare state*?
- What is neoliberalism, and how did it lead to the decline of the welfare state?
- What is the relationship between nation-states and global institutions such as the World Trade Organization or the United Nations?
- What are some of the tensions that have resulted from the process of globalization?

The argument was made in the previous chapter that the state is a class-based institution, generally giving priority to the interests of the class with economic power. And yet it is obvious that the three levels of government in Canada often do things that benefit the rest of us. In the developed capitalist world, this is partly because all governments have to legitimate the overall class system to maintain stability and ensure the continuity of class relations. If they supported only the ruling class, no capitalist society would last for long. However, in the last half of the twentieth century Canadians won many additional rights and benefits. It is therefore important to take a closer look at the reasons for the rise in government social supports in Canada following World War II, and why such supports began to decline starting in the 1970s.

The Erosion of the Commons
Despite the fact that we live in a capitalist society—one in which the concept of private ownership of property is central—there are still a great many areas of life that have remained in the public domain. These areas have traditionally been considered out of bounds for private ownership or trade because they have been accepted as collective property, existing for everyone to share as they have for millennia. These elements are sometimes described as **the commons**.

This term, as noted in Chapter 4, was used in feudal Europe to describe the public grazing lands shared by all until the feudal aristocracy enclosed them in the eighteenth century to secure personal profits. However, this term has been revived in recent years. Today, the commons includes such natural elements as the air we breathe, the water we drink, the oceans, and the genetic matter of living things. It also includes our public spaces, our shared languages and culture, our informal community support systems, and modern technological developments such as the broadcast spectrum and the Internet.

As capitalism advanced, some components of the commons transferred to private ownership. In many parts of the world, the commonly held lands of indigenous peoples were stolen from them and transferred to private individuals or companies. For example, the Canadian Pacific Railway was granted huge tracts of land in the nineteenth century by the Canadian government, lands formerly held by indigenous peoples across the country. In spite of this trend, many peoples around the world remained outside of capitalist development and continued to survive through communal sharing of land and other natural resources.

Even in the developed capitalist world, many elements of society remained in the public domain and were socially valued. Governments of all levels in Canada built bridges, roads, tunnels, harbours, government buildings, public schools, libraries, water filtration plants, and so on. Many of these public works projects are renowned today as major architectural accomplishments of their time. In addition, many parks, beaches, and other Crown lands were kept from private development. The commons also includes activities undertaken by various levels of the state to serve the public good, such as health care, education, sewage and water treatment, as well as care of the elderly, the poor, the unemployed, and so on.

Think About It

Graffiti artist Banksy has argued that it is corporate advertising that defaces our buildings and buses, while graffiti artists are actually trying to respond to these ads. Do you think that graffiti art is an attack on the commons, or, as Banksy argues, are they subversive political statements about the erosion of public spaces?

After the 1970s, the privatization and commodification of the commons became a major component of government policies, as we shall see later in this chapter. Many Crown corporations—such as Air Canada, CN Rail, and PetroCanada—were sold to private companies at very low prices, and the management of some public corporations and spaces was also handed over to private companies. Many other aspects of the commons formerly thought of as unacceptable for private ownership or trade have now been transferred into the capitalist marketplace. This trend has happened both within Canada and across the globe.

The Growth of the Welfare State

There was a short period during the latter half of the twentieth century when it seemed as if the commons—particularly with respect to its social aspects—was expanding and that governments were taking the interests of their citizens more seriously. It was a time of relative economic stability and improved living conditions for many in the developed capitalist world. It is for these reasons that the period between approximately 1946 and 1971 is sometimes referred to as the "golden age of capitalism" even though it was far from "golden" for everybody.

Nonetheless, it was during this period that the global economy expanded dramatically. The transnational corporation appeared on the scene and grew in size and dominance. The most powerful of the TNCs were based in the United States, although Germany and Japan became key players as well. The power of these new economic giants went far beyond the merely economic. With mass production and the global expansion of consumer goods came the spread of American advertising and American culture, and culturally related products from the United States (such as films, television shows, and popular music) became their largest area of export. Economic globalization led to cultural globalization.

During this period, what is commonly referred to as the *welfare state* expanded rapidly. That is, the Canadian state took a greater role as a provider and protector of individual well-being and security. The growth of the welfare state involved the expansion of the **social wage**. When we hear the term "wage," most of us automatically think of money we receive directly from our employer, which we then use to purchase the things we need. But there is another way that we can acquire the things we need. The social wage is part of the surplus value produced by workers, transferred to the state in the form of taxes and then given back to workers, not in the form of money, but through the provision of social necessities such as health care, education, unemployment insurance, old-age pensions, and so on. The state provides these services to us collectively rather than us having to purchase them in the private marketplace. If we receive something as part of the social wage (such as our health benefits), then we don't have to pay for them out of our real wages. The term *social wage* is useful because it reminds us that the funding for these social benefits comes mainly from the productive activities of working people. It also reminds us that it can be worthwhile to pay taxes to the government if the major part of it is returned to us in the form of needed services.

Think About It

Can you think of anything that is not currently part of the social wage in Canada that might be worth having? (Here's one to get you started: free postsecondary education and grants for all qualified students.)

The obvious question that must be asked here is why the capitalist owning class—if the analysis of the previous chapter is correct—would suddenly have agreed to having a larger share of government funds transferred back to the workers, rather than continuing to resist any expansion of the social wage as they did in the early twentieth century.

To make sense of this change of heart on the part of capital, it is important to understand the context in which it occurred. We must also recall that the owning class has both long-term and short-term goals. While the short-term goal is profit maximization, the long-term goal is maintenance of the system that allows it to secure its profits. It is this long-term goal that is of particular importance here. There were a number of serious problems that capitalists faced following World War II. One serious concern was the expansion and consolidation of the socialist world. Suddenly, the capitalist part of the world had to face the reality that the other (now expanded) part was trying to build a social system not dominated by capital. In a sense, the capitalist owning class had to prove that "its" system was the better of the two, and the expanding social wage was one means of legitimating capitalist rule.

In addition, workers in the capitalist world were putting pressure on governments to help them. Many had just fought in defence of their country and now thought their country owed them something in return. Even those who hadn't actually gone overseas had suffered through a long depression and then lived through the deprivations of a wartime economy. Citizens had high expectations of their governments. Employers, on the other hand, needed these individuals—relatively "de-politicized" and eager to work—to fill the jobs in a rapidly expanding postwar economy. In this context, the capitalist owning class and organized sector of the working class reached what has been termed an "accord."

The main underpinning of this accord was an agreement that the state would act as a mediator in the struggle between capital and labour. Corporate leaders agreed—grudgingly and in a limited way—to recognize greater rights for workers and citizens and to accept the labour movement's demands for higher wages, collective bargaining rights, and an increase in the social wage. The labour movement, in return, agreed to accept the control of employers over production and investment, to confine class struggle primarily to collective bargaining in the workplace, and to isolate or expel radicals from their midst. They also agreed to work toward social reforms within capitalist political and economic structures instead of struggling for any type of more radical alteration of the capitalist system.

Organized labour saw this accord as a great victory. In the ten years following World War II, union membership in Canada rose from 24.2 percent of the non-agricultural workforce to 33.7 percent. Fringe benefits—including pensions, paid holidays, shorter work weeks, sick pay, and disability benefits—became more common for workers, and seniority became the key for distributing job-related benefits (Fudge and Tucker 2001, 303–4). In addition, the low unemployment rates through the 1950s and 1960s gave workers more power because of their ability to negotiate improved wages and working conditions with their employers (Black 1998, 80). However, as a result of the accord, unions became more mainstream and less radical.

At the same time that the state took a greater role in regulating workers, it also increasingly regulated capital. The notion of state regulation, known as **Keynesianism** after British economist John Maynard Keynes (1883–1946), led to greater state intervention in the economy. Keynes was no socialist; after the crisis of the Great Depression in the 1930s, he and other economists argued that increased state intervention in capitalist economies was necessary to protect them from their own excesses, to control for the inevitable crisis of overproduction, and to reduce the instability created by capitalist business cycles. Following World War II, the owning class was more willing to agree to a Keynesian welfare state. The booming economy and growing productivity resulting from new technologies meant that profits could rise even as workers were able to get a bigger share of the social surplus. Indeed, the social safety net, creating healthier and happier workers, could actually help raise productivity.

Of course, every country has its own unique history, and the degree to which each country adopted Keynesian policies and expanded the welfare state varies. Europe, particularly the Scandinavian countries, saw a much expanded social safety net, while the United States scarcely developed a safety net at all. While it is impossible here to detail all the reasons for the differences, the political strength of the working class in each of these countries was certainly a key variable in its ability to win social supports from the state.

Neoliberalism and the Decline of the Welfare State

Unfortunately, greater government intervention in the economy could not permanently eliminate the contradictions of capitalist economies. By the mid-1970s, the so-called golden age came to a rapid end as capitalism entered a permanent state of economic crisis. As a result, the ruling class tried ever harder to increase the rate of profit by introducing new technologies, downsizing corporations, merging, seeking additional benefits from national governments, and advancing globalization. New computer-based and microelectronic technologies gave many TNCs increasing geographical flexibility and the ability to truly globalize—that is, to move capital to those global sites with the most favourable conditions for profitability.

In this context, the accord between corporate employers and organized labour collapsed. Starting in the mid-1970s, inflation—in which the cost of commodities, including money itself, increases—became a chronic problem in much of the capitalist world, and inflation increased the debt load for governments. For the corporate elite, inflation is always a concern, not only because it fuels worker demands for higher wages, but also because it raises the cost of borrowing money. During this period, most capitalist governments shifted away from Keynesian policies to a new set of economic and political policies that were more favourable to the needs of major corporations. The combination of increasing rates of unemployment, stagnating wages, and growing global competition weakened the ability of workers to respond to the power of capital.

This new set of policies is referred to as **neoliberalism**. Neoliberalism is the rejection of the Keynesian welfare state and its replacement with free-market doctrines and practices. It is, in essence, the political side of the economic transformations discussed in Chapter 6, the alteration of political structures to fit the needs of global capital. The current period of global competition requires that capital institute an all-out assault on workers and ordinary people to protect its own interests.

The term *neoliberalism* links this approach to classical liberalism, such as that of Jeremy Bentham and John Stuart Mill, which saw government's role as minimal, the market as the central determinant of social values, and the individual as the core unit of society. When she was prime minister of Great Britain, Margaret Thatcher went so far as to state that "there is no such thing as society. There are individual men and women and there are families." However, although neoliberalism expressed strong opposition to government intervention, it was, ironically, national governments that advanced the neoliberal agenda. According to one author (McQuaig 1992, 13), the underlying goal of this agenda was straightforward: it was simply a massive transfer of wealth and power to the corporate sector.

For the average Canadian, this has meant a rapid decline in the social wage. For example, in 2001 Canada spent 11 percent of its gross domestic product (GDP) to help those in financial need, down from 14.3 percent in 1992. Health care spending fell from 7.3 percent of GDP in 1992 to 7 percent in 2001, while education spending fell in the same period from 7.7 percent of GDP to 5.9 percent (Little 2003). Canada now ranks last among developed nations in spending on early childhood development (Rushowy 2007). As government supports have declined, particularly for the economically disadvantaged, there has been a widening gap between the rich and poor, as we will see in the next chapter.

There are a number of distinct but interconnected components to neo-liberalism, which have been enforced around the world via what have been termed **structural adjustment policies**. These policies were implemented by the World Bank and the International Monetary Fund. Their purpose—in theory to help poorer nations advance their economies and to create a single global market—is actually to increase the private accumulation of capital on a global scale. Governments around the world have been pressured to remove any restrictions that they have placed on TNCs; to increase productivity and lower wages by disciplining workers; and to provide new sources of investment that help deal with the global excess of capital.

It is impossible in the short space of this chapter to give a detailed picture of all the elements that constitute the neoliberal agenda. However, a few key policy components of this process (adapted from Teeple 2000, and McBride and Shields 1997) will be presented here:

- *"Free trade," global trading blocs, and international treaties.* As capital internation-alizes, it requires economic rules and regulations that are international as well. Although they are often called "trade rules," they are really about the free movement of capital. Any legislation that gives protection to specific countries or individuals is weakened or eliminated. Global non-elected bodies such as the World Trade Organization increasingly set limits on decisions

Table 9.1 The Public-Private Continuum in Canada

Fully Public	Contracted Out	P3s	Privatized
The people own and have stewardship over a public asset, through their local, provincial or federal governments.	Components of a public asset or service are handed to a private party, who operates the service for a profit.	Government agrees to pay a private partner to fund, build, and/or operate a facility or service that would normally have been in the public domain.	Governments sell a public institution to the private sector for its own use and profit.
A. Citizens have a say in determining how the facility or service is built, funded, operated and made accountable.	A. Private partner accountability is limited to meeting its contractual obligations. The private partner is not accountable to the public.	A. Accountability of the private partner is limited to meeting its contractual obligations. The private partner is not accountable to the public.	A. Private owners are not accountable to the public except through laws, the courts, etc.
W. Workers are usually unionized and paid family-sustaining wages.	W. Workers are less likely to be unionized or paid a family-sustaining wage.	W. Workers risk being shifted into non-union or low-paying variations of their old jobs.	W. Vast disparity between low-waged workers and corporate CEOs.
$$ No profit made by the private sector.	$$ Some public money goes to private profit.	$$ Profits to the private sector are often guaranteed.	$$ Unlimited.
E. Most existing Canadian schools, hospitals and public works facilities.	E. Services like janitorial, laundry, or payroll.	E. A growing number of new schools, hospitals, and public works facilities.	E. Some facilities or services that were formerly Crown corporations or otherwise in the public domain, such as B.C. Gas, Air Canada, C.N. Rail, some health services in Alberta.

A. = Accountability, W. = Workers and wages, $$ = Profit potential, E. = Examples
Source: Adapted from "The True Cost of P3s," Canadian Centre for Policy Alternatives, April 2003.

that can be made by nation-states.

- *Privatization.* Privatization involves selling off various aspects of the commons. The push to privatize sectors of the economy formerly under state control is part of the corporate sector's need to find new sources for investment. This is particularly true in the areas of health and education, where billions of dollars stand to be made as various components are shifted to for-profit services. Governments don't always fully privatize a sector, but, rather, create public private partnerships or P3s (see Table 9.1). At their core, P3s allow corporations to make large profits while governments absorb most of the financial risks.

- *Deregulation.* Rules and regulations of national governments that were created to protect citizens or limit the rights of corporations are either eroded or removed entirely. This includes legislation that protects workers, the environment, or national industries, and laws that keep capital—particularly international capital—from maximizing profits.
- *Decline in the social wage.* Government funding to many social programs is cut drastically. This includes spending on health care, education, old-age pensions, and various forms of social assistance such as welfare. It can also include cuts to public support for the arts. Eligibility for many benefits is severely tightened and the universality of certain programs is eliminated.
- *Shift from government support to charities.* Help for the poor and the sick, as well as support for education and the arts is increasingly via voluntary, tax-deductible "gifts" rather than the social wage. Charities, unlike government services, can be selective in what or whom they choose to support.
- *Tax reforms.* Changes to taxation are instituted that primarily benefit the rich and large corporations. Governments increasingly turn to regressive forms of taxation (such as sales tax and user-pay schemes) while cutting income tax, the most progressive form of taxation. Initially, tax reforms put small amounts of money in the pockets of ordinary working people. However, the privatization of government services and increases in regressive forms of taxation ultimately mean less income for the average person.
- *Attack on labour.* Legislation protecting workers and the workplace—for example, union rights, minimum wages, employment standards, and worker health and safety—is weakened or removed entirely. This process increases profits by reducing the cost of production, increasing the intensity of labour, and restraining labour activism.
- *Decline in democracy and civil rights.* Sweeping new legislation is created that gives vastly expanded powers to the repressive state apparatus, while legislation that protects the individual from arbitrary measures on the part of the state is weakened. Police become less accountable, while access to information about government activities declines. Funding cuts are made to human rights organizations, legal aid services, and groups defending the rights of the disadvantaged.
- *Decrease in the size and scope of the state.* As all the processes noted above occur, the size of the state sector declines. Any state function that does not further the ability of corporations to secure their profits is seen as "waste." As a result, governments reduce the number of agencies, and the number of workers in the public sector declines. The exception is the repressive state apparatus—including the police and prison system—which expands.

There are also a number of aspects of neoliberalism that are specific to Canada. Two important elements are these:

- *Increasing integration with the United States.* Our economy and our military are ever more closely tied to the United States and its interests. In addition, Canada's social, political, cultural, and economic institutions are becoming increasingly similar to those of the United States. Canadian sovereignty in all spheres declines.

- *Transformation of the relationship between the federal state and the provinces.* The role of the Canadian government in protecting Canadian institutions, balancing inequalities among the provinces, and promoting sovereignty declines. More independence is granted to the provinces, which may then advance their own neoliberal agendas. However, certain federal powers—specifically those that enhance corporate interests—are actually strengthened, as national governments must now ensure that provinces comply with the rules of economic agreements such as the North American Free Trade Agreement (NAFTA) and those enforced by the World Trade Organization.

While the elements of neoliberalism have been separated out here for the purposes of analysis, it should be made clear they are all are interconnected. For example, with regard to postsecondary education, both the federal and provincial governments made massive funding cuts through the 1990s, a decrease in the social wage. As universities and colleges faced reduced funding, they successfully appealed to governments to totally, or partially, deregulate tuition fees. As a result, tuition fees at most Canadian universities skyrocketed, while postsecondary institutions began to spend increasing amounts of time and money on private fundraising. Postsecondary education increasingly became market-driven, with most universities and colleges now advertising to attract students and research dollars. Faculty spend more and more time writing research proposals because there is less money to go around and find themselves working harder in an increasingly competitive environment.

It should also be noted that while neoliberalism meets the needs of the corporate sector *in general*, there can be occasional disputes and differences between different sectors of capital on specific issues. For example, a number of provinces have already, or plan to, deregulate and privatize the provision of electricity and natural gas. This might be very profitable for those who may come to control that industry, as well as those in the financial and legal sectors who stand to make millions through the sale of shares of newly privatized companies in the marketplace. However, those industries that use large amounts of energy in production may be uneasy about the likely increase in their costs, as well as the possible instability of delivery. As a result of tensions between different sectors of capital, neoliberalism does not advance in a straightforward and simplistic manner.

Nonetheless, as globalization proceeds, governments around the world, regardless of the party in power, have been under pressure to adopt at least some of the components of the neoliberal agenda. Canadians find themselves in a particularly difficult position regarding this agenda. On the one hand, since Canada borders the United States and is its biggest trading partner, there is strong pressure to adopt these policies in an effort to harmonize the economies of the two countries. On the other hand, as a result of its distinct geography and history, Canada has always had greater dependency on state intervention as well as values that supported such intervention.

Think About It
Do you think Canadians have a different attitude than Americans to changes brought about by the neoliberal agenda?

Thus there is an ongoing tension between the traditional expectations Canadians have about the role of their governments and the new assumptions of a minimalist state that are part of the neoliberal agenda (McBride and Shields 1997, 31–32). However, few countries have been able to resist the global drive toward neoliberalism. Most countries, whether they want to or not, have increasingly adapted to the needs of the corporate ruling class.

Selling the Corporate Agenda to Canadians

Despite the fact that the state generally promotes the corporate agenda, the welfare state that expanded in the so-called golden age of capitalism certainly did provide many benefits to ordinary Canadians. How does the state subsequently cut back on such things as unemployment insurance, health care, public education, workers' rights, and care for disadvantaged groups? Why didn't more Canadians protest these cuts? If people are going to accept an erosion of their standard of living and an attack on those things they hold dear, they must be convinced that such cuts are being done in the name of a higher good and that everyone will ultimately benefit from such activities.

Starting in the mid-1970s, Canadians were bombarded with various messages from business and government leaders, as well as corporate-supported think tanks such as the C.D. Howe Institute and the Fraser Institute. In the Trudeau era, the main issue was the high wages of workers that were supposedly the root cause of inflation. By the 1980s, the key issue became huge government deficits that Canadians were told were going to destroy the future for young Canadians. Indeed, governments and businesses became seized with "deficit-mania" until 1997, by which time most governments had eliminated their deficits. Along with the deficit scare came the attack on public services, which people came to believe were inefficiently run by lazy and overpaid civil servants, followed by an intensive and prolonged campaign to promote tax cuts. All of these campaigns had a specific goal: to lower the expectations of Canadians about what the state could do for them (Dobbin 1998).

Many myths were advanced to sell this negative view of the state to Canadians. One of the biggest myths, still being advanced to this day, was that the Canadian government had been spending too much on social benefits. The data simply do not bear this out. As noted in the previous chapter, Canada allocates less for social spending than most developed capitalist countries (OECD 2006).

Moreover, when comparing two ways of funding health care, Canada's largely public system actually costs far less and is more effective than the privately run system in the United States (*CCPA Monitor*, May 2002, 16).

The intense and constant promotion of the neoliberal agenda must be understood as part of the ideological hegemony of the dominant class in capitalist societies. It is not that Canadians are too dimwitted to understand their real interests. Rather, if people are repeatedly told by supposed "experts" that something is true, they are apt to believe it, at least in the short run, particularly if the issues are complex and the alternative view is not readily available.

However, ideological mystification can mask reality only to a certain extent. While Canadians may have accepted cuts to social spending in general during the 1980s and 1990s, they increasingly opposed further erosion of public services, particularly publicly funded health care. Unfortunately, the areas of health, labour legislation, and education are under provincial jurisdiction in Canada. Thus a number of provincial governments have been able to advance aspects of the neoliberal agenda while few citizens understand the implications. Moreover, with many people facing longer work hours, more stress, and stagnating wages, there is simply no time in their lives to be involved in political activities.

> [A] large part of my message as a politician is to say: we have to put an end to rising expectations. We have to explain to people that we may even have to put an end to our love for our parents or old people in society, even our desire to give more for education or medical research.
> —Prime Minister Pierre Trudeau, 1977

Globalization and the Changing Role of the State

The rapid expansion of globalization has forced social scientists to rethink the role of the nation-state in developed capitalist societies. In the past, the Canadian state has traditionally played an important role in nation building, in mediating squabbles between and within classes, in moderating the worst excesses of capital, and in promoting the specific interests of Canadian-based corporations. Social scientists are now debating the extent to which the state will be able to continue to play this type of role. Some theorists feel that the power of nation-states will weaken; others feel that nation-states will align themselves more closely with international capital, so that their role will change rather than decline.

In order to make sense of the changing role of the state, we should recall that, as explained in Chapter 4, the capitalist owning class has always had the need to expand beyond its own national borders. Capital moves around the globe to maximize profits, and those who own and control it turn to governments to help in that quest. Economic domination requires political and military domination, so capitalists turn to their governments for support. As capital expands around the world in an attempt to increase the rate of profit, the most dominant nation-states gain control over the economies of other nation-states. This is why it is more accurate to speak of the process as imperialism rather than globalization. In the eighteenth and nineteenth centuries, England and the countries of Western Europe became the dominant imperial powers as they colonized many countries around the world. Direct colonial rule ended in the second half of the twentieth century, but most nations remained economically dependent on the larger players in the global economy.

Thus globalization is not a recent phenomenon, nor is it a benign and inevitable process resulting from the expansion of trade. What has changed in the past half-century is that new technologies have allowed capital to move around the world in greater volumes and at faster speeds than ever before. While England and the Western European states were the dominant imperial powers in the nineteenth and early twentieth centuries, the United States became the pre-eminent imperial power, or empire, following World War II.

We saw in the last chapter that two key functions of the state are those of accumulation and coercion. As capital becomes increasingly global, both of these functions must be redirected to a certain extent from nation-states to organizations that are themselves global in scale. With regard to the accumulation function, a number of such bodies play a central role in advancing the needs of global capital. With regard to the repression function, the United States military has become the world's police officer. Both of these points require some understanding of the key role played by the United States, beginning in the second half of the twentieth century.

The United States as Global Superpower

From the period following World War II until the fall of the Berlin Wall in 1989, the world spoke of two contending superpowers, the United States and the Soviet Union. However, in the decade that followed the fall of the Berlin Wall and the subsequent break-up of the Soviet Union, it became clear that the Soviet Union had never been a match—economically, politically, or militarily—for the United States. In reality, the last half of the twentieth century was dominated by only one global superpower, and that power has continued into the twenty-first century.

Prior to World War II, corporations usually turned to their governments for economic and military support as they expanded globally. However, the competition between these nations as each promoted their own spheres of influence inevitably led to outcomes—including internal economic problems and international wars—that were destructive not only to human life and property, but also to capital itself. In the same way that workers and employers within countries reached an accord following World War II, corporations also needed to reach an accord with each other so that the global capitalist economy could continue to expand without nation-based corporations destroying each other in the competitive marketplace. This New World Order, as it came to be called, was dominated by the United States.

At first, the United States government mainly represented U.S. capitalist interests. However, as corporations gradually merged to form transnational corporations, the U.S. government increasingly came to represent capital as a whole as well. Global capital now shared a common set of interests that went beyond narrow national interests, and the key goal was to create a single world economy of competing corporations (Teeple 2000, 54). The government of the United States played a central role in creating global structures that would advance that goal.

The Role of Global Institutions

In 1995, David Korten published a book entitled *When Corporations Rule the World*. In it he argued that the interests of the corporate ruling class were coming to dominate the world, with negative consequences for the average citizen. How did this happen? In Chapter 5 we saw the ways capital tries to coordinate its activities through such organizations as the Council on Foreign Relations, the Bilderberg Group, and the Trilateral Commission. As was noted in that chapter, these organizations are not the outcome of some "secret plot" on the part of those with power, but rather reflect their need to act collectively on the basis of their shared class interests.

The post–World War II period saw the creation of a number of international agencies—dominated by the United States—that reflected the desire of capital to create global political, economic, and military structures as well as policies. On the military side, the United States became the dominant force in the North Atlantic Treaty Organization (NATO), formed in 1949 as the international agency to coordinate military operations of the North American and European powers. On the political side, the United Nations was created as an umbrella organization to help coordinate the activities of nation-states. While in theory it was a democratic body representing all nations of the world, in reality its structure gave dominance to the United States. Moreover, the U.N. was financially dependent on the United States, as were most of its member nations. The global economic dominance of the United States thus came to be reflected in its global political and military dominance as well.

On the economic side, a number of global agencies and institutions were created in the second half of the twentieth century. Recommendations from the Council on Foreign Relations led to the Bretton Woods conference in 1944, at which the World Bank and the International Monetary Fund (IMF) were created. Their goal was to help stabilize and integrate world economies, to develop programs that would allow for greater capital investment in the less-developed countries, and to create an international monetary system that would improve global capital flow. In recent years, both the World Bank and the IMF have played a key role in imposing structural adjustment programs on the less-developed countries.

The World Trade Organization

Throughout this book we have talked about power existing in both the proximal (nearby) realm and the distal (distant) realm. One of the most powerful organizations in the distal realm in recent years has probably been the World Trade Organization (WTO). The WTO was established in 1995 as an international body

---

Box 9.1 Opposition to the WTO

Many individuals and groups have opposed the activities of the World Trade Organization. The main criticisms are as follows:

- The WTO is not a democratic organization. Members to the body are not elected, and its hearings on trade disputes are closed to the public and the media.
- The WTO is too powerful. It has been given a mandate to compel sovereign states to change their country's laws because they are in violation of free trade rules.
- The WTO is biased against poorer countries. Countries in the developing world have found that protectionist policies in much of the developed world, particularly with regard to agriculture, have prevented their products from competing fairly in the global economy. Many developed countries also provide large subsidies to their farmers. For example, between 2001 and 2005, the U.S. government spent $42.7 billion a year on various farm support programs (Reynolds 2007).
- The United States ignores WTO rulings when it chooses. This happened with the softwood lumber dispute between Canada and the United States—the United States lost several rulings at the WTO but refused to implement the decisions.
- The WTO has ignored the impact of its policies on child labour, the environment, and workers' rights.

As a result of such concerns, the WTO found itself in 2007 still unable to conclude the Doha Round of talks, begun in 2002, that were supposed to further expand the global economy. Whether the WTO will eventually conclude these talks and expand its mandate over time remains to be seen.

---

that would effectively set the rules for global trade and investment. While few of us know much about this organization, it is having an enormous influence on our communities and our everyday lives.

Currently 150 countries, including Canada, are members. However, the real decision-making power lies primarily with the United States, the European Union, and Japan. The WTO is the administrator of a number of treaties that govern world trade, including the General Agreement on Tariffs and Trade (GATT), the General Agreement on Trade in Agriculture, and the General Agreement on Trade in Services (GATS). The WTO is in some ways the world's highest judicial and legislative body, with the powers of an international state. Its agenda is very clear—to open the entire world to the TNCs so that they can maximize profits, without constraints from laws or procedures of nation-states that might put limits on corporate goals. Not only is the WTO closely linked to a number of big-business coalitions, but in many cases the WTO rules have actually been written directly by global corporations themselves.

While the World Trade Organization is clearly an effort on the part of big business to reconfigure world economies to its benefit, the competition between various groups—particularly companies within nations—continues. Large corporations still press their national governments to support them in the increasingly competitive global marketplace at the same time as governments are feeling the pressure to endorse free trade and the promotion of a variety of global bodies. Thus while the creation of various international agencies has helped minimize the worst effects of capitalist economies, including global wars, for more than sixty years, the underlying contradictions now seem to be escalating once again.

This tension can be seen clearly when one examines some decisions of the U.S. government under George W. Bush. On the one hand, the U.S. government was instrumental in pushing for the expansion of free trade and promoting organizations such as the WTO. However, while demanding the removal of trade barriers around the world, Bush increasingly protected U.S.-based industries from foreign competitors and opted out of many global agreements. For example, the U.S. government refused to sign the Kyoto Protocol on climate change, refused to sign the treaty banning anti-personnel mines, rejected the Comprehensive Nuclear Test Ban Treaty, and unilaterally withdrew from the Anti-Ballistic Missile Treaty that it had signed in 1972. It has also refused to become part of the International World Court and voted in the U.N. General Assembly to oppose limitations on both biological warfare and weapons in space.

At the same time that it became more independent in its economic and political policies, the United States became more aggressive in its global military activities. The escalation of such activities increased rapidly following the attacks on the World Trade Center and the Pentagon in 2001, but the strategies advancing such activities were first proposed many decades earlier. In 2003 the United States, with only a few allies and without support from the U.N. Security Council, began the war in Iraq. This demonstrated that the United States was going to ignore international decision-making bodies in the military sphere just as it already had in the economic and political spheres.

The United States as Global Police Officer

As noted throughout this chapter, the second half of the twentieth century saw the rapid expansion of the global economy, primarily to meet the needs of capital. Transnational corporations arose and rapidly expanded both in size and geographical reach, while international agencies were created to oversee and structure the new economic order. At the same time, however, some kind of repressive apparatus was required to guarantee that the creation of a global economy open to the needs of capital would go according to plan. That role was increasingly carried out by the U.S. military, with direct support from the U.S.

> The hidden hand of the market will never work without a hidden fist. McDonald's cannot flourish without McDonnell Douglas, the designer of the U.S. Air Force F-15. And the hidden fist that keeps the world safe for Silicon Valley's technologies to flourish is called the U.S. Army, Air Force, Navy and Marine Corps.
> —Thomas Friedman,
> *New York Times Magazine,* 1999

Central Intelligence Agency (CIA) via a number of covert activities.

While we often hear that people around the world hate the United States because they oppose its freedoms, this is rarely the case. Unfortunately, the history of U.S. foreign interventions in the twentieth century left a sad legacy in many countries. Leaders who have been assassinated with U.S. complicity since World War II include Abdul Karim Kassem in Iraq (1963), Patrice Lumumba in the Republic of the Congo (1961), and Salvador Allende in Chile (1973). From 1945 until 1999, the U.S. government was involved in attempts to overthrow more than forty foreign governments and to crush more than thirty people's movements that were struggling against repressive regimes. In most cases it succeeded. In the process, millions of people lost their lives and at least that many suffered untold agonies and social dislocation.

> We have about 60 percent of the world's wealth but only 6.3 percent of its population. Our real task in the coming period [will be] to maintain this position of disparity. We need not deceive ourselves that we can afford the luxury of altruism and world benefaction.... The day is not far off when we are going to have to deal in straight power concepts. The less we are hampered then by idealistic slogans the better.
> —George Kennan, head of U.S. State Department Planning, 1948

What was the goal of these actions? One author (Blum 2000, 13–14) argues that there are four key imperatives driving U.S. foreign policy:

- opening the world to transnational corporations, particularly U.S.-based ones;
- justifying and increasing the size of government military spending necessary to sustain the profitability of defence contractors;
- preventing the rise of any society that might serve as a model for economic independence by wanting to opt out of the global capitalist economy; and
- preventing the rise of any other government that might challenge U.S. economic, political, or military global dominance.

In advancing these imperatives, the United States has helped replace elected governments in many countries with repressive regimes and often supported or trained some unsavoury characters. One of these individuals was Saddam Hussein. Another was Osama bin Laden.

Think About It

Why do you think we learn so little about the history of U.S. intervention in countries around the world? If we do hear of certain interventions undertaken by the United States, how are they portrayed?

Bin Laden—the son of a wealthy Saudi Arabian family with connections to the Bush family in the United States—was part of a large group of radical Islamic rebels who, in the 1980s, went to Afghanistan to oppose Soviet intervention there. The United States was well aware of the violent and aggressive acts being committed by these mujahideen, as they were called, but they were seen as "friendly" terrorists. The United States supported these mujahideen, who were referred to at the time as "freedom fighters." When that war in Afghanistan ended, tens of thousands of veterans of this war—now trained in battle and armed—spread around the world to inflame and train a new group of Islamic radicals (Blum 2000, 33). Some of these militants were almost certainly part of the group that organized the September 11, 2001, attacks. Shortly afterward, George W. Bush declared that the United States was entering a prolonged war in which anyone not agreeing with U.S. policy was to be considered an enemy.

A number of authors have begun to refer to the current policies of the United States as "new imperialism." While in many ways it remains the same as the old form of imperialism, there are a few key transformations. As noted in Box 9.2, the United States is by far the largest military spender in the world. However, as one author (Mooers 2006, 4) notes, "Its superiority in firepower vastly exceeds its economic supremacy." In other words, the United States is no longer at the head of the global economy, and countries such as China and India are expanding rapidly. The United States has never before had such a large trade deficit. Its job growth has been falling behind population growth and there has been no recent growth in consumer real incomes (Roberts 2006). And its growing need for natural resources can be seen, in part, in the desire of the United States to gain control of the major oil-producing regions of the world. With declining economic power, overwhelming military might has become the only way for the United States to protect global capitalist interests. The result is a permanent state of warfare.

Why have Americans and their allies (including Canada) accepted the huge cost—both in human and financial terms—of such a highly militarized society? Why has there been so little response to the global corporate agenda in North America until recently? Why do so few of us even know about this agenda? The answer to these questions requires us again to remember the key role played by ideology in sustaining structures of power.

We must start with something very simple: no government—whatever its political orientation—is going to justify its policies by announcing that it is doing something most people would find unacceptable. For example, no government will ever say, "We are going to war because we want to control the natural resources of that country" or "We are helping our transnational corporations expand." It is not hard to understand that when a government prepares a population to send its young people to their possible death, at great financial cost, it must always be done in the name of good, not evil.

Every government justifies its push to war and conquest with positive values such as overthrowing dictators, bringing rights and freedoms to the country in

Box 9.2 U.S. Military Spending

In early 2007 the Bush administration released its budget request for fiscal year 2008. As part of this request, the White House asked for $644 billion for the military—$502 billion for the Pentagon and the nuclear weapons-related activities of the Department of Energy, and an additional $142 billion for the "global war on terrorism." In 2006, military spending (including costs for past, present, and future activities) accounted for 41 percent of the U.S. budget. In comparison, 5 percent was spent on social policy; 5 percent on community and economic development; 2 percent on science, energy, and the environment; and 1 percent on non-military international programs.

The United States is far and away the global leader in military spending:

- The United States spends more than the next 42 highest-spending countries in the world on the military.
- The United States accounts for 47 percent of the world's total military spending.

- The United States spends five times more on the military than China, and eleven times more than Russia.
- The United States outspends the remaining "Axis of Evil" countries—Iran and North Korea—on military spending by a ratio of 72 to 1.
- The United States and its allies—the NATO countries (which includes Canada), Japan, South Korea, and Australia—spend $950 billion combined on their militaries, 70 percent of the world's total.

Source: Adapted from "U.S. Military Spending vs. the World," 5 Feb. 2007, Center for Arms Control and Non-Proliferation, <http://www.oldarmscontrolcenter.org/archives/002279.plp> and *Friends Committee on National Legislation*, <http://www.fcnl.org/issues/item.php?item_id2336&issue_id=19>.

question, or promoting the glory of a higher power. Earlier European and British imperial conquests were justified in part because they were said to be bringing superior western civilization and religion to inferior populations. In the period following World War II, successive U.S. governments and the media promoted the notion of a world communist conspiracy in order to justify aggressive international policies. As late as 1987, just a few years prior to the fall of the Berlin Wall and the subsequent collapse of the Soviet Union, 60 percent of Americans agreed with the statement that there was an international communist conspiracy that was attempting to rule the world (Blum 1998, 12). Blum describes the way North Americans thought of this supposed conspiracy:

> ...a great damnation has been unleashed upon the world, possibly by the devil himself, but in the form of people; people not motivated by the same needs, fears, emotions, and personal morality that govern others of the species, but people engaged in an extremely clever, monolithic, international conspiracy dedicated to taking over the world and enslaving it; for reasons not always clear perhaps, but evil needs no motivation save evil itself.

Now, re-read this quote, but instead of thinking of it as a description of how we viewed communism in the past, think of it as a description of how we view global terrorism today. Surprisingly, the description fits exactly.

With the socialist world in disarray, the United States needed a new enemy that would allow it to continue—indeed expand—its global activities on behalf of capital, and "terrorism" became the new code word for this enemy. That is not to say that there are no terrorists in the world. However, the term is used in particular ways for particular ideological outcomes. For example, the term terrorism excludes any acts of governments and their military that are able to inflict large-scale terror on civilians. It also excludes economic terrorism, such as trade embargoes, which may restrict food, medicines, or other necessities from reaching a population. Moreover, some terrorists seem more acceptable than others. For example, Luis Posada Carriles was convicted of planting the bomb on an Air Cubana flight in 1976 that took the lives of seventy-three passengers, and he was also likely responsible for the 1997 bombing at a Cuban hotel that killed an Italian tourist. He escaped from prison in Venezuela in the 1980s and in 2005 he made his way to the United States. A U.S. immigration judge refused to extradite him to Venezuela on the grounds that he might be tortured there.

While the United States remains the world's foremost "global police officer," other countries—including Canada—have played important supporting roles. For example, Canada's military was a significant participant in the 2004 U.S.-led "regime change" in Haiti that forced President Jean Bertrand Aristide into exile (Sanders 2007). The Canadian military has also been an essential part of the "war on terrorism" in Afghanistan, which allowed the U.S. military to focus on Iraq. Both the Liberals and Conservatives justified Canadian participation in this war—and its concurrent escalation of military spending—by arguing that they were trying to help the people of Afghanistan. However, most analysts agree that conditions have seriously worsened for the Afghan people since 2001 (Joya 2007). Meanwhile, military spending rose under the Harper government as Canada became more closely aligned with the United States. Canada spent over $1 billion on its Afghanistan mission in 2007 (Smith 2007).

Globalization: Growing Tensions

At the same time as the world is increasingly being integrated both economically and culturally as a result of globalization, there is a simultaneous tendency of countries in various parts of the world to experience growing internal tensions. Some of these tensions have led to long and protracted civil wars, "ethnic cleansing" of minorities, or the breaking up of nation-states into smaller units. Some countries have become what are referred to as "failed states." Failed states can no longer perform basic functions such as education, security, or governance, usually as a result of violence or extreme poverty. Their failure can be the result of internal factors or intentional destabilization from foreign governments. When we look at the entire globe, it seems, then, that the world is both coming together and breaking apart at the same time. Both of these opposing tendencies can be linked to the rise of capitalism and its development into a global entity.

The concept of the nation-state is relatively new. Prior to the industrial era, most people lived in small communities, identifying primarily with their family, clan, or tribe. Groups of individuals who lived together were relatively homogeneous, with most of them sharing the same language, religion, cultural traditions, and history. With the growth of capitalism and the nation-state, diverse groups of people had to be forged into a somewhat artificial entity called a "nation." In order for governments to create a loyal population, they actually had to create the nation, with citizens now being pressed to share a common language, history, and culture. War often played an important role in binding populations together, uniting diverse peoples and groups against a common enemy.

Canada provides an interesting example of how nation-states were forged from groups with extremely different histories, languages, and cultures that were not easily brought together. Two competing European peoples colonized Canada, with one of these groups defeated in war by another. Both played a role in conquering the indigenous population. These historic residues left lingering tensions. In many parts of the world, as a result of war or conquest, national boundaries were arbitrarily drawn or re-drawn, and some cultural and linguistic groups suddenly found themselves living as minority populations in one or more nation-states.

Often, then, it was not particularly easy to bring together the various cultural groups within a single country, and underlying tensions remained. Usually the economic, political, and intellectual elite consisted mainly of one dominant ethnic, linguistic, or racial group. Under certain conditions, those with power used divide-and-rule policies in combination with every attempt to encourage traditionalism, tribalism, and superstition to divide and weaken the oppressed masses of the population. Many of the hostilities of the twentieth century and onward are rooted in the attempts of the ruling elite or the European colonizers to play one nationality, tribe, or religion against another—Tamil against Sinhalese in Ceylon (now Sri Lanka), Hindu against Muslim in India, Jew against Arab in the Middle East, Tutsi against Hutu in East Africa, and so on.

Another factor leading to increasing tensions around the world has been the large-scale migration of populations. As capitalism expands globally it creates "push-pull" conditions that lead naturally to the migration of populations. Sometimes this movement is within a country, as people who can no longer survive through the decline of agricultural labour are pushed into cities where they hope to find work in expanding industries. In other cases, the migration is between countries, as people seek to better their conditions of life. In the case of Canada, aside from the indigenous peoples, almost all of us are relatively recent immigrants or descendants of immigrants, going back less than a few hundred years.

Today, Canada continues to receive immigrants from around the world. However, some analysts are concerned that Canada is now taking the best-educated individuals from less-developed countries, leaving these countries with shortages of professionals in key areas. Others are concerned about the increasing numbers of workers that are brought to various parts of the developed capitalist world as "guest workers." This is a polite term for low-paid workers (in Canada they most commonly work in the agricultural sector, although some are currently doing industrial work) who have few of the rights and privileges guaranteed to citizens. When their term of work is finished, they are expected to return to their country of origin.

Sometimes migration is forced upon people against their will. Probably the largest involuntary migration of people resulted from the slave trade, with untold millions of Africans forcibly transported to the western hemisphere. Today in many parts of the world, millions of people are refugees or internally displaced persons who have had to leave their homes as a result of civil wars or natural disasters. Others become victims of human trafficking and effectively become slaves against their will. One component of "failed states" is the massive movement of people, which creates major humanitarian crises.

While employers may benefit from the large influx of immigrants and guest workers willing to take any job for relatively low pay, working people may have mixed feelings about the next wave of newcomers to their country. Not only are foreign workers often used by employers to drive down the cost of labour, but they have at times also been used to break strikes. Rather than blaming employers for using immigrants in this way, it is more common for people to blame the victim, seeing immigrants as the cause of a country's ills. Whether it is rising unemployment, rising crime rates, or a decline in traditional values, immigrants have regularly been turned into scapegoats to explain a variety of social problems.

Think About It

Ask family members and friends (even if they were once immigrants themselves) what they think about immigrants now coming to Canada. Should immigrants be forced to adapt to Canadian ways?

Rapid social change brought on by the spread of global capitalism has also had negative consequences for the less-developed parts of the world. Here locals often view the inundation of modern Western values and culture as a serious problem. The fear of some people that their ancient traditions and religious beliefs are disappearing often gives rise to radical religious or nationalist movements. Ironically, some of these organizations and some of their leaders have received support from the United States, which saw them as a countervailing force to local non-religious political movements that might have threatened the interests of global capital.

In sum, while the expansion of globalization draws increasing numbers of diverse populations together via a shared economy, culture, and governance, there is a simultaneous growth of tensions that pit groups of people against one another. These tensions have frequently led to the death or dislocation of large numbers of people. Once again we can see the ways in which capital seeks stability to carry out its activities, but in seeking to secure its profits, the outcome has often been instability.

Toward the Future: Globalization and the Changing Role of the Nation-State

It became clear with the U.S.-led attack on Iraq in 2003 that the U.S. government was prepared to act independently, without the support of multilateral organizations such as the United Nations. As the world's most powerful military power, the United States felt emboldened to advance its own agenda.

At the same time, there are sectors of the capitalist ruling class that are concerned about increasing U.S. willingness to act alone or with only a few allies, rather than with the support of other nations. These are the sectors of the dominant class that understand the need for international stability if global capitalism is to thrive and develop. The entire last half of the twentieth century can be seen as a delicate and prolonged attempt to create a world that would be friendly and open to the advances of global capital. If the United States increasingly opts out of global agreements and global organizations, then many fear that other countries will follow suit. The World Trade Organization has been stalled over the past few years as a number of countries feel excluded from decisions. This could lead to a return to rising tensions between nation-states similar to those that led to economic instability and war in the first half of the twentieth century.

There are also growing indications that ordinary people around the world are not only dissatisfied with an increasingly aggressive and unilateral U.S. government, but are also organizing to resist it. The global protests that took place in early 2003, opposing the U.S. war in Iraq before it began, were unique in human history, not only in their numbers, but also because never before had so many people stood together—across nations, religions, and classes—to express shared opposition to war and corporate greed.

It is currently unclear whether the neoliberal corporate agenda itself will lead to the very opposite of what capital seeks. The major part of the twentieth century saw the state playing a larger and larger role in capitalist economies, primarily to guarantee their stability. If neoliberalism continues unabated; if the TNCs continue to increase their global power at the expense of national governments and people's needs; if public expenditures continue to be reduced and thus the social wage diminished; if environmental degradation and climate change are allowed to continue; if capital can maintain its rule only through increasing repression and war—then the long-term viability of capitalist economies must be cast into doubt. We shall return to this complex issue in the final chapter of the book.

Key Points

1. Although the state is a class-based social institution, all levels of government in Canada have provided many rights and benefits to ordinary Canadians.

2. Even though capitalism promotes the concept of private property, many elements of society remained in the public domain until recently.

3. The welfare state grew after World War II, as the capitalist owning class and the organized sector of the working class achieved an "accord" that was mediated by the state.

4. The decline of social reform began in the 1970s as capitalism entered a permanent state of economic crisis and the accord between capital and labour began to collapse.

5. By the 1980s, most capitalist governments around the world began to shift to policies more sympathetic to the needs of the corporate sector. The package of changes is commonly referred to as neoliberalism.

6. From the mid-1970s on, Canadians were bombarded with a number of myths meant to convince them to accept fewer social benefits from all levels of government.

7. The nature and role of nation-states has been changing with the advance of a globally integrated capitalist economy, but social scientists are still debating where these changes are headed.

8. The United States has become the leading force—economically, politically, and militarily—in an increasingly integrated global capitalist economy.

9. In order to allow a single world economy of competing corporations to function properly, a number of global agencies and institutions were created in the last half of the twentieth century.

10. There is an increasing tension between the global dominance of the United States, with its propensity to act unilaterally in its own interests, and the need for countries to work together to advance the development of an integrated global economy.

11. The U.S. military has increasingly played the role of "global police officer" in order to ensure the creation of a global capitalist economy dominated by its own corporate sector.

12. Although there has been an increasing integration of people around the world, there has concurrently been an increase in tensions between groups of people, both within countries and between countries.

Further Reading

Bezanson, Kate, and Meg Luxton, eds. 2006. *Social Reproduction: Feminist Political Economy Challenges Neo-Liberalism*. Montreal and Kingston: McGill-Queen's University Press.
Contributors to this work show that neoliberal policies have had particularly negative consequences for women, who continue to be the main caregivers in society.

Blum, William. 2000. *Rogue State: A Guide to the World's Only Superpower*. Monroe, ME: Common Courage.
A straightforward analysis of the role played by the United States over the past half-century in opening the world to transnational corporations. Easy to read, yet full of detailed examples.

Klein, Naomi. 2007. *The Shock Doctrine: The Rise of Disaster Capitalism*. Toronto: Knopf.
Canadian journalist Klein argues here that neoliberalism thrives on wars, terror attacks, natural catastrophes, poverty, trade sanctions, market crashes and other economic, financial and political disasters.

Harvey, David. 2007. *A Brief History of Neoliberalism*. London: Oxford University Press.
A concise history of the roots of neoliberalism, the reasons for its global spread, and the prospects for more socially just alternatives.

Johnson, Chalmers. 2007. *Nemesis: The Last Days of the American Republic*. New York: Metropolitan Books.
This is the last book in a trilogy that included *Blowback* and *The Sorrows of Empire*. In this book Johnson continues his argument that various forms of military activity have led to unintended but negative consequences for the United States.

McBride, Stephen. 2005. *Paradigm Shift: Globalization and the Canadian State*, 2nd ed. Halifax: Fernwood.
A thorough examination of how the Canadian state has changed in the face of globalization and neoliberalism.

Mooers, Colin, ed. 2006. *The New Imperialists: Ideologies of Empire*. Oxford: Oneworld Publications.
The various articles in this book examine the "New Imperialism" of the United States, and its devastating consequences for the freedom and democracy it claims to be defending.

Toussaint Eric. 2005. *Your Money or Your Life: The Tyranny of Global Finance*. Updated Edition. Chicago: Haymarket Books.
A detailed examination of neoliberalism's effect on economies around the world, particularly those of the poorer nations. Full of facts and figures.

10 Inequality of Wealth and Income

In This Chapter

- Why is the gap between rich and poor growing in Canada and globally?
- How easy is it to move up the ladder of success in our country?
- What is the extent of poverty, and who are the poor in Canada?
- Is it true that "the poor will always be with us"?

Of all the topics students study in introductory sociology courses, probably the most emotionally difficult and controversial are those regarding various forms of social inequality. It is not that students are surprised about inequalities, either in Canada or globally. One doesn't have to take a course in sociology to realize that there are gross inequalities of wealth and status in our society. Rather, the debates regarding social inequality arise from disagreements about both its causes and its possible solutions.

Social inequality is a topic that dominates the discipline of sociology. Sociologists generally focus on the extent of such inequalities, whether inequalities are expanding or shrinking, and why inequalities seem to exist in every modern society. For the order theories, a number of explanations have been proposed that explain the existence of social inequality. Two approaches noted earlier in this book are the biological determinist arguments, discussed in Chapter 2 (and further discussed in Chapters 11 and 12), and the functionalist approach, which will be explained in more detail in this chapter. While very different in content, both these theoretical frameworks conclude that social inequality is inevitable.

In contrast are the change theories, which link inequalities of wealth and income to the economic structure and class relationships. Change theorists accept that there will always be differences of ability among people. However, for these theorists the more important issue is how inequalities become structured in particular ways at certain times in history. Change theorists tend to emphasize the linkage of various forms of modern social inequality to the capitalist economic system,

> The very nature of globalization has an inherent bias toward inequality.
> —former Prime Minister Paul Martin

as well as to the structures and beliefs that arise within that system. Some of these theorists have also looked at the ways in which the recent expansion of globalization and neoliberalism has increased the divide between the haves and have-nots, both in Canada and around the world.

Because our society puts so much emphasis on the individual, it should not be surprising that most of us connect inequalities of wealth and power not to structural arrangements but, rather, to individual characteristics. Conversely, of course, inability to succeed is seen to be the result of some failure on the part of the individual. Without knowing it, most of us adhere to liberal notions of inequality. Liberalism, as we saw in Chapter 7, is the underpinning of almost all belief systems within capitalist societies.

Think About It

Why do you think most of us really *want* to believe that income and wealth inequality are the result of individual differences rather than being rooted in the nature of capitalist societies themselves?

The eighteenth and nineteenth centuries witnessed rapid social change, with the rigid feudal order gradually replaced by the new capitalist economic order. Throughout the feudal era, social inequalities were seen as the inevitable working out of God's plan; they required no explanation and certainly were not open to change. The growth of markets and of capitalist productive relations gave rise to a new way of thinking about social inequality. The new and expanding bourgeois class was certainly not satisfied with a notion that only those born at the top had a right to be there; thus this class promoted the argument that anyone should be able to attain the wealth, prestige, and power that was formerly held only by those of noble birth. The new owning class believed that the market, rather than an accident of birth, should determine one's place in the system of inequality, with equality of opportunity for all. The bourgeoisie, of course, was not opposed to structured inequality, but rather to their own exclusion from the highest ranks within such a system. Soon other people who saw themselves as marginalized or oppressed took up the rallying cry of liberalism.

The essence of liberalism is fairness, in the particular sense of equal ability to compete. Life itself is seen as a marketplace in which all individuals get to compete for places in the status hierarchy. If we imagine all humans as competing in "the race of life," liberal ideology sees equality when everyone gets chance to "run" in this imaginary race in the hopes of achieving wealth, prestige, and power. As everyone knows, there are always winners and losers in a race. Thus within liberal ideology, structured inequality is acceptable as long as the "race" for positions within the hierarchy appears to be a reasonably fair one.

Change theorists, in contrast, argue that the "race of life" under the conditions of capitalism is never truly fair. True equality of opportunity is not possible because a small number of individuals—those with great wealth and power—

Box 10.1 Winners and Losers: A Core Capitalist Notion

Our society is so dominated by competition that it is hard for us to accept that it is specific to capitalist societies. While there may be some genetic component of our desire to compete, and while other societal forms certainly had competitive elements in them, capitalism is unique in having competition between individuals and groups as a core cultural value. In today's world we are surrounded by competition. Businesses—even the largest transnational corporations—constantly compete for markets, investors, raw materials, and so on. The political arena is also a hotbed of competition, with candidates and political parties spending more and more money to win our vote.

At the individual level, competition begins when we enter the school system, if not before. We get graded by our teachers, and we pass or fail our year. More and more school systems across Canada are introducing province-wide tests at the elementary level so that schools themselves can be graded. By the time students leave high school, they have begun to be sorted into winners and losers. Of course, this process continues in university, as students compete for grades, scholarships and bursaries, and entrance into graduate programs. Schools increasingly compete with each other to get top students, professors, and research dollars. Once students graduate, they enter the work world, where they compete with each other for jobs and promotions.

In our spare time, most of us are at some point involved in competitive activities. This can range from sports—where there are always winners and losers—to electronic games or various forms of gambling. Some of the most popular television shows involve competition. This includes sporting events, game shows, and entertainment shows such as *Canadian Idol*. Increasing numbers of awards are given out annually to the best films, books, music, plays, architecture, entrepreneurs, and so on, and there is a "top ten" of the week for everything from book sales to cellphone rings. You can even rate your professor. Whether the winners are actually better than the losers is ultimately irrelevant.

Canadians are not a heartless people. Most of us care about those less fortunate than ourselves and often wonder why there is so much poverty in a world where some have more money than they can possibly spend in their lifetime. However—given our culture of competition—it is not surprising that most of us accept the idea that winners and losers are just a natural part of life.

---

effectively control the competition between individuals, just as they control the competition between economic units. As a result, the race of life is set up in such a way as to prevent most people from winning. For change theorists, liberalism actually masks structural inequality because it gives the impression that everyone gets a reasonably fair chance to run the race. With this assumption, any failure to achieve wealth, prestige, or power appears be the fault of the individual.

Thus liberalism—like capitalism itself—is full of contradictions. On the one hand, it draws us toward such admirable goals as equality, democracy, and individual human rights and freedoms; on the other hand, liberalism helps mask the structural basis that sets limits on these very aspirations.

Symbolic Markers of Social Inequality

Humans are pre-eminently a symbol-creating species, and we have always symbolically represented difference, either between individuals or between groups. Once social classes came into existence, it became important for those who owned the means of production to distinguish themselves publicly from the masses that did not. With their control of the surplus, vast sums could be spent on clothing, housing, and other indicators of their place in the status hierarchy. In today's society—where most people live in large, anonymous cities and their place in such a hierarchy is unknown—the external markers of one's status become particularly important. Such markers are referred to by sociologists as **status symbols**. They refer not only to one's housing and manner of dress, but also to speech, mannerisms, hobbies, food preferences, favourite alcoholic beverages, and so on.

It is important to note that such markers are socially created and can change over time and place. Indeed, in advanced capitalist societies, where cheap imitations of the symbols of wealth can be mass-produced very quickly, status symbols, particularly in the area of fashion and style, are constantly changing. Somehow people come to understand these shared meanings. One very interesting example is skin colour. During the period prior to and at the beginning of the Industrial Revolution, pale skin was a sign of high status: it distinguished wealthy people from poor peasants who had to work in the sun. Gradually, as peasants became factory workers whose faces rarely saw the light of day, tanned skin became an indicator of someone with leisure time and money. This became particularly true by the second half of the twentieth century, when air travel to tropical climes became possible. (Of course, because of the persistence of racism, an acquired tan was a symbol of high status while naturally dark skin was not.) In recent years, as tanning has increasingly become associated with cancer and premature aging of the skin, a tan no longer is the status symbol it once was.

> Blessed with riches and possibilities far beyond anything imagined by ancestors who tilled the unpredictable soil of medieval Europe, modern populations have nonetheless shown a remarkable capacity to feel that neither who they are nor what they have is quite enough.
> —Alain de Botton, *Status Anxiety*

Think About It

Much has been written about the status hierarchies that develop in high schools. Can you think of status markers, such as clothing styles, that distinguished one group from another at your high school?

Many books and articles have been written detailing the lifestyles of various status groups, particularly those at the top. Such analyses are very much in line with the early theoretical work of Thorstein Veblen, an American economist who wrote with biting wit about the patterns of what he termed "conspicuous

228

consumption" of the "leisure class" (Veblen [1899] 1994). Veblen and other social analysts have argued that wealth comes to be reflected in something far more complex than simply social position, something we generally label "style" or "taste." Demonstrating to others one's place in the status hierarchy required, according to Veblen, both leisure and the consumption of conspicuous goods. Writing at the turn of the twentieth century, Veblen could have had no idea how accurate his analysis would prove. Today, mass advertising convinces us to buy more and more products that serve no purpose other than as status symbols.

More recently, a wide-ranging work by British writer Alain de Botton about status anxiety over several thousand years achieved bestseller status. Botton is particularly interested in the high degree of such anxiety in today's society. Why, for example, do the very wealthy feel so insecure that they continue to accumulate totally unnecessary and ridiculously expensive material objects? Like Veblen, Botton feels that humans need affirmation from others, and in today's society wealth and material objects are the things that are valued (Botton 2004, 7).

Analyses such as those of Botton and Veblen are useful in explaining how human behaviour can be understood only by examining both our objective conditions and our subjective interpretations of these conditions. In other words, economic inequality always becomes embedded with cultural meaning. However, if we are not careful, such studies can direct our attention exclusively toward status differences and distinctive patterns of consumption, and away from the key issue of class relations and inequality of power. We must always recall, therefore, that the underlying basis for structured inequality is more than style. Unequal allocation of our society's resources is the result of the private appropriation of surplus value. Unfortunately, this is difficult for many of us to see, as the dominant world view of capitalism directs our attention to individual differences rather than to the structural bases of inequality.

Inequality in Canada: The Growing Gap

There are two key ways of measuring social inequality. The most common way is to measure differences in **income**, that is, the money that is acquired through wages, salaries, or various forms of government assistance. Social scientists can also study differences in **wealth**, which comprises all assets—including real estate holdings and money in bank accounts, stocks, bonds, and so on—minus debts. Most data on social inequality tend to focus on income for the simple reason that data on income are more readily available. However, examining income alone ignores the fact that a small number of people can legally acquire huge amounts of wealth, not through their labour but via a surplus produced by the labour of others. Wealth, therefore, is more clearly a measure of true economic power and command over a country's resources (McQuaig 1999, 134).

There are few people in Canada who would argue for a society where there is no inequality of income or wealth whatsoever. The issues that interest most of us are whether inequality is moderate or extreme, and whether the gap between those at the top and those at the bottom is growing or shrinking. Recent data indicate—for both income and wealth—that the inequality gap has been growing over the last thirty years.

During the 1980s and onward, all levels of government in Canada asked citizens to participate in a great social experiment. As we saw in Chapter 9, the shift away from the welfare state and toward a more free-market economy was promoted. Canadians were told that if the economy were allowed to expand, freed from government constraints, all citizens would benefit. "A rising tide lifts all boats" was what we were told.

However, as we advance through the first decade of the twenty-first century, the data do not indicate improved incomes for all Canadians. For example, wages in the 2000 census revealed a polarization between high-paying and low-paying forms of employment. While the average wage of Canadians had risen 7.3 percent during the 1990s and the number of earners in higher income brackets soared, four in ten income earners continued to make only $20,000 a year or less (Statistics Canada 2003a, 1). This growing gap reflects the expansion of the hour-glass labour market, with well-paid "good jobs" for some, and poorly paid "bad jobs" for many others.

> In 2005, corporations banked $130 billion more in gross profits than they would have if the profit share had remained at 1991 levels. Sharing those earnings with workers could have gone a long way to reducing Canada's growing income gap.
> —Ellen Russell and Mathieu Dufour, *Rising Profit Shares, Falling Wage Shares, 2007*

> The gap between the very richest and very poorest Canadians rivals anything seen in the Third World.
> —Steve Kerstetter, *Rags & Riches*

A more recent examination of incomes from 1976 to 2004 indicates that the gap between rich and poor increased in periods of both economic recession and economic growth (Yalnizyan 2007). In 1976, the richest 10 percent of Canada's families raising children had incomes that were thirty-one times that of the poorest 10 percent. By 2004, their incomes were eighty-two times that of the poorest 10 percent. Clearly the rising tide of a booming economy was not lifting all boats. As Figure 10.1 indicates, the total share of earnings has been shifting from the bottom half of income earners to the top half. While we might assume that the top 10 percent has seen their incomes soar as a result of harder work, the data indicate exactly the opposite: everybody *except* the richest 10 percent of families have seen their work time in the paid workforce increase (ibid., 21).

A worrying trend is the growing generational gap in income. Of course, younger workers traditionally earn less, on average, than older workers. However, the 2000 census indicated that younger workers seemed to be on a consistently lower earnings track than older, more experienced workers. For men, this divide occurred at the age of forty, while the dividing line for women was the age of thirty (Statistics Canada 2003a, 10). It now seems that younger workers start

Figure 10.1 Top Getting Bigger Share of Earnings; Bottom Share Is Shrinking

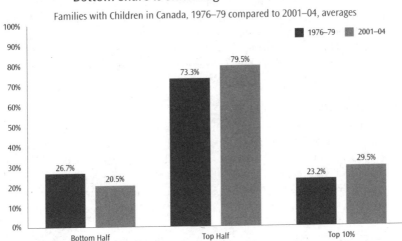

Families with Children in Canada, 1976–79 compared to 2001–04, averages

Source: Armine Yalnizyan, "The Rich and the Rest of Us: The Changing Face of Canada's Growing Gap," *CCPA Monitor* April 2007: 11. A project of the Canadian Centre for Policy Alternatives, Ottawa.

their careers earning less than their counterparts who started work thirty years earlier and make slower progress for at least the first ten years of their working lives. These figures help explain why the number of young people aged twenty to twenty-nine living at home has jumped from 27 percent in 1981 to 41 percent in 2001 (Statistics Canada 2003a, 11).

Another group that has lost ground is immigrants to Canada. Even after ten years in the country, they still earned less than the average income earned by Canadian-born workers. This inequality persisted whether they worked in a high-skilled or a low-skilled occupation. For example, for those in management, men aged twenty-five to fifty-four who immigrated during the 1990s and held a university degree earned between 50 and 60 cents for every dollar earned by their Canadian-born counterparts (Statistics Canada 2003a, 12–13).

An examination of wealth inequality rather than income inequality reveals the same pattern—from the 1970s onward, the rich got much richer while the poor got poorer (Morissette and Zhang 2006). In 2005 the wealthiest 10 percent of families held 58 percent of total household wealth, up from 52 percent in 1984. Meanwhile, 24 percent of families in 2005 had no financial wealth at all compared to 18 percent in 1984; 14 percent of families in 2005 had more debts than assets, up from 11 percent in 1984. As with income, wealth inequality statistics reveal a generational gap, with wealth falling substantially among those in which the major income recipient was aged twenty-five to thirty-four. In 2005, these families had a median wealth of $13,400 (in 2005 dollars), compared to $27,000 in 1984 (ibid.).

231

Think About It

In 2004, according to Statistics Canada, the median total income (before taxes) was $29,500 for lone-parent families. Try to imagine how you would budget if that was your income and you had one child. Be sure to consider taxes, housing, food, travel, clothing, and so on.

Explaining Social Inequality

While pre-capitalist societies are relatively "closed" class systems, with economic inequalities based on heredity, modern societies are generally thought of as "open" societies where one's class or status is based on merit. A society where advancement is based on individual ability or achievement is commonly referred to as a **meritocracy**. Most of you reading this book probably believe that our country is a meritocracy and that success is the inevitable reward for getting an education and working hard.

Order theories generally see capitalist societies as meritocracies. One of the predominant order theories is that of functionalism. Functionalism (or structural functionalism), a theoretical framework that has been discussed in several chapters in this book, tries to explain how certain components of a society serve particular functions. It starts with the assumption that there are no sharp cleavages, such as classes, within a society, but rather there are simply differences of ranking or privilege. With regard to inequality, functionalists argue that since social stratification is so prevalent in various types of society, it must serve an essential social function.

In the second half of the last century, functionalist explanations of social inequality attained some prominence in North America. Such explanations essentially tried to demonstrate the value of structured inequality, primarily by showing how inequality guaranteed that the "top jobs" would be filled by those most qualified to fill them. Of all the functionalist analyses of structured inequality, the best known is probably that of Kingsley Davis and Wilber E. Moore (1945). The Davis-Moore thesis, as it came to be known, sparked a great debate among sociologists at the time. While it is now largely rejected by sociologists, it continues to reflect the common-sense view that assumes that societies such as ours are meritocracies.

Davis and Moore looked at the division of labour to explain inequality. They argued that the unequal allocation of societal rewards, both material and social, is both universal and functionally necessary in all societies, since there has to be some motivation to get individuals in a society to fill the most important and difficult occupations. Some jobs require exceptional talent, while others require a long and costly training process. Thus the unequal rewards of the occupational structure ensure that all jobs that are "functionally necessary" for society are filled. In this argument, a medical doctor—to use one example—should be paid more than a hospital orderly because it is a more specialized and important job that requires dedication and many years of training.

One critique of the Davis-Moore thesis centres on the notion of what a society sees as a "functionally important" occupation. Are commodity traders, stockbrokers, real estate agents, or lawyers earning hundreds of thousands of dollars a year really more functionally important to a society than artists or childcare workers, most of whom can barely eke out a living? Since few people have the talent to become great artists of some sort, one might assume that this rare breed would be highly remunerated.

The functionalist analysis ends up being a circular one. In our society, where wealth determines value, salaries are automatically assumed to be connected to job importance, whether or not this is actually the case. Those occupations that receive high salaries come to be *seen* as the most important jobs. This becomes particularly clear when we look at jobs that have historically been deemed to be "women's work." These positions—such as childcare worker, nurse, or social worker—have consistently been undervalued and underpaid, even though many require a high level of training and all are, without a doubt, functionally important. Clearly, in such cases, ascribed status is as important a variable in determining wages as the functional importance or level of training.

Such issues indicate some of the problems with the functionalist analysis. By ignoring the fact that both financial rewards and access to job opportunities develop within an already-existing structural inequality, cause and effect are turned on their heads. By addressing only differential rewards within the division of labour, Davis and Moore fail totally to explain the expansion of such inequality in recent years.

In contrast to the functionalist argument, class analysis sees Canadian society as only a partial meritocracy, for it argues that a true meritocracy is not possible within current social arrangements. This approach stresses the privileges held by those at the top of the social hierarchy, who are able to obtain the best education for their children in addition to making the important social connections that help them get the right jobs. These individuals also have easier access to money—through inheritance, family trusts, or loans—that help them get a head start. From this point of view, one's structural position is as much a determinant of success as, if not more than, any inherent capabilities one might have. Moreover, within the current arrangements of capitalist societies, certain status groups—the poor, recent immigrants, Aboriginal people, women, the disabled, and people of colour—have consistently been disadvantaged. Thus everyone does not have an equal opportunity to achieve wealth and power. Those born into privilege have a distinct advantage over those who lack it.

It should also be pointed out that wages are determined, in large measure, in the marketplace. In capitalism, as we have seen, there is not equality within this marketplace. For corporate owners, some jobs are of marginal interest, while others are highly valued. For example, few of the top-earning jobs in Canada are in the helping professions or the arts. Moreover, as noted earlier in this book, those in the very highest circles of corporate power can pay themselves outrageously high incomes and bonuses simply because they have the ability to do so. In recent years corporate compensation packages in North America have grown enormously. In 1980 CEOs in the United States were paid an average of 42 times more than production workers; by 2005 that figure had risen to 411 (United for a Fair Economy 2007). In 2006, the average CEO salary and bonus in Canada was $11.48 million, with the top ten CEOs averaging approximately $26 million in total compensation (*Globe and Mail*, 4 June 2006, B4).

Thus for change theorists, while a hierarchy of inequality with rewards based strictly on merit is possible in theory, the nature of capitalism severely limits this possibility. The interests of the dominant class are to maximize profits and to maintain, in the long run, a system that will allow it to continue to do so. Financial compensation for work performed is not the result of some collective society-wide decision-making process, nor does it reflect either the quality of the work performed or its value to society.

The Degree of Social Mobility in Canada

The degree to which we will tolerate economic inequality of any kind in our society must to a fair extent be related to our feeling regarding our ability to move from a position with few rewards to one with greater rewards. Obviously, we may be willing to tolerate even major inequalities as long as we feel that we, or our children, will have a chance to move up the status hierarchy. It is important, therefore, that we examine the data regarding social mobility in Canada.

"Rags to riches" stories have always been part of North American mythology, and, by and large, people are fascinated by them. Such stories are appealing because, of course, if someone else can start with nothing and make it to the top, then so can we. For social scientists, the issue is whether such stories are the exception or the rule. In order to answer that question, they study patterns of **social mobility**, or movement of people from one social position to another. Sociologists are interested in two forms of mobility: *intragenerational mobility*, which is the status change that occurs within an individual's lifetime, and *intergenerational mobility*, or changes between the occupational status of parent and child.

Such studies, both in Canada and internationally, indicate that mobility is certainly possible within capitalist systems, and mobility in Canada has been greater than in other countries. On the other hand, research in all capitalist countries has repeatedly indicated that achievement is not based on merit alone; there seems to be a fair amount of status inheritance. People with some wealth and privilege are able to pass on their advantages to their offspring. Ascribed statuses such as gender, race, ethnicity, and national origin also affect the degree of occupational mobility.

In addition, it should be noted that most occupational movement is very modest. Only a small percentage of Canadians experience rags-to-riches mobility, and even fewer fall to the bottom from lofty heights. Thus the very top and the very bottom of the status hierarchy remain relatively closed, and most occupational mobility is mainly small movements in the middle. A Statistics Canada study

Box 10.2 Planning for Your Retirement?

For most of you reading this book, the last thing on your mind is how you will live after retirement. At the moment, your most urgent financial concerns are probably getting through college or university, covering current expenses, or saving money for future purchases. However, once we hit our forties, many of us start to wonder, "Hmmm, when I eventually stop working, what will I live on?"

Many young people, if they have considered this issue at all, assume they will automatically receive some kind of pension from the Canadian government. The government does administer a number of different pensions and benefits for older people. However, the amount that most people over the age of sixty-five receive is not substantial. In 2007, it was $864 per month. Financial advisers often tell people to plan on a retirement income that is around 70 percent of their pre-retirement income to maintain their standard of living. Clearly, most Canadians are not prepared to live on CPP alone.

Most unionized workers also receive some type of pension (which they partially contribute to during their working years) because their union negotiated this as part of a benefits package. While most public-sector workers have occupational pension plans, only 27 percent of workers in the private sector are covered by such plans. However, many companies have recently ceased offering plans where a pension related to earnings and years of service is guaranteed. In its place, new hires are put into plans where retirement income depends on investment returns and no particular pension is promised.

For those without any pension plan or for those who wish to top up their occupational plan, there is always the option of private investment. Canadians have been increasingly told to plan for their retirements by investing in Registered Retirement Savings Plans, and the Canadian government encourages such private investment by allowing citizens to deduct the cost of RRSP purchases from their incomes, thus reducing their taxes. However, even with that incentive, little more than a third of those eligible actually put money into an RRSP. Moreover, the median value of RRSPs held by Canadians totals around $30,000, which will "buy" them a monthly pension of about $175.

Canadians' main form of investment today is now their housing. As many older people age, they may sell their homes to pass wealth on to offspring. The wealthy in Canada, of course, can also leave large inheritances. Poorer people have little in the way of savings and are more likely to be renters, and thus have less to pass on to their children. Thus the gap between the "haves" and "have nots" is not only maintained through the life span, but can continue through generations.

Sources: Keith Ambachtsheer, "Mutual Funds: How to Remedy the $25-billion Pension 'Haircut'," *Globe and Mail*, 21 May 2007: B2; Jim Stanford, "Forget RRSPs: Home Is Where the Wealth Is," *Globe and Mail*, 15 Jan. 2007, <http://www.theglobeandmail.com/servlet/story/LAC.20070115.COSTANFORD15/TPStory/TPComment/?query=> (accessed May 21, 2007); Statistics Canada, "Registered Retirement Savings Plan Contributions," *The Daily*, 22 Nov. 2006, <http://www.statcan.ca/Daily/English/061122/d061122f.htm> (accessed 21 May 2007).

(Corak and Heisz 1996) confirmed this finding. The study tracked 400,000 men between the ages of sixteen and nineteen from 1982 to 1993. This study concluded that, while there is a good deal of movement on the income scale, the richest and poorest tend to inherit their income levels from their fathers. According to one of the authors, "You are three times more likely as a young man to move from rags to rags than rags to riches. And moving from riches to riches is the most likely of all" (quoted in the *Globe and Mail*, 26 January 1996, A1).

Education and Meritocracy

At the core of our liberal belief in the existence of a meritocracy is the assumption that our education system will help to overcome ascribed status barriers and be the key to social mobility. Certainly the data does show that a university education is correlated with higher wealth and income on average, regardless of one's ascribed status. However, averages can mask particular cases. For example, one recent study of census data concluded that various racialized groups in Canada consistently earned less than their white counterparts even when they had postsecondary education. Blacks in particular earned lower wages than all other racialized groups; indeed, this group did not seem to benefit at all with regard to earnings as a result of obtaining a postsecondary education (Gosine 2000). This example gives us a hint that the education system in Canada does not eliminate existing inequalities. As one sociologist (Forcese 1986, 102) has noted, "As presently constituted, the educational system favours the already privileged, and screens out the already disadvantaged. Rather than defeating stratification, formal education is a cause of persisting and increasingly rigid stratification."

Order and change theories agree that a key function of the education system is "sorting," as it channels young people into the different jobs required by society. However, the order theories generally see the process as a relatively straightforward one in which everyone competes within an educational structure that provides equality of opportunity. From this point of view, public education is the primary agent of social equalization; any inequality of outcome must, by default, be linked to individual differences. Change theories, on the other hand, see the school system as generally reproducing inequalities that already exist. In other words, inequality of outcome is primarily the result of inequality of condition. Those with wealth, power, and prestige have an unfair advantage in pursuing success, and in most cases the school system simply serves to justify and maintain the already-existing inequalities.

The maintenance of inequalities comes about in a number of complex ways. Many students—particularly African-Canadians and those from lower socioeconomic backgrounds—are "streamed" into lower-level programs (Curtis et al. 1992; James 1990). In addition, exclusionary curricula, texts, and teacher-student interactions, as well as the overall culture of the school system, alienate many young people (Brathwaite and James 1996; Gaskell 1993). Students (and parents) who do not see the school as their own are less likely to feel committed to it. Marginalization can create feelings of self-doubt and shame, which can interfere with both learning and motivation (Roberts-Fiati 1996, 73).

A Statistics Canada study (Frenette 2007) found that only 31 percent of those in the bottom 25 percent of the income distribution attend university, compared to 50 percent of young people in the top 25 percent. The data indicated that many factors influenced the probability of going to university. Those that mattered most were standardized test scores, high school marks, parental education, parental expectations, high school quality, and financial constraints. Youths from well-to-do families ranked higher on all these variables. In other words, while all of us have a legal and moral right to pursue a university education, those who are born in financially advantaged circumstances have a better chance of actually doing so than others. Put simply, the "race of life" is not a completely fair race, because all of us are not starting at the same starting line.

> Some teachers give more attention to the slower learners. I actually prefer to help the students who are better at reading. After all, the others are just going to end up watching TV anyway, aren't they?
> —comment by a Grade 1 teacher at a parent–teacher meeting

By the time we enter elementary school, economic inequalities have already had an effect. One study from the United States, for example, found that students from lower-income families entering kindergarten already had significantly lower cognitive skills than their more advantaged counterparts (Lee and Burkham 2002). Schools can do only so much to eliminate existing inequality of condition. As one study notes about children from low-income families, they are "less healthy, have less access to skill-building activities, have more destructive habits and behaviours, live more stressful lives, and are subject to more humiliation" (Ross et al. 2000, 2).

It would be unfair and inaccurate to attribute total failure to public education with regard to providing the key to social mobility. Certainly, more women, racial and ethnic minorities, and economically disadvantaged individuals are attending postsecondary institutions than was the case thirty years ago. However, it is unclear whether the patterns of the last thirty years will continue into the next thirty. Governments have massively reduced funding to education, while corporations have been gaining a more direct foothold in the education system. As noted in Chapter 7, dramatic changes to education seem to be leading increasingly to a two-tiered system—one for the privileged and one for everyone else. Such changes include the expansion of private schools, more "back to the basics" curricula, cuts to equity and anti-racism programs, more parental fundraising for individual schools, and an increase in formalized streaming and standardized testing. While all Canadians are affected by such changes, the most seriously affected are those at the lowest levels of income in Canada.

Poverty in Canada

What is meant by the term *poverty*? On the one hand, the question seems absurd—poverty is when you're poor! However, both social scientists and government bureaucrats require a more precise and empirical measure of poverty. The question is no mere academic matter, since the definition of the term may affect who qualifies for various forms of government assistance targeted at the poor, or how humane (or how fiscally responsible, depending on the values being emphasized) a particular government appears.

There are two different ways of defining poverty. The first is referred to as absolute poverty. Using this approach, only those who are not getting their most basic daily needs met—that is, who are not able to acquire a minimum of nutrition, basic shelter, and adequate clothing—would be defined as poor. From this point of view, favoured by corporate think tanks such as the Fraser Institute, there are relatively few poor people in Canada. The second approach, which sees poverty more as a form of social exclusion, is referred to as relative poverty. In this definition, those whose incomes are far less than the average in their locale are deemed to be poor, even if they are above the barest subsistence level. Using this relative definition, a much greater number of Canadians live in poverty.

There is no official Canadian government definition of poverty. The Statistics Canada annual survey of incomes probably comes closest to being such a measure, although it now has three different measures related to low income.[1] The best known and most commonly used measure of poverty in Canada is based on a set of low-income cut-offs (LICOs) below which people are said to live in "straitened circumstances." The LICO, a compromise between measures of absolute and relative poverty, determines a threshold below which families spend a disproportionate share of their income on food, clothing, and shelter (see Table 10.1). The threshold is calculated on the basis of what other Canadians are spending on their basic necessities and varies according to family size and geography.

The second measure, called the low-income measure, is a second way that Statistics Canada measures poverty. It is a simple calculation that draws the line at half the median income in Canada. While not well known or used by social services or academics, this mainly statistical definition allows comparisons with other countries that often use this measure to express their rates of low income.

The newest Statistics Canada measure of low income is based on an absolute "market basket" approach to defining poverty. A shopping basket of basic life necessities has been developed, and those with incomes prohibiting them or their family from acquiring all the necessities in the basket are defined

---

1. It should be pointed out that data from Statistics Canada excludes those living in the Yukon, Nunavut, and Northwest Territories, as well as those in homes for the aged or prisons, and Aboriginals on reserves. This point is important to note, because Aboriginals constitute one of the poorest groups in Canada. Thus, the Statistics Canada data necessarily underestimates the full extent of poverty in Canada.

Table 10.1 Before-Tax Low-Income Cut-Offs (LICOs), 2005

Population of Community of Residence

Family Size	500,000+	100,000–499.999	30,000–99,999	Less than 30,000*	Rural
1	$20,778	$17,895	$17,784	$16,273	$14,303
2	$25,867	$22,276	$22,139	$20,257	$17,807
3	$31,801	$27,386	$27,217	$24,904	$21,891
4	$38,610	$33,251	$33,046	$30,238	$26,579
5	$43,791	$37,711	$37,480	$34,295	$30,145
6	$49,389	$42,533	$42,271	$38,679	$33,999
7+	$54,987	$47,354	$47,063	$43,063	$37,853

Note: This table uses the 1992 base. Income refers to total pre-tax household income.
*Include cities with a population between 15,000 and 30,000 and small urban areas (under 15,000).
Source: Prepared by the Canadian Council on Social Development using Statistics Canada's Low Income Cut-Offs, from *Low income cut-offs for 2005 and low income measures for 2004* Catalogue #75F0002MIE <http://www.ccsd.ca/factsheets/fs_lico05_bt.htm>.

as low income. Some social analysts worried that the shift to a market-basket approach—that is, an absolute measure of poverty—would reduce the number of people defined as low income. However, when the data was released in 2003, the new measure actually *increased* the number of people in poverty, with 13.9 percent of Canadians—almost four million people—defined as poor, compared to 10.9 percent as defined by the LICO. For those under eighteen, 16.9 percent were defined as poor using the market basket measure, while the LICO considered only 12.6 percent to be low income (Philp 2003).

The fact that Statistics Canada has three quite different measures of low income is a clear indicator that defining poverty is not as easy as it first appears. The definition is made even more complex in Canada because social assistance is provided primarily by provincial or local governments rather than by the federal government, although the federal government shares some of the costs of these programs via transfer payments from the one level to another level of government. The cut-off lines for social assistance vary from locality to locality and have recently been reduced in a number of jurisdictions. The current evidence, including the numbers of the homeless and of welfare recipients using food banks, indicates that the income provided by social assistance is inadequate to allow most families to get by.

It should also be noted that many people not officially defined as poor are also barely able to meet their basic needs. Such people, who do not get government assistance and who may even consider themselves middle class, are living from paycheque to paycheque, with no money put away for the future. Paying for a university education is out of the question; a sudden illness, rise in mortgage rates, or unexpected emergency could push them over the brink into serious poverty. Many young people with low-income part-time jobs and large student debt loads are increasingly forced to live with their parents. They may not think of themselves as poor because they see their low income as a temporary phenomenon.

The rapid growth of debt in Canada has also placed many Canadians in highly vulnerable economic conditions. While the richest 20 percent of family units in Canada in 1999 had enough financial assets to replace normal income for more than four years, the poorest 20 percent had only enough to keep the family going for around five weeks (Kerstetter 2003, 5). Most middle-income families also lack financial security because, as already noted, the wealth of Canadians is tied up in housing.

Think About It
Obviously, few of us plan to be poor. Can you think of a number of unexpected occurrences that might push you into poverty at some point in your life?

Who Are the Poor in Canada?

Data from the 2001 census indicates that pre-tax poverty levels using the low-income cut-offs (LICOs) remained basically the same as in 1990 at 16.4 percent, in spite of the fact that the economy grew through the latter half of the decade. The overall number of Canadians living in poverty actually increased over the decade, from 4.28 to 4.72 million (Canadian Council on Social Development 2003).

At one time, those at greatest risk for poverty were the elderly. While 17 percent of the elderly are still below the LICOs, the age group now most likely to be poor is children. Although in 1989 the House of Commons passed a resolution to end child poverty by 2000, more than 18.4 percent were still living in poverty that year, up slightly from 18.2 percent in 1990. The situation is even worse for children of immigrant families who have arrived in Canada within the previous ten years. Poverty among children from two-parent families in this situation expanded to 39 percent in 2001, up from 33 percent in 1990 and 22 percent in 1980 (Canadian Council on Social Development 2003). In 2006, 41 percent of food bank users across the country were children even though they made up only one-quarter of the population (Canadian Association of Food Banks 2007).

Visible minorities (most notably recent immigrants), Aboriginals, and people with disabilities have much higher rates of poverty than the national average. Particularly at risk are Aboriginal children and youth. And while seniors in Canada are no longer at greatest risk for poverty, they are hardly well off. Despite gains, the rate of poverty among unattached elderly individuals remains high, particularly for women. Indeed, many social scientists have noted a development that is referred to as the *feminization of poverty* because an increasing proportion of the poor are women. Women in all categories are at greater risk for poverty than men, but it is particularly serious in lone-parent families headed by women.

Throughout the 1990s, the poverty rate for this group varied between 55 and 60 percent (Ross et al. 2000, xxi). If there is a single factor that reduces the chances of ending up poor, it is having two wage earners in the family.

And while a large number of poor lack postsecondary education, the data does not support the fact that people are poor simply as a result of low educational levels. Growing numbers of those who are poor have at least some postsecondary education. For recent immigrants to Canada, having a degree does not seem to protect them from the rising probability of becoming low income. Indeed, 2001 census data indicate that the gap in low income rates between Canadian-born and recent immigrants is actually highest among degree holders, particularly those with engineering and applied science degrees (Picot and Hou 2003, 17).

Inequality and poverty are not new. What is of concern today is that the growing gap is making it harder for particular groups of "have-nots" to move permanently out of their state.

Why Does Poverty Exist?

The data in the previous section gives us a clue that poverty, at least in part, is connected to a number of structural realities that go beyond personal inadequacies. One major source of poverty is the inevitable existence of unemployment. Without work, many must live on the margins of society. In addition, many workers, particularly women, cannot find affordable childcare and are therefore unable to work. Poverty can also be linked to the increase in precarious forms of employment, inadequate minimum wages, massive cuts to unemployment insurance, and wage discrimination against recent immigrants, racial minorities, and women. For example, as a result of changed legislation, the number of unemployed workers eligible for unemployment insurance (now called Employment Insurance) fell from 87 percent in 1989 to just 36 percent in 1998 (Robinson 1999, 14). Declining rates of unionization, the decline of well-paid public-sector jobs, as well as the growing inability of Canadians to secure adequate incomes from fishing or farming must also be noted.

> When I feed the poor, they call me a saint. When I ask why they are poor, they call me a communist.
> —Brazilian Bishop Dom Helder Camara

Four in ten Canadians with employment income in 2000 earned less than $20,000. Of these, more than 22 percent, or nearly one and a half million people, were working on a full-year, full-time basis. It should also be noted that 11 percent of earners with less than $20,000 who were working full-year, full-time had completed a university education and 16 percent had accreditation from a college (Statistics Canada 2003a, 8). Although obtaining a postsecondary education increases your chances of financial success in Canada, it by no means guarantees it.

However, few of us see structural realities as the causes of poverty. As we have discussed throughout this book, most of us tend to focus on individual

Box 10.3 How We Blame the Victim

In one of my introductory sociology classes, students were asked to write a short response to the question "Why do we want to believe that the people we see asking for money on the street are the cause of their own misfortune?" However, so deeply held are many students' attitudes about the causes of poverty that about 20 percent of the class didn't answer that question at all; instead they told me why such individuals were indeed the cause of their own misfortune. Below are some sample student responses to my question. Notice the recurring themes of personal choice and that anyone can succeed if they want to:

- "I believe that if you are strong you can accomplish anything you desire."
- "There are opportunities out there, it is only a matter of taking advantage of it and take the first step."
- "I believe that the homeless are the cause of their own misfortune simply because they choose to live that way. We live in a country where we are taken care of by the government.... Therefore there should be no reason,

other than choosing to live like that, should someone be on the street."
- "If they really try to find work they can find at least some work to do. Even if they don't have education, still they can work somewhere, where you don't actually need any qualification."
- "Because they had the right to make their own choices, and as a result of those choices, that's why they're in the circumstance of living on the streets."
- "How could one let themselves stoop to that level.... One would not allow themselves to reach that social status, simple as getting a minimum wage job...."
- "The society... that we live in today, gives a chance to everyone to work and study.... It is up to us to try and survive through these circumstances...."
- "We want to believe that it is their own fault because it is their own fault. They don't want to work and rather sit on the sidewalk and ask for money."

characteristics as the primary basis for understanding human behaviour. In the case of poverty, it is not surprising that we tend to focus on certain inherent characteristics of those who are poor—their supposed laziness, lack of education, lack of ambition, and so on (see Box 10.3). Such an approach reflects the ideology known as "blaming the victim," first delineated by American author William Ryan in 1971.

Ryan compared this ideology with the views of biological determinists, who see social inequality as the result of natural differences. In contrast to biological determinism, the emphasis in the blaming-the-victim ideology is on environmental or cultural causation, and the analysis is couched in terms that may even display deep concern for the victim and a sincere commitment to reform. However, in the final analysis, the approaches of the biological determinists and the victim blamers end up in the same place. According to Ryan, "The stigma that marks the victim and accounts for his victimization is an acquired stigma, a stigma of social, rather than genetic, origin. But the stigma, the defect, the fatal difference—though derived in the past from environmental forces—is still located within the victim" (1971, 7).

In recent years, the term *poor-bashing* has been used to describe the process first noted by Ryan. It is not just others who blame the poor. What is particularly troubling about this process is that it is often the poor who blame themselves for their condition. With low self-esteem, the poor often turn to self-destructive coping mechanisms such as smoking, alcohol abuse, or substance abuse. With the poor internalizing the blame, it often becomes more difficult for them to get out of poverty (Morris 2002).

Blaming the victim, like the belief in a meritocracy, is an integral component of liberal ideology. Because most of us believe that everyone gets a fair chance at the "race of life," those who lose must simply be inadequate runners. The race itself is not in question; it is the losers of the race who need "fixing." Put in more sociological terms, the individual, rather than the social structure, is seen as the problem. It is therefore assumed that it is the poor who must be changed if poverty is to be reduced. Across Canada the expansion of neoliberalism also saw the return of a nineteenth-century notion—the "deserving" and the "undeserving" poor. For those deemed by governments to be deserving—such as children, the disabled, or the elderly—a bare minimum of social assistance is provided. For all the rest, the state provides practically nothing. Help for the poor is provided on a "case by case" basis via charitable or religious organizations, with the onus being on the poor to prove they are deserving. In major cities across Canada, many of the poor—such as panhandlers and the homeless—have increasingly been criminalized.

Can Poverty Be Eradicated?

Because we see inequalities as linked solely to individuals, we lose sight of the fact that an unrestrained marketplace will inevitably lead to extremes of wealth and poverty, so aptly described by Charles Dickens and others in nineteenth-century England. While the corporate elite secure great personal wealth, the majority are left to face the possibility of unemployment or underemployment, low wages, and inadequate social supports.

Moreover, capital will flow where it can get the best return on its investment. In the long term, the production of luxury items can generate greater profits than the production of necessities, because greater mark-ups

> To eradicate poverty and to prevent its recurrence, it is necessary to have a true explanation of the cause of poverty: Poverty is primarily caused by wealth.
> —Richard Ziegler

can be attached to the price of the former. If capital flows out of the production of necessities, then, as a result of supply and demand, the price of necessities will rise. As the prices of these commodities rise, a certain percentage of the population will simply not have the "extra" money to pay for the increase. Such individuals will no longer be able to afford the necessities of life.

An example can be seen in the housing market. Governments at all levels have been letting market dynamics provide for housing needs—they have provided little publicly funded social housing, and all provinces have abolished or weakened rent regulation. When rents escalated rapidly in many Canadian cities, some people absorbed the extra cost by skimping on other expenses. However, for some, any increase was too much: they simply could not afford the increase, because they had no "extra" to draw on. As a result, some people were driven into homelessness. In 2007 there was a core of about 150,000 homeless people across Canada (Laird 2007). Others, not quite so badly off, obtained their rent money by cutting into their food budget. Over 750,000 Canadians were forced to use food banks for at least one month in 2006 (Canadian Association of Food Banks 2007).

The persistence of poverty must also be connected to the growing constraints that the corporate sector has placed on governments regarding any attempts to either redistribute wealth (for example, via taxation) or provide adequate social supports to the poor. Many social analysts have noted that one of the main functions of the welfare state was to reduce inequality through a variety of social policies. It is not surprising, then, that the neoliberal policies that led to an erosion of the welfare state have also led to an increased disparity between rich and poor. Without the government to moderate the worst excesses of an unrestrained market, we are seeing a return to the unfettered capitalism of the nineteenth and early twentieth centuries. As one author writes, "A shrinking government means a growing gap" (Yalnizyan 1998, 65).

While the total elimination of poverty may not be possible in any capitalist society, it is certainly possible to moderate it, if governments have the political will to do so. There are many policy options and initiatives that can reduce inequality in Canada. For example, a report by the Canada Millennium Scholarship Foundation concluded that federal and provincial tax credit programs for postsecondary students, valued at $1.8 billion annually, are not helping the neediest students. In fact, the entire system of tuition and education credits primarily benefit those from high-income families who are more likely to attend university (Church 2007). A much more effective approach to help less affluent families would be to give the same amount of money directly to students in the form of grants.

In addition, governments could improve market incomes by improving minimum wages, enhancing the ability of workers to organize unions, and granting part-time workers equal rights and benefits. Governments could also help increase the number of "good" jobs by, for example, expanding public-sector employment, rewarding those employers who provide well-paying full-time employment, and legislating a shorter work week. They could also help families meet their basic needs by developing a national childcare program, increasing social and cooperative housing, expanding public transportation systems, and ensuring that all Canadians have equal access to health care and education (Curry-Stevens 2001, 42–45). There is no lack of money to undertake these programs, and a return to a more progressive tax system would provide the financial means to build a more equitable and sustainable society. Unfortunately, no political party wants to risk losing votes by raising taxes.

Why Poverty Affects All of Us

William Ryan notes that a major component of blaming the victim is the separating out and identification of a particular population of victims as a special group different from the rest of us. In his terms (1971, 9), we define such people as "the Different Ones," who are perceived as "less competent, less skilled, less knowing—in short, less human." This attitude can be seen in the comments of students in Box 10.3. Of course, this tendency is not unique to current victim-blamers. Throughout history, the dehumanization of particular groups of people has been used to justify their abuse, maltreatment, enslavement, or even extermination. To return to a point made in an earlier chapter, humans have always had the propensity to create a world of "us" and "them." The current demonization of the poor in Canada is part of a process that has allowed us to tolerate, and even actively support, government cuts affecting the most vulnerable in our society.

It is therefore important to point out that the poor are not different from us; they *are* us. At a psychological level, this is not something most of us want to hear. We want to believe that poverty is the result of a personal failing that, of course, we ourselves lack. Students in particular want to believe they cannot be poor. After all, they are laying out a large sum of money for tuition, something most have been told is an investment in their future—a protection against ending up as a "have-not." However, the reality is that any of us (or our relatives and friends) may at some time in our lives find ourselves just a paycheque or a divorce away from poverty, particularly if we are women.

Poverty means far more than simply the lack of money. It affects all aspects of an individual's life; it is linked to a number of variables, including mortality rates. According to the National Council of Welfare (1993, 479), "[W]ell-off Canadians live longer and healthier lives on average than low-income Canadians." People in the poorest income group in Canada can expect to have more children die before their first birthday, have more ill health throughout their lifetime, have more years of illness so severe it inhibits major activities, and die at an earlier age. These patterns are consistent with those in other developed capitalist countries.

It is important to note that international data indicate that the key variable to determining one's outcome in life seems to be the distribution of income within a society rather than the attainment of a particular amount of income. For example, Sweden, Norway, and the Netherlands, with more equitable income distribution, had the highest average life expectancies, while the United States, with its extremes of wealth and poverty, had the second-lowest average life expectancy among developed countries.

Why should those of us who may never be poor be concerned about the

---

Box 10.4 What It Means to Be Poor

Reflections from Working with the Women at the Ottawa Council for Low Income Support Services

To live in poverty is a struggle for survival filled with tension, fear, and frustration. It is to be robbed of pride, for people living in poverty can't afford the luxury of pride. To stand in line for food or Christmas toys or beg for a special clothing allowance leaves little room for pride.

It is the deep pain which comes with the knowledge that you must deprive your children of opportunities and experiences other children receive as their right.

It's the humiliation of going to your child's school to explain why you can't afford the expensive running shoes that don't mark the gym floor.

It's the look of sadness in your child's eyes when you say no to a school trip or to the purchase of school pictures. Young children don't understand the concept of money. As one parent put it, "They just think you don't love them as much as

other parents love their kids."

Poverty is the dread lurking ever in your consciousness. Dread of the day your kids realize their family is different and somehow not as good. Dread of the day your children are ashamed of you. Dread of the end of the month with no money and no food.

Poverty is living a "no-name, no frills" existence amidst a world in which materialism runs rampant. It's listening to non-poor people make false judgements about you, devalue your existence, question your integrity, label you "poor" as though that's all there is to you.

Poverty is a demoralizing existence which saps the hopes and dreams upon which the rest of us build our lives.

Source: Andrew Jackson and David Robinson, with Bob Baldwin and Cindy Wiggins, *Falling Behind: The State of Working Canada 2000*. Ottawa: Canadian Centre for Policy Alternatives, 2000, 132.

---

poor? Even if for the moment we lay aside humanitarian reasons for caring for those more disadvantaged than ourselves, we all still need to be concerned about the existence of poverty. If we begin to see that poverty is a structural rather than an individual problem, then it becomes easier to understand how the existence of poverty affects us all.

In straight capitalist terms, poverty costs us all a lot of money. The costs of poverty come in two forms: lost output and diverted output (Economic Council of Canada 1969, 109–10). Lost output is connected to the fact that the poor represent, in economic terms, unutilized or underutilized resources of human capital. Not only are many of them not producing goods and services, but also with low incomes they are unable to purchase a variety of goods and services. Diverted output means that poverty adds costs to the economy that would not be required if poverty did not exist. These costs include additional demands on the health care system resulting from greater rates of illness among the poor; substantial costs for government to administer a wide variety of public welfare and assistance programs; large amounts of voluntary labour to assist the poor that could be put to more productive use; increased expenditures to protect individuals and property, as well as additional demands on the entire criminal justice system; and additional costs to the education system in its attempts to deal with children living in poverty. One recent study estimated that homelessness alone costs Canadians between $4.5 and $6 billion dollars annually (Laird 2007).

In addition, the growing gap between rich and poor leads to a decline of social solidarity, an essential component of civil society. In the United States, with its greater extremes of wealth and poverty, the middle and upper strata are increasingly moving into walled communities with security gates to keep the "unwanted element" out of sight and out of mind. Such communities have also begun to appear in Canada. Greater equality means a more vibrant, socially integrated society.

... *And the Poor Get Prison*

Although the Reiman quotation is describing the United States, the same description would hold for Canadian prisons as well. As noted in the previous chapter, the entire criminal justice system—from what behaviours are defined as illegal to who gets incarcerated—favours the privileged and works against those at the bottom of the socioeconomic scale. Given the high poverty rates of Aboriginals in Canada, it should not be surprising that they are highly over-represented in the prison population. In 2005, Aboriginals made up 4.4 percent of the Canadian population but accounted for 17 percent of the people in prison (CBC.ca 11 April 2005).

It might be thought that the extent of poverty is of no interest to those in power. However, the poor and long-term unemployed may be seen as a threat to the stability of the capitalist system. They are not being well served by the current economic arrangement; in fact, they have every reason to oppose it. In addition, the poor make capitalism look bad to the rest of us. In the midst of an economic boom, many of Canada's largest cities are full of homeless people, making the extremes of wealth and poverty highly visible. In a more concrete way, the poor are more likely to commit petty crimes of property and make the middle classes afraid to visit areas where they congregate. Since poverty as a whole is not going away, it is now the poor themselves who are being made to go away. In some cities in Canada, the poor have been given free bus tickets to go elsewhere. Another trend has been to harass the poor so they will move to outlying parts of the city. When these types of efforts fail, there is always prison.

This is not to say that those in prison are innocent. Rather, it is to argue that the entire criminal justice system works against the poor, guaranteeing that many of them end up in prison. It is also worth noting that the United States, with one of the greatest extremes of wealth and poverty in the world, also leads the world

> When we look in our prisons to see who really threatens us, all we see are poor people. By that time, virtually all the well-to-do people who endanger us have been discreetly weeded out of the system.
> —Jeffrey Reiman, *The Rich Get Richer and the Poor Get Prison*

in the number of prisons and imprisonment. In the United States, the number of people in prison quadrupled in just over twenty years, from approximately 500,000 in 1980 to more than two million in 2000. At the end of 2005, a record seven million people—one in every thirty-two U.S. adults—were behind bars, on probation, or on parole (*Washington Post*, 1 December 2006, A3). Many of those in jail have been found guilty of minor drug offences, and a large number are either Black or Hispanic.

The current criminal justice system serves many positive functions for those with wealth and power within our system. First, our attention is directed away from failures of our social system or our inequitable distribution of wealth to the poor, who we fear may kidnap our children, break into our houses, and so on. During elections, many of us find a "law and order" platform very appealing. Second, it convinces the middle strata that the poor are deserving of their condition, and that they are *not* "just like us." Third, it demobilizes the poor as a potential political force. Fourth, it brings down unemployment rates, as those in prison are not counted as part of the unemployed.

In addition, following the U.S. model, increasing numbers of prisoners in Canada are being exploited as cheap labour. Federal prisoners are currently making office furniture, textiles, and farm products, as well as doing printing and data entry work. Prison labour can be very profitable: wages can be extremely low because governments cover costs of food, housing, clothing, and shelter. There is also a growing trend—begun in the United States but now happening in Canada as well—to privatize prisons, creating what has been called a "prison-industrial complex." Thus, prisons are becoming a growth industry, and crime does pay—to the shareholders of companies that run private prisons!

Inequality on a Global Scale

Until this point, we have largely been discussing unequal allocation of resources and power within Canada. However, inequality also exists on a global scale. All of us are aware that there are countries in the world where life is much harder and the standard of living much lower than in Canada. These countries are referred to as underdeveloped, developing, the Third World,[2] or the South. The United Nations uses the term "less developed countries" (LDCs). Such countries share a number of common traits, including low per-capita income, high rates of unemployment, a large gap between rich and poor, unrepresentative governments, increasing populations, rural-based economies, and a high level of political instability (Basran 1993, 468).

The explanations for the existence of inequality between countries mirror those for inequality within Canadian society. Hence, the biological determinists see the underdevelopment of some nations as proof that certain groups—notably those with dark skins—are biologically inferior. In contrast, the various liberal

---

2. This term first appeared in the 1960s. It was used to distinguish the majority of countries in the world that were neither part of the developed capitalist West (the First World) nor the Soviet Bloc countries of the East (the Second World).

theories see global inequality as the result of some inherent disadvantage that keeps certain countries from fairly competing in the "race of life." While ostensibly neutral, such theories end up blaming the victim; that is, the causes of underdevelopment are linked to various tendencies within these countries. Such failings include overpopulation, corruption and nepotism, traditional cultural values, low achievement motivation, under-developed markets, low levels of technology, and so on. From the liberal perspective, if underdeveloped countries can be given help in overcoming such prob-lems, they will move along the path to development and wealth.

> The globalisation of poverty in the late 20th century is unprecedented in world history. This poverty is not, however, the consequence of a "scarcity" of human and material resources. Rather it is the result of a system of global oversupply predicated on unemployment and the worldwide minimisation of labour costs.
> —Michel Chossudovsky, *The Globalisation of Poverty*

Change theories, in contrast, focus on the structural basis for global inequality. In this analysis, developed and underdeveloped countries are not compared to each other, but rather are seen as being in a relationship of structural inequality. Countries suffer from "underdevelopment" because of the mas-sive export of surplus value from their countries to the developed world, which deprives them of the benefit of their natural resources and labour (Rodney 1972, 22). As Chossudovsky's quote notes, gross inequalities on a global scale result from the ongoing needs of the corporate sector. Just as inequalities *within* countries must be understood as relationships of power and domination, so must inequali-ties *between* countries be seen that way.

Change theorists argue that the problems noted by liberals are the *result*, not the *cause*, of underdevelopment. We have already seen that capitalism grew as a result of European expansionism. In this competitive process, the European nations seized territories in Africa, Asia, Australia, and North and South America. By the end of the nineteenth century, the European states had established total control over their territories, and the era of imperialism had begun.

The colonial powers were also active behind the scenes within the colonies to secure their political and economic control. First, they undertook to gain support from the most conservative elements in these societies. These included feudal landlords and royalty, traders who were often agents for foreign companies, and, at first, the small group of educated individuals drawn from the local population. At the same time, divide-and-rule policies—in combination with every attempt to encourage traditionalism, tribalism, and superstition—were used to divide and weaken the oppressed masses of the population.

The end of direct colonial rule did not change the situation of the less developed countries in any way, as their economies had become extremely distorted and dependent on the imperialist powers. Moreover, internal political instabilities, an impoverished or underpaid workforce susceptible to graft and corruption, as well as continued alliances between the imperialist powers and the local elites, meant little true independence or advancement for the majority of people in the Third World. Thus the imperialist powers, led by the United States in the second half of the twentieth century, retained effective domination over the poorest nations of the world through political, economic, social, military, and technical means.

The economies of the lesser developed countries, particularly those in Africa, have continued to stagnate, in large measure because of massive debt load. Much of the foreign loan moneys that were transferred to the Third World in the post-war era either were wasted on inappropriate or cost-inflated technologies, were spent on military hardware, were transferred directly to banks in the developed world, or were spent on wasteful conspicuous consumption. Rising oil prices and interest rates also aggravated the debt crisis (George 1989, 11–46). The bottom line for the debt-ridden poorest nations is that, to pay off their debts, they are now exporting more wealth than they receive from abroad.

Just as there has been an increase in the gap between the "haves" and "have-nots" *within* capitalist countries, there has also been an increasing gap between the "have" and "have-not" countries, and economic conditions in the less developed countries continue to be bleak. In 1960 the top 20 percent of the world's people in the richest countries had 30 times the income (measured by total GDP) of the poorest 20 percent. This grew to 32 times in 1970, to 45 times in 1980, and to 59 times in 1989. By 1999, the top 20 percent received 74 times the income of the bottom 20 percent (Lee 2002, 28). Although a small number of the LDCs, such as China and India, are seeing their overall economies grow as a result of an integrating world economy, globalization and trade liberalization have not improved the lives of the majority of people around the globe. Moreover, in countries such as China a rapidly developing economy has led to a massive growth in disparity between the rich and poor *within* that country, particularly a disparity between rural and urban populations. It should also be noted that the poor countries are most vulnerable to growing environmental risks resulting from extreme weather conditions caused by climate change. Since 1991, two-thirds of disaster victims have lived in countries with a low level of development (Toussaint 2005, 51).

Imperialism—the more precise term for what is commonly known as globalization—is not, in the end, a relationship between nations. Rather, it is the same unequal class relations found within capitalist economies but on an international scale. Working people in the developed capitalist world are not the beneficiaries of imperialism. While some small amount of the total wealth taken from the developing world may return to some workers in the form of higher wages, cheaper goods, or better working conditions, the ultimate beneficiary is the capitalist owning class. Thus all inequalities of wealth and income—whether within countries or between them—must be understood within a particular set of class relations.

Key Points

1. Because we live in a society that puts so much emphasis on the individual, we usually connect social inequalities to individual characteristics, rather than to structural arrangements.

2. Humans have always symbolically represented differences between groups or individuals. In capitalist societies, mass advertising convinces us to buy products that serve as symbols of high status.

3. Liberalism, the dominant ideology of capitalism, stresses fairness and equality of opportunity, but actually masks structural inequality.

4. Functionalist theories argue that unequal allocation of societal rewards is both universal and necessary in all societies. Change theorists, on the other hand, argue that structured inequality unfairly advantages those at the top, while the majority do not benefit from such arrangements. From the class perspective a true meritocracy cannot exist in capitalist societies.

5. Movement from one social position to another is referred to as social mobility. While some upward mobility is possible in Canada, most mobility is occupational, relatively modest, and occurs within the "mass middle."

6. Although education is assumed to be the primary agent of social equalization, in reality it more or less sustains the already-existing inequalities of socioeconomic status, race, and gender. In today's economic climate, it is likely that such inequalities may increase.

7. There is no single definition of poverty in Canada, although Statistics Canada creates low-income cut-offs (LICOs); individuals and families below these cut-offs are said to be in "straitened circumstances." Social assistance is provided mainly by the provinces, and cut-off lines are fairly arbitrary.

8. Poverty is not equally distributed across all groups in Canada. Visible minorities (most notably recent immigrants), Aboriginals, and people with disabilities have much higher rates of poverty than the national average. Poverty rates are also higher than average among female-headed lone-parent families with dependent children.

9. The ideology referred to as "blaming the victim" directs our attention to the poor and their particular environments as the cause of poverty. In reality, poverty is the inevitable result of the economic arrangements within capitalist societies.

10. It is possible for governments to reduce the degree of social inequality in Canada.

11. Inequality also exists on a global scale. Like inequality within nation-states, global inequality must be understood within particular class relations.

Further Reading

Chossudovsky, Michel. 1998. *The Globalisation of Poverty: Impacts of IMF and World Bank Reforms*. Halifax: Fernwood.
This book discusses the ways in which economic reforms and structural adjustment programs are having a devastating effect on humans and the environment.

Laird, Gordon. 2007. *SHELTER—Homelessness in a Growth Economy: Canada's 21st Century Paradox*. Calgary: Sheldon Chumir Foundation. <http://www.chumirethicsfoundation. ca/files/pdf/SHELTER.pdf>.
This short work details the degree of homelessness in Canada and what can be done about it.

Mirchandani, Kiran and Wendy Chan. 2007. *Criminalizing Race, Criminalizing Poverty: Welfare Fraud Enforcement in Canada*. Halifax: Fernwood.
These authors argue that the poor in general, and racialized people in particular, are most often the victims of government cutbacks; these individuals are stigmatized and discriminated against within the welfare system.

Reiman, Jeffrey. 2007. *The Rich Get Richer and the Poor Get Prison: Ideology, Class, and Criminal Justice,* 8th ed. Upper Saddle River, NJ: Allyn & Bacon.
A critical examination of the criminal justice system in the United States, a country with the highest incarceration rate in the world.

Swanson, Jean. 2001. *Poor-Bashing: The Politics of Exclusion*. Toronto: Between the Lines.
A non-academic work that examines how the poor are being demonized in Canada. Of particular interest is Swanson's analysis of how the media teach us to attack the poor.

Yalnizyan, Armine. 2007. *The Rich and the Rest of Us: The Changing Face of Canada's Growing Gap*. Ottawa: Canadian Centre for Policy Alternatives, March.
A brief overview of the growing economic disparity in Canada. The CCPA regularly produces many studies and reports that provide up-to-date information on a wide variety of topics. Their website is <www.policyalternatives.ca>.

Zawilski, Valerie, and Cynthia Levine-Rasky, eds. 2005. *Inequality in Canada: A Reader on the Intersections of Gender, Race, and Class*. Don Mills, ON: Oxford University Press.
A reader that examines the way various inequalities in Canada —including those of race, gender, sexual orientation, and socioeconomic status—are interconnected.

11 Race and Ethnicity

In This Chapter

- What is racism and what are its roots?
- Do racism and other forms of social intolerance exist in Canada?
- How do various social theories explain the persistence of racism?
- What is the outlook for the future?

There are many differences between human beings, but only some seem to be socially significant. One difference that is consistently noted in our society is that of gender. Another is race and ethnicity. With regard to race and ethnicity, the very categories of analysis have been hotly debated, and there is no consistency in their usage. For example, people of Jewish origin have variously been described as a race, ethnic group, nation, religion, or people. Moreover, individuals often have their own interpretations of how they see themselves and others. Thus it can be said that issues of race and ethnicity are perhaps the most complex in the social sciences. Such debates give us a clue that we are dealing with social categories, rather than self-evident biological ones.

Let's begin with the concept of race. All humans belong to a single species, *Homo sapiens*, which likely evolved in Africa millions of years ago. Over time, some members of our species, isolated within particular gene pools, developed certain distinctive physical characteristics. Such characteristics were likely the result of natural selection: for example, while dark skins would provide benefits in hot climates, such as better protection from the sun, lighter skins would be advantageous in moderate and cold climates, allowing for more absorption of vitamin D (Leakey

> It always amazes me when people express surprise that there might be a "race problem" in Canada, or when they attribute the "problem" to a minority of prejudiced individuals. Racism is, and always has been, one of the bedrock institutions of Canadian society, embedded in the very fabric of our thinking, our personality.
> —Adrienne Shadd "Institutionalizing Racism and Canadian History"

and Lewin 1977, 137). However, over time people moved about and came into contact with new gene pools. This process advanced in the modern period, as new modes of transportation developed. As a result, there are no genetically "pure" races, and modern-day distinctions between people are more cultural than physical. Nonetheless, humans continue to try to prove the biological reality of "race."

The concept of race first appeared in the English language around 500 years ago. In its initial usage, it referred to a class or group (of people, plants, or animals) possessing some common characteristics. It was not until the eighteenth century that the term began to refer more narrowly to a category of people with shared physical or biological characteristics. The scientific categorization of people into races was the result of two interconnected developments: the expansion of capitalism with its imperial domination of non-European peoples, and the growth of science, particularly, in the nineteenth century, the field of physical anthropology.

Exactly how many races are there? One scientist in the eighteenth century suggested that there were four: Europeans, Asiatics, Africans, and American Indians. This categorization was based on skin colour and the subjective assessment of behavioural differences. In 1781, a German physiologist, Johann Friedrich Blumenbach, proposed a categorization based on head or skull shape. By the nineteenth century, physical anthropologists became seized with the question of categorizing people into racial categories, and new divisions and subdivisions appeared as new populations became known. While such research was supposedly neutral, it was occurring in a particular social context in which it was assumed that some racial groups were innately superior or inferior to others. This context helps us understand that the obsession with race is a social phenomenon particular to a specific time and place.

Think About It

The next time you're sitting in a classroom, consider the following: have you ever paid attention to which students in the class are left-handed? Blue-eyed? Wearing glasses? Compare this to the way we notice skin colour or other physical characteristics linked to racial difference.

What Is Racism?

From a strictly genetic standpoint, it can be said that there is no such category as a race. The genetic variation between two people described as being of the same "race" may actually be larger than between two people of different races. Nonetheless, certain individuals with particular physiological characteristics have been disadvantaged, in spite of the fact that race has no scientific validity. Race, therefore, is important as a social, rather than a physiological, reality. In this context, **race** can be defined as a category of people who share certain common physical traits deemed to be socially significant. Many sociologists now prefer to speak of **racialized groups** because this term highlights the social process by which certain groups of people are singled out for unequal treatment on the basis of real or imagined physical characteristics (Li 1990, 7). Race, then, should be distinguished from **ethnicity**. Ethnic groups are distinguished by socially selected *cultural* traits, rather than physical ones. These cultural traits may include language, religion, ideology, ancestry, or historical symbols.

In reality, of course, there is some overlap between the two concepts of race and ethnicity. Some groups that may share common physical traits and may be defined socially as a race may also share distinctive cultural traits. On the other hand, some European ethnic groups have been racialized at certain times in Canada's history. For example, Ukrainian immigrants at the turn of the century were considered "racially" suited for the difficult work of pioneer farming on the prairies, while Italian immigrants were brought into Canada in the postwar era in part because they were considered "racially" suited to the difficult and dirty work in the construction industry (Satzewich 1999, 323).

> We speak so blithely about "race" and yet the concept is as unstable as water.... To speak personally, I am tan-tinted, and of African and Aboriginal and European heritage, and grew up "Black" in Nova Scotia. Yet, in South Carolina, a woman declared I was Filipino, or Chinese; in Quebec, a man swore I was Arab; in Ontario, another man presumed I was Portuguese. To some, I am African (but pallid); to others, Caucasian (but swarthy); to still others, Asian (but with curly hair). I am "Black"—but can pass easily for "Cuban" or, post-9/11, "Middle Eastern," and my loud "Yankee" laughter gets me thrown out of restaurants.
> — George Elliott Clarke, Canadian poet and novelist

However, the most commonly racialized groups today are those with darker skins. The Employment Equity Act of 1986 used the term *visible minority* to describe "persons other than Aboriginal peoples, who are non-Caucasian in race and non-White in colour." The following groups are considered visible minorities: Chinese, South Asians, Blacks, Arabs and West Asians, Filipino, Southeast Asians, Latin Americans, Japanese, Koreans, and Pacific Islanders. The 1996 census was the first to ask Canadians if they felt they were members of one of these groups.

As noted in Chapter 3, social groups and cultures tend to evaluate themselves and their way of life favourably in relation to others. This tendency is referred to as *ethnocentrism*. In and of itself, ethnocentrism is not a negative social characteristic, but rather reflects group solidarity. Indeed, its absence can be a sign of social disintegration, as when a chronically disadvantaged and oppressed group thinks so little of itself that individuals see the culture of outsiders as superior to their own.

Under certain conditions, ethnocentrism becomes more virulent and hateful, taking on a quality of hostility, aggression, and antagonism toward non-members of a particular group. If this hostility is directed toward people on the basis of their membership in a particular ethnic group—for example, Greeks, Irish, or Ukrainians—it is referred to as **ethnic chauvinism**. If it is directed toward people with particular physical characteristics—such as skin colour, eye shape, or hair texture—it is referred to as **racism**. The term **anti-Semitism** is used to refer to hostility directed specifically at those who are of Jewish origin, while **Islamophobia** is a relatively recent term that refers to hostility directed at Muslims and their religion, Islam.

Two more terms are worth noting here. **Prejudice** is an attitude of dislike or hostility toward individuals on the basis of their membership in particular groups. On the other hand, **discrimination** refers to the denial of equal treatment or opportunities to these same social groups. While these two phenomena are usually connected, they can be distinguished from each other. Some people might be highly prejudiced, but unable to discriminate because they have no structural means of doing so. On the other hand, others might find themselves in a position where they must discriminate, although they are not in fact prejudiced (for example, a restaurant worker might be told not to serve Black customers). Discrimination is generally the more serious of the two processes since it will inevitably hurt the victim's life chances, such as getting a job or finding a place to live. However, because prejudice can also lead to hurtful acts—including those of a violent nature—it too can have negative consequences for the victim.

The lack of clarity of terminology has often led to imprecision of analysis. For example, race and ethnicity are often used interchangeably or conflated into the term "minority group." Prejudice and discrimination are sometimes conflated, and antagonisms toward a variety of social groups are commonly described as forms of racism. In part, this reflects the fact that the consequences of ethnic chauvinism, anti-Semitism, Islamophobia, and racism are often similar, and the existence of one can at times mean the existence of the other.

Racism, unlike other forms of social intolerance, is always linked to real or perceived physiological traits. As Bolaria and Li (1988, 18) note: "It is the combination of physical traits and social attributes that makes racial oppression unique. Since the permanence of physical features is unquestionable, racial minorities carry a social stigma along with their experience of oppression that becomes indistinguishable from their physical appearances." Most importantly, racism differs from other forms of social intolerance because it is rooted in very specific historical and economic conditions.

Think About It

Sometimes we confuse responses to racism with racism itself. For example, racialized groups are sometimes accused of being racist because they don't associate with the dominant group. At your high school, did kids from racialized groups hang out together? If so, can you think of some social reasons why you/they might have done this?

Box 11.1 "Us" versus "Them" Revisited

Some years ago I was standing in a check-out line at a local store. The line was moving very slowly, and I complained to the woman in front of me that they needed to hire more staff. The woman told me she didn't mind the wait. "I like that woman at the cash," she said, "she's Black but she's very nice."

How we categorize others—how we decide who will be part of "us" and who will be considered "them"—is largely determined by those with power and the ideological constructs that support them. Once these categories are created, we use them without thinking too much about it. Because most of those with power in Canada have historically been European, it should not be surprising that "us" is often assumed to be people of European ancestry, while "them" refers to any non-Europeans.

With regard to the comment made to me by the woman at the check-out line, what is disturbing is not just the underlying racism, but also her assumption that she could talk to a total stranger that way—in her mind we both shared a category different from the woman at the cash register, since we were both White. The assumption that "White" is normal—a kind of default category—is so much part of our culture that we rarely notice it. For example, we rarely hear comments such as "I really like my new sociology teacher—she's White and very smart" or "A new corner store just opened up in the neighbourhood that's run by a nice White family." Even among non-racialized people who profess to be "colour-blind," race is a category that we all note, and people who are not White are still considered to be different from "us."

In recent years, many analysts have begun to address the issue of *White privilege*. Of course, there is no real biological entity as a "white" person, and many actually have darker skin colours than individuals from racialized groups. "White," however, is more than descriptive; it also has positive linguistic connotations as it is a colour usually connected to cleanliness, purity, and even holiness. It has been argued that being perceived as White guarantees various social advantages that most people in this category take for granted:

> White people can count on certain things: they are not routinely intercepted by police while going about their business…; vacancies do not suddenly disappear when they seek housing; their bad behaviour is seen in individual terms rather than as a reflection of their group identity; they are not regularly asked to explain "the white view of things" or to speak on behalf of their "race"; they regularly see people like themselves represented in media, in professions, and in positions of authority; they do not need to make special efforts to find children's literature, dolls or toys that feature people who look like themselves;… they are not routinely followed by store clerks watching that they do not steal; they do not need to wonder if the obstacles they face are based on racism or if their appearance will count against them if they seek legal or medical aid. (Sorenson 2003, 47–8)

Whether we acknowledge it or not, our social world is divided along racial lines. Those with light skins are considered Canadians, while those with racialized characteristics—even if their family has been in Canada for generations—are still considered "outsiders" (see Box 11.1).

The Roots of Racism

There is a great deal of debate about the origins of racism. The debates generally centre on whether the various forms of social intolerance prior to the capitalist era can be defined as racism. It will be argued here that racism as we know it is a relatively recent phenomenon, and its emergence as a systematic world view developed with the rise of capitalism and its global expansion.

It was common for foraging peoples to define themselves as "chosen people." However, outsiders could achieve acceptance by simply acquiring a kinship tie, whether real or symbolic. During the period of antiquity, slavery was based on capture in war rather than on any particular physical characteristics. There is no evidence of racism among the ancient Egyptians, Babylonians, or Persians. The Greeks viewed all outsiders as barbarians, inferior as a result of cultural and linguistic, rather than physical, differences; those who acquired Greek culture, particularly its language, were welcomed into Greek society. Among the Romans, distinction was based on citizenship, which was extended to all people defined as "free" throughout the empire, regardless of physical traits. Slaves were not distinguished by their physical characteristics (Cox 1970, 322–23).

In medieval Europe, the fundamental distinction between people was that of Christian and non-Christian. Anti-Semitism was persistent and widespread because of its basis in the Christian dogma of the period, rather than any specific physical traits attributed to Jews. Likewise, the expansion of the Islamic world into Europe during the Middle Ages can be linked to economic and religious goals, rather than any racist assumptions. Of course, people in the pre-capitalist period could observe physical distinctions between peoples. However, nowhere did such differences become central or even important in defining particular social institutions or social structures.

The beginnings of racism can be traced to the expansion of European economies—first under a mercantilist and later an industrial capitalist system. This early globalization by the imperial capitalist powers, dominated by Britain, was primarily into countries where people had skin colours different from those of Europeans. Imperialism

> With the British leading the way, European capitalism invaded Ireland, the Americas, Asia and Africa, exhibiting a barbarity and cruelty that is almost incomprehensible.... In the process, a colonial system and an ideology of modern racism were constructed— abominations that continue to haunt the world in which we live.
> —David McNally,
> *Another World Is Possible*

could then be morally justified by arguing that those affected were somehow inferior and that the Europeans were actually there to help them. This argument came to be known as the "White man's burden"—the title of British poet Rudyard Kipling's poem published in 1899 regarding the U.S. conquest of the Philippines—which refers to the conquered as "new-caught sullen peoples/ Half-devil and half-child." In the name of "civilizing the heathen," people of colour around the globe were robbed of their resources and their cultures and forced to work in the mines, fields, and forests to create great wealth for rich Europeans. This wealth became the economic basis for the development of capitalism.

It is impossible in the short space of this book to give adequate attention to the horrors that were inflicted on people of colour around the globe at this time. Everywhere the European colonists settled, from the Americas to India, from Africa to Asia, indigenous populations suffered untold miseries. Populations were decimated by a combination of mass murder, disease, and maltreatment; some peoples—such as the Beothuk of Newfoundland and the Tasmanians of Australia—were completely eradicated. This period also saw the widespread reintroduction of the social institution of slavery. Slavery was the result not of racism, but rather of the economic requirements of the exploiters; however, once slavery developed, a complex belief system developed to maintain it.

The first forced labourers in the New World were actually the indigenous populations of the Spanish, English, and French colonies. However, their numbers were never adequate and their sustained resistance led to perpetual uprisings. Thus the enslavement of these populations came at a very high social and economic cost. As the Anglo-American colonies expanded, the planter class needed a larger and more secure source of cheap labour. At first, a large number of bonded or indentured workers were brought from the mother country. When the numbers of such workers also proved insufficient, plantation owners sought a new source of labour. Millions of workers brought from Africa—kidnapped and transported for sale to the New World—proved most suitable, not because of their race, but because they were abundant and they were cheap.

The British and Europeans certainly believed that darker-skinned peoples were uncivilized and distinctly inferior to themselves. In the mid-eighteenth century, however, an additional notion began to appear: racial minorities, primarily Blacks, were no longer seen as simply culturally or socially inferior to Europeans; they gradually came to also be considered *biologically* inferior, not fully human (Miles 1989, 28–30).

Prior to the eighteenth century, it was rare for European-Americans to refer to themselves as "White." Usually they thought of themselves in terms of their country of origin or with reference to their religion. As the concept grew of Blacks as biological inferiors, the concept of "Whiteness," with its natural superiority, grew as well. This rigid separation of Blacks and Whites proved very useful to plantation owners. In the classic divide-and-rule fashion, the slave-owning class encouraged White workers to identify with their White masters, rather than their Black fellow workers. By giving certain privileges and the perception of a shared "Whiteness" to poor British and European labourers, they could minimize the class identification of these people with Black slaves, and thus lower the risk of a successful rebellion (McNally 2002, 113–24).

Within the economic reality of colonialism and slavery, racism as an ideology grew and flourished, reaching its full development in the latter half of the nineteenth century, ironically just at the time that the formal institution of slavery was coming to an end. The belief in the "natural" inferiority of Blacks was now reinforced by the pseudo-science of the biological determinists.

Why would such an ideology advance just at the time when slavery was ending? Unlike all class societies that preceded it, capitalism was the first socio-economic formation that, in theory, did away with the privileges of birth. And yet social inequality and classes still existed. Since capitalism did provide a degree of upward mobility, there had to be some ideological justification for the failure of most people to move upward in the social hierarchy. What better explanation than the social Darwinist notions that some were naturally superior to others? Notions of racial inferiority, which were a basic element of social Darwinist thought, thus constitute a major component in the ideological underpinning of all modern capitalist societies.

In Chapter 2, both the prevalence and invalidity of biological determinist arguments were noted. It was pointed out that biological determinism sees the hierarchical arrangements of society—in which some receive more power and wealth than others—as simply a reflection of innate differences between people. Biological determinist arguments have been used to justify the unequal treatment of women, the poor, immigrants, and—most persistently—racial minorities. For well over a hundred years, some social scientists have tried to prove that there is a hierarchy of races, and that Blacks in particular form a natural underclass. Yet legitimate biological, behavioural, and social scientists, using universally replicable data, have repeatedly discredited such attempts. Nonetheless, many Canadians continue to believe that certain groups constitute a "natural" underclass.

A History of Racism in Canada

Some Canadians like to believe that, in comparison to the United States, Canada is a country with little history of overt racism. Others believe that racism exists, but that it is a relatively recent phenomenon linked to modern immigration patterns. In reality, racism in Canada has a long and sordid past, described by one author (Wright 1993, 313) as "an unsightly history swept under the threadbare rug of its national myths." This history begins with the subjugation of Canada's Aboriginal peoples, a tale that is nothing less than one of state-directed cultural genocide, domination, and control (Frideres 1988).

Aboriginal Peoples[1]

The first British and French colonists made contact with Aboriginal peoples primarily to exploit their labour power in the fur trade. The Aboriginal peoples were paid pitifully low prices for their pelts or given worthless objects in trade; at the same time, alcohol was introduced into their societies. The Hudson's Bay Company eventually gained monopoly control over the fur trade and, in the process, made indigenous peoples totally dependent on them for survival. Despite the evidence of the destructive effects of alcohol on Native societies, company traders commonly bartered alcohol for furs. Indigenous people received none of the huge wealth they created for the Hudson's Bay Company; rather, large numbers of them perished from famine or were ravaged by diseases introduced by the Europeans.

As the fur trade declined and agriculture expanded, the colonists, no longer needing the labour of indigenous peoples, now sought the increasingly valuable lands inhabited by them. After Confederation, the Canadian government used various means to gain control over Native lands. In the end, assimilation was seen as best, for it was thought that if Aboriginals could be absorbed into the broader population, there could be no land claims. The tool used to promote this end was the Indian Act of 1876. Although there have been some subsequent changes to this act, it set a framework of domination over Aboriginal peoples that continues to the present day.

The Indian Act created sweeping legislation that controlled every aspect of the lives of Native people and, in effect, made them wards of the state under the superintendent of Indian Affairs. It also laid out who would be bound by the act: Indians enrolled in the register of the Department of Indian Affairs were (and continue to be) defined as "status Indians." (The groups not included under the act are non-status Indians, Métis, and Inuit.) Under the terms of the original act, status Indians were prohibited from owning land, from voting, and from purchasing or consuming alcohol, and they were forcibly segregated on reserves. Although the reserves were generally in areas long occupied by various bands, they were much smaller than previous Native territory, were often poorly suited for farming or other economic activity, and could not be disposed of without permission from the federal government.

Traditional Native governments were eventually replaced by band councils that had little real power or influence. Amendments to the act in 1884 prohibited Indians from engaging in certain traditional cultural activities, such as the potlatch and sun dance. The goal of the legislation was to encourage assimilation through contact with White "civilization"—through such institu-

---

1. Since racial categories are social rather than biological entities, the terminology used to describe them is also a social creation. Because of structured inequality, the terminology used by others may not reflect the self-definition of the oppressed group. As a result, there is no totally satisfactory terminology when speaking collectively of the first peoples of Canada. In this book, the terms *Aboriginal people*, *Native people*, *indigenous people*, and *First Nations people* are used interchangeably. The term *Indians* refers to those defined by the federal government as status Indians under the Indian Act.

tions as missionary-run residential schools—while concurrently dissolving Native culture and political structures. Children were taken away from their families and communities and spent many years getting inferior educations in an environment of neglect and disease, as well as physical, sexual, and emotional abuse (see Box 11.2).

Residential schools deprived children of healthy parental role models and weakened the community and family structure upon which traditional Native life was built. The legacy of these schools has been profound. The Canadian government estimates that there are 80,000 people alive today who attended residential schools, and so many display a constellation of symptoms—similar to those of post-traumatic stress disorder—that it has recently been given its own medical name: residential school syndrome (Brasfield 2001). Some argue that the residential school policies were part of an overall pattern of genocide, because the government was consciously attempting to eradicate Indians as a cultural group.

Government policies over the years were largely contradictory. Native peoples were simultaneously segregated from the dominant culture while being expected to integrate into it. They were often unable to continue their traditional means of subsistence, but were not allowed to draw on the resources or services of White settler communities. Meanwhile, the provincial and federal governments gradually acquired massive tracts of valuable Aboriginal lands, often through expropriation, which sometimes required the forcible resettlement of Native communities. Thus, the indigenous peoples of Canada saw the theft of both their resources and their culture. At the same time, they were marginalized from the dominant economy and its culture and were forced to become dependent on the Canadian state.

> I quite often hear from the Indians that they do not want to send their children to school as it is a place where they are sent to die.
> —W. M. Graham, Indian Commissioner for Saskatchewan, 1925
>
> [If] I were appointed by the Dominion Government for the express purpose of spreading tuberculosis, there is nothing finer in existence than the average residential school.
> —N. Walker, Indian Affairs Superintendent, 1948

That marginalization continues up to the present. More than three centuries of prejudice and discrimination against the First Nations of Canada have left a scandalous legacy. Although there has been some improvement in the last twenty-five years, massive inequities remain. Just over 40 percent of Registered Indians live at or below the poverty line, and the unemployment rate for Aboriginal Canadians is twice the rate for non-Aboriginal Canadians. On reserves, the unemployment rate is more than triple the Canadian rate. High rates of poverty and unemployment lead to many other negative outcomes, including ill health, lower life expectancy, and higher rates of infant mortality. Youth suicide among

Box 11.2 The Legacy of Trauma

Maggie Hodgson is a member of the Carrier First Nation. She has co-authored a number of books, including The Spirit Weeps, Healing Voices, *and* A Healing Place. *She has received numerous awards for her work in healing, including the Aboriginal Achievement Award and an award from the United Nations. Here she describes life in residential schools and the consequences for individuals, their families, and their communities:*

Perhaps the most pervasive form of abuse was verbal violence from nuns and priests. Children were called "dirty Indians," "savages." My mom was called a "bastard" because she didn't have a family to go to until her aunt and uncle started to take her during the holidays.

There was also physical violence, stemming from the accepted belief in mainstream society that if you "spare the rod," you "spoil the child." This was foreign to children who had come from a society where discipline meant you learned from your own mistakes and from your grandparents and other role models. The rod spelled fear and alienation.

Violence affected not only individual children, but also whole families and future generations. In one community where I conducted a sexual abuse workshop, a woman came in with big scars all over her face. Her nose had nearly been cut off. Her husband, who had beaten her, was a convicted sexual abuser. He was a victim of abuse in residential school. In the workshop, participants, including members of the husband's family, talked about sexual abuse they had suffered when they were young.

The violent brother, the man who had cut up his wife, told the non-abused brother a story from residential school. "Remember how I used to get you up every night to go pee?" he asked. "I did that because when I wet the bed, the priest would take me to his room and rape me, then beat me for wetting the bed. I never wanted that to happen to you, so I used to get you up to pee."

The brother he had saved from abuse had gone on to be a successful athlete, a non-drinker and a leader. But the man who had heroically protected his brother was a violent alcoholic, locked in pain and had abused his wife with knives and fists.

In his book, *Le Suicide*, French sociologist Émile Durkheim writes that when you reach into a culture and pull out the values, rituals, and societal norms, then try to inject new values, rituals, and norms, the result is often disorientation and the absence of values. Our people who have difficulty adjusting, who are in jail, who are alcoholics, who suffer from poor self-esteem, are reflecting Canadian policies and laws that restricted native religious practices, changed our traditional leadership, and forced native children to attend residential schools. The institutionalization of Aboriginal peoples in foster homes, youth detention facilities and jails continued our community's legacy of trauma.

Source: From *Nation to Nation, Aboriginal Soverignty and the Future of Canada* by Bird/Land/Macadem, 2001. Reprinted with permission of Nelson, a division of Thomson Learning: www.thomsonrights.com. Fax 800-730-2215

the First Nations population is almost double the Canadian average (Indian and Northern Affairs Canada, 2003).

Blacks in Canada[2]

Ironically, the commonality that brings all people of colour together is not their shared cultural or biological origins but, rather, their experience of racism (Bolaria and Li 1988, 18). This is particularly true with regard to Blacks. On the one hand, utilizing concepts such as "African-Canadians" or "Blacks" masks the vast range of differences—in culture, length of time in Canada, national origin, socioeconomic status, and so on—within these categories. On the other hand, such terminology is required to point out their shared experiences as the victims of racism.

African-Canadians have had a long presence in Canada. The first Black slaves were brought to Canada by the French in the seventeenth century. Although the kind of agricultural production in Canada did not lend itself to the wide-spread use of slave labour, the practice of slavery continued. Approximately 10 percent of Loyalists who came to British North America after the American Revolution were Black. The Black population of Canada subsequently increased as many runaway slaves from the United States found their way north on the Underground Railroad. In 1860, the Anti-Slavery Society estimated there were 60,000 Blacks in Canada (Walker 1980, 56).

Far from finding Canada a refuge, Blacks faced overt prejudice and dis-crimination and were tolerated mostly as a source of cheap labour. They were restricted in their ownership of property as well as their ability to educate their children. Both Ontario and Nova Scotia legislated racially separate schools (Shepard 1991, 16); indeed, segregated schools continued in Nova Scotia until the 1960s. Racism was both pervasive and public and could be seen not only in schools, but also in government, the media, the judiciary, the workplace, and elsewhere in society.

Such racism continues into the twenty-first century. At the time of the 2001 census, Blacks constituted the third-largest visible minority group in Canada, with the majority centred in Toronto. Discrimination against Blacks in the labour force continues to be a reality. An analysis of census data found that Blacks experience lower employment rates and employment income and higher unemployment rates regardless of educational level. As one author (Mensah 2002, 129) notes, "The unabashed racial discrimination in the job market impacts Blacks more than any other form of bigotry." Overall, Blacks are more likely than other visible minorities to feel discriminated against or treated unfairly because of their ethnicity, culture, race, skin colour, language, accent, or religion (Milan and Tran 2004, 7).

---

2. As has already been noted, there is no terminology that adequately describes socially constructed racial categories. In this book the terms *Black* and *African-Canadian* are used interchangeably. The terms *people of colour* and *racialized groups* are generally used to refer to all people—including South Asians and Hispanics—who experience racial discrimination on the basis of their skin colour.

Immigration from the Nineteenth to the Twenty-first Century

While a wide variety of immigrants have historically met with discriminatory treatment on their arrival in Canada, those who faced the greatest hostility in the late nineteenth and early twentieth centuries were from China, Japan, and India. As many as 14,000 Chinese men were brought to this country in the late nineteenth century to build the Canadian Pacific Railway. The work was arduous and dangerous, the living conditions appalling, and the wages pathetic. The men were not allowed to bring their families, nor were they allowed to establish relations with White women. Many died from malnutrition, disease, and construction accidents. When the railway was completed in 1885 and their labour was no longer needed, politicians tried to force the Chinese to leave Canada. Some did return to China; of those who remained, most lived in British Columbia.

To discourage further Chinese immigration, the federal government imposed a "head tax" of $50 on every Chinese immigrant in 1886; by 1904 it had risen to $500, which was equivalent to a year's wages for steady work. In 1923, the Chinese Immigration Act (also referred to as the Chinese Exclusion Act) was passed, which virtually ended Chinese immigration. Meanwhile, the Chinese in Canada faced blatant discrimination. They could not serve in public office or on juries, could not vote in provincial or municipal elections, and were barred from the higher-paying professions. As a result, most ended up in small businesses, restaurants, or laundries.

The Japanese in Canada faced similar hostility. Like the Chinese, they encountered economic exploitation and job restrictions and were not allowed to vote. Their schools and housing were segregated, and they were not allowed access to many public places. One of the most shameful examples of racism in Canadian history was the treatment of the Japanese during World War II. After the bombing of Pearl Harbor in 1941, the federal government gave the order to detain all Japanese Canadians living within a hundred miles of the Pacific Coast. In early 1942, more than 20,000 people—more than half of whom had been born in Canada—were forced from their homes and transferred to camps in Alberta, Manitoba, and the B.C. interior. Meanwhile, the federal government sold all their property at a fraction of its value. No comparable actions were taken against German or Italian Canadians, although Canada was also at war with Germany and Italy at the time. In 1946, with the war over, the federal government tried to deport 10,000 Japanese, but a large public outcry forced them to back down.

The third group that endured racial discrimination in immigration policy during this period was from India. Although only a small number of Indians had settled in British Columbia by the early twentieth century, this did not stop the press in that province from attacking what was referred to as a "Hindu invasion." Like the Chinese and Japanese, those of Indian origin were exploited economically, denied the franchise, and restricted from certain occupations and property ownership. In 1908, the government implemented the Continuous Passage Act, which made immigration from India virtually impossible. The argument used to justify the exclusion of immigrants from China, Japan, and India was their inability to assimilate; underlying such arguments was the assumption that such individuals were both different and inferior.

Anti-Semitism has also been a persistent undercurrent in Canadian society. Most Jewish immigration came after 1880, when hundreds of thousands of Jewish refugees fled the virulent anti-Semitism of Eastern Europe. Having been denied the right to own land in Europe they were unfamiliar with farming, and most ended up in larger urban centres, either as workers in the expanding sweatshops or, if they were more fortunate, as owners of small businesses. Anti-Semitism was widespread: Jews were prevented from working in certain occupations, and there were quotas limiting the number of Jewish students allowed to enroll at universities. Jews fortunate enough to find their way into the professions often had to hide their identities. Signs that said "No Jews or Dogs Allowed" or "Christians Only" could be seen in various clubs, resorts, and vacation areas. Canada has a shameful record in regard to providing sanctuary for Jewish refugees from Europe in the 1930s and 1940s (Abella and Troper 1982).

Following World War II, there was some lessening of clearly discriminatory immigration policies in Canada and a decline in overt racial and ethnic discrimination. In part, this was due to the growth of international human rights legislation following the war, as well as the struggles of various groups to end discriminatory practices. The changing economic conditions of the time also helped push such struggles forward. The 1950s and 1960s were times of economic growth in Canada, which led to a rapid expansion in the need for workers; at the same time, improved conditions in postwar Europe led to a decline in immigration from the formerly "preferred" groups of northern Europe. To fill the void, the government loosened its policy with regard to immigrants from non-European countries.

While overt forms of racism and discrimination were in some ways less acceptable, they by no means disappeared. From the 1970s onward, hostilities toward immigrants and people of colour increased. For example, South Asian immigrants in a number of cities were the victims of vandalism and assaults. Blacks continued to face job and housing discrimination, as well as unfair treatment in the criminal justice system, and "racial profiling" by police of both Blacks and indigenous peoples has become a major controversy in many Canadian cities.

Since the events of September 11, 2001, there has also been increasing hostility toward Muslims. This hostility is not new. It has been a feature of European societies since the eighth century and took on a particular form after the expansion of European imperialism into predominantly Muslim countries. The term *Islamophobia* developed in the 1990s, because at that time there was an increase in the negative treatment of Muslim immigrants in a number of European countries. However, after 9/11 and the U.S. government's response to it, Islamophobia became widespread; one particular aspect of Islamophobia took hold—the belief that Islam is a violent, aggressive religion, supportive of terrorism around the world.

While the current attack on Muslims in Canada is similar to the treatment of Jews in nineteenth-century Europe—that they are the "others" who do not have beliefs or values in common with "us"—it has an additional element. Because many (although not all) of those who practise the Muslim faith have darker skins, there is also a strong aspect of racism inherent in Islamophobia. Indeed, other racialized groups such as Sikhs have falsely been attacked for being Muslims. Because of this racist element, many Muslims in Canada today have experienced an increase in prejudice and discrimination. One recent focus of Islamophobia has been on the Islamic tradition of women wearing head coverings. At McMaster University in 2007, a Jewish professor had an anti-Muslim (and pornographic) comment spray-painted across her office door as a result of organizing a "Wear a Hijab Day" on campus in support of Muslim women. However, it is not just a few racists who oppose head coverings for women; some government agencies have recently taken positions prohibiting them in certain situations.

This brief overview of Canadian history suggests that racism involves more than simply the personal biases of individuals. Rather, what we begin to see is a pattern of **institutional racism** (also referred to as systemic racism) in which whole social institutions—such as education, the judiciary, the media, and so on—are embedded with racist ideologies and help sustain them. Moreover, the history of racism and other forms of social intolerance in Canada points out the central role played by the various levels of the state. Not only have governments repeatedly turned a blind eye to waves of social intolerance, they have at times been the perpetrators of such actions.

The Liberal Perspective: Focusing on Culture

Liberalism is one of the many order theories that try to explain why racial inequality exists. The central variables of social analysis from the perspective of liberalism are values, attitudes, and cultural differences. The liberal perspective does not ignore structural inequities; rather, it argues that structural inequities are a result of cultural problems.

Such arguments are pervasive within the social sciences. In contrast to those theories that focus on the psychological bases for prejudice, sociologists have tended to focus on racism and other forms of discrimination in the cultural sphere. In the period that followed World War II, most North American sociologists saw social intolerance as a temporary phenomenon that would disappear as various groups assimilated over time into the broader culture. This approach, commonly referred to as **assimilationism**, starts with the assumption that industrial societies—which tend to promote individual freedom and initiative—will naturally discourage discrimination. From this point of view, since modern societies tend to promote equality, the persistence of racism must be the result of certain groups clinging to traditional values, attitudes, and beliefs.

Similar to, but distinct from, the assimilationists are those theorists who have focused on the cultural or psychological characteristics of the oppressed groups themselves. One of the early examples of this approach (Rosen 1959) maintained that ethnic groups differ in their achievement motivation, their value orientations, and their educational-vocational aspiration levels. Rosen maintained that the greater social mobility and economic success of some groups resulted from their greater achievement motivation.

Perhaps the best known of these early theories was that of Oscar Lewis (1966), who advocated a "culture of poverty" approach to explain social inequality. Lewis, an American anthropologist, felt that living in poverty creates a culture imbued with a number of characteristics, including a low level of social organization, hostility toward representatives of the broader society, and feelings of despair, dependence, and inferiority (Satzewich 1995, 101). It is this culture of poverty, according to Lewis, that keeps certain groups from attaining economic success.

In Canada, such arguments have been used to explain the condition of Aboriginal people. One author (Nagler 1972), for example, believed that a century of life on the reserves, with its forced idleness and isolation, helped create a culture of poverty that left Native people ill-prepared to adapt to urban living. From this point of view, the basic value system of indigenous people conflicts with the values dominant in North American society, such as "the value of punctuality, saving, future orientation and the work ethic" (134). The conflict between these two value systems, according to this author, keeps Aboriginal people from assimilating or attaining equality.

Such arguments, although popular, have a number of serious failings. One of the main problems with such arguments is that they confuse cause with effect: the values and cultural orientations of particular groups are seen to be the source of the problem, rather than the result of it. (Perhaps, for example, high rates of poverty and unemployment among indigenous people have led to a poor work ethic, orientation to the future, or ability to save money.) As such, the assimilationist and culture of poverty theorists end up blaming the victims for their own oppression. As was noted in Chapter 10, theories that focus on the victims of social problems draw attention away from the structural bases of such problems. The solution to these problems, then, is seen as being some alteration of the victim's attitudes or behaviour, rather than any necessary change in the social structure itself.

More recent liberal theories acknowledge the existence of institutional racism and direct attention away from the victims toward the broader society. While such approaches no longer focus on those oppressed by racism, liberal theories continue to see racism as a cultural problem rooted in values, beliefs, and attitudes. Language and discourse are the means by which these cultural elements are transmitted, and the various social institutions become embedded with racist ideology. The solution, therefore, is directed at eliminating racial prejudice, which is seen to be the basis for discrimination.

The Class Perspective:
The Structural Basis of Racism

Unlike the liberal perspective, which focuses on the cultural roots of social intolerance, the Marxist or class perspective looks at the material basis for such behaviour and beliefs. Class analysis accepts that racism is sustained by a body of ideas. However, Marxists try to explain how such ideas come to be pervasive in our society, and why they are so resistant to change. The class perspective, unlike liberalism, focuses first and foremost on structures of power.

Extra Profits from Discrimination

From the Marxist perspective, the capitalist owning class benefits from racial inequality in a number of ways. First, and most directly, the underpayment of racialized groups is a major source of extra profits for those who employ them. Moreover, underpayment of one sector of the labour market serves to keep all wages down. Members of these groups (as well as recent immigrant groups) also constitute an important part of the reserve army of the unemployed first described in Chapter 6. A greater percentage of racial minorities not only are unemployed, but also are underemployed or work part-time. These groups exert a downward pressure on wages. There is substantial evidence that this is the case in the United States (Bonacich 1976; Perlo 1976; Gordon et al. 1982), and a similar situation exists with regard to racialized groups in Canada (Henry and Ginzberg 1985; Mensah 2002; Galabuzi 2006).

Data indicate that Whites earn more than racialized minorities (see Table 11.1). Indeed, one author (Galabuzi 2006) speaks of Canada as having a system of economic *apartheid*, a term used to define the institutionalized system of racism in South Africa from the 1960s to the early 1990s. Using Statistics Canada income figures from 1996 to 1998, Galabuzi concludes that racialized groups in Canada tend to do less well than Whites in income, employment, and poverty levels. Among the worst off are visible-minority women, immigrant women, and Aboriginal women.

There is no single explanation for the persistence of lower wage rates for racial minorities. In the past, it could be linked to such easily identifiable realities as government immigration policies, hiring restrictions, and other legalized forms

Table 11.1 Inequality in Median Incomes, 1998

	Total Population	Racialized Group (a)	Non-racialized Group (b)	Difference (a/b) $	%
Less than high school	$12,414	$9,727	$12,666	2,939	24
University degree	$31,408	$24,485	$32,074	7,589	24

Source: Grace-Edward Galabuzi, *Canada's Economic Apartheid: The Social Exclusion of Racialized Groups in the New Century.* Toronto: Canadian Scholars' Press, 2006: 95.

of racism. While such overt forms of racism are generally unacceptable today in Canada, more subtle forms of discrimination in the labour market continue. Many companies have also excluded racial minorities by demanding "Canadian experience," by disallowing foreign credentials, or by using excessively narrow job recruitment channels. Data from the 2001 census indicate that while the earnings of immigrants used to improve with length of time in Canada, immigrants now continue to have lower wages than Canadian-born workers even after ten years in the country. Moreover, the racialized employment gap persists among both low- and high-income earners, and among those with both low and high educational attainment. This gap lessens only in unionized workplaces (Galabuzi 2006, 91–119).

The Ideology of Racism

Racism provides more than short-term economic benefits for capital. We should recall that capital has two goals: in the short term, profit maximization; in the long term, the maintenance of a system that allows it to achieve its short-term goal. As an ideology, racism goes beyond the immediate function of enhancing profitability. Racism and other forms of ethnic hostility also serve to separate workers in the classic divide-and-rule pattern, as was noted earlier in this chapter. The more that various racial and ethnic groups are pitted against each other, the less likely it is that they will be able to unite in a common struggle to oppose those with power. In addition, if racial minorities become scapegoats they can direct attention away from the real bases for social problems.

However, to say that capital benefits in general from racism is not to deny that individual capitalists or companies may work toward eroding racism. There are many reasons—hiring more qualified workers, hiring workers that reflect the diversity of their customers, or simply personal values—that individual employers may work against discrimination in the workplace. Indeed, it has been argued that when the Chinese were facing entry restrictions to Canada early in the twentieth century, they found that capitalist employers were among their strongest allies because the employers saw them as a source of cheap labour (Satzewich 1999, 324).

Conversely, one cannot mechanically assume that all workers will oppose racism. Indeed, White workers have often been the perpetrators of racist actions. In the early twentieth century, racist attitudes permeated the whole trade union movement, both in Canada and in the United States, and many unions barred specific minorities from becoming members. The unions justified their opposition to certain groups by the fact that employers frequently hired racial minorities or recent immigrants (at lower wage rates) and used them to bust unions or to break strikes. The perpetuation of racism did give many White workers a certain short-term advantage in wages, job security, working conditions, and promotions. In the end, however, racism among workers actually eroded their conditions and played into the hands of the employers.

At the moment, many working people are susceptible to racism and ethnic chauvinism. People are not innately cruel or prejudiced; however, since capitalism turns workers into commodities who must sell their labour in the market, it makes workers rivals who must compete against one another. In a world where jobs constitute a scarce resource, there are many people who are open to arguments that would exclude certain groups from direct competition for these resources. In bad economic times, as jobs become even scarcer, racism and other forms of group hostility will generally increase (Seccombe and Livingstone 1996, 163–67). Educational opportunities and affordable housing are also scarce resources in capitalist societies. Competition for these resources in the face of government cutbacks and declining wages can set the stage for increased social intolerance.

In addition, working people feeling the negative effects of a competitive, individualistic capitalist workplace may be looking for some sense of community. As a result, many may turn to their ethnic, religious, or racial group for solidarity. While this can certainly be a positive response, there is a danger that, under certain conditions, such solidarity can turn to anger or hatred against those who are "outsiders." Again, such hostility is likely to increase in bad economic times, as globalizing tendencies make people feel increasingly powerless, as fear and frustration grow, and as people look for easy explanations for their deteriorating conditions. In such circumstances, people can become susceptible to arguments that place them above some other supposedly naturally inferior minority.

Think About It

Do you think racism and other forms of social intolerance are increasing or decreasing in Canada? Have you personally encountered such acts? If you are not Canadian-born, would you say social intolerance is worse or better than where you lived previously?

The Struggle for Racial Equality: How Far Have We Come?

Given the history of racism in Canada, it does appear that there has been a major advance in the struggle for racial equality in recent years. Certainly, it is now the exception for a public figure to openly make a racial or ethnic slur, something that was quite common only fifty years ago. African-Canadians and other racialized groups are gradually gaining visibility on television and in other media. Blacks in professional sports and in popular music have become heroes to many young people of all backgrounds. Racism within the school system has been acknowledged and, while there are variations across the country, anti-racist education is gaining ground. Since the report of the Royal Commission on Equality in Employment (1984), there has been some equity legislation passed federally.

On the other hand, it can also be argued that the struggle for racial equality has not come very far. There is substantial evidence that racism is widespread in the criminal justice system (Henry et al. 2000, 145–205). Our popular culture remains permeated with racist images and negative stereotypes. Racialized groups, especially recent immigrants, continue to face discrimination in housing and employment, and hate groups continue to exist across the country, now using the Internet as a means of promoting their ideologies.

In Chapter 8, it was argued that the state generally acts on behalf of the ruling class. If this is correct, and if—as argued earlier—this ruling class is the primary beneficiary of racial inequality, then we should expect to see the state playing its role in the maintenance of racial inequality. Certainly, this can be seen most sharply in Canadian government policies prior to World War II. Following the war, such blatant and open evidence of racial or ethnic intolerance by governments became unacceptable in the international community. This does not mean, however, that the various levels of government in Canada ceased to play a role in the maintenance of racial inequality. While the federal and provincial levels of government have given lip service to fighting racism, their actions have been limited and of a very specific nature.

It is true that the Canadian government has ratified the United Nations International Convention on the Elimination of All Forms of Racial Discrimination, and has, under the Constitution Act of 1982, created a Charter of Rights and Freedoms, which outlaws discrimination on the basis of—among other things—race, ethnic origin, colour, and religion. In addition, the federal government, all provinces, and the territories have human rights codes, and most have human rights commissions to administer the codes.

However, there has been much criticism of the overall approach to discriminatory practices in Canada. The onus is generally on the victims of discrimination to pursue charges, either through human rights commissions or, in the case of alleged Charter violations, through the courts. The adversarial nature of the process; the cost in time, money, and effort; the prolonged delays; and the stringent requirements for the complaint system have together made official challenges to discrimination an unrealistic option for most people. Most importantly, current government legislation focuses on individual acts of discrimination, rather than on broader and more pervasive forms of institutional racism. Individual rights, rather than collective rights, are emphasized.

The federal government adopted the Employment Equity Act in 1986, which applies to approximately 1,250 federally regulated companies. Employers designated under the act are required to submit an employment equity plan annually, which sets out goals and timetables for hiring persons from designated groups (women, racial minorities, Aboriginal people, and people with disabilities); the ultimate goal is ostensibly that the workforce should eventually reflect the diversity within the broader Canadian population. However, the act has proven to be ineffectual in bringing about real change (Henry et al. 2000, 344). It contains no penalties for failure to implement programs, no criteria for measuring success, and no provisions for enforcement, except with regard to failure to comply with the reporting documents. Even more revealing, the federal government has exempted itself from the provisions of the act.

The area where the federal government has shown itself to be most proactive is in the sphere of multiculturalism, as it actively promotes ethnic diversity in many spheres. Multiculturalism as government policy was first introduced by Prime Minister Pierre Trudeau in 1971 and in 1988 became enshrined in the federal Multiculturalism Act. While it certainly was an advance, in that it did recognize ethnic diversity within Canada, its emphasis has been on promoting cultural traditions rather than the eradication of systemic racism and other forms of discrimination. Multicultural policies, like liberalism in general, transform complex political and economic problems—including the relationship between Canada's two charter groups, the English and the French, in addition to the historic oppression of Aboriginal people—into mere cultural and linguistic differences. By so doing, multiculturalism has drawn attention away from inequities of power and the root causes of differences within the Canadian mosaic.

The First Nations Struggle

For more than a century, Canadian government policy has left Aboriginal people with little structural power. Moreover, the pervasiveness of institutional racism against the First Nations people, the devaluation of their culture, the limited opportunities for economic development, the legacy of residential schools, and the persistence of widespread racial stereotypes have all had a debilitating effect on Aboriginal self-worth and their ability to struggle against the conditions of their lives. Nonetheless, there are some pockets of resistance across the country. For example, protestors from the Six Nations have occupied land in Caledonia, Ontario, since early 2006, arguing that it was part of a large land grant given to them in 1784.

Changing the conditions for Aboriginal people in any major way requires that they be given true control over their lives and the ability to obtain their fair share of Canada's wealth. This requires the settling of land claims and provision of a stable land base as a starting point. But even that first step has not been achieved by most indigenous peoples, and large areas of Canada continue to be the subject of Aboriginal land claims. Such claims are based either on traditional Aboriginal use and occupancy of the land or on assertions that the Canadian government did not fulfill historical treaty obligations. In 2007 there were still approximately 800 outstanding claims, and there is some indication that settlements may turn out to be less than satisfactory for the First Nations.

The various levels of government do not seem to be particularly interested in resolving many of the land claims. There is even some suspicion that they may actually be trying to co-opt, divide, and depoliticize the

> We have to have sustained systemic change on the part of the governments to avoid conflict. The young people, if we don't, are going to rise up.
> —Shawn Atleo, B.C. regional chief for the Assembly of First Nations, 2007

Box 11.3 The Life and Death of the Kelowna Accord

Starting in 2004, representatives from many Aboriginal organizations along with provincial, territorial, and federal governments met numerous times to hammer out a plan that would help to "close the gap" between Aboriginal and non-Aboriginal Canadians. The Kelowna Accord, as it was called, was signed in November 2005. Its goal was to provide $5.1 billion over ten years for education, health, housing, and economic opportunities, with a view to raising the living standard for Aboriginal peoples up to that of other Canadians by 2016.

Right after the Accord was signed, a federal election was called. The Liberal government was not able to bring down a new budget before the election, so no money had yet been set aside to fund the measures agreed to in the Accord. The Conservative Party won the election of early 2006 and shortly thereafter they cancelled the Accord. The new budget allocated a fraction of the money that would have gone to Aboriginal people under the Kelowna Accord.

Sources: Jeff Gray, "Native Spending Falls Millions Short of Pact," *Globe and Mail*, 3 May 2006; Lisa L. Patterson, "Aboriginal Roundtable to Kelowna Accord: Aboriginal Policy Negotiations, 2004-5," 4 May 2006. PRB 06-04E. Library of Parliament, Parliamentary Information and Research Service).

---

leadership of the First Nations. This is not surprising, since much of the land under dispute is now quite valuable and often occupied by others. Moreover, major corporations covet the resources on Aboriginal lands and generally oppose any settlements that give the First Nations increased control over these lands. It seems likely that the Aboriginal struggle will continue for some time.

The Issue of Gender

The modern women's movement has quite correctly noted that race and gender are intertwined in complex ways. Women who are members of racial minorities face simultaneous discrimination as a result of both their gender and their race. In general, women of colour are the most exploited workers in the world.

Aboriginal women in Canada faced a particularly notorious example of this double jeopardy. The Indian Act of 1876 determined that Indian women who married non-Indian men would lose their rights under the act. Indian men, on the other hand, suffered no such consequences if they married non-Indian women—indeed, they endowed their non-Native wives with Indian status. On marriage to a White man, an Indian woman had to leave the reserve and could no longer own property on the reserve. Her children were not recognized as Indian and were therefore severed from their cultural heritage and from any programs or prerogatives limited to status Indians. She could be prevented from returning to live with her family on the reserve, even if she were subsequently to become ill, divorced, or separated. Upon her death, she could not be buried with her kin on ancestral lands (Jamieson 1978, 1). After a long struggle—including one within the Aboriginal community itself—this inequity was finally repealed in 1985, although the problem has not totally been resolved within Aboriginal communities.

Other women of colour also often find themselves torn between choosing what is best for themselves, their families, their communities, or the men in their lives. For example, many—even those experiencing violence at the hands of their partners—will avoid going to the police for fear of subjecting the men in their lives to the criminal justice system. They may also avoid getting help because they are afraid of reinforcing negative stereotypes about their community.

The Outlook for the Future

A recurring theme throughout this book is that capitalist societies are full of contradictions. Such contradictions are reflected in the area of racial inequality. On the one hand, capitalism emphasizes the free movement of capital and labour. In this sense, both the struggle for economic advantage (i.e., for employers to get the best worker for the job, regardless of physical or cultural characteristics) and the ideology of liberalism ought to lead to an erosion of racism. Likewise, the shift toward democracy and multiculturalism should play a role in lessening racial inequality.

There is some evidence to indicate that racial and ethnic prejudice in Canada has been in decline in recent years, as those under age thirty seem to hold less biased attitudes than their elders. They value Canadian multiculturalism, the Charter of Rights and Freedoms, bilingualism, and having people from differing cultural backgrounds living in peace. They believe immigrants are having a positive effect on the country, and no longer think that a similar ethnic background is important when choosing a spouse or friends (Mendelsohn 2003).

Nonetheless, racism and other forms of social intolerance persist in all advanced capitalist societies. This is because the benefits of racism for the capitalist ruling class obviously outweigh the costs. In spite of changing attitudes and values, many minorities in Canada continue to face prejudice and discrimination. As noted in Chapter 5, the "bad" jobs available in the restructured capitalist economy disproportionately go to, among others, certain racialized groups and immigrants. Moreover, recent cuts to public education and social services have the most negative consequences for those who are already disadvantaged.

As long as jobs, educational opportunities, and affordable housing constitute a scarce resource, people and groups will be forced to compete against each other in the marketplace. In such a context, employment equity programs and other government initiatives that might limit structural racism are likely to face a backlash.

This chapter has argued that the persistence of racism can be understood only within the broader framework of capitalist class relations. As American writers Baran and Sweezy (1966, 271) note, "It was capitalism, with its enthronement of greed and privilege, which created the race problem and made it the ugly thing it is today. It is the very same system which resists and thwarts every effort at a solution."

Key Points

1. From a strictly genetic standpoint, there is no such thing as race. The concept of race, therefore, reflects a social rather than a physiological reality.

2. Racism, while connected to other forms of social intolerance such as ethnic chauvinism and anti-Semitism, must be seen as distinct from them.

3. Prejudice is the holding of biased beliefs toward individuals on the basis of their membership in particular groups. Discrimination is the denial of equal treatment or opportunities to these same social groups. Discrimination generally has more serious consequences for the victim than does prejudice.

4. Racism as we know it began to develop after 1492, as the European powers began their global expansion and competition. Racism grew and flourished within the economic conditions of colonialism and slavery.

5. At the same time that slavery was disappearing, biological determinist arguments about racial inferiority became increasingly popular. Racism reached its full development by the end of the nineteenth century.

6. Canada has a long history of state-supported racism, particularly against the First Nations people.

7. Liberalism sees the cause of racial inequality as rooted in values, attitudes, and cultural differences. In contrast, class analysis focuses on the material basis for such ideas, that is, the way they are rooted in our society's economic and political structures.

8. From the Marxist perspective, racism continues to be pervasive because the dominant class in capitalism benefits from its existence.

9. While there have certainly been some advances in the struggle against racism, there is substantial evidence to indicate that racism remains pervasive in Canadian social institutions. The anti-racist policies of the government are very weak.

10. The struggle for self-government and for the settlement of long-standing land claims remains central for First Nations people.

11. The variables of race, gender, and socioeconomic status are intertwined in complex ways.

12. There is some evidence that Canadians have become more tolerant of racial and ethnic minorities. On the other hand, the capitalist structure has limited economic and social advances for racialized groups.

Further Reading

Boyko, John. 1995. *Last Steps to Freedom: The Evolution of Canadian Racism*. Winnipeg: Watson & Dwyer.
This book asks readers to face their racist past by offering short pieces regarding past discrimination against six groups in Canada.

Fanon, Frantz. [1961] 2004. *The Wretched of the Earth*. New translation by Richard Philcox. New York: Grove Press.
This is a re-issue of a class work on colonialism, revolution, and racial difference. Fanon's work, while not well known today, has been very influential, both in academia and in the arts

Frideres, James S., and René R. Gadacz. 2001. *Aboriginal Peoples in Canada: Contemporary Conflicts*, 6th ed. Toronto: Prentice Hall.
A comprehensive and detailed textbook that offers a thorough examination of Aboriginal issues.

Galabuzi, Grace-Edward. 2006. *Canada's Economic Apartheid: The Social Exclusion of Racialized Groups in the New Century*. Toronto: Canadian Scholars' Press.
An examination of the extent of racism in Canada, with many statistics provided.

Ighodaro, MacDonald E. 2006. *Living the Experience: Migration, Exclusion, and Anti-Racist Practice*. Halifax: Fernwood.
An examination of the issues faced by refugees, immigrants, and other racialized minorities, both in Canada and around the world.

Mensah, Joseph. 2002. *Black Canadians: History, Experiences, Social Conditions*. Halifax: Fernwood.
This book provides both a brief history of Blacks in Canada and an overview of current issues and controversies.

Milloy, John S. 1999. *A National Crime: The Canadian Government and the Residential School System, 1879–1986*. Winnipeg: University of Manitoba Press.
This book uncovers the full extent of the government's complicity for nearly a century in destroying the lives and cultures of Aboriginal people.

Tator, Carol, and Frances Henry. 2006. *Racial Profiling in Canada: Challenging the Myth of "A Few Bad Apples."* Toronto: University of Toronto Press.
The authors demonstrate the pervasiveness of racial profiling as practised by police and other social institutions, examine its effects on both individuals and society as a whole, and offer some solutions.

12 Gender Issues

In This Chapter

- To what extent does gender inequality exist in Canada?
- What are the theoretical explanations for its persistence?
- When did gender inequality begin?
- What are some key gender issues in Canada today?

When a child is born, one of the first things we want to know is its sex. Indeed, as a result of new medical technologies, many of us want to know the sex of our child before it is born. Clearly, then, the status categories of male and female are central to our lives. While humans hold many statuses at any given moment, gender constitutes such an elemental status—its recognition begins so early, its socialization is so intense, and its imposition on all other components of human development and status achievement is so total—that we could term gender a *core status*.

One of the foremost analysts of human behaviour in the twentieth century was Sigmund Freud. Freud believed that anatomy was destiny: he argued that women's lack of the male sex organ inevitably led to certain negative behavioural consequences for them. But Freud was far from being the first, or the only, man to believe in the natural inferiority of women. Indeed, as far back as Aristotle one can find philosophical justifications for women's inequality. A century after Freud we continue to speak of men and women as "the opposite sex," while pop psychologist John Gray, the author of *Men Are from Mars, Women Are from Venus*, tells us that the two sexes "think, feel, perceive, react, respond, love, need, and appreciate differently (1993, 5)."

Around the world, *gender difference* has been used to justify *gender inequality*. This chapter will examine both the beliefs we have about gender difference and the consequences of these beliefs regarding gender

> What are little girls made of?
> Sugar and spice and everything nice, that's what little girls are made of.
> What are little boys made of?
> Snakes and snails and puppy dog's tails, that's what little boys are made of.
> —nursery rhyme

inequality. It should be noted that, technically speaking, the word *sex* refers to the physiological categories of male and female, while the term *gender* refers to the socially created categories of masculine and feminine. However, in recent years gender has come to encompass both meanings. Some social scientists argue that this is reasonable, since in reality it is impossible to separate the physiological from the cultural.

Gender Inequality in the Twenty-first Century

In 1970, the Royal Commission on the Status of Women in Canada tabled a report that contained 167 recommendations. Canadians were beginning to acknowledge that in the workplace, the home, the justice system, religious institutions, and everyday life, women and men were not equal. On the surface, it may appear that the issue of gender inequality is no longer relevant. Certainly, since 1970 there have been many advances for women in Canada. They have entered the paid labour force in large numbers, with their participation rate now very close to that of men, and women today can make many personal choices that were considered radical only forty years ago. However, while Canadian women now have equality protection in the Charter of Rights and Freedoms, it is clear that full gender equality does not yet exist:

- In Canada today there are still men's jobs and women's jobs. In 2004, practically unchanged from 1996, 67 percent of all employed women were working in teaching, nursing and related health occupations, clerical or other administrative positions, and sales and service occupations. This compared with just 30 percent of employed men (Statistics Canada 2006b).
- Women's and men's wages also continue to differ. In 2003, the pre-tax income of women was $24,400, just 62 percent of that earned by men (Statistics Canada 2006c, 133).
- In the 2001–02 academic year, 57 percent of full-time university students were female. However, women were only 30 percent of all university students in mathematics and physical sciences, and just 24 percent of those in engineering and applied sciences (Statistics Canada 2006c, 92).
- The percentage of female directors on the boards of Canada's 300 largest companies has remained at about 8 percent for the past ten years (McFarland 2007).
- Although the number of self-employed women grew by 50 percent between 1989 and 2004, one-third of the companies run by women generated less than $50,000 in annual revenue, double the number for firms run by men. At the other extreme, more than 20 percent of businesses owned by men generated annual income of more than $500,000, almost twice the number for firms run by women (Lima 2006).
- Most of the poor in Canada are women, with one in five women living in poverty. In 2003, almost one-third of unattached women aged sixteen and over lived in a low-income situation. In the same year, 38 percent of all

families headed by lone-parent mothers had low incomes, triple the rate for families headed by lone-parent fathers (Statistics Canada 2006b).

- Despite the fact that increasing numbers of women are in the paid labour force, they continue to do the majority of unpaid housework, home maintenance, childcare, and care of the elderly. For individuals aged twenty-five to forty-four, daily participation rates for housework continue to be significantly higher for women than for men in all family types (Statistics Canada 2006a).

- While both men and women experience spousal violence, women are more likely to experience more serious forms of violence as well as repeated violence. In the 2004, one in four Aboriginal women reported being a victim of spousal abuse, compared to 7 percent of non-Aboriginal women (Statistics Canada 2006c, 161–63).

- In 2004, women were charged with committing 17 percent of all crime in Canada, but were about half of all victims. There were over six times as many female victims of sexual assault as male victims. And while women are less than half as likely as men to be murdered, of the 873 spousal homicides that occurred between 1961 and 2004, 97 percent of the victims were wives (Statistics Canada 2006c, 164–65).

Everywhere we look, we can see the concrete manifestations of gender inequality. Far fewer women than men run for, and are elected to, public office. For example, in the 2006 federal election, only 20.8 percent of those elected to sit in the House of Commons were women. While women can now be ordained in some religious faiths, few are headed by women, and many still promote women's place as being inside the home as wife and mother. In the media women continue to be portrayed as sex objects, and traditional female roles are still widely promoted.

Think About It

Spend a day observing the gendered world around you. Watch for differing behaviours of men and women on public transportation, at school, or in your family. Watch TV or look at magazines to see how men and women are portrayed. What differences do you observe? What are the similarities?

In other parts of the world conditions for women are far worse than in Canada. Of the nearly two billion people living in poverty, 70 percent are women, while two-thirds of illiterate adults are women (van der Gaag 2004, 12). With regard to health, women still face many health dangers—including death from childbirth, illegal abortions, and HIV/AIDS—while the global preference for sons over daughters remains widespread. In some parts of the world brutal mass rape has become a common part of modern warfare, in some cases in an attempt to make women pregnant as a form of ethnic domination (ibid., 110). In addition, while some countries have extended anti-discrimination provisions to include sexual orientation, homosexuality remains illegal in many countries, and sexual minorities—both men and women—continue to face unfair arrest, persecution, torture, or even death.

Is Biology Destiny?

Gender inequality is often assumed to be the result of gender difference. Biological determinists, as we have seen throughout this book, argue that certain biological differences inevitably lead to inequality. And yet how different are the sexes? If we carefully examine a group of women and men, their similarities far outweigh their differences. Even more surprising, while most of us assume that there are two clear gender categories—an unambiguous classification based on obvious biological distinctions—a number of traditional societies in fact have three or four gender categories (Martin and Voorhies 1975, 84–107). Such diversity reminds us once more that biology is always invested with cultural meaning.

> The very creation of difference is the foundation on which inequality rests.
> —Barbara Risman, *Gender Vertigo*

One of the major focuses of research on male-female differences has been on intelligence and brain function. This perspective saw women as lacking the intellectual capacity to compete as equals with men. In the nineteenth century, the research into intelligence was mechanical and crude, usually comparing brain sizes and weights of men and women. For example, in 1879, Gustave Le Bon, a Parisian, wrote, "In the most intelligent races, as among the Parisians, there are a large number of women whose brains are closer in size to those of gorillas than to the most developed male brains. This inferiority is so obvious that no one can contest it for a moment; only its degree is worth discussion" (quoted in Gould 1981, 104–5).

As noted earlier in the book, analyses that emphasize biological or genetic differences to explain social inequalities are very popular, particularly in the mass media. Such arguments are also now commonly used to explain the existence of homosexuality. Even many within the gay and lesbian community subscribe to this view. Yet there is no clear scientific evidence that homosexuality is "caused" exclusively by either hormones or genes. While same-gender eroticism and different-gender eroticism have always existed in every society, specific behaviours and attitudes about them have varied widely (Kinsman 2001, 214–5). This is another example of the way biology is filtered through culture.

Connected to, but somewhat distinct from, biological determinist arguments is the functionalist approach. If we recall, functionalism (or structural functionalism) examines existing structures within a given society and then tries to explain their existence by looking at their functions for that society. With regard to gender, the argument would go something like this: men and women are biologically different, which has led to their doing different tasks in all societies. Since this gender division of labour seems to exist in all societies, it must serve some societal need. The best-known functionalist explanation of differing gender roles in modern societies is probably that of Talcott Parsons.

Parsons argued that the nuclear family in industrial societies gives rise to two different, but complementary, roles for men and women. The male takes on what Parsons refers to as the instrumental leadership role, taking part in life outside the family. The female, on the other hand, plays an expressive role, raising and socializing the young inside the household. Both roles, it is argued, are necessary to maintain the social order. The different roles for each sex, thought Parsons, were linked to the biological fact that women bore the children and nursed them in their early years (1955, 23).

Thus, for Parsons, the gender division of labour was both rooted in biology and functional for modern industrial society as a whole. Whether it was functional for individual women and men was not considered a relevant question. Moreover, Parsons' description of the "typical" American family, with the father as breadwinner and the woman at home raising the children, described only a portion of the American population even at the time he was writing. Today, such families constitute a small minority in modern industrial societies, and few social analysts accept the functionalist approach to gender inequality.

The question of physiological difference between the sexes requires closer examination. Social scientists are agreed that there are a few real physiological differences between males and females—chromosomes, gonads, internal and external reproductive organs, hormones, and secondary sex characteristics. Women lactate and menstruate. However, there is no clear dichotomy between the sexes. For example, men and women have both male and female sex hormones; indeed, some men may have more female hormones than some women and vice versa. In addition, as was noted in Chapter 2, biology itself can be affected by the external environment, making absolute boundaries difficult to determin.

Numerous studies have been undertaken to investigate possible innate differences between the sexes, including activity levels, nurturing behaviour, aggression, and mathematical and visual-spatial ability. Taken as a whole, this research suggests that—both biologically and psychologically—there are few obvious, consistent, and recurring differences between men and women (Armstrong and Armstrong 1994, 142–43). In other words, there is simply no concrete evidence to support the argument that biology alone is the basis for gender inequality. In the end, such arguments, like all biological determinist arguments, are more *justifications* of inequality than legitimate explanations of them. That is not to say that the biological difference between men and women plays *no* part in gender inequality; however, biology must always be understood within a social context.

Think About It

In what ways is the notion that the difference between men and women is natural or eternal reinforced within our society? Think of what you have learned in school as well as from your religion, parents, peers, and the media.

Feminist Theories of Gender Inequality

If biology alone cannot explain gender inequality, why has it been so widespread? Various theories have attempted to answer this question. We have seen how the growth of capitalist economies brought about a new world view known as liberalism, an ideology that emphasizes individual freedom, equality, and choice. This ideology developed because it suited the new growing bourgeoisie, but it was taken up by others who also aspired to these laudable goals. One of these groups was women. From the mid-nineteenth century and onward to the present day, groups of women (and some men) have taken on the question of gender inequality. The term **feminism** is used to broadly describe both the belief in the social, political, and economic equality of the sexes, as well as the various social movements organized around this belief.

When we hear the word *feminism* today, many of us have a distorted negative perception of its meaning, linking it to some mythical unhygienic man-hating extremist women. In reality, feminism includes a broad spectrum of beliefs or social activities, and most feminist research today examines the implications of gender inequality for both men and women. A number of writers now speak of three "waves" of feminism. First Wave feminism developed in the mid-nineteenth century, at first in Britain and later in North America. It consisted mostly of privileged White women who wanted to improve their own life situations; the focus was on gaining equal rights for women, especially the right to vote. These women did not refer to themselves as feminists.

This term really developed during the Second Wave of feminism, which began in the late 1960s. Second Wave feminism developed out of other social movements that arose at this time, including the student, anti-war, and civil rights movements in the United States; the revolutionary youth movements in Europe; the Quiet Revolution in Quebec; and various nationalist and socialist movements across Canada (Rebick 2005, 7–8). This period of the twentieth century saw the development of a number of theories about gender inequality. As has been noted in previous chapters, the key theoretical frameworks in social analysis in the course of the twentieth century have been linked to liberalism and Marxism, and two strands of Second Wave feminist theories can be linked to these traditions. However, the 1960s also saw the development of a new approach to gender inequality that came to be known as *radical feminism*, which will be examined later in this chapter.

Second Wave feminism must also be understood in the context of two developments that occurred at that time: first, middle-strata young women in North America started to attend university in increasing numbers, and second, the birth-control pill appeared on the scene. As women were increasingly given occupational choice, they also began to value greater personal choice as well. Many women in this period thus began to challenge the traditional family structure and their expected role of wife and mother; because of the pill, women also began to have expanded choices regarding sexual activities and childbearing.

In this context, women began to oppose the state's right to control their bodies—particularly with regard to reproduction—and, thus, issues relating to contraception and abortion were high on the feminist agenda. Both men and women also began to challenge **heterosexism**, the ideology that heterosexual sex within a state-sanctioned marriage—primarily for the purpose of reproduction—is normal, while all other forms of sexual behaviour are deviant. Lesbians, gay men, bisexuals, and transgendered people (individuals who move from one gender to another or defy gender boundaries) have made great strides in the last thirty years, although many forms of prejudice and discrimination remain.

Culture as the Basis of Gender Inequality: The Liberal View

The most broadly accepted form of feminism that advanced during the Second Wave was that of liberal feminism. For liberal feminists, the main source of gender inequality is the process of socialization. As has been discussed earlier in this book, socialization is the learning process by which we acquire our society's cultural components and social expectations. This process is carried out by various social institutions such as the family, schools, peers, mass media, and so on. While it begins in childhood, it continues throughout our life.

In Chapter 3, we discussed how Margaret Mead's work challenged the taken-for-granted assumptions about the biological basis for men's and women's roles in society. In fact, the cross-cultural research done by many anthropologists has demonstrated that the gender behaviours that seem so natural in our own society may be quite different in other times and places. In a broader investigation of more than 200 societies, George Murdock (1937) also found a large degree of cultural variation in the division of labour. While all societies had some division of labour based on gender, what was considered a male or female activity was not consistent. However, some patterns did appear: for example, hunting and warfare were generally male activities, while cooking and childcare were more often defined as female tasks. Works such as those of Mead and Murdock refuted the biological determinist approach and put emphasis on the cultural basis of gender difference. These early studies were part of the broader liberal tradition.

Humans learn accepted gender behaviours from the various agents of socialization. For example, social scientists have noted that parents treat their male and female children differently, even within the first twenty-four hours after birth. In general, baby girls are thought to be more fragile than boys and are held more (MacDonald and Parke 1986). Ample data have also demonstrated the differential treatment of boys and girls in school classrooms, not only by their teachers but via stereotyping in school materials. Outside the classroom, boys are socialized to participate in highly competitive rule-oriented games, while girls have traditionally been socialized to play in small groups, with activities involving a minimum of competitiveness (Adler et al. 1995). Meanwhile, from children's cartoons to adult drama, the mass media continue to portray stereotyped images of men and women. Advertising reinforces the centrality of physical attractiveness for women. One study (Cortese 1999) noted that women were commonly shown in advertising as being young, beautiful, and seductive.

Box 12.1 What Sports Teaches Boys

Through sports, boys are expected to learn to control their emotions, and particularly to suppress those culturally labeled as "feminine." Anger and feelings of aggression are to be channeled into appropriate actions designed to further individual or team goals. Fear and feelings of physical pain cannot be displayed, but must be contained behind a veil of stoicism ("tape an aspirin to it and get back out there") lest those feelings be exploited for competitive disadvantage. The image of European-trained athletes writhing on the soccer pitch or arena ice is widely regarded as an object of disdain for the truly masculine Canadian male. Athletes permanently disabled physically by their participation in sports are offered admiration and respect, but empathy and compassion for an opponent are generally forbidden. "Big boys" may cry at the thrill of victory but losers in the agony of defeat are supposed to weep only in private, and preferably not at all.

Competitive sports are also expected to reinforce the conquest theme for boys and men. Given the small size and low profile of our peacetime armed forces, sports has become one of the major socially acceptable contexts for instilling and reinforcing the Warrior image of masculinity in Canada. The language of a variety of sports, football in particular, contains numerous military references. One Canadian professional football team (Roughriders) was named after a famous military fighting unit and another (Blue Bombers) implicitly maintains a military theme.

The weekend Warrior is aided in his task by wearing a uniform with a team name emblazoned on his chest that invokes the imagery of barely controlled aggression channeled into annihilating opponents. Young boys and older adolescents perform on teams that frequently model their names on professional sports franchises. The language of team nicknames, particularly in hockey and football (also found in basketball, e.g., Grizzlies and Raptors), is dominated by ferocious, masculine-identifying, animal names such as the currently existing: Panthers, Cougars, Jaguars, Tiger Cats, Bengals, Lions, Bruins, Falcons, Eagles, Ravens, Seahawks, Sharks, Broncos, and Coyotes. Even the Mighty Duck has an evil scowl on his face. Rarely do boys find themselves donning the uniforms of Pooh Bears, Pussy Cats, or Daffy Ducks.

Sports imagery and participation teaches boys directly and indirectly that competing is not sufficient in and of itself. Our playing fields from Corner Brook to Victoria are supposedly governed by the noble sentiment of "it matters not whether you win or lose, it's how you play the game." Yet, those fields, tracks, pools, and arenas all have scoreboards that record scores or times or rankings. Following such immersion in peer sports subculture, men tend to treat almost every activity, such as playing a game with a child or a female partner, as a competitive challenge rife with implications for their masculinity.

Source: Excerpted from Adie Nelson and Barrie W. Robinson, 2002. *Gender in Canada*, 2nd ed., 139–40. Pearson Education Canada. Reprinted with permission by Pearson Education Canada, Inc.

Think About It

Look at a magazine rack as if you were a social scientist studying gender. Which sex is most often on the cover of magazines? What do men and women on the cover of these magazines look like? Do they look like people you know?

Surprisingly, role expectations are in some ways narrower for boys than for girls. Little boys learn very early on not only that they must not simply behave as boys, but also, more importantly, that they must not behave as girls (David and Brannon 1976, 14). This makes sense, since males in our society have a higher status than females: it is more acceptable for those with the lower status to emulate the behaviour of those above them; conversely, it is less permissible for men to act in ways that are seen in our society as "beneath them." Thus in the last thirty years, the struggle for gender equality has seen more women entering male-dominated professions than the converse. While the women's movement brought to the fore the negative consequences of narrowly defined social roles for women, more recent works have also begun to notice that traditional expectations of masculinity have negative, although different, consequences for men (see Box 12.1).

The study of gender role socialization has helped social scientists understand that both women and men have a societal "script" imposed on them, and both women and men pay a price for the various restrictions on their behaviour. However, while the study of gender role socialization is fascinating, it helps us understand only one piece of the puzzle. For example, if social behaviour is merely the result of the process of socialization, how do we explain social change? Most of the women who initiated the modern women's movement in the 1960s and 1970s were raised in the very traditional family forms of the 1950s, just as many of you will reject some of the traditional family norms and values you learned as children.

One additional question remains: Where did our ideas about gender come from in the first place? As we noted with regard to race, the question is more than an academic one, for if we fail to eradicate the basis for such ideas then we will never achieve full gender equality. Liberal feminism and its arguments regarding gender role socialization are valuable in helping us understand how gender inequality is reinforced; however, it fails to pinpoint both the reasons for its development and the power structures in the distal sphere that help maintain it.

Structural Analyses of Power: Radical Feminism and Marxism

As women's issues came into public awareness in the 1970s and onward, a number of writers advanced arguments that tried to move beyond liberal feminism by explaining the root cause of gender inequality. Two core theories were Marxism and **radical feminism**. Both were structural analyses in the sense that they both saw gender inequality as rooted in something beyond simply beliefs. For radical feminists, gender inequality is connected to the biological difference between men and women. As Shulamith Firestone (1972, 16) argues, "Sex class sprang directly from a biological reality: men and women were created different, and not equal. The biological family is inherently an unequal power distribution." Theories such as Firestone's were quite popular among feminists in the 1970s.

While there is much diversity among radical feminists, their shared focus has been on the subordination and oppression of women. Thus radical feminists commonly speak of Western societies as a form of **patriarchy**, or rule by men. In this power relationship, which may be sustained by the broader legal and cultural institutions, men are the main beneficiaries and thus are predisposed to maintain gender inequality. Because radical feminism emphasized the unequal power structures in the proximal sphere of the traditional family and male-female relationships, it touched the real experiences of many women.

Since radical feminists saw inequality as rooted in our biology, the difficult issue was how to attain gender equality. For many radical feminists, the struggle for social change came to be centred on a separatist solution—that is, the elimination of men and traditional family structures from women's lives—since *compulsory heterosexuality*, a term first coined by Adrienne Rich (1980), was seen as a key way in which women's subordination was maintained. As a result, some lesbian feminists directed their struggle for change mainly in the sphere of personal relationships rather than broader societal issues.

Traditional Marxism, like radical feminism, sees the problem of gender inequality as a structural one rather than one simply based on ideology. However, unlike radical feminists, Marxists see gender inequality as rooted in the change in power relationships between the sexes that arose with the development of class-based societies. Friedrich Engels, drawing on the work of anthropologist Lewis Henry Morgan, was the first to present a fully developed Marxist position on gender inequality in *The Origin of the Family, Private Property, and the State* ([1884] 1972). According to Engels, the monogamous family with the man at the head was the result of the growth of private property and the transformation of the family form into a means through which property could be inherited. For Marxists, then, gender inequality—past and present—is interconnected to class relationships.

During the 1970s, there was a heated debate amongst feminists, particularly those in academia, about the cause of women's oppression. By the late 1970s, many feminists became increasingly dissatisfied with what they saw as the narrowness of both radical feminism and classical Marxism. They developed a new framework, which came to be known as **socialist feminism**. Socialist feminists attempted to combine the best insights of both radical feminism and Marxism, with varying degrees of success. In general, socialist feminism stresses the intersection of class and gender as well as the intersection of the public sphere of the economy and the state with the private sphere of the family and household (Hamilton 1996, 19). Many Canadian socialist feminists broadened and deepened the traditional Marxist analysis of gender.

While socialist feminism retained a link to the materialism of traditional

Box 12.2 Immigrant Women and Domestic Abuse

While Second Wave feminism focused on the general oppression of women, Third Wave feminism pays greater attention to the differing experiences of women. For example, immigrant women in Canada, especially those from racialized groups, face particular challenges regarding violence in the home. While it is easy to blame particular cultures for their patriarchal values, domestic abuse in immigrant communities can be linked to certain structural realities.

Immigration legislation itself usually sets up an unequal power relation within the family, enhancing the potential for abuse. Women are often economically dependent on their husbands, may lack language skills or accreditation for their qualifications, and may face discrimination in the workplace. Unable to find childcare, many are unable to enhance their language skills, upgrade their education, or in some cases find any employment at all. In 2000, over one-third of women who had immigrated to Canada in the previous ten years were in a low-income situation. Immigrant women also often suffer trauma from migration (or from the violence experienced prior to immigrating), isolation, and fear of deportation. These problems are even more serious for women who are sponsored or are refugees.

If women in these situations do suffer violence in the home, their options are few. Many come from cultures that see the family as sacrosanct and woman's role as one of holding the family together. They may have a fear of police or of being condemned by their communities. They may be blackmailed by their husbands or worry about the loss of their children. They may not know which services to access and may face discrimination or cultural insensitivity that reinforces their already existing feelings of insecurity.

The needs of these women are physical, emotional, social, economic, and legal. Economic independence is central to preventing abuse, but these women also need special support services. These might include language classes, childcare, more women's shelters, and various culturally sensitive social and legal supports. Unfortunately, major government funding cuts to social services in recent years have decreased or eliminated many of these necessary services.

Sources: Yasmin Jiwani et al., "Intersecting Inequalities: Immigrant Women of Colour, Violence and Health Care," July 2001 <http://www.harbour.sfu.ca/freda/articles/hlth02.htm>; Maria Rosa Pinedo and Ana Maria Santinoli, "Changes in Laws and Policies: Immigrant Women and Wife Assault," 2001 <http://www.womanabuseprevention.com/html/immigrant_women.html>; Samantha Sherkin, *Community-based Research on Immigrant Women: Contributions and Challenges.* Community Social Planning Council of Toronto, CERIS Working Paper No. 32 (May 2004) ; Statistics Canada, *Women in Canada: A Gender-based Statistical Report,* 5th ed. No. 89-503-XPE. Ottawa: Ministry of Industry, 2006 .

Marxist analysis, a number of other new theoretical frameworks that developed from the mid-1990s and onward moved in different directions. These theories are often described as Third Wave feminism. One strong theme of this new wave is diversity. This approach has been given various names, including multicultural feminism (Jaggar and Rothenberg 1993, 123) and inclusive feminism (Nelson and Robinson 2002, 96). Inclusive feminism argues that radical feminism and Marxism—by focusing on broad categories such as "women" or "workers"—often ignores the lived experiences of individuals who are not only discriminated against as women but are additionally marginalized because of their race, ethnicity, socioeconomic status, age, ability, or sexual preference (see Box 12.2). Third Wave feminism is also connected to *postmodernism*, a broad analytical framework that is now found in most universities. Unlike the earlier approaches of Second Wave feminism, postmodernism rejects what are often called grand narratives or totalizing theories. Because postmodernism focuses on cultural elements such as the media, language, and ideas, it is in some ways similar to liberal feminism.

The Roots of Gender Inequality

In general, neither liberal feminism nor Third Wave feminism is concerned with the origins of gender inequality. For these two approaches, the ways that today's culture reinforces inequality is of greater interest than its historic roots. In contrast, the origin of gender inequality is at the core of Marxist and radical feminist theoretical analyses and constitutes one of the major differences between these two frameworks. For radical feminists, biology is the basis for gender inequality. If biological determinists and radical feminists are correct, then, minimally, this inequality should be seen in all societies. If, however, the Marxist position is correct, then structured gender inequality will appear only with the rise of permanent surpluses and social classes.

While not all social scientists agree, most of the evidence seems to indicate that gender inequality was minimal in foraging societies. As was noted in Chapter 3, foraging societies emphasized cooperation, sharing, and mutual support. Family structures in these societies helped to ensure social stability, maximize life chances for offspring, and decrease the likelihood of social conflict. The family linked women to men, children to adults, and individuals to other individuals in often-complex kin networks. Survival depended on the interdependence of men and women.

Certainly there must have been a preference among women for tasks compatible with pregnancy and lactation. While this gave differing tasks to women and men, it in no way implied an unequal distribution of power. The distinction between the public world of men's

> Monogamous marriage comes on the scene as the subjugation of one sex by the other; it announces a struggle between the sexes unknown throughout the whole previous prehistoric period.... The first class opposition that appears in history coincides with the development of the antagonism between man and woman in monogamous marriage, and the first class oppression coincides with that of the female sex by the male.
> —Friedrich Engels, *The Origin of the Family, Private Property and the State*

289

work and the private world of women's domestic labour had not yet developed, because essentially the collective household was the entire community (Leacock 1972, 33).

Most anthropologists and historians seem to concur with Engels's proposition that dramatic changes in women's status began to occur with the production of food surpluses and the gradual transition to agrarian-based modes of production. As noted in Chapter 3, permanent surpluses led to the growth of structured social inequality, the state, warfare, and ultimately the development of class societies. Gender inequality, beginning about 7,000 to 10,000 years ago, took about 2,500 years to develop (Lerner 1986, 66). Although we do not know the exact chain of events, we do know that over time productive property passed from collective ownership to family ownership, with the parallel development of the monogamous, or patriarchal, family. The main economic activity of farming came to be dominated by males. In this process, women became a form of property owned by the male.

Central to the changes in women's condition was the rise of slavery, and indeed one author (Lerner 1986, 78) argues that the first slaves were women and children. Thus the concept of women as property is tied to the notion of property in general, and the inequality of the female develops with the rise of social inequality in general.

As classes developed, only a few families became the owners of productive property, which included slaves. The central role for women of this ruling class was solely to provide "legitimate" offspring to inherit property; their productive role became irrelevant since there were slaves to perform the work tasks. But even for small land-holding peasants, the question of heirs became important, since land could not be divided infinitely. There was only one way to maximize the likelihood that offspring who could make a claim on property were, indeed, "legitimate": the husband had to have full control over his wife to prevent her from having sexual access to other men.

Public and private spheres became increasingly separated, with women generally restricted to the household. In addition, the perceived role and value of men and women gradually changed. In foraging societies, the supernatural life-giving force was, logically, female. With the growth of gender inequality came gradual changes in religious beliefs. Female goddesses were gradually joined and eventually replaced by male gods, as in Greece and Rome, culminating in the widespread acceptance of the unitary, patriarchal god of the Old Testament, who created all living things and who created the first woman out of the first man (Lerner 1986, 145–46). These notions can be tied to the religious beliefs of Jews, Christians, and Muslims.

Such beliefs were connected to other changing assumptions about men and women: that God had created men and women as different and ultimately unequal; that men were naturally superior, stronger, and more rational, while women were naturally weaker, intellectually inferior, more nurturing, and emotionally unstable; that men's natural characteristics made them suited to explain and order the world, while women's made them suited to household activities and childcare (Lerner 1993, 4). Women were excluded from the world of ideas and, as a result, became invisible. Living in a form of slavery, they were—like all slaves—seen as less than fully human. Masculine behaviour came to be seen as "normal," while feminine was "abnormal." Thus to a greater or lesser degree, all modern societies became infused with notions of **misogyny**, or the hatred of women. These changing notions evolved gradually, as the roles of men and women—and social inequality in general—changed over time. In this way, the various beliefs about the sexes both resulted from societal changes and reinforced them.

The growth of the state also played an important role in legitimating gender inequality. With the development of private property, families became connected to a state system. Marriage, divorce, rights of inheritance, legitimacy of children, and so on, came to be legal as well as moral matters. In this process, women's sexuality also came under increasing control of a public and coercive apparatus—what had previously been a private matter was now regulated by the state (Lerner 1986, 121). Of course, the issue regarding who actually "owns" a woman's body continues to the present day.

Think About It

The issues about the state's rights to control a woman's body are very complex. For example, do you think the Canadian government should have the right to prohibit pregnant women from smoking, drinking, or taking drugs?

The state enforced by law what religion enforced by belief, with violators severely punished. As forms of chattel like slaves, women had no, or very few, legal rights until recent times. Both legally and ideologically, women were seen as the property of men. At birth, a woman belonged to her father and remained so until she was "given away" in marriage to her husband. And, until very recently, like any form of property, she was the owner's (man's) to do with as he pleased, including rape, assault, and, in some jurisdictions, even murder.

Many anthropologists have argued that conditions for women reached their lowest point in agrarian societies. In these societies—which still exist in many parts of the world—women are kept ignorant and often isolated in the family unit from which there is no escape. In addition, while they may hold a certain degree of power in the domestic sphere, they are legally under the control of their fathers or husbands. Historically, maintaining control over women often involved such acts as foot binding (practised in China for almost a thousand years), suttee (a Hindu custom in which the woman was expected to throw herself on the funeral pyre of her dead husband), and various forms of genital mutilation still practised by many religious groups in North and West Africa.

The industrial era saw women around the world begin their long struggle out of horrific conditions of oppression. Capitalism, from the earliest stages, drew women out of the home. Women were actually sought out by the textile industry in the eighteenth and nineteenth centuries because they had small hands and worked for lower wages. However, it was not until the early 1960s that a large number of women, particularly married women with children, began to enter the paid labour force. This integration of women into paid labour has raised women's status in society and has helped break down the notion of "man's place" and "woman's place," as well as the different value assigned to each.

Gender and Power

We have noted throughout this book that inequalities of power exist at both the distal level and the proximal level. Power at the distal level is rooted in the relationships between classes; in contrast, it is status differentials that largely determine power relationships at the proximal, or nearby, level. It is often power at the proximal level that we experience most directly and most intensely: on a day-to-day level, one is more likely to feel, and have to respond directly to, the power wielded by one's parents or boss as opposed to that wielded by, say, the prime minister or the CEO of a major corporation.

When we look at the statuses of male and female, it is obvious that, on all accounts, males have the higher status. It should be noted that this status inequality is so far from being "natural" that it must constantly be reaffirmed in symbolic ways. Even today, men are still expected to date and marry women who are shorter, smaller, younger, and less educated and who have a lower occupational status.

Think About It

What would you think if you saw an older woman walking arm-in-arm with a much younger man? Why do you think my students always giggled when I asked this question in class?

Radical feminists emphasized male power over women that is the result of this unequal status relationship. This power can most clearly be noted in the many forms of physical and psychological violence that men have long inflicted on women. Both in Canada and around the world, women report a much higher incidence of domestic abuse than men. In addition, women who report being abused are more likely to report being physically injured or require medical attention and are much more likely to fear for their lives or the lives of their children. However, while an abused woman may see her abuser as very powerful, men as a group actually have very little structural power. In much of their daily lives—in their world of work, in their control over the world—the majority of men are actually quite powerless.

Radical feminists also argued that men hold on to their power because they benefit in so many ways from their higher status, and many feminists continue to speak of male privilege. On one level, it seems obvious that men are the main beneficiaries of gender inequality. In the workplace, men have traditionally been able to obtain the better jobs, higher salaries, more promotions, and so on. In the domestic sphere, women still do the majority of housework and childcare. But while men do indeed achieve some real benefits from gender inequality, they have also paid a high price for them, a fact that has now been noted by many men. At the economic level, the lower wages of women exert a downward pressure overall on men's wages as well (Armstrong and Armstrong 1990, 84). Moreover, since most men are members of family units, the lower wages of women reduce their total family income.

Men also pay a high price in physical health and safety. Proportionally more men than women die as a result of heart attacks, strokes, suicides, and automobile accidents, and many more are killed or injured every year in job-related accidents (Human Resources Development Canada 2000, 24). We should also not forget the large number of men who die every year in war. The psychological price men pay for their few privileges is much harder to measure, but no less consequential. From a young age most boys are taught not to display those characteristics deemed "feminine," including the ability to express feelings and show vulnerability (Pollack 1998). This can stunt personal relationships, sexual intimacy, and emotional experiences. For many men, a life devoted to occupational mobility has meant higher death rates from diseases of stress and less time to participate in family life.

Moreover, although men are raised to feel powerful, many men do not actually feel very powerful. Because many men in society are denied access to legitimate sources of power within broader social institutions, they may try to assert it elsewhere (see Box 12.3). For example, Connell (1989, 295) argues that male students who don't succeed at school may claim other sources of power via prowess in sports, physical aggression, or sexual conquest. A study of a group of young Black men in England argued that being male and being Black was about asserting control, publicly over women and other groups of young men, particularly White men, and privately over women (Alexander 1996, 143).

However, although men as a group do not hold the reins of power, they have traditionally had greater *access* to the positions of power than have women. Put differently, we might say that the "access gates" to positions of power within capitalism have been more open to men than to women, even though the reality for most men is that, like most women, they will never hold such structured positions of power. In this way, we can speak of male privilege just as we can speak of White privilege, without assuming that all males, any more than all White people, have all the power.

For Marxists, the main beneficiary of gender inequality is the ruling class in capitalist society. Gender inequality, as noted in this chapter, long predates capitalism; the bourgeoisie inherited a social system with a long history of gender inequality and a deeply held set of beliefs and values that justified and maintained it. Nonetheless, the capitalist owning class has benefited from this already-existing inequality and as a result has had little motivation to eliminate it.

In the previous chapter we saw how capital benefits from the maintenance

Box 12.3 The Paradox of Men's Power

The very ways that men have constructed our social and individual power is, paradoxically, the source of enormous fear, isolation, and pain for men ourselves. If power is constructed as a capacity to dominate and control, if the capacity to act in "powerful" ways requires the construction of a personal suit of armor and a fearful distance from others, if the very world of power and privilege removes us from the world of child-rearing and nurturance, then we are creating men whose own experience of power is fraught with crippling problems.

This is particularly so because the internalized expectations of masculinity are themselves impossible to satisfy or attain. This may well be a problem inherent in patriarchy, but it seems particularly true in an era and in cultures where rigid gender boundaries have been overthrown. Whether it is physical or financial accomplishment, or the suppression of a range of human emotions and needs, the imperatives of manhood (as opposed to the simple certainties of biological maleness), seem to require constant vigilance and work, especially for younger men.

The personal insecurities conferred by a failure to make the masculine grade, or simply the threat of failure, is enough to propel many men, particularly when they are young, into a vortex of fear, isolation, anger, self-punishment, self-hatred, and aggression. Within such an emotional state, violence becomes a *compensatory mechanism*. It is a way of re-establishing the masculine equilibrium, of asserting to oneself and to others one's masculine credentials. This expression of violence usually includes a choice of a target who is physically weaker or more vulnerable. This may be a child, or a woman, or, it may be social groups, such as gay men, or a religious or social minority, or immigrants, who seem to pose an easy target for the insecurity and rage of individual men, especially since such groups often haven't received adequate protection under the law. (This compensatory mechanism is clearly indicated, for example, in that most "gay-bashing" is committed by groups of young men in a period of their life when they experience the greatest insecurity about making the masculine grade.)

What allows violence as an individual compensatory mechanism has been the wide-spread acceptance of violence as a means of solving differences and asserting power and control. What makes it possible are the power and privileges men have enjoyed, things encoded in beliefs, practices, social structures, and the law.

Men's violence, in its myriad of forms, is therefore the result both of men's power, the sense of entitlement to the privilege, the permission for certain forms of violence, and the fear (or reality) of not having power.

Source: Michael Kaufman, "The Seven P's of Men's Violence." © Michael Kaufman, 1999. The full text is available at: <www.michaelkaufman.com>. Used with permission.

of racism. To some extent, the benefits to capital of gender inequality are similar. First and most directly, the underpaid labour of women provides huge profits for the employer. There are, of course, historical and societal variations. While wage differentials are universal in all capitalist societies, the actual extent of it may vary. Nonetheless, capital in general does benefit from wage inequality. More women than men are unemployed, underemployed, or work part-time, ready to take whatever work is available out of economic need. This underpayment of women—as already noted—exerts a downward pressure on all wages, further enhancing profits.

Some women are particularly disadvantaged in the workplace. For example, foreign-born women, on average, earn less than those born in Canada. Other variables that can negatively affect a woman's place in the workforce include race, socioeconomic status, age, and the existence of a disability. Aboriginal women have the lowest labour force participation rates of all, particularly for full-time employment, and the lowest average income of any group (Statistics Canada 2006c). In addition, women in the less-developed countries continue to constitute a major source of cheap labour. In the domestic sphere, the unpaid labour done by women is also of benefit to the capitalist owning class. Women continue to be the primary caregivers for the next generation of workers, at little cost to this class that might otherwise have to pay more taxes to provide an extensive state-supported childcare system.

The gender division of labour—with the male as the breadwinner and the female as homemaker taking care of dependent children—became so economically and ideologically dominant following World War II that it actually came to be regarded as the "traditional" family model, with the assumption that it had existed throughout history. In reality, this model of family life developed only in the nineteenth century, spreading to increasing numbers of families in the twentieth. As part of the development of this family form, the notions of "muscular masculinity" and "domestic femininity" were promoted (Sears 2003, 159–60).

Despite changing gender roles in the workplace in the late twentieth century, males and females have continued to be socialized into these traditional roles. Muscular masculinity is linked to participation in sports, as well as the ability to fight, endure pain, and master machines (Connell 1995). Governments and traditional religions that adhere to historical gender roles have promoted this notion of masculinity to prepare men for their role in the family, their possible role on the battlefield, and for work.

Domestic femininity, meanwhile, prepares women for their role as household workers and family caregivers. Even if women work outside the home, their primary activity is still commonly seen as that within a heterosexual marriage with offspring. A high value is also placed on women's appearance, and a "beauty myth" has helped sustain gender inequality. Although the latter half of the twentieth century saw women's and men's work activities change substantially, notions of the "traditional" family and gender roles—if modified somewhat to reflect new realities—continue to the present day. Indeed, Wolf (1991) has argued that the growing independence of women has actually led to an escalation of the beauty myth, with women more preoccupied with their self-image than with changing structures of power.

Think About It

Do you agree with Wolf's argument that, despite widespread participation in the labour market, most women in Canada today spend more time worrying about their appearance than being involved in social change? Do you think it is any different for men?

Most of us would agree that men today have also become absorbed with their appearance. However, while young women tend to focus on breast size and thinness, young men focus on muscularity. As one author (Kimmell 2003, 234) writes:

> The increasing packaging of men's bodies in the media—it is now common to see men's bodies displayed in advertising in ways that were conceivable only for women's bodies a generation ago—coupled with increased economic anxiety (which leads us to focus on things we *can* control, like how we look), has led to a dramatic shift in men's ideas about their bodies.

It is interesting to note that while Second Wave feminists sought to discredit the media's hyper-sexualized images of females, today's young women have embraced these images. In the late 1960s the "unisex" look was the rage, and it was sometimes hard to tell if the young person walking past you on the street was a male or female. As women have struggled to advance gender equality—entering the paid labour force and attaining higher levels of education—the idealized body type and fashion style for both men and women have returned to an emphasis on their physiological differences. Such differentials, in their own way, help maintain the notion of gender difference.

These images have also proven very profitable to capital. The need of males and females to live up to these images has both women and men spending billions on clothing, gym memberships, make-up, weight-loss products, steroids, plastic surgery, and so on. And of course, because most of us need money to buy these products as we seek the temporary gratification that comes through their purchase, we are likely to accept our deteriorating workplace conditions. In this way, distinct gender roles and the images that go with them remain very profitable to capital.

How Far Has the Struggle for Gender Equality Come?

From the viewpoint of the early twenty-first century, it may appear that Canadian women of today actually have it pretty good. However, in some ways the main advances for women have come in the personal realm—increasing freedom of lifestyle choices as well as sexual liberation—while certain important structural transformations have been limited.

For example, there continues to be occupational gender segregation, with the labour market divided into male and female segments. As one textbook on work notes, "A potent combination of gender-role socialization, education, and labour market mechanisms continue to channel women into a limited number of occupations in which mainly other females are employed" (Krahn et al. 2007, 182). These female job ghettos often have lower wages, fewer benefits, little job security, and little opportunity for advancement.

Moreover, some of the growing equality between the sexes has come not from women's advances but rather from men's deteriorating position, particularly regarding the increasing numbers of men working in low-wage jobs. Such data are in line with the argument made by Pat Armstrong (1996) that using a male standard to evaluate women's progress often exaggerates women's gains while masking the deteriorating condition for some men. While some women—like some men—are doing better than ever, more women and more men are finding themselves in "bad" rather than "good" jobs. Moreover, even those who remain in the good jobs find that they are working harder and are under more stress. Both men and women are working longer hours (Statistics Canada 2006a).

And while girls are surpassing boys at all levels of education—females get higher grades in high school, are more likely to graduate from high school, and are more likely to attend postsecondary institutions—their achievements may be coming at the expense of some males. Across North America, the data seems to indicate that white, middle-, or upper-income males are doing as well as, or better than, ever before. However, some racial and ethnic minorities and lower-income males are finding themselves increasingly marginalized at an early age. With some "good" and many "bad" jobs, many disadvantaged students—as noted elsewhere in this book—are being streamed out of programs that would give them access to the postsecondary education required for the high-paying good jobs (Sears 2003).

For both males and females, there is a link between paid employment and work done in the home. However, unlike men, many women continue to make career choices that they feel will be compatible with child-rearing. Men, in contrast, are more likely to see themselves as the breadwinners and choose careers that fit with this assumption. The unequal wages that persist in the workplace simply reinforce differing roles in the heterosexual household, which then reinforce differing roles in the workplace.

Think About It
How did you decide what program to choose when you entered university or college? Do you think your choice was at all gender-related?

Gender inequality persists in male-female households, despite women's increased participation in the paid labour force. For example, when men do participate in housework, they tend to do the more pleasant chores, such as playing with children or shopping (Coleman 1991, 248; Luxton 1990, 48). Among heterosexual couples, a central variable affecting the gender division of labour in the home seems to be the wages of the woman relative to those of the man. That is, the narrower the wage gap between male and female partners, the more equal the household division of labour seems to be. A 2005 study of Canadian households concluded that the division of paid labour and housework for male-female couples is more likely to be split equally when wives have an income of $100,000 or more (Statistics Canada 2006a).

The household continues to be seen as privatized and outside of the public sphere, primarily under the control of those within it. For this reason, domestic violence and violence against children have taken so long to be seen as more than a personal problem, while the burdens of child-rearing and household management have seen declining support from the state, particularly in Canada. In 2006, shortly after taking power, the Conservative government of Stephen Harper cancelled plans for the $2.2 billion National Child Care strategy that had been over ten years in the making; instead the government returned to a system of funding families, with every child under six receiving a paltry $1,200 per year. (The sole exception to this policy is the province of Quebec, which increased family benefits some years ago and instituted an accessible and afford-able childcare system.) Care for the sick and elderly is also being shifted back into the private sphere of the household.

In all these activities, women constitute the majority of caregivers. Those with higher incomes are increasingly hiring paid workers such as nannies, cleaners, or caregivers for the aged to do such work. Of course, most of these paid household workers are other women—often immigrant women—with low wages, poor working conditions, few benefits, and low status. In many cases these women are forced to leave their own children behind in the care of others while they work abroad.

In recent years both women and men have felt increasing pressures in trying to balance work and home tasks. The "work-family crunch" is currently being aggravated by a number of tendencies. The stagnating wages of men have pres-sured more women to stay in or rapidly re-enter the paid labour force. Declining government supports for children (particularly in the areas of childcare and education) also mean that two wages are required for parents to acquire some measure of financial security. At the same time, both men and women are finding that they are under increasing pressure from employers to be more productive, which has resulted in longer hours and more intensified work.

Achieving a balance is a particularly serious concern for women, who per-form the major share of domestic tasks. Researchers at Laval University found that the combination of high-stress jobs and child-rearing responsibilities was driving women's blood pressure to persistently high levels, putting them at a much higher risk of stroke and heart disease (Picard 1999). Some women opt to become full-time mothers after their children are born. However, one study found that women who stayed at home to raise children actually experienced *more* symptoms of depression, such as irritability and sleep disorders, than those who worked outside the home (*Globe and Mail*, 25 June 1999, M1). Moreover, staying at home is not a realistic option for most women. In the current economic climate, the majority of women—whether living with a partner or not—have to work and find themselves working harder than ever before. Clearly these stresses are magnified for lower-income earners and in lone-parent families.

Many men are now taking on more child-rearing responsibilities. For example, between 2001 and 2006, the proportion of fathers who took a leave from work for the birth or adoption of their child rose from 38 percent to 55 percent. This rise was likely due to changes in government eligibility for benefits (Statistics Canada 2007b). However, the stresses are different for men, who often find themselves in jobs where no accommodation is made for their family life. Moreover, while men are under pressure to more equitably share household tasks, they are still expected to be "good providers" (Conway 1997, 210).

The Outlook for the Future

Unlike earlier pre-industrial societies, it is now possible to have full equality between men and women. And yet gender inequality continues to exist. Since this inequality has had negative consequences for *both* men and women, why is change so slow? The process of change is by no means an easy one. Even for many women change does not come easily. This should not be surprising, given that notions of gender inequality have existed for thousands of years and constitute an inherent part of many of our strongly held religious or moral belief systems. Moreover, because those with power continue to benefit from gender inequality, changes in the ideological underpinnings, government policies, and the process of socialization have nowhere matched the speed of change in the material preconditions for gender equality.

Governments at all levels have a key role to play in this respect. One key area lies in support for families. Countries that provide the most social and financial supports to families, such as Sweden where 83 percent of children aged one to six get state-funded daytime care, also have the greatest social equality, including gender equality. Such government supports, including adequate subsidies for single parents, improved minimum wages, and so on, would advance gender equality both in the home and in the workplace. Unfortunately, the neoliberal policies of various levels of government in Canada have eroded some of the previous gains made by women, and many policies have had a devastating effect on the family as social supports were reduced or removed. The massive spending cuts over the last twenty-five years at all levels of government have been particularly hard on women, in part because so many find themselves in poverty.

But there are other concerns for women, not only those who are poor. Women's paid employment occurs in a relatively narrow range of occupations, primarily the service sector. These are the very occupations—such as nurses, early childhood educators, teachers, social workers, and government clerical workers—that were most under attack by governments during the late 1990s. Some women also find themselves having to take care of aging parents as social supports to the elderly and the sick have declined. Globalization and the elimination of trade barriers have also had a particularly negative effect on women.

Many of the jobs held by women in manufacturing (clothing, footwear, textiles, and electrical products) have been lost to cheaper global competition.

The declining rate of unionization is another worrying trend. There is substantial agreement that collective bargaining improves wages and benefits for unionized workers when compared to non-unionized workers, particularly for those with lower skills, while promoting greater equality of wages and working conditions within the unionized sector (Jackson and Schellenberg 1999, 247). Not only do women in unionized workplaces generally earn higher wages than do women in comparable employment who are not unionized, but they also have greater protection via collective-agreement provisions such as maternity leave and sexual harassment.

The same factors that are holding back gender equality in Canada—global capitalism and neoliberalism—have been having a negative effect on women in other parts of the world, and many recent advances for women have been eroded. The transformation of countries of the former Soviet Union to free market economies meant an end to a range of government supports for women—including free health care and education—which drove many into poverty. In the developing world, global pharmaceutical companies have marketed unsafe or experimental contraceptives to women. Meanwhile, the current backlash against Western society and values in many parts of the world has frequently meant a backlash against women's rights (van der Gaag 2004, 12). Many of the countries that have repressive laws against women continue to severely restrict and punish homosexuality as well.

As emphasized in this chapter, the erosion of women's conditions generally means worsening conditions for men. Such analyses tell us that the struggle for gender equality is not one of women versus men, nor is it simply a struggle to change ideas or gender images. Gender inequality is bound up in the unequal and highly segregated worlds of work, both in the paid labour force and in the household. Gender inequality is inevitable in a society that puts corporate needs ahead of the needs of people.

In the short term, a number of policy changes would lead to greater gender equality in Canada, improving the lives of both women and men. This would include a national childcare program, more affordable housing, minimum wages that are above the Statistics Canada LICO poverty line, the expansion of public-sector jobs, improvements to unemployment (employment) insurance, union contracts that limit the ability of companies to hire contingent workers, and more protections and benefits for part-time workers.

In the longer term, there is a need for a shorter work week so that both men and women can better combine paid labour with family obligations, the reduction of part-time and contingent workers, and increased rates of unionization. Overall, all family forms require greater financial and social supports from the various levels of government and from employers. Such demands constitute a collective challenge to the present ruling class, which currently sets the limits on such possibilities through its ownership and control of the means of production.

Key Points

1. Assumptions about gender difference have led to gender inequality around the world.

2. Despite gains over the past thirty years, gender inequality continues to be a reality in Canada.

3. Biological determinists and functionalists believe that anatomy is destiny. Overall, the research suggests that there are few obvious, consistent, and recurring differences between men and women.

4. Since the nineteenth century, various feminist theories have developed to explain gender inequality. Many writers now speak of three "waves" of feminism.

5. Liberal feminism sees the main cause of gender inequality within a society's culture, that is, in the ideas we have about men and women and in the way children are socialized. What is missing in this argument, however, is the roots of these cultural elements.

6. Both radical feminism and traditional Marxism see gender inequality as a structural problem, linked to the allocation of power. While radical feminists feel gender inequality is rooted in biology, Marxists argue that it began with the rise of social classes and the patriarchal family.

7. Most anthropologists agree that the development of classes led to the growth of the state, warfare, a changing religious system, and the development of the patriarchal family. All of these played a role in magnifying gender inequality.

8. While men's higher status does lead to some male privilege, most men have little structural power. The real power is held by the capitalist owning class. Traditionally men have had greater access to positions of power, but most men—like most women—seldom achieve such positions.

9. Many of the recent advances made by women in Canada are currently under attack as a result of globalization and neoliberal government policies.

10. Both women and men have felt increasing pressures in trying to balance work and home tasks; these stresses are magnified for lower-income earners and in lone-parent families.

11. Gender inequality has had negative consequences for both men and women. The Canadian government could make a number of policy changes that would improve the lives of both men and women.

Further Reading

Barndt, Deborah. 2002. *Tangled Routes: Women, Work, and Globalization on the Tomato Trail*. Aurora, ON: Garamond.
This book traces the journey of a tomato from Mexico to Canada. An innovative approach that looks at the effects of globalization on real women.

Engels, Friedrich. [1884] 1972. *The Origin of the Family, Private Property, and the State*. Ed. Eleanor Burke Leacock. New York: International Publishers.
Not an easy read, but this work is the classic Marxist statement on the rise of gender inequality. The introduction by Eleanor Leacock is informative.

Hesse-Beiber, Sharlene Naigy, and Patricia Lina Leavy. 2006. *Feminist Research Practice*. Sage Publications.
This book introduces a number of feminist theories and explains how feminist research is done.

Kimmel, Michael S. 2004. *The Gendered Society*. New York: Oxford.
An easy-to-read textbook that looks at the various aspects of gender in today's world. Although it is American, most issues would apply to Canada as well.

Lerner, Gerda. 1986. *The Creation of Patriarchy*. New York: Oxford University Press.
This is probably the most thorough examination of the evolution of gender inequality in the region of the Middle East. Essential reading for those interested in the way religious beliefs about men and women transformed over time.

Tyyska, Vappu. 2007. *Action and Analysis: Readings in the Sociology of Gender*. Toronto: Thomson Nelson.
This book of readings does a nice job of showing how the various feminisms of our time have each added to our understanding of modern gender issues.

van der Gaag, Nikki. 2004. *The No-Nonsense Guide to Women's Rights*. Toronto: New Internationalist Publications.
This small book provides a brief, fact-filled examination of gender inequality around the world and the global struggle for women's equality. Also in this series is Vanessa Baird's *No-Nonsense Guide to Sexual Diversity*.

13 Looking Toward the Future

In This Chapter

- Where is capitalism headed?
- Can the problems within capitalist societies be corrected without any radical transformation of the entire system?
- Will Canada survive as a country?
- How do societies change from one form to another?

We currently live in a world where change is all around us. However, although we know that change is constant, it often seems that change is both unpredictable and out of our control. In this context, the notion of being able to make predictions about where our society is headed seems an absurdity. Social scientists, of course, are not mystics. Like all scientists, we predict the future based on past patterns.

> The philosophers have only interpreted the world; the point however is to change it.
>
> —Karl Marx, *Theses on Feurbach*

European social thought of the late nineteenth and early twentieth centuries, including sociology, largely developed out of the turbulent changes brought about by the Industrial Revolution and the transformation to capitalism. From the outset, there was a tension in the social sciences about the ultimate purpose of social analysis. This tension is noted in the quote from Marx that opens this chapter. On one side are those analyses—the order theories—that supposedly seek simply to describe the social universe. While society may need a bit of fixing up here and there, social arrangements are seen as both inevitable and permanent—"The world is just." In contrast are the change theories, generally linked to the works of Marx and Engels. For such theorists, as for the little fish, "There is no justice in the world," and the current social arrangements need to be changed.

These two approaches to the social world are reflected in the political sphere. Generally speaking, the politics of the Right is the politics of order, while the politics of the Left is the politics of change. Liberalism, the dominant ideology of capitalism, gives the appearance of being neutral, in the centre of the political spectrum; in reality, as we have seen, liberalism is part and parcel of current class relations and thus falls into the category of the order approach to social reality. At the same time, however, just as capitalism itself is full of contradictions, so is its dominant ideology, liberalism. We saw in earlier chapters that liberal ideology has advanced notions of democracy, human rights, and social equality, ideas not prevalent in the pre-capitalist period.

Few of us today can imagine a world that might exist without capitalist economic relations. Despite all the economic, political, and social turbulence that has faced the world over the past century, the mass media have uniformly limited any debate about possible alternatives to our current economic arrangements. As one author (Shutt 1998, 206) notes, "Any suggestion that the capitalist system might after all need to be fundamentally reshaped, if it is to survive at all, [is dismissed] as an example of old-fashioned Marxist thinking unworthy of serious consideration."

In addition, since we live in an era that emphasizes rational thought and personal choice, we generally think that capitalism and the culture within it, as well as any alterations to it, are the result of a conscious choice. Most of us believe that somehow the majority of people in Canada and the world have chosen to live in a capitalist system. In the same way, most of us assume that the main reason that capitalism would change in the future would be because people want it to.

In reality, the question of whether capitalism will transform into something else, how and when it will change, as well as what might follow capitalism are actually linked to two elements: the real, material conditions within capitalist societies and the way humans act on and change such conditions. In other words, change must be understood in terms of both the *objective* and the *subjective* components in any given society at any particular point in time. This chapter will examine some of the growing and increasingly visible contradictions within capitalist systems and the way people are responding to these contradictions.

Will Capitalism Last Forever?

It has been noted throughout this book that humans, interacting both with each other and with the natural world, inevitably alter the world in which they live. Most of the changes humans make are within the existing relations of production. Any such change—which can be of a social, legal, economic, or political nature—is generally referred to as a **reform**. Reforms can be of benefit to ordinary people (for example, human rights legislation) or work against their interests (for example, government cuts to social spending).

Reforms can sometimes be major transformations within a society and therefore can be quite controversial. In Canada, the last half century has seen the social institutions of both marriage and the family change in dramatic ways. The expansion of divorce, the right to disseminate birth control information, the right of women to obtain legal abortions, and the right of gays and lesbians to marry were all very controversial developments in their time.

Even when reforms involve major alterations to a social institution, they must be distinguished from the rare instances of **revolution**. This term has been co-opted and trivialized in recent years by the advertising industry and political movements. At times it has been used to refer to any kind of major social, political, or technological change. However, social science requires greater precision of terminology. For this reason, revolution should more correctly be defined as a radical transformation of the social order. In the traditional Marxist definition, it is legitimate to use the term *revolution* only when there has been a basic alteration in the relationships between social classes. Even dramatic political events that result in some form of "regime change" without altering the existing class structure are not revolutions.

No social transformation, however radical, totally eliminates that which came before. Humans are an essentially conservative species, always building the new on the foundation of the old. Many of our current religious and philosophical beliefs are thousands of years old. Capitalism itself is rooted in the European feudal order, and advanced capitalism still has a number of feudal remnants, such as a queen of Canada.

It should also be pointed out that there is nothing in the concept of revolution that requires physical violence as a necessary component. If a ruling class is defeated by a previously subservient class (or classes), then this is a revolutionary change no matter whether it occurred peaceably or through armed force. While historically all revolutions have included some violence, the actual degree of it—for example, the presence or absence of civil war—can vary. Frequently, the revolution itself has been relatively peaceful, but the counter-revolution instigated by the defeated ruling classes has been quite ruthless and of considerable duration. This is exactly what happened following the Russian Revolution of 1917.

There is a dialectical relationship between reform and revolution. If we recall that dialectics notes change as moving from the quantitative to the qualitative, then reforms constitute the quantitative component of change, while revolution constitutes the qualitative. Radical transformations of society do not happen out of the blue any more than water instantaneously converts from a liquid to a gas. People do not just wake up one day, say to themselves simultaneously, "Hey, I've got a great idea—how about a new socioeconomic formation?" and then go out and overturn the old order. On the other hand, water being heated just doesn't keep increasing in temperature indefinitely: at a certain point, it is transformed into something that is qualitatively distinct. Likewise, reforms within a given socioeconomic formation cannot simply go on forever. When the "boiling point" of a society is reached, when the contradictions within it have become so great that it can no longer continue in its present form, then a qualitatively distinct moment for change has arrived.

Of course, to speak of revolution in the present Canadian context seems an absurdity for most of us, clearly an indication that the boiling point for radical change in this country is not yet at hand. That is not to say that the failings in our society are not recognized. Even a superficial glance at the daily news in Canada—with its stories about crime, poverty, corruption, racism, homelessness, violence against women, and so on—tells us that something is terribly amiss within our society. Yet most of us continue to believe either that certain social problems are inevitable—the result of individual failings or some unchangeable human nature—or that reforms alone will improve our social world.

The view that we can change the world through reforms alone is referred to as **reformism**. This approach acknowledges the imperfections of our society but denies the class nature—and therefore the power inequities—of capitalism. Reformism is reflected in the political tendency known as *social democracy*. Social democrats acknowledge the inequities and unfairness created by capitalist systems. While they are likely to identify with workers and disadvantaged groups, they believe that the worst tendencies of capitalism can be brought under control. For social democrats, the primary solution to the excesses and inequities of capitalism is to put their political party into power. In Canada, social democracy is embodied in the New Democratic Party.

At certain moments in history, social democratic parties have been one of the leading political forces for change that helped ordinary people. In recent years, however, many of these parties have been almost indistinguishable from their more conservative opponents. Social democratic parties are commonly spoken of as "socialist" parties. However, although social democrats have achieved parliamentary majorities in a number of provinces and in many countries, often for considerable periods of time—for example, Saskatchewan, Manitoba, Sweden, Great Britain, and New Zealand—the capitalist ruling class has retained both its wealth and its power, and the private appropriation of surplus has continued unabated.

In opposition to the social democrats are those on the left who feel that, in the end, capitalism cannot be reformed to any great extent. If we examine history, it is clear that all socioeconomic formations up to the present have come into being, developed for a time, decayed, and finally disappeared. On the other hand, capitalism has shown itself to be an extremely flexible societal form. Marxists have frequently predicted the imminent demise of capitalism, and yet it still dominates the globe. Nonetheless, the increasingly visible contradictions within capitalist systems give us a clue that capitalism may now be on the decline.

The Contradictions of Capitalism

More and more analysts—not simply those with a Marxist orientation—are noticing a number of disturbing developments within modern capitalist societies. None of them are new, but there seems to be an increased visibility of such tendencies, as well as escalating discomfort with them. Many are beginning to question whether the interests of corporate leaders mesh with the interests of the rest of us. A look beneath the surface of our society reveals a troubling and uncertain future for capitalism.

Doomsday scenarios that see a society declining economically or morally and headed into a "dark age" are not new, and the prevalence of this theme—among religious leaders, philosophers, or cultural critics—may make some of us

306

wonder about their legitimacy. Nonetheless, there do seem to be a number of major fault lines in our current social arrangements. Morris Berman (2006), an American sociologist, sees the United States heading into a "dark age," which he links to such elements as cultural deterioration, erosion of both civil liberties and the rule of law, the development of a permanent state of war, and the decline of the United States as a global economic and moral power. Jane Jacobs (2004, 163), focusing on broader North American culture, argues that a decay in the five central pillars of our society—community and family; higher education; science and technology; governmental representation; and self-regulation of the learned professions—are leading to what she calls an "unprecedented crisis."

> It must be recognised that organised capital has become—together with, but to an even greater extent than organised crime—a parasite so voracious that it is killing the body it feeds off.
> —Harry Shutt, *The Trouble with Capitalism*

As was noted in Chapter 1, dialectics teaches us that change is the result of the unity and struggle of opposites—that, in effect, all societies contain the seeds of their own destruction. Capitalism certainly displays such tendencies. Strangely, the inner contradictions of capitalism are escalating at the very time when its supposed enemies—that is, Marxist political movements, the Soviet empire, the trade union movement, and so on—have either disappeared or are weak.

Growing Social, Political, and Economic Instability

The capitalist owning class seeks stability, but, in carrying out its competitive activities in the marketplace, it always ends up with its opposite, growing instability. New policies and directions are sought in an attempt to restore stability, until the inevitable instability appears again. This is the irresolvable crisis of capitalism. Capitalism inevitably suffers from excess production—of goods, of workers, and of capital itself, and overproduction leads to growing economic instability, which in turn creates increasing social and political instability. The highly competitive global economy of today has increased economic instability and the risk of global economic collapse.

Some government policies were developed in the late nineteenth and early twentieth centuries in an attempt to control the worst tendencies of the ruling class, in particular, its propensity to do anything required to maximize profits, regardless of the consequences. Nonetheless, the first half of the twentieth century was marked by two world wars and one global depression. In an attempt to prevent such major upheavals from happening again, the governments of the developed world became more involved in economic issues in the second half of the twentieth century. This role played by governments was not simply to help the average citizen—although it often did that—but, rather, to keep capitalist economies from destroying themselves.

In Chapter 9 we saw that, following World War II, two other important changes occurred within the world capitalist economies. First, the United States gained ascendancy, becoming the pre-eminent global superpower economically, politically, and militarily. Second, a wide range of organizations such as the United Nations and World Bank were developed in order to integrate the various capitalist nations of the world. The goal was to prevent a repeat of the economic collapse in the earlier part of the century and to remove all constraints on the ability of capital to move anywhere in the world to secure profits.

In some senses, these two key developments are in opposition to each other. Although the United States was a key force in the development of various international organizations and agreements, it is now increasingly opting out of decisions by these entities when it feels such decisions work against its own interests. The unwillingness of the United States to be bound by these international bodies and agreements undermines the credibility of the very entities created to maintain stability. Thus there is an increasing tension between the needs of globalized capitalism in general, and the needs of the most powerful capitalist country in the world, the United States.

In addition, the push by the owning class to maximize profits has created what has been termed *hypergrowth*, the ever more rapid and expanding corporate economic growth that is caused by the search for new markets, cheaper labour, and new resources (Cavanagh et al. 2002). To achieve this end, corporations called for increasing "free trade." However, trade was never the issue. In reality, what corporations sought was the freedom to secure profits anywhere in the world without the constraints of governments. As neoliberal agendas around the world deregulated and freed corporations from "impediments"—such as laws that protected the environment, workers' rights, public health, and national sovereignty—nation-states and local governments have been less able to protect their resources and their citizens. In this way, the tension between the needs of the few in the ruling class—to secure and constantly expand their profits at any cost—and the rest of us are becoming more visible and more direct.

Social and political instability can only be aggravated by a growing disparity between rich and poor, environmental degradation, and the loss of a shared sense of social values. Moreover, in a world that appears to be out of our control with increasing competition for scarce resources, people tend to turn inward—to their clan, ethnic group, language group, religion, or region. As noted in Chapter 9, this leads to increasing tensions, an increase in social instability, and increased violence.

As part of this process, we are seeing a growing threat of terrorism around the world. Although terrorism usually refers to small groups using violent means to achieve their goals, we should also include the expansion of state terrorism. As noted in Chapter 8, the repressive arm of the state has been growing in most countries, and there is greater criminalization of dissent. Moreover, the United States has increasingly asserted its military might against any government it perceives as unacceptable. But rather than stabilizing the world, this growing use of military force threatens to destabilize not only particular regions but also the entire globe.

Many of us are also terrified of the new diseases spreading around the world. The globalization of industrial agriculture, factory farming practices, and the global movement of people and goods have brought frightening diseases to our doorstep. The spread of avian flu, mad cow disease, severe acute respiratory syndrome (SARS), and West Nile virus must all be linked to the growth of a global capitalist economy. These diseases not only are dangerous to our health but also can destabilize whole economies. In addition, in the rush to import cheap products from China, many countries overlooked their poor standards. In 2007, after a number of dogs died from tainted pet food, journalists uncovered the fact that much of the foodstuffs imported from that country may be unsafe for human consumption.

The contradictions and irrationality of capitalism are so embedded in our society—and in our psyches—that we rarely even notice them. For example, we rarely think about the fact that people around the globe are suffering untold misery as a result of unemployment and underemployment, while there are an enormous number of jobs that need to be done. For example, there are housing shortages, deteriorating roads, overcrowded classrooms, illiterate children, rampant diseases, short-staffed hospitals, and so on. Thus there is no shortage of tasks to be done, nor is there a shortage of money to train and employ people to do these tasks, as the wealthiest individuals are financially better off than ever before. However, aside from the occasional act of charity, those who have the means to fund various work-creating and socially useful projects do not do so because they will not make sufficient return on such investments. Not only is this perfectly legal in all capitalist countries, but we actually reward the corporate leaders who cause massive human and social destruction by constantly seeking to maximize their profits.

The Limits of Growth

We have seen throughout the book that a basic underlying element of all capitalist economies is perpetual growth. This growth is the inevitable result of individual units of capital, in competition with each other in the marketplace, constantly self-expanding. In the capitalist marketplace, "you grow or you die." Without thinking about it, most of us see this never-ending growth as a positive thing. The media are always reporting that it is good when the GDP increases, bad if the economy shrinks. This notion is not totally incorrect, for in a capitalist system, an expanding economy is more likely to see the number of jobs increase than a shrinking one. Moreover, many Canadians have investments or pensions that depend on the success of specific corporations and the stock market in general. If corporations are losing money or go out of business, this may, indeed, be bad for some Canadians. And a serious economic downturn could prove disastrous for many.

However, events of the last thirty years have called into question whether perpetual growth, in and of itself, is good for Canadians or the world as a whole. The advance of the neoliberal agenda has seen an improvement of life conditions for some while others have seen their standard of living stagnate or decline. This has occurred even when the economy is in a boom period, as companies cut costs by downsizing and outsourcing. While "good" jobs continued to be available for some, more and more "bad" jobs—insecure and poorly paying—have appeared on the scene. While some individuals have been able to secure huge amounts of wealth, many others cannot get their most basic needs met.

> For more than 20 years we have exceeded the earth's ability to support a consumptive lifestyle that is unsustainable and we cannot afford to continue down this path.
> —James Leape, World Wildlife Fund Director-General, 2006

> Unless we are brave enough to challenge the notion that growth is good, the world will shop until it drops.
> —George Montbiot

There has been a growing critique of the effects this agenda has had on ordinary people. Some critics are advocating a return to the "golden age," when governments intervened more directly in economies to moderate the worst effects of capitalism for the average Canadian. Others are criticizing corporations for their excessive greed and lack of social conscience, urging them to be more socially responsible. Such individuals believe that mere reforms can improve the lives of most people in this country. They accept that capitalism is an essentially workable system that has simply lost its bearings and has become more and more unfair and unjust. From this point of view, a few adjustments—both political and economic—can create a better world for all.

In contrast are those who feel that the perpetual growth required by capitalist economies has reached its limits; indeed, many now feel perpetual growth is itself one of the major problems of the twenty-first century. Many scientists have noted that, beginning in the 1970s, global economic growth began to surpass the capacity of the planet's ecosystems to sustain it. If economic growth and population increases continue at their current rate, it is unlikely that the Earth—and the humans that occupy it—will survive the next hundred years (see Box 13.1). For those who see capitalism and its need for perpetual growth as the core problem, the whole socioeconomic system will have to be transformed.

The Consequences of Perpetual Growth

Humans have always had to exploit nature in order to survive. Foraging peoples realized that they were in a delicate balance with the natural world and, indeed, considered nature holy. If nature didn't provide, these people would not survive. The rise of social classes and the growth of technology changed the relationship between humans and nature. For the first time, the environment was seen as something to be dominated and conquered. However, it was not until the industrial age that advancing technologies made massive environmental destruction a

Box 13.1 Environmental Costs of a Global Economy

The central feature of an export-oriented production model is that it dramatically increases transport and shipping activity. In the half-century since Bretton Woods, there has been about a twenty-five-fold increase in global transport activity.

As global transport increases, it in turn requires massive increases in global infrastructure development. This is good for large corporations like Bechtel, which get to do the construction work: new airports, seaports, oil fields, pipelines for the oil, rail lines, high-speed highways. Many of these are built in areas with relatively intact wilderness, biodiversity, and coral reefs, or they are built in rural areas. The problems also occur in the developed world. In the United Kingdom a few years ago, there were protests by two hundred thousand people against huge new highways jammed through rural landscapes so that trucks could better serve the global trading system.

Increased global trade increases fossil fuel use as well, contributing to global warming. Ocean shipping carries nearly 80 percent of the world's international trade in goods. The fuel commonly used by ships is a mixture of diesel and low-quality oil known as "Bunker C," which is particularly polluting because of high levels of carbon and sulfur. If not consumed by ships, it would otherwise be considered a waste product.

Increased air transport is even more damaging than shipping. Each ton of freight moved by plane uses forty-nine times as much energy per kilometre as when it's moved by ship. A physicist at Boeing once described the pollution from the takeoff of a single 747 like "setting the local gas station on fire and flying it over your neighbourhood." A two-minute takeoff by a 747 is equal to 2.4 million lawnmowers running for twenty minutes.

Ocean pollution from shipping has reached crisis levels, and there have been direct effects of these huge ships on wildlife and fisheries. Even more serious, possibly, is the epidemic increase of bio-invasions, a significant cause of species extinction. With the growth of global transport, billions of creatures are on the move. Invasive species, brought by global trade, often outcompete native species and bring pollution or health crises.

Ocean shipping also requires increased refrigeration—contributing to ozone depletion and climate change—and an increase in packaging and the wood pallets used for cargo loading; these are little-noted but significant factors in increased pressure on global forests.

The central point is this: if you are going to design a system built on the premise that dramatically increased global trade and transport is good, you are guaranteed to bring on these kinds of environmental problems. They are *intrinsic* to the model.

reality. Capitalist growth is infinite, but the planet's resources are finite.

Evidence is mounting that our natural world—without which there can be no life—is seriously under threat. In the twentieth century, the world population increased by more than four billion, over three times what it was at the beginning of the century. However, the use of energy and raw materials grew more than ten times (Brown and Flavin 1999). Our planet simply cannot sustain its current level of environmental degradation. In this context, we are coming to realize that environmental protection is a global issue. Whether it is the disappearance of the Amazon rainforest, the depletion of ozone in the Earth's atmosphere as a result of fluorocarbons, the destruction of the oceans from oil spills and other chemical contamination, the air pollution resulting from automobile exhausts, the irreversible contamination resulting from nuclear accidents, or the decline of safe drinking water—all of us, regardless of nationality, are affected by environmental degradation.

The need for corporations to seek new sources for profit expansion has led to the increasing privatization of the commons, as was discussed in Chapter 9. Some of the commons can be thought of as global—the atmosphere, the oceans, outer space, or plant and animal biodiversity; other elements of the commons can be thought of as community commons, such as public spaces, common lands, local knowledge and wisdom, and the gene pool of populations. All of these elements are now under threat as transnational corporations seek to privately own and control that which has historically been shared by all.

One worrying trend, particularly for Canadians, is the privatization of fresh water. The supply of available fresh water represents less than half of one percent of the world's total water stock. Thirty-one countries face water scarcity and more than a billion people lack adequate access to clean drinking water (Barlow 2000). For those who bottle and sell water, increased consumption that generates higher prices is a central goal, rather than the promotion of water conservation. Companies that control water resources are not local enterprises, but rather giant transnationals. Governments are often required to financially support these corporations with public money.

Another serious concern is the threat to the genetic commons as a result of recent advances in genetic engineering and the patenting of life forms and biodiversity. Corporations such as Monsanto, Novartis, DuPont, Pioneer, and others are now scouring the globe for life forms they can own or engineer. Monsanto has intellectual property rights to more than 80 percent of all genetically engineered seeds. It also owns broad species patents on cotton, mustard, and soybeans, species that were developed over thousands of years in small farming communities. Even the genes of humans are in the process of being patented. This process is sometimes referred to as "biopiracy" (Shiva, in Cavanagh et al. 2002, 87).

Many people are concerned about the introduction of genetically modified (GM) foods. At the moment, few of us in Canada are even aware that we are consuming such foods, because there is no requirement that they be labelled. However, since soybeans, canola oil, and corn are among the key foods currently being modified, and since such products find their way into almost all packaged products, it is likely that the vast majority of Canadians have already consumed them. No one can be sure of the long-term consequences of such crops either for the consumers or the environments in which they are grown.

The commons is also being appropriated as a free dumping ground for the waste materials produced by corporations. The need to secure profits pushes corporations toward planned obsolescence, for there is more money to be made if your car or computer has to be replaced every few years. Not only does this use up our limited natural resources at a rapid pace, it also leads to the increasing problem of where to store the ever-mounting waste. And increasingly, that waste is full of toxic ingredients. One solution has been the shipping of waste to the poorest countries in the world, which are becoming toxic dump sites for the excesses of corporate capitalism. Citizens in Canada and other developed countries are also facing the problem of dealing with waste materials. For example, approximately two million television sets, 1.1 million VCRs, and 348,000 CD players—most only a few years old—were thrown out in 2002. In addition, Canadians discarded approximately 155,000 tonnes of personal computers. Each television can contain up to two kilograms of lead, a dangerous substance that has been linked to learning disabilities in children; mercury, used in the backlight display panel of stereos, is also becoming more common in the country's landfills (Friscolanti 2003).

Lastly, we are all increasingly aware that human activities have led to global warming. It has already, at least in part, affected food supplies and caused severe storms, droughts, and forest fires in many parts of Canada. If the planet continues to warm, as most scientists are now predicting, we can look forward to rising sea levels, the disappearance of the rainforests, major social dislocation, massive species extinction, and global malnutrition. Most of us are concerned about these frightening scenarios and want our three levels of government to take action. To some extent, our governments have been limited by the policies of our neighbour to the south.

Will Canada Become Part of the United States?

For Canadians, a key issue that will face us in this century is whether we will survive as a nation. The first half of the twentieth century saw Canada slowly separate from Britain. By the 1960s Canadians had their own flag and got their own constitution in 1982. Ironically, the 1980s was also the time when neoliberal policies began to dominate in Canada. One key aspect of neoliberalism in Canada has involved an increasing integration with the United States, politically, economically, militarily, and culturally.

In poll after poll, the majority of Canadians have indicated that they like the Canadian way of life and want to protect Canadian sovereignty. When asked in a 2000 *Maclean's* poll whether Canada should "move closer to the United States in its laws and attitudes," 72 percent said no, while only 21 percent agreed (Hurtig 2002, 120). And yet almost imperceptibly over the last thirty years, Canada has become increasingly Americanized.

If Canadians want to retain their independence from the United States, why does there seem to be growing integration with that country? The answer involves understanding the interests of those with power, the corporate owning class, and the politicians who support them. In the nineteenth century, the majority of Canadian corporate leaders saw U.S. businesses as worrying competitors. They sought to build a sovereign country where their smaller units of capital would not be threatened by the much bigger competitors to the south. However, maintaining Canadian independence from the United States has never been easy, given our shared border, language, and cultural elements. Numerous governments created policies to try to promote and protect Canadian economic and cultural entities. Things began to change drastically when Prime Minister Brian Mulroney pushed greater economic integration with the United States via the North American Free Trade Agreement (NAFTA) as part of the overall neoliberal agenda.

Economic protection for Canadian-owned companies began to decline with the advance of free trade, and some key sectors of our economy became increasingly owned by U.S. and other international corporations. Many Canadians have begun to wonder whether, in a time of crisis, Canadian oil, gas, and water will be shipped south of the border, while Canadians could face shortages of their own natural resources. It is now known that the governments of Canada, the United States, and Mexico have been meeting regularly—sometimes in secret—to proceed with what is referred to as *deep integration*. **Deep integration** is the harmonization of policies and regulations between the three North American countries in the interest of the corporate sectors of these countries. Canadian and American regulations and standards governing health, food safety, and the environment have already moved toward harmonization (Barlow 2007). One analyst (Dobbin 2007) describes deep integration as "the most treacherous plan for the country yet devised" by Canada's ruling class.

Meanwhile, various regions of the country feel alienated from the dominance of the government in Ottawa. For many years people outside Quebec saw that province—with its strong separatist tendencies—as the biggest threat to Canada's existence. In more recent years, many in western Canada, particularly in Alberta, began to talk about separation. In 2003, with the total collapse of the cod fisheries, many in Newfoundland began to wonder whether they had made a bad bargain joining Confederation in 1949, while in 2007 the whole Atlantic region felt it was being unfairly treated by the Harper Conservatives. It is unclear whether the fragile nation-state that binds the diverse regions of Canada together will be able to resist the onslaught from the south over the next fifty years.

Think About It

Do you care whether Canada continues as a country? Why or why not?

The Changing Nature of Classes

It comes as no surprise that Marx and other social critics of the nineteenth century disliked the capitalist owning class. It was felt that this class, in the name of profits, committed horrible crimes against the vast majority in the capitalist world. However, while many people in the nineteenth and early twentieth centuries may have hated the capitalist class, it was the only class at that time that had the capacity to advance the productive forces. Thus moral opposition to the capitalist system could not be transferred into viable economic alternatives.

A century later, this is no longer the case. The concentration and centralization of capital has led to a decline in the size of the owning class, as well as a separation of the function of ownership from the function of management. For example, in an interview a number of years ago, Thomas Bata of Bata Shoes described a day in his life:

> There's always a briefing session at 10 o'clock at which information is passed around…. This happens whether I'm around or not: one of our greatest strengths is that throughout the world we have such a team of people that I can be away for weeks on end and things just carry on. (*Star Weekly Magazine*, 18 August 1979)

If, as Bata notes with pride, he can be away for weeks without negatively affecting production, can he be away for months, years, forever? In other words, it seems that we have now reached a stage in social development where the owning class no longer performs the essential economic role it once did. In many cases today, groupings of capital purchase large corporations without any real interest at all in the productive process. Their goal is to restructure or simply hold on to a company until, it is hoped, share prices rise, and then re-sell it in the marketplace at a hefty profit.

Nor is the owning class, on the whole, any longer seen by the rest of us as the arbiter of societal values. Indeed, there are many who see a moral vacuum in both the economic and political spheres. Capitalism as a whole is increasingly facing a crisis of legitimacy that is the result of the widespread incidence of fraud, corruption, scandals, organized crime, and abuses of power within both the corporate and political spheres.

Concurrent with changes to the ruling class are changes to the working class that occurred over the course of the twentieth century. No longer the unskilled, uneducated workers of a hundred years ago, an increasing proportion of working people are now highly trained and educated. People are educated not simply in specific skills, but in the general capacity to work with others collectively, in an organized and disciplined fashion, to achieve a particular set of goals. Working people also constitute a proportionally larger sector of the population, as more people on a global scale have to sell their labour power for a wage. It is these characteristics—size, organizational capacity, education, and discipline—that led Marx and Engels to argue that the working class, created by the bourgeoisie, would be "the gravediggers of capitalism."

Moreover, the notion that the state can be directly involved in the economy is no longer an alien or frightening notion. In the nineteenth and early twentieth centuries, large-scale economic intervention by the state seemed like a foreign and dangerous concept, impossible to bring into reality. It is hard for us to believe that the early proponents of a state-run health care system in Canada were attacked for being "communists." The growth of the welfare state in the latter half of the twentieth century made a large number of people less fearful of state intervention in the economy. Canadians have seen that their governments can lessen the worst effects of unfettered capitalism, and in general Canadians have supported government-provided social services. Moreover, the number of people working directly or indirectly for the government rapidly expanded in the second half of the twentieth century. Even with the recent cuts to the public sector, almost every Canadian knows someone who is connected, through wages or transfer payments, to some level of government.

On the other hand, there are many Canadians who continue to disapprove of policies promoting direct government involvement in the Canadian economy. There is a strong libertarian sentiment (that is, one that gives priority to individual freedoms over government intervention) in Canada, particularly in the west. Such opposing views regarding the state and its role, which is part of the larger political and social instability within many capitalist societies, will be discussed later in this chapter.

Where Is Capitalism Headed?

For thousands of years, religious leaders and philosophers have envisaged a better world, often a paradise to be reached after death. Given the limited life chances of most humans, it is not surprising that so many have needed to believe in a better tomorrow. Thomas More created the word *utopia* in the sixteenth century, and since that time many writers have described their visions of a heaven on Earth. If the real world were one of exploitation, oppression, poverty, injustice, inequality, cruelty, and hatred, a future utopia would be one with equality and social justice, where humans were kind, cooperative, and loving.

By the end of the eighteenth century, a number of utopian socialists, such as Claude Henri Saint-Simon, Charles Fourier, and Robert Owen, were describing their vision of an alternative to capitalism. Owen, a British factory owner, actually put his ideas into practice by creating more humane conditions for his workers, reducing the working day, setting up nurseries for workers' children, and raising wages. In the end, the utopian socialists failed because they did not understand the class relations of power within capitalist societies. They thought socialism could be attained simply by winning people over to their vision of a more humane society.

Today few of us have even heard of such individuals, let alone read their work. Yet the names of Karl Marx and Friedrich Engels are known around the globe. While they acknowledged their debt to the utopian socialists, Marx and Engels stood apart from them. It sometimes comes as a surprise to learn that Marx and Engels wrote relatively little about exactly what the alternative to capitalism would look like. In this sense, they were being true both to their philosophical materialism and to the methods of science. Unlike the mystics who conjured up the future from crystal balls or tea leaves, or the intellectuals who imagined a better world inside their heads, the first "scientific socialists" (as they called themselves) felt that the only way to predict the future was to look for past patterns. Thus Marx and Engels concentrated on studying the history of human societies, the political economy of human social life, and the patterns of social change.

Marx and Engels felt that the conditions within capitalism—the development of the working class, the large-scale socialization of production, and the growing tension between the needs of an ever-shrinking ruling class and an expanding working class—set the stage for the next socioeconomic formation, which they thought would be socialism.

What does the word "socialism" conjure up for you? Whatever the image, it is almost certainly not a positive one. This should not be surprising, if we recall the degree of control that the dominant class will always have in the sphere of ideas: no group with power would encourage the dissemination of ideas that might lead to its own eradication. In addition, attempts to build socialist societies in the twentieth century were—for a variety of complex reasons—a failure and not models most of us would like to see for our own country. As a result, not only do we not feel positively disposed to the notion of socialism, most of us are actually downright hostile to it, in spite of the fact that many of us have only the vaguest notions of what the concept means.

It will be possible here to touch only briefly on the question of how Marx and Engels viewed socialism. Simply put, Marx and Engels thought that capitalism, a system in which the bourgeois class had power, would be replaced by a socioeconomic formation where the working class would become the ruling class. They certainly did not imagine that a socialist society would be one of perfection, for they were not utopian socialists. They also did not see socialism as a society where everyone earned the same wages. The jobs that need to be done in any society would necessarily involve differing levels of skill, knowledge, risk, and importance to society, and such differences would have to be acknowledged in the form of differential wages and benefits. However, they felt it was possible to narrow the range of salaries from the highest to the lowest. Indeed, whatever we may think of twentieth-century socialism, this was one of its greatest successes (Cereseto 1982).

What is most clear in the writing of Marx and Engels is that they saw socialism as a socioeconomic formation in which the interests and goals of ordinary working people would dominate in all spheres—the economic, the social, and the political. They believed that current class relations would be replaced by a new set of class relations in which power—via the state—would be transferred to the working class, that is, the vast majority. Production would no longer be for corporate profits and personal gain but rather to meet human needs. Marx and Engels thought this new socioeconomic formation would appear when capitalism had reached its limits of development; that is, when the forces of production could no longer advance under the current capitalist class relations.

It is worth noting that this was not the case for the socialist societies that appeared in the twentieth century. While a complete explanation for the failure of such societies would constitute a book in itself, the low level of development of the forces of production must certainly be one key factor. At the time of its revolution, Russia was largely a backward, peasant-based society. All twentieth-century socialist societies had to focus on advancing their forces of production, including the development of a workforce with appropriate skills and knowledge. Many were devastated during World War II. While this by no means fully explains the failure of such societies, it certainly points out the vast difference between these and any future socialist society that would develop out of advanced capitalism.

Despite the fact that many of us feel, as we have been told so many times by those with power, that "There Is No Alternative" (sometimes referred to simply by its acronym TINA), there are increasing numbers of individuals and groups who are pondering what will follow capitalism. Many are reclaiming and renewing a vision of socialism to fit with the world in the twenty-first century.

As modern-day historians and social analysts look back on the feudal period, many developments can be noted that set the stage for the ultimate transition to a new set of class relations. In the same way, it is not simply ideas of a few great thinkers that will pave the way for a new society; rather, it will be a set of conditions that develop within capitalism itself. While the objective preconditions for social transformation may currently exist within the developed capitalist world, the actual process of transformation will depend on the willingness and capacity of the people within these societies to act for change.

Modern Social Movements for Change

To this point we have been discussing the *objective* factors that may lead to future social transformations. We should now briefly address the *subjective* element of how real people come to change the conditions of their lives. Dialectics helps us understand that societies contain opposing tendencies and that elements within a society give rise to their opposites. Humans persistently join together to oppose the negative conditions that arise in societies.

We can begin to examine this process by thinking of a simple situation that any one of us might experience. Suppose you are taking a course in sociology and you fail a major term paper. What do you do? You might see the teacher, appeal the grade, complain to your friends, or, perhaps, you might do nothing at all. Now suppose you find out the next week that the teacher has failed two-thirds of the class. Moreover, you also discover that this professor has been failing most of her students for years. At this point, you have discovered that what started out (in C. Wright Mills's terms) as a "personal trouble" is actually a "public issue."

What do you do now? You may still decide to do nothing, but it becomes more likely that you will get together with some of the other students who failed and plan a strategy—perhaps you will start a petition, get a group to speak to the chair or dean, or go to the student newspaper. The more radical among you might suggest staging a sit-in at the president's office or hiring a lawyer. Perhaps you will do all of these things or just some of them. What you have probably realized is that, in order to oppose someone with more power than yourself, you have to act in a collective and organized fashion.

This is exactly how opposition to structures of power occurs in the broader society. People lose their jobs, get sexually abused, get hurt in industrial accidents, are denied housing because of their skin colour, are harassed for being gay, and so on. Given the nature of power and the lack of understanding most of us have about our social world, a good many of us will direct our anger or frustration at ourselves or others. Not being able to grasp the power that exists at the distal realm, we are likely to see ourselves as the victims of personal problems rather than as being a part of broader public issues.

Obviously, as long as most people can get their needs met within a given socioeconomic formation, they will not be particularly interested in risking what they have for some unknown future. At the moment—both in Canada and across the developed capitalist world—it is likely that a good proportion of people want to keep their privileges and do not want the world to change in any major way. However, it is likely that this world of privilege will change in the next fifty years. In times of increasing social and economic deterioration or uncertainty, more and more people may feel frustrated by failed attempts to achieve the reforms that would better, or simply maintain, the conditions of their lives. At this point, many formerly passive individuals will join the struggle for change, and organized attacks on the social order will grow. What no one can predict at the moment is whether sufficient changes will occur in time to save our planet from ecological destruction.

Think About It

Read Box 13.2. Are you prepared to make any lifestyle changes to help minimize climate change? Why or why not? Ask your friends and relatives what they might be prepared to do. Do you think individuals alone can bring about needed changes, or do we need governments to take charge?

Organizing for Change

There are many ways that people struggle to change elements within a society. Some people feel that the only way to effect change is by altering their own personal behaviour. Others will decide that the best way to change existing social institutions is to become involved in the political structures of society in the hopes of creating new social policies.

However, there are many who see the necessity of collective action but prefer

Box 13.2 An Imaginary Letter to Her Grandson, 2046

Looking back, Tom, I remember that 2006 was the time when climate change really became a mainstream issue. The mistake at that point was obvious even at the time: the politicians were still pretending that tackling climate change wouldn't require a big change in lifestyle.

For a long time the politicians were understandably reluctant to spell out the kind of state intrusiveness and personal self-denial that was going to be necessary. Around 2006 they began to impose light penalties on those huge cars. The drivers complained: one woman insisted that she had three children to get to school, I remember. It was absurd, the effort she was making for these children that at the same time was contributing to the destruction of their future.

But none of us can claim to be guilt-free. How can I explain to you why I drove thousands of miles every year, and lived in a draughty old house that pumped central heating on to the pavement? Why weren't we all clamouring on the streets for the politicians to do more, demanding that our government impose sanctions and launch boycotts of the countries refusing to collaborate in cutting emissions? All of this eventually happened, but by then it was too late.

A debate developed between those who believed it was possible to change our lifestyle without pain and those who disagreed, arguing that this was a moral issue and that it would involve concepts such as self-denial and self-sacrifice. The latter were deeply unpopular—even alien—to a consumer culture built on entitlement. "Because you're worth it" ran an ad slogan, and we really believed we "needed" the foreign holidays and the repeated buzz of consumer novelty.

The problem was that we were intoxicated with an idea of individual freedom. With hindsight, that understanding of freedom was so impoverished that it amounted to little more than a greedy egotism of doing whatever you wanted whenever. We understood freedom largely in terms of shopping and mobility. The idea that the most precious freedom of all was freedom from fear gained force much later.

Fear in the end was the only mechanism that was able to cut through the complacency and force the cultural change, the political pressure and the global cooperation necessary. We are all haunted by the fact that human beings were unable to use the benefits of our own intelligence—we had the knowledge—to avert disaster.... In the end it was catastrophes that prompted change. But, as you would point out, by then it was too late.

Source: Adapted from Madeline Bunting, "It's Hard to Explain, Tom, Why We Did So Little to Stop Global Warming," copyright Guardian News & Media Ltd. 2006.

to struggle for change in what are sometimes referred to as *civil society groups*, that is, voluntary organizations that are outside of both the corporate world and the state. There are a wide variety of such groups currently advocating for change across Canada. Some may develop because of a local issue and exist only for a short period of time, such as those opposing a new highway or struggling for more social housing. Others may be larger, may be more permanent, and may have broader aims. The Council of Canadians, for example, has more than 100,000 members and supporters across the country. It describes itself as an independent, non-partisan, public interest organization that provides a critical voice on key national issues.

Social movements are broader networks of groups and individuals that work for change, and there are many such movements in Canada, including those struggling for social justice, peace, environmental protection, and the advancement of women, minorities, and Aboriginals. In the last ten years or so, many groups opposing the various negative consequences of globalization and free trade have linked together, both within Canada and around the world. There has also been a growing integration between those opposed to the negative effects of globalization and the various movements for peace.

Think About It

Have you ever been involved in a movement for social change? Why or why not? Why do you think most young people are not involved in such movements?

Populist Movements

For most of this book we have examined the two dominant classes in capitalist society, the corporate ruling class and the class of working people. However, in times of increasing social instability (such as the period we are now in), we need to understand the important place of the "middle fish," the ones who think "There is some justice in the world." In the real world, the middle fish are the middle strata, consisting of the small-business class (the petite bourgeoisie) and the upper strata of working people.

It is not hard to guess that such individuals will generally like the system that has rewarded them with relatively high wages, high status, or the privileges of ownership. However, we have seen in earlier chapters how increasing numbers of those in the middle have felt increasing stress: self-employed individuals feel increasing financial strain, highly paid workers suddenly find themselves out of work, and small businesses feel increasingly squeezed by taxes, cut-throat competition with big business, and employee demands. Such individuals may continue to support the system, even though they feel their share in it is declining. Their goal, therefore, is to change *market* relations rather than *class* relations, in the hopes of getting a bigger piece of the economic pie. White males, in particular, may feel their share has been declining because others—women and racial minorities, for example—have been getting a bigger share.

Some of the middle strata will be drawn to the movements for democracy and social justice, as well as those trying to preserve the social safety net. However, many of these individuals, particularly the petite bourgeoisie, may be drawn to right-wing social movements that espouse an ideology known as **populism**. Populism comes from the Latin word *populi*, meaning "of the people." It presents itself as a movement of "the little guy," opposing big government, big business, and (for the right-wing variant of populism) big unions. Western Canada has long been fertile ground for populist movements of both the Left (the Co-operative Commonwealth Federation, forerunner of the NDP) and the Right (Social Credit, forerunner of the Reform Party, which became the Canadian Alliance and later merged with the federal Progressive Conservative Party).

The other group that is often drawn into right-wing movements, particularly those of the far right, is the underclass, or what Marx referred to as the *lumpenproletariat*. These people, who are largely outside of productive relations, are the most marginalized in society. Historically, such individuals—extremely oppressed and cut off from any means of large-scale collective action—have played a role in such movements as the Ku Klux Klan or the fascists in Hitler's Germany and Mussolini's Italy. Such groups give isolated individuals a collective to belong to as well as scapegoats to attack (Blacks, Jews, gays, immigrants). In other words, they give some sense of power to the relatively powerless. When extreme right-wing groups attain some legitimacy, they may also become appealing to the middle strata.

Right-wing populist political parties have increased their support by appealing to the real fears of the middle strata. For example, some political parties, such as the Reform Party and subsequently the Canadian Alliance, gained popularity primarily by promoting the notion that individuals were being held hostage by "special interest groups," such as the poor, women, racial minorities, or the disabled (Harrison et al. 1996, 174). Right-wing populist movements also tend to be connected to a broader social and religious conservatism, such as hostility to feminism and gay rights, opposition to sex education in the schools, and so on. In times of social instability, when many people feel that moral standards and traditions are rapidly eroding, such views can have wider appeal.

Although populist movements of both the Left and the Right often express philosophical opposition to big business, their actual policies are not generally hostile to the owning class, and variations of the corporate agenda can be found in all the mainstream political parties. Moreover, their focus on problems with government policies masks the real power that resides in the largest corporations.

New Social Movements: "A Better World Is Possible"

Humans have long struggled against the oppressive conditions of their lives. Slavery gave rise to anti-slavery movements, imperialism to anti-imperialist movements, war to anti-war struggles, and so on. It should not be surprising, then, that the advances of globalization since the 1980s have given rise to anti-globalization movements around the world. The recent international movements to oppose current economic, social, and political transformations are not against globalization itself. What these groups oppose is the capitalist model for global development, a model that benefits the major transnational corporations at the expense of local communities and people's democratic rights and freedoms.

This anti-corporate social movement has brought together many individuals and groups, including activists organizing around issues as varied as peace, the environment, poverty, racial discrimination, genetically modified foods, and workers' rights. Linked to these anti-corporate groups are those working on issues concerning climate change and environmental degradation that exist locally, across Canada, and around the world. Increasing numbers realize that our constant-growth economy will have to change drastically if we are to save the planet. While their general goals may be similar, however, their tactics for change are varied. This movement is much more complex than Marx and Engels imagined, although at the core it does question the very basis of capitalist economies.

In recent years there has been expanded global organizing for change. In opposition to the World Economic Forum—a meeting of the global corporate elite that gathers annually in Davos, Switzerland—the World Social Forum was created and met a number of times in Puerto Alegre, Brazil. In 2007, over 75,000 participants gathered in Nairobi for the seventh World Social Forum under the banner "People's Struggles, People's Alternatives." Later that same year, the first Social Forum was held in the United States, with over 10,000 participants, most of them poor or working class (Rebick 2007). In other parts of the world—particularly in South America—governments have recently been elected that oppose the neoliberal agenda and corporate dominance within their countries.

Marx and Engels understood more than a century ago that working people would be drawn together in an increasingly globalized capitalist system. This, of course, was the core contradiction of capitalism: the privatization of ownership in tension with the socialization of production. But change would not happen unless the "small fish" got together to oppose their condition. Thus Marx and Engels ended their *Communist Manifesto* with the rallying cry, "Workers of All Countries Unite!" It is worth noting that, until recently, this was extremely difficult, given the enormous power of both the transnationals and the various governments around the world. However, new computer technologies—which allow people to communicate easily and inexpensively—have increased the ability of groups around the world to coordinate their actions on a broad scale. Indeed, the Internet itself has increasingly become a means of publicly promoting alternative viewpoints and promoting social change.

Think About It

How are protest movements generally portrayed in the mass media? Do such portrayals make you want to be a participant in future protests?

One of the interesting aspects of these new movements is that they are not simply opposed to various negative aspects of capitalism; they are beginning to draw a blueprint of what a future society not dominated by the interests of global corporations would look like. Another interesting feature of the new social movements is the coming together of old and new types of activists. Labour unions—the organized sector of the working class—continue to be at the heart of most such movements because of their centrality to the productive process. However, a wide spectrum of new groups has become involved in opposition to corporate globalization as well. Despite somewhat differing agendas and different strategies, there is a commonality of goals. Most groups are fighting for an advance of democratic rights along one or more of the following lines: subsistence rights, economic rights, environmental rights, social rights, cultural rights, and human rights. Within these demands is the call for a fundamental redistribution of wealth and power (Barlow and Clarke 2001, 207).

Conclusion

People in general, and Canadians in particular, are not especially prone to rebelliousness; given alternatives, most of us will accept the social order and our place in it. Moreover, many of you reading this book may feel that you simply want to graduate, get a good job, buy a house or car, and live the good life promised in the ads; changing the world may be the last thing on your mind. However, we have now reached a point where the need for dramatic social change is no longer a debatable question. If our planet is to survive, we must come up with creative and immediate solutions to major economic, social, and political problems.

As noted in this chapter, we are reaching the limits of capitalist growth. The two central issues that now face humankind, climate change and global militarization, are both being fuelled by the greed of transnational corporations and their government supporters. The issue of whether humans can continue in the destructive manner of the last two centuries is literally one of life or death.

It is easy to feel powerless in the face of the growing concentration of global capital, and at the moment there can be no question that the power of capital remains ascendant. However, history has shown that even the most powerful can be defeated by determined and persistent opposition. All the territorial empires of the last few hundred years—regardless of their military might—such as the Austro-Hungarian empire, the Ottoman empire, and the colonial empires of Europe, have declined or disappeared entirely. These empires have declined primarily because of political and civil resistance from within, rather than via defeats on the battlefield. Indeed, the nature of the technology of modern warfare makes it increasingly necessary to seek non-military solutions to global crises. With regard to opposition to capitalism itself, there has certainly been some very successful opposition to corporate rule around the world, although such opposition up to this point has been erratic and mostly localized. As this book has demonstrated, it is distal relations of power that are both hardest to understand and most difficult to oppose.

The problem, of course, is that most of us

> The apparent power of governments and corporations is in fact fragile; it rests on the obedience of the citizenry, and when that obedience is withdrawn, extraordinary change can take place.
> —Howard Zinn, U.S. historian

> If you want to know who is going to change this country, look in the mirror.
> —Maude Barlow, National Chairperson, Council of Canadians

do not want to be—or are unable to be—activists. Most people around the world spend their days caught up in the problems of their lives in the proximal realm—working, spending time with family and friends, getting their basic daily needs met, and so on. It is therefore unreasonable to expect a majority of people in any country to be swept into a struggle for social change until conditions of their lives have eroded to the point where they cannot continue as they are. One thing Marx and Engels could not have predicted is the rapid destruction of our physical environment. Unfortunately, current scientific evidence seems to indicate that—with regard to climate change—if we wait until our lives are negatively affected to the point where we are prepared to struggle for change, it may be too late.

We are living in a time of great cynicism and despair. Many of us feel that the world is changing rapidly, but that such changes are beyond our understanding and out of our control. Although some young people are front and centre in the struggle for change, many more continue to be quite detached from both the new social movements and mainstream social institutions. This detachment, of course, is exactly what the ruling class prefers, as it ensures the maintenance of relationships of power and inequality. Nonetheless, this book has shown that there is every reason to be optimistic rather than pessimistic about the future. Humans are social animals; as history has confirmed again and again, people—organized and united—can determine the future course of their lives.

Key Points

1. There has always been a tension in sociology between those theorists who focus on simply describing society and those who feel the social world needs to be changed.

2. These two approaches to the social world are reflected in the political sphere. Generally speaking, the politics of the Right is the politics of order, while the politics of the Left is the politics of change.

3. While the real material conditions of capitalism set the stage for social transformation, the future will depend on how human beings act on and change such conditions.

4. Changes that occur within a given socioeconomic formation are referred to as reforms, while a revolution is a radical transformation of the social order in which there is a basic alteration of the relationship between social classes. There is a dialectical relationship between reform and revolution.

5. The view that reforms alone will eventually eliminate the problems of working people in capitalism is referred to as reformism. Social democracy is reformism in the political sphere.

6. Around the world, there is growing instability and an escalation of the inner contradictions of capitalist systems.

7. Many analysts feel that the perpetual growth required by capitalist economies has reached its limits and may be one of the major problems of the twenty-first century.

8. For Canadians, a key issue that will face us in this century is whether we will survive as a nation.

9. The nature of both the owning class and the working class in capitalist societies has changed dramatically over the past century.

10. Many individuals get involved in the struggle for change outside the formal institutions of the state in civil society groups and social movements.

11. In times of social instability, many of the middle strata may shift to the political right, rather than the left. They are often drawn to the ideology known as populism. The underclass may also be drawn into right-wing social movements.

12. Since 1999, there has been the expansion of a broad and diverse anti-corporatist social movement, dedicated to the belief that "a better world is possible."

Further Reading

Ashford, Mary-Wynne, with Guy Dauncey. 2006. *Enough Blood Shed: Solutions to Violence, Terror and War.* Gabriola Island, BC: New Society Publishers.
Part One of this book argues that a world without violence and war is possible. Part Two offers concrete solutions for individuals, organizations, and governments.

Berman, Morris. 2006. *Dark Ages America: The Final Phase of Empire.* New York: W.W. Norton.
A thorough examination of the "decline and fall" of the U.S. empire, linking large-scale processes to the deteriorating everyday lives of its citizens.

Cullis-Suzuki, Severn, et al., eds. 2007. *Notes from Canada's Young Activists: A Generation Stands Up for Change.* Vancouver: Greystone.
Twenty-five young activists explain how they were inspired to become active in an attempt to make the world a better place.

Dobson, Charles. 2003. *The Troublemaker's Teaparty: A Manual for Effective Citizen Action.* Gabriola Island, BC: New Society Publishers.
A "how-to" book for those who want to help change the world.

Foster, John Bellamy. 2002. *Ecology Against Capitalism.* New York: Monthly Review Press.
Foster argues that Marxism—properly understood—provides the best framework for understanding current ecological issues.

Lebowitz, Michael A. 2006. *Build It Now: Socialism for the Twenty-First Century.* New York: Monthly Review Press.
In this short optimistic work, the author tries to lay out what socialism in this century might look like, and uses Venezuela as a case study for social change.

McNally, David. 2002. *Another World Is Possible: Globalization and Anti-Capitalism.* Winnipeg: Arbeiter Ring.
This clearly written book offers both a critique of globalizing capitalism and a set of proposals for change.

Finding Useful Resources on the Web

The rapid expansion of the Internet and the World Wide Web has meant that we have easy access to more information than ever before. However, many of us are simply overwhelmed by the amount of material now available and have trouble identifying legitimate sites. Below are some interesting sources that can be found on the Web. Many of these sites have extensive links to other interesting sites. Of course, the Web is constantly changing, so it is possible that some of the sites listed below may no longer exist, and it is certain that there will be new sites not listed here.

For statistics on and analysis of various aspects of Canadian society, go to:
Caledon Institute of Social Policy: http://www.caledoninst.org/
Canadian Centre for Policy Alternatives: http://www.policyalternatives.ca/
Canadian Council on Social Development: http://www.ccsd.ca/home.htm
Canadian Research Institute for the Advancement of Women: http://www.
    criaw-icref.ca/
Centre for Social Justice: http://www.socialjustice.org/
Growing Gap: http://www.growinggap.ca./
National Council of Welfare: http://www.ncwcnbes.net/en/home.html/
Parkland Institute (re Alberta): http://www.ualberta.ca/%7Eparkland/
Statistics Canada: www.statcan.ca/

For statistics and analysis of international issues, go to:
International Forum on Globalization: http://www.ifg.org/index.htm
New Internationalist: http://www.newint.org/
Organization for Economic Co-operation and Development (OECD): http://
    www.oecd.org
United Nations: http://www.un.org/english/

For a library of resources connected to Marxism, go to:
The Marxists Internet: http://www.marxists.org/

For an alternative to free-market economics in Canada, go to:
The Progressive Economics Forum: http://www.progressive-economics.ca/

For a guide to sociological resources on the Web, go to:
http://www.socioweb.com/~markbl/socioweb/

For websites that offer alternative news and analyses, go to:
Alternet: http://www.alternet.org/
Briarpatch: http://www.briarpatchmagazine.com/
Canadian Dimension http://www.canadiandimension.com/issues/v41n4/
CommonDreams: http://www.commondreams.org
CounterPunch: http://www.counterpunch.org/
Fairness and Accuracy in Reporting: http://www.fair.org/index.php
Monthly Review: http://www.monthlyreview.org/
New Left Review: http://www.newleftreview.org/
Our Times, Canada's Independent Labour Magazine: http://www.ourtimes.ca/
Rabble.ca: http://www.rabble.ca
Straight Goods: http://www.straightgoods.ca/
The Tyee: http://thetyee.ca/
This Magazine: http://thismagazine.ca/
Znet/Z Magazine: http://www.zcommunications.org/

For sites that offer a critical analysis of corporate capitalism, go to:
Corporate Watch: http://www.corpwatch.org/
Corporate Welfare (U.S.): http://www.progress.org/banneker/cw.html
The Corporation: www.thecorporation.com
Critical look at Wal-Mart: http://thewritingonthewal.net/
Multinational Monitor: http://multinationalmonitor.org/
Sweatshop Watch: http://www.sweatshopwatch.org/

For some sites connected to social action and social change, go to:
Amnesty International: http://www.amnesty.ca/
Canadian Civil Liberties Association: http://www.ccla.org/
Canadian Federation of Students: http://www.cfs-fcee.ca/
Climate Change Action Network: http://www.climateactionnetwork.ca/e/
Coalition to Oppose the Arms Trade: http://coat.ncf.ca/
Code Blue for Child Care: http://www.buildchildcare.ca/
Council of Canadians: http://www.canadians.org/
David Suzuki Foundation (re environment): http://www.davidsuzuki.org/
Democracy Watch: http://www.dwatch.ca/
Egale Canada: http://www.egale.ca/
Friends of Canadian Broadcasting: http://www.friends.ca/
Friends of Medicare: http://www.friendsofmedicare.ab.ca/
Greenpeace Canada: http://www.greenpeace.org/canada/en/
Homeless Nation (a website created by and for homeless Canadians): http://
    homelessnation.org/?lang=en
National Anti-Poverty Organization: http://english.napo-onap.ca/
Polaris Institute: http://www.polarisinstitute.org/
Science for Peace: http://scienceforpeace.sa.utoronto.ca/
Stop Racial Profiling: http://www.stopracialprofiling.ca/
Women's International League for Peace and Freedom: http://www.wilpf.org/
Worldwatch Institute: http://www.worldwatch.org/

Glossary

Numbers in parentheses refer to the chapter(s) containing the main discussion of the term.

Absolute poverty
A way of measuring poverty, in which only those who are not getting their most basic daily needs met—that is, those who are not able to acquire a minimum of nutrition, basic shelter, and adequate clothing—are defined as poor. (10)

Alienation
In Marxist terminology, the separation of workers from their labour, and all that this entails. In capitalist societies, workers lose control over the workplace, the product, and the surplus value that they produce. In non-Marxist terminology, the term is used to describe more general feelings of powerlessness, meaninglessness, or isolation. (6)

Anarchy of production
In Marxist terminology, an inevitable consequence of capitalist production, with each individual productive unit making production decisions on the basis of maximizing profit. For this reason, production cannot be planned, which leads inevitably to the crisis of overproduction. (5)

Anti-Semitism
Hostility directed toward those of Jewish origin. (11)

Assimilationism
A theory proposing that particular racial or ethnic groups will cease to be disadvantaged once they integrate into the dominant group. (11)

Biological determinism
Any theoretical explanation of human behaviour that focuses on the biological or genetic basis for that behaviour. (1, 2)

Bipedalism
The ability to stand upright on two feet. (2)

Bourgeoisie
The class in capitalist society that owns and controls the means of production and hires workers to produce the surplus value that is converted into profits. This class is also referred to as the owning class, the ruling class, or capitalists. (4)

Capital
Money invested with the purpose of increasing its value. (4)

Capitalism
An economic system in which all production is subordinated to the imperatives of the market, i.e., accumulation, labour productivity, competition, and profit maximization. (4)

Change theories
Theories that critique the current dis-

tribution of power and focus on how societies change. They are generally linked to a Marxist analysis. (1)

Class
See Social class. (3)

Class conflict
Conflict that occurs as a result of the direct opposition of the interests of the owning and producing classes. (3)

Class consciousness
A person's understanding of her or his place in the class structure and of shared interests with others in the same class. (5)

Commodity
Any object that is exchanged in the marketplace. (4)

Commons
Areas of a society that have traditionally been considered out of bounds for private ownership or trade because they have been accepted as collective property, existing for everyone to share. (9)

Concentration and centralization of capital
An inevitable process in capitalism, it is the coming together of small aggregates of capital to form huge enterprises located in a few centres around the globe. (4)

Convergence
The merging of the technology and content of the telecommunications, computer, entertainment, publishing, and broadcasting industries, among others. (7)

Credentialism
The use of paper credentials as a means of limiting access to certain job categories, even if the credentials are of questionable utility in actual job performance. (7)

Crisis of overproduction
In Marxist terminology, an inevitable consequence of the anarchy of production in all capitalist societies. As individual productive units compete in the marketplace in an attempt to maximize profits, there will ultimately be overproduction of goods. Capital tries to solve this problem in a variety of ways, but the crisis keeps recurring. (5)

Culture
The complete way of life shared by a people, including both the material and non-material elements. (3)

Deep integration
The harmonization of policies and regulations between Canada, the United States, and Mexico in the interest of the corporate sectors of these countries. (9)

Dialectics
A philosophical approach to the world that emphasizes the constancy of change and the interrelationship of elements. A concept first developed in ancient Greece, it was advanced as a tool for modern social analysis by Karl Marx and Friedrich Engels. (1)

Discrimination
The denial of equal treatment or opportunities to individuals on the basis of their membership in a particular social group. (11)

Distal relations of power
Relations of power that exist in society as a whole rather than within personal social relationships. This is a term used to describe the power wielded by governments or corporations that affect both individuals or groups. The opposite of *proximal relations of power*. (1)

Division of labour
The assigning of tasks to particular individuals or groups of people. All

societies have minimally had a division of labour by sex and by age. (2)

Ethnic chauvinism
Hostility directed toward people on the basis of their membership in a particular ethnic group. (11)

Ethnicity
A collectivity of people with shared cultural traits, including language, religion, or ancestry. (11)

Ethnocentrism
The tendency of people to see the world in terms of their own culture, and to evaluate their group or culture favourably in relation to others. (3)

Eugenics
First developed by Francis Galton, a theory and later a social movement that believed in the improvement of the human species through selective mating. Eugenics theories were used to sterilize thousands of individuals considered "feebleminded" and became the basis for the mass exterminations undertaken by the Nazi regime. (2)

Exogamy
Rules or social preference for marriage outside the immediate group.(2)

Fascism
Capitalism in its most repressive, undemocratic, and militaristic form, with a police state to control populations while corporations increasingly control the economy. As an ideology, fascism emphasizes a strong leader and a strong state, while opposing egalitarianism, democracy, pacifism, or collectivism. (8)

Feminism
A term that broadly describes the belief in the social, political, and economic equality of the sexes, as well as the various social movements organ-

ized around this belief. (12)

Feudalism
A socioeconomic formation that grew out of the ruins of the old slave societies in the Middle Ages, which centred on duties and obligations between individuals. The major classes were the appropriating class, the aristocracy, and the producing class of peasants, or serfs. (4)

Fordism
A term used to describe that period of capitalist development marked by intensive production, maximum use of machinery, and minute divisions of labour. Such developments were combined with higher wages that would allow workers to buy the mass-produced goods created through these new production techniques. (6)

Free enterprise
An economic system in which no single buyer or seller can affect the price of a commodity by withdrawing purchasing power or a product. (4)

Functionalism
Also referred to as structural functionalism. A sociological framework that sees society as similar to an organism, with a number of interrelated and necessary elements. Each element, or structure, is seen as having an equally important function for the maintenance of a particular society. (1)

Gemeinschaft
A term created by Ferdinand Tönnies to describe traditional societies, where social relationships were based on personal bonds of family or friendship that were held together by shared moral values usually tied to religion. The opposite of *gesellschaft*. (6)

Gender division of labour
Assigning different tasks in a society to

men and women. (2)

Gesellschaft
A term created by Ferdinand Tönnies to describe large urban societies where social bonds were eroded by the complex division of labour, individualism and competitiveness. The opposite of gemeinschaft. (6)

Heterosexism
The ideology that heterosexual sex within a state-sanctioned marriage—primarily for the purpose of reproduction—is normal, while all other forms of sexual behaviour are deviant. (12)

Ideological hegemony
The control of the ruling class over a society's belief system. The term, developed by Antonio Gramsci, has embedded in it the notion that the dominant class maintains its power through a combination of coercion and persuasion. (7)

Ideology
A body of assumptions, ideas, and values that coalesces into a coherent world view. In Marxist terminology, ideologies are connected to specific social classes and their particular class interests. (7)

Imperialism
The global stage of capitalism in which large monopolies come to control the economy, and capital—rather than commodities—becomes the primary export. (4)

Incest taboo
A societal rule that forbids sexual relations between those defined as kin, or family. (2)

Income
The economic gain derived from wages, salaries, or various forms of government assistance. (10)

Instinct
An inborn complex pattern of behaviour that must exist in every member of a species and, because it is embedded in the genetic code, cannot be overcome by force of will. (2)

Institutional racism
Racism that is embedded within a society's various social institutions, such as the education system, the judiciary, and the mass media. (11)

Islamophobia
The fear of or prejudiced viewpoint toward Islam, Muslims, and matters pertaining to them. (11)

Keynesianism
An approach to capitalism that advocates increased levels of state intervention and regulation of the economy. Named after economist John Maynard Keynes, it was adapted by many capitalist countries after World War II to help maintain economic and social stability. (8)

Labour power
The sum total of all a worker's physical and mental capacities that go into a particular work task. In capitalist societies it is a commodity that is purchased by the employer because workers add value to the business. (4)

Labour union
A group of workers who join together to bargain with an employer or group of employers with regard to wages, benefits, and working conditions. (5)

Laissez-faire capitalism
An early stage of capitalism, when free enterprise still dominated, there were many small or medium-sized productive units, and there was only moderate state intervention to control the worst excesses of capital. (4)

Liberalism
The dominant ideology of capitalism, it emphasizes individual freedom, equality, and choice, all perceived within the framework of a capitalist market economy. (7)

Lumpenproletariat
In Marxist terminology, the underclass within capitalist societies, made up of those marginal to production, such as the long-term unemployed, who historically have been used by the bourgeoisie against the organized working class (as strikebreakers, for example). (5)

Macrosociology
The branch of sociology that primarily examines societies as a whole, with analysis focusing on large-scale and long-term social processes. (1)

Market
People offering goods and services for sale to others in a more or less systematic and organized way. The concept of the market embodies not simply a physical place but rather a set of social relationships organized around the buying and selling of objects. (4)

Means of production
The various items that humans use in order to produce what they need. These include tools, natural resources, the land on which production occurs, and the buildings (if any) where production takes place. (3)

Mechanical solidarity
A term developed by Émile Durkheim to describe a society with a minimal *division of labour* and people united by shared values and common social bonds. The opposite of *organic solidarity*. (6)

Meritocracy
A society where advancement is based on individual ability or achievement. (10)

Microsociology
The branch of sociology that examines primarily individual and small-group behaviour, with analysis focusing on individual perceptions and communications. (1)

Misogyny
The hatred of women. (12)

Mode of production
The economic underpinning of a society, it is composed of the forces of production and the relations of production. (3)

Monopolization
An economic situation where there are so few companies in a given industry that free-enterprise competition no longer effectively exists. There is a high degree of monopolization in the current world economy. (4)

Nation
An aggregate of people within a particular territory who share a common history, language, and culture, and who possess—or seek to possess—a politically independent unit. (4)

Neoliberalism
The theoretical underpinning of the modern corporate agenda, it argues for the centrality of the individual, the importance of the marketplace, and a minimal role for government intervention. (9)

Neolithic Revolution
The historical technological transformation beginning about 10,000 years ago that led to the growth of agrarian societies. (3)

Norms
Actions that go against the expected patterns of behaviour. (1)

333

Order theories
Theories that ultimately support the current arrangements of power within a society. (1)

Organic solidarity
A term developed by Émile Durkheim to describe a society with a complex division of labour, with people performing highly specialized tasks, and people united by their interdependence. Such patterns were to be found in industrial societies. The opposite of mechanical solidarity. (6)

Patriarchy
In radical feminist analysis, a social system characterized by male dominance and female subordination, with men in control of the political, economic, and ideological spheres. The term is also used more generally to mean any society where males as a category have social advantages over women (for example, access to better jobs or higher wages). (12)

Petite bourgeoisie
The class that owns some means of production, but not a sufficient amount to survive by ownership alone. This class includes small-business people, farmers, fishers, and self-employed professionals. (4)

Philosophical idealism
An analytic framework that asserts that the mind, idea, or spirit is primary, and the basis for the material world. In the social sciences, idealists begin by looking at the beliefs and values of people; these are seen as central to understanding a society's culture and social organization. (1)

Philosophical materialism
A framework for analysis that asserts that the material world is primary, and that mind or consciousness is a property of matter. In the social sciences, materialists begin by looking at the real material conditions of people; these are seen as central to understanding the belief system and various cultural elements within a given society, as well as a society's form of social organization. (1)

Pluralism
A theoretical position that argues that power in capitalist societies is spread among a wide number of equally influential interest groups and associations, which guarantees that no one group can dominate the others. (8)

Populism
A political orientation that presents itself as a movement of "the little guy," opposing big government and big business. Its ideology is rooted in the petite bourgeoisie. (13)

Post-Fordism
The stage of capitalist development characterized by more flexible forms of work that differ from the rigid Fordist assembly-line model. Post-Fordist production is centred on new information-based technologies. (6)

Power
The ability of an individual or a group to carry out its will even when opposed by others. Power is largely a result of the control one has over the resources of a society, including its "human resources." (1)

Precarious employment
Those forms of work characterized by limited social benefits and statutory entitlements, job insecurity, low wages, and high risks of ill health. (6)

Prejudice
The holding of biased attitudes and beliefs toward individuals on the basis of their membership in particular

social groups. (11)

Progressive taxation

A form of taxation in which citizens are taxed on the basis of their ability to pay. The opposite of *regressive taxation*. (8)

Proletariat

The class in capitalist societies that does not own any means of production. As a result, members of this class must sell their labour power for a wage in order to survive. (4)

Proletarianization

The process in which higher status jobs, such as those of professionals, increasingly take on the characteristics of factory workers. (5)

Proximal relations of power

Relations of power that exist between individuals within social groups—for example, the power a parent has over a child in the family. The opposite of *distal relations of power*. (1)

Public private partnerships (P3s)

A growing part of the neoliberal agenda. Governments do not fully privatize a state-owned sector of the economy. Rather, they have private corporations build needed infrastructure such as roads or hospitals. The corporations usually sign extended contracts to service them after they are built. (9)

Race

A category of people who share common physical traits deemed to be socially significant. Racial categories are most commonly linked to differences in skin colour. (11)

Racialized groups

Groups of people that are singled out for unequal treatment on the basis of real or imagined physical characteristics. (11)

Racism

Hostility directed toward those with real or perceived physiological traits, most centrally skin colour. (11)

Radical feminism

A theory that sees gender inequality as rooted in *patriarchy*, or the power men hold over women in society. (12)

Reformism

The belief that a series of reforms to the current structure can eliminate the major contradictions of capitalism, create societies where social justice reigns, and, in the long run, eventually lead to socialism. (13)

Reforms

Any change to society—whether legal, political, social, or economic—that occurs within a particular socioeconomic formation. There is no change in class relations. (13)

Regressive taxation

A form of taxation in which there is no connection between the amount of wealth or income one has and the tax paid. The opposite of *progressive taxation*. (8)

Relations of production

The type of relations that occur between humans in the process of production and are the result of their relationship (ownership or non-ownership) to the means of production. (3)

Relative poverty

A definition of poverty in which those whose incomes are far less than the average in their locale are deemed to be poor, even if they are above the barest subsistence level. (10)

Reserve army of the unemployed

In Marxist terminology, a group of people who exist in all capitalist societies as a result of the anarchy of production. They move in and out of the labour force as they are required by capital and are frequently unemployed for long periods of time. (6)

Revolution
Any major social transformation. In Marxist terminology, revolutions can be said to have occurred only when there is a transformation of class relations in a society. (13)

Rule of law
A formally determined set of rules or principles that applies, in theory at least, to all within its jurisdiction. (8)

Scientific management
A concept of managerial control of workers that developed in the early twentieth century. The goal was increased worker efficiency in order to maximize worker output and, therefore, profits. (6)

Social capital
The social networks connecting individuals to each other that are based on reciprocity, shared norms, and trust. (6)

Social class
A group of people with a common relation to the means of production. Where private appropriation of surplus occurs, there must always be a minimum of two classes: a superor class that, through ownership or control of the means of production, appropriates the surplus; and a subordinate class that produces the surplus. (3)

Social Darwinism
Any theoretical approach arguing that social inequality is based on biological differences and is simply the working out of the laws of nature. Often this refers specifically to a group of theories justifying social inequality

that came out of the United States in the late nineteenth and early twentieth centuries. (2)

Socialist feminism
A theory that attempts to explain gender inequality by combining insights from both *radical feminism* and Marxism. In this framework, power is linked to both gender and class. (12)

Social mobility
The upward or downward movement of individuals in terms of their class position or their socioeconomic status. (10)

Social wage
The part of surplus value that is used, via transfers to the state, to provide such social necessities as health care, education, unemployment insurance, old age pension, and so on. (9)

Socialization
An ongoing process by which individuals learn a society's cultural components and social expectations. (3)

Society
A group of people within a limited territory who share a common set of behaviours, beliefs, values, material objects (together referred to as culture), and social institutions, all existing together as a coherent system. (1)

Sociocultural system
A term commonly used by anthropologists, it embodies the same meaning as society. (1)

Socioeconomic formation
In Marxist terminology, a society with a specific mode of production. Marxists sometimes refer to the mode of production as a society's base, and the other components—ideological, political, and social—as its superstructure. (3)

Socioeconomic status (SES)

The position one has in society, usually based on some combination of occupation, income, and education. Often used interchangeably—but incorrectly—with social class. (5)

Sociological imagination

The ability to go beyond the personal issues that all humans experience and connect them to broader social structures. Put differently, the sociological imagination is the ability to link distal relations of power to our immediate life situations. (1)

State

An organized political structure that carries out tasks required by more complex societies as their population and geographic size increase, as warfare and trade expand, and as social inequalities become more extreme. The state also acts as a major institution of social control. (8)

Status

A position within the social structure; statuses are usually ranked in relation to each other. Status can also be used to mean honour or prestige. (1, 5)

Status symbols

Those cultural objects, primarily although not totally material, that reflect an individual's socioeconomic status. (10)

Structural adjustment policies

A set of policies implemented by the World Bank and the International Monetary Fund that are linked to the expansion of neoliberalism. Its guiding principles include export-led growth; privatization and trade liberalization; and the efficiency of the free market. (9)

Structural functionalism

See Functionalism. (1)

Surplus value

That which is created by the unpaid labour of workers. In Marxist analysis, the production of surplus value and its appropriation by capitalists is the motive force of the capitalist mode of production. (4)

Symbol

Any object or act that has a socially shared meaning. It is anything that stands for or represents something else. (2)

Systemic racism

See Institutional racism. (11)

Transfer payments

Payments from one level to another level of government. It can also be used to describe payments made from one level of government to a family or an individual. (8)

Transnational corporations (TNCs)

Large capitalist monopolies, national in their capital, but international in the sphere of economic activity due to the export of capital. Such companies generally conduct at least 25 percent of their business outside of their own country. (4)

Wealth

All one's assets—including real estate holdings and money in bank accounts, stocks, bonds, and so on—minus debts. (10)

Welfare state

A form of capitalism in which governments played an increasing role in economic affairs, the public sector and social safety net expanded, and there was general economic prosperity for large numbers of working people. Most developed capitalist economies developed this form following World War II until the 1970s. (4, 8)

References

Abella, Irving, and Harold Troper. 1982. *None Is Too Many: Canada and the Jews of Europe, 1933–1948*. Toronto: Lester and Orpen Dennys.

Adler, Patricia A., Steven J. Kless, and Peter Adler. 1995. "Socialization to Gender Roles: Popularity Among Elementary School Boys and Girls." In E. D.Nelson and B. W. Robinson (eds.), *Gender in the 1990s*. Scarborough, ON: Nelson.

Agrell, Siri. 2007. "The Science of Soul." *Globe and Mail*, May 3: L1.

Alexander, Claire. 1996. *The Art of Being Black: The Creation of Black British Youth Identities*. Oxford, U.K.: Clarendon.

Anderson, Mitchell. 2003. "The Cod's Gone, yet the Deadly Draggers Remain." *Globe and Mail*, 30 April: A17.

Anderssen, Erin. 2007. "Cut Your Spending, Save the World." *Globe and Mail*, April 21. Available at <www.theglobeandmail.com> (accessed 23 April 2007).

Anisef, Paul, and Norman Okihiro. 1982. *Losers and Winners: The Pursuit of Equality and Social Justice in Higher Education*. Toronto: Butterworths.

Armstrong, Pat. 1996. "Feminization of the Labour Force." In Isabella Bakker (ed.), *Rethinking Restructuring: Gender and Change in Canada*. Toronto: University of Toronto Press.

Armstrong, Pat, and Hugh Armstrong. 1990. *Theorizing Women's Work*. Toronto: Garamond.

———. 1994. *The Double Ghetto: Canadian Women and Their Segregated Work*. 3rd ed. Toronto: McClelland and Stewart.

Association of Workers' Compensation Boards of Canada. 2007. *National Work Injury, Disease and Fatality Statistics (2004-2006)*. Mississauga. Available at < http://www.awcbc. org/english/NWISP_Stats.asp> (accessed January 2008).

Azmier, Jason J. 2005. "Gambling in Canada 2005: Statistics and Context." June. Canada West Foundation <www.cwf.ca> (accessed March 28, 2007).

Bagdikian, Ben. 2004. *The New Media Monopoly*. Boston: Beacon.

Baran, Paul A., and Paul M. Sweezy. 1966. *Monopoly Capital: An Essay on the American Economic and Political Order*. New York: Monthly Review Press.

Barber, Bernard. 1957. *Social Stratification: A Comparative Analysis of Structure and Process*. New York: Harcourt, Brace World.

Barlow, Maude. 2000. "The Fight for Liquid Assets." *Globe and Mail*, 16 August: A14.

———. 2007. "INTEGRATE THIS! A Citizen's Guide to Fighting Deep Integration."Available at <http://www.canadians.org/DI/issues/guide/index.html> (accessed 7 July 2007).

Barlow, Maude, and Heather-Jane Robertson. 1994. *Class Warfare: The Assault on Canada's Schools*. Toronto: Key Porter.

Barlow, Maude, and Tony Clarke. 2001. *Global Showdown: How the New Activists Are Fighting*

Global Corporate Rule. Toronto: Stoddart.

Basran, G.S. 1993. "Development and Under-development." In Peter S. Li and B. Singh Bolaria (eds.), *Contemporary Sociology: Critical Perspectives*. Toronto: Copp Clark Pitman.

Berman, Morris. 2006. *Dark Ages America: The Final Phase of Empire*. New York: W.W. Norton.

Black, Errol. 1998. "The 'New' Crisis of Unemployment." In Wayne Antony and Les Samuelson (eds.), *Power and Resistance: Critical Thinking About Canadian Social Issues*, 2nd ed. Halifax, NS: Fernwood, 76–94.

Blau, Peter M., and Otis Dudley Duncan. 1967. *The American Occupational Structure*. New York: Wiley.

Blum, Jeffrey M. 1978. *Pseudoscience and Mental Ability: The Origins and Fallacies of the IQ Controversy*. New York: Monthly Review Press.

Blum, William. 1998. *Killing Hope: U.S. Military and CIA Interventions Since World War II*. Montreal: Black Rose.

———. 2000. *Rogue State: A Guide to the World's Only Superpower*. Monroe, ME: Common Courage.

Bolaria, B. Singh, and Peter S. Li. 1988. *Racial Oppression in Canada*, 2nd ed. Toronto: Garamond.

Bonacich, Edna. 1976. "Advanced Capitalism and Black–White Race Relations in the United States: A Split Labor Market Analysis." *American Sociological Review* 41.

Bowles, Samuel, and Herbert Gintis. 1976. *Schooling in Capitalist America*. New York: Basic Books.

Boyd, Monica, John Goyder, Frank E. Jones, Hugh A. McRoberts, Peter C. Pineo, and John Porter. 1985. *Ascription and Achievement: Studies in Mobility and Status Attainment in Canada*. Ottawa: Carleton University Press.

Brannigan, Augustin. 1984. *Crimes, Courts and Corrections*. Toronto: Holt, Rinehart and Winston.

Brasfield, Charles R. 2001. "Residential School Syndrome." *BC Medical Journal* 43(2) (March). Available at <http://www.bcma.org/public/bc_medical_journal/BCMJ/2001/march_2001/ResidentialSchoolSyndrome.asp> (accessed 31 January 2007).

Brathwaite, Keren S., and Carl E. James, eds. 1996. *Educating African Canadians*. Toronto: Lorimer.

Brent, Paul. 2007. "Say Hello to Big Media." *Marketing Magazine*, Sept. 24. Available at <http://www.marketingmag.ca/magazine/current/media/article.jsp?content=20070924_70241_70241#> (accessed 25 September 2007).

Brown, Lester, and Christopher Flavin. 1999. "It's Getting Late to Switch to a Viable World Economy." *International Herald Tribune*, 19 Jan.

Brownlee, Jamie. 2005. *Ruling Canada: Corporate Cohesion and Democracy*. Halifax: Fernwood.

Burke, Mike, and John Shields. 2002. "The Hour-Glass Workforce: Measuring the Deterioration of Job Quality in Canada." Paper presented at the Annual Meeting of the Society for Socialist Studies, 30 May.

Canadian Association of Food Banks. 2007. "Hunger Count 2006." Available at <http://www.cafb-acba.ca/documents/HUNGERCOUNT_ENGLISH_2006.pdf> (accessed 23 May 2007).

Canadian Council on Social Development. 2003. "Census Shows Polarization of Income in Canada." Available at <http://www.ccsd.ca/pr/2003/censusincome.htm> (accessed 1 June 2003).

Canadian Taxpayers Federation. 2007. "On the Dole: Businesses, Lobbyists and Industry Canada's Subsidy Programs, January 10." Available at <http://www.taxpayer.com/

pdf/2007_corporate_welfare_report.pdf> (accessed 23 March 2007).

Carey, Elaine. 2003. "Gambling a Real Growth Industry." *Toronto Star*, 23 April:A4.

Carroll, William K. 2004. *Corporate Power in a Globalizing World: A Study in Elite Social Organization*. Toronto: Oxford University Press.

———. 2007. "Tracking the Transnational Capitalist Class: The View From on High." Paper presented at Hegemonic Transitions and the State, Simon Fraser University, February.

CAUT. 2002. "Release Communiqué: Tuition Fee Hikes Deplorable." Available at <http://www.caut.ca/english/publications/news_releases/20020821TuitionFee.asp> (accessed 20 July 2003).

Cavanagh, John, Jerry Mander, et al. 2002. *Alternatives to Economic Globalization: A Better World Is Possible. A Report of the International Forum on Globalization*. San Francisco, CA: Berrett-Koehler.

Cereseto, Shirley. 1982. "Socialism, Capitalism, and Inequality." *Insurgent Sociologist* 11 (Spring).

Chase, Allan. 1977. *The Legacy of Malthus: The Social Costs of the New Scientific Racism*. New York: Alfred A. Knopf.

Cheng, Maisy, Maria Yau, and Suzanne Ziegler. 1993. *Every Secondary Student Survey*. Parts 1, 2, and 3. Toronto: Research Services, Toronto Board of Education.

Chernomas, Robert. 1999. "Improved Social Conditions the Best Cure for Most Diseases." *CCPA Monitor* 5 (June).

Church, Elizabeth. 2007. "Tax credits provide little help to low-income students, study finds." *Globe and Mail*, May 29: A7.

Clark, Terry N., and Seymour M. Lipset. 1991. "Are Social Classes Dying?" *International Sociology* 6.

Clement, Wallace. 1975. *The Canadian Corporate Elite: Economic Power in Canada*. Toronto: McClelland and Stewart.

———. 1983. *Class, Power, and Property: Essays on Canadian Society*. Toronto: Methuen.

Clement, Wallace, and John Myles. 1994. *Relations of Ruling: Class and Gender in Postindustrial Societies*. Montreal: McGill-Queen's University Press.

Coleman, Marion Tolbert. 1991. "The Division of Household Labor: Suggestions for Future Empirical Consideration and Theoretical Development." In Rae Lesser Blumberg (ed.), *Gender, Family and Economy*. Newbury Park, CA: Sage Publications.

Cohen, Lizabeth. 2003. *A Consumers' Republic: The Politics of Mass Consumption in Postwar America*. New York: Vintage.

Collins, Randall. 1994. *Four Sociological Traditions*. New York: Oxford University Press.

Connell, R.W. 1989. "Cool Guys, Sots and Wimps: The Interplay of Masculinity and Education." *Oxford Review of Education* 15, 3.

———. 1995. *Masculinities*. Berkeley, CA: University of California Press.

Contenta, Sandro. 2007. "'Aye, Spy' to Street Cameras." *Toronto Star*, 5 May. Available at <http://www.thestar.com/article/210720> (accessed 6 May 2007).

Conway, John. 1997. *The Canadian Family in Crisis*. 3rd ed. Toronto: Lorimer.

Corak, Miles, and Andrew Heisz. 1996. *The Intergenerational Income Mobility of Canadian Men*. Analytical Studies Branch no. 89. Ottawa: Statistics Canada.

Cortese, Anthony. 1999. *Provocateur: Images of Women and Minorities in Advertising*. Latham, MD: Rowman & Littlefield.

Cox, Oliver C. 1970. *Caste, Class, and Race*. 1942. Reprint, New York: Monthly Review Press.

Cribb, Robert. 2006. "What Right Does the Public Have to Know?" *Globe and Mail*, 23 September: A11.

Curry-Stevens, Anne. 2001. *When Markets Fail People: Exploring the Widening Gap Between Rich and Poor in Canada*. Toronto: CSJ Foundation for Research and Education.

Curtis, Bruce, D. W. Livingstone, and Harry Smaller. 1992. *Stacking the Deck: The Streaming of Working-Class Kids in Ontario Schools*. Toronto: Our Schools/Our Selves Educational Foundation.

Daniels, Ronald J., Patrick Macklem, and Kent Roach. 2001. *The Security of Freedom: Essays on Canada's Anti-Terrorism Bill*. Toronto: University of Toronto.

David, Deborah, and Robert Brannon, eds. 1976. *The Forty-Nine Percent Majority: Readings on the Male Role*. Reading, MA: Addison-Wesley.

Davis, Kingsley, and Wilber E. Moore. 1945. "Some Principles of Stratification." *American Sociological Review* 10.

de Botton, Alain. 2004. *Status Anxiety*. London: Viking.

de Wolff, Alice. 2000. *Breaking the Myth of Flexible Work: Contingent Work in Toronto*. Toronto: The Contingent Workers Project.

Diamond, Jared. 1999. *Guns, Germs and Steel: The Fates of Human Societies*. New York: W. W. Norton.

———. [1992] 2006. *The Third Chimpanzee: The Evolution and Future of the Human Animal*. New York: Harper Perennial

Dicker, John. 2005. *The United States of Wal-Mart*. London: Penguin Books.

Dobbin, Murray. 1998. *Charter Schools: Charting the Course to Social Division*. Ottawa: Canadian Centre for Policy Alternatives.

———. 2007. "The Plan to Disappear Canada." June 8. TheTyee.ca. Available at <http://thetyee.ca/Views/2007/06/08/DeepIntegrate/> (accessed 7 July 2007).

Domhoff, G. William. 1983. *Who Rules America Now? A View for the '80s*. Englewood Cliffs, NJ: Prentice Hall.

Durkheim, Émile. [1897] 1951. *Suicide*. New York: Free Press.

———. 1933. *The Division of Labor in Society*. New York: Free Press.

Economic Council of Canada. 1969. *Sixth Annual Review*. Ottawa: Minister of Supply and Services.

Ehrenberg, Margaret. 2001. "The Role of Women in Human Evolution." In Caroline Brettell and Carolyn Sargent (eds.), *Gender in Cross-Cultural Perspective*. NJ: Prentice Hall.

Engels, Friedrich. [1884] 1972. *The Origin of the Family, Private Property, and the State*. Eleanor Burke Leacock, ed. New York: International Publishers.

Epps, Ken. 2002. "Canadian Military Exports 2000." *Ploughshares Monitor* (Spring). Available at <http://www.ploughshares.ca/CONTENT/MONITOR/monm02.g.html> (accessed 2 June 2003).

Erman, Boyd. 2007. "Merger Mania Forecast to Continue in 2007." *Globe and Mail*, 25 Feb. Available at <http://www.theglobeandmail.com/servlet/story/RTGAM.20070223.wmergers0223/BNStory/Business/home> (accessed 10 March 2007).

Ferrie, J. E., M. J. Shipley, M. G. Stansfeld, and G. D. Smith. 1995. "Health Effects of Anticipation of Job Change and Non-employment: Longitudinal Data from the Whitehall II Study." *British Medical Journal* 311.

fifth estate. "The Denial Machine." Broadcast 15 November 2006. Available at <http://www.cbc.ca/fifth/denialmachine/> (accessed 25 September 2007).

Finkel, Alvin, Margaret Conrad, with Veronica Strong-Boag. 1993. *History of the Canadian Peoples: 1867 to the Present*. Toronto: Copp Clark Pitman.

Finn, Ed. 1983. "Labour Reporting in Canada." *The Facts*. Ottawa: Canadian Union of Public Employees, June.

Firestone, Shulamith. 1972. *The Dialectic of Sex*. Frogmore, U.K.: Paladin.

Fleming, James. 1991. *Circles of Power: The Most Influential People in Canada*. Toronto: Doubleday.

Forcese, Dennis. 1986. *The Canadian Class Structure*. 3rd ed. Toronto: McGraw-Hill Ryerson.

Francis, Diane. 1986. *Controlling Interest: Who Owns Canada?* Toronto: Macmillan.

Frenette, Marc. 2007. *Why Are Youth from Lower-income Families Less Likely to Attend University? Evidence from Academic Abilities, Parental Influences, and Financial Constraints*, February. Statistics Canada Analytical Studies Branch Research Paper Series, 11F0019MIE – No. 295. Available at <www.statcan.ca>.

Frideres, James S. 1988. "Institutional Structures and Economic Deprivation: Native People in Canada." In B. Singh Bolaria and Peter S. Li (eds.), *Racial Oppression in Canada*, 2nd ed. Toronto: Garamond.

Friesen, Joe. 2006. "Where Clothes Don't Always Make the Man." *Globe and Mail*, 27 July:A3.

Friscolanti, Michael. 2003. "A Toxic Electronic Wasteland." *The National Post*, 7 October.

Fudge, Judy. 2005. "Beyond Vulnerable Workers: Towards a New Standard Employment Relationship." *Canadian Labour and Employment Law Journal* 12(2).

Fudge, Judy, and Eric Tucker. 2001. *Labour before the Law: The Regulation of Workers' Collective Action in Canada, 1900–1948*. Don Mills, ON: Oxford University Press.

Galabuzi, Grace-Edward. 2006. *Canada's Economic Apartheid: The Social Exclusion of Racialized Groups in the New Century*. Toronto: Canadian Scholars' Press.

Gaskell, Jane. 1993. "Gender Equity in the Curriculum." In James Curtis, Edward Grabb, and Neil Guppy (eds.), *Social Inequality in Canada: Patterns, Problems, Policies*, 2nd ed. Scarborough, ON: Prentice Hall.

George, Susan. 1989. *A Fate Worse Than Debt*. Harmondsworth: Penguin.

Glasbeek, Harry J. 1993. "Commercial Morality through Capitalist Law: Limited Possibilities." *La Revue Juridique* 27, 2-3.

———. 2002. *Wealth by Stealth*. Toronto: Between the Lines.

Goleman, Daniel. 2006. *Social Intelligence: The New Science of Human Relationships*. New York: Random House.

Gordon, David M., Richard Edwards, and Michael Reich. 1982. *Segmented Work, Divided Workers*. Cambridge: Cambridge University Press.

Gosine, Kevin. 2000. "Revisiting the Notion of a 'Recast' Vertical Mosaic in Canada: Does a Post Secondary Education Make a Difference?" *Canadian Ethnic Studies Journal* 32,3 (Fall).

Gould, Stephen Jay. 1977. *Ever Since Darwin*. New York: W.W. Norton.

———. 1981. *The Mismeasure of Man*. New York: W.W. Norton.

———. 1989. *Wonderful Life*. New York: W.W. Norton.

Gray, John. 1993. *Men Are from Mars, Women Are from Venus*. New York: HarperCollins.

Grusky, David B. 1994. "The Contours of Social Stratification." In David B. Grusky (ed.), *Social Stratification: Class, Race, and Gender in Sociological Perspective*. Boulder, CO: Westview.

Guppy, Neil, and A. Bruce Arai. 1993. "Who Benefits from Higher Education? Differences by Sex, Social Class, and Ethnic Background." In James Curtis, Edward Grabb, and Neil Guppy (eds.), *Social Inequality in Canada: Patterns, Problems, Policies*, 2nd ed. Scarborough, ON: Prentice Hall.

Gwyn, Richard. 2007. "The Rich Get Their Own Nationality." *Toronto Star*, 26 June. Available at <http://www.thestar.com/comment/article/229382> (accessed 26 June 2007).

Hall, Emmett, and Lloyd Dennis. 1968. *Living and Learning*. Toronto: Newton Publishing.

Hamilton, Roberta. 1996. *Gendering the Vertical Mosaic: Feminist Perspectives on Canadian Society*.

Toronto: Copp Clark.

Harding, Jim. 2004. *After Iraq: War, Imperialism and Democracy.* Halifax: Fernwood, 2004

Harris, Marvin. 1989. *Cows, Pigs, Wars and Witches.* New York: Random House, 1974. Reprint, New York: Vintage Books.

———. 1991. *Cannibals and Kings.* New York: Random House, 1977. Reprint, New York: Vintage Books.

Harrison, Trevor, Bill Johnston, and Harvey Krahn. 1996. "Special Interests and/or New Right Economics? The Ideological Bases of Reform Party Support in Alberta in the 1993 Federal Election." *Canadian Review of Sociology and Anthropology* 33, 2 (May).

Henry, Frances, and Effie Ginzberg. 1985. *Who Gets the Work?* Toronto: Urban Alliance on Race Relations and the Social Planning Council of Metropolitan Toronto.

Henry, Frances, Carol Tator, Winston Mattis, and Tim Rees. 2000. *The Colour of Democracy.* 2nd ed. Toronto: Harcourt Brace.

Henton, Darcy. 1996. "Faith in Eugenics Ran Deep in Alberta." *Toronto Star*, 11 Feb.: F1.

Herman, Edward, and Noam Chomsky. 1988. *Manufacturing Consent: The Political Economy of the Mass Media.* New York: Pantheon.

Higham, Charles. 1983. *Trading with the Enemy: An Exposé of the Nazi-American Money Plot, 1933–1949.* New York: Dell.

Howe, P. 2002. "Where Have All the Voters Gone?" *Inroads* 12. Available at <http://www.inroadsjournal.ca/pdfs/Inroads_12_howe.pdf> (accessed 11 April 2007).

Hubbard, Ruth, and Elijah Wald. 1993. *Exploding the Gene Myth.* Boston: Beacon Press.

Human Resources Development Canada. 2000. "Work Safely for a Healthy Future." Available at <http://info.load-otea.hrdc-drhc.gc.ca/~oshweb/naoshstats/naoshw2000.pdf> (accessed 30 June 2003).

———. 2003. "National Day of Mourning." Available at <http://info.load-otea.hrdc-drhc.gc.ca/~oshweb/events/mourning.shtml> (accessed 28 May 2003).

———. 2007. "Labour Policy and Workplace Information." Available at <http://www.hrsdc.gc.ca/en/lp/wid/union_membership.shtml> (accessed 10 April 2007).

Hurtig, Mel. 2002. *The Vanishing Country: Is It Too Late to Save Canada?* Toronto: McClelland and Stewart.

Indian and Northern Affairs Canada. 2003. "Some Fast Facts on the Funding of Aboriginal Programs." Available at <http://www.ainc-inac.gc.ca/sft/facbk_e.html> (accessed 13 May 2003).

Innis, Harold Adams. 1964 [1951]. *The Bias of Communication.* Toronto: University of Toronto Press.

Jackson, Andrew, and Grant Schellenberg. 1999. "Unions, Collective Bargaining and Labour Market Outcomes for Canadian Working Women: Past Gains and Future Challenges." In Richard P. Chaykowski and Lisa M. Powell (eds.). *Women and Work.* Montreal and Kingston: McGill–Queen's University Press.

Jacobs, Jane. 2004. *Dark Age Ahead.* Toronto: Random House Canada.

Jaggar, Allison M., and Paula Rothenberg, eds. 1993. *Feminist Frameworks*, 3rd ed. New York: McGraw-Hill.

James, Carl. 1990. *Making It: Black Youth, Racism and Career Aspirations in a Big City.* Oakville, ON: Mosaic Press.

Jamieson, K. 1978. *Indian Women and the Law in Canada: Citizens Minus.* Ottawa: Minister of Supply and Services.

Jin, R. L., C. P. Shah, and T. J. Svoboda. 1995. "The Impact of Unemployment on Health: A Review of the Evidence." *Canadian Medical Association Journal* 153, 5.

Johnson, Leo. 1972. "The Development of Class in Canada in the Twentieth Century." In Gary Teeple (ed.), *Capitalism and the National Question.* Toronto: University of Toronto Press.

Joya, Malalai. 2007. "The US has Returned Fundamentalism to Afghanistan." CommonDreams.org, April 12. Available at <http://www.commondreams.org/archive/2007/04/12/468/> (accessed 11 May 2007).

Kendall, Diana, Jane Lothian Murray, and Rick Linden. 2007. *Sociology for Our Times*. 4th ed. Toronto: Nelson-Thomson.

Kerstetter, Steve. 2003. *Rags and Riches: Wealth Inequality in Canada*. Ottawa: Canadian Centre for Policy Alternatives.

Kimmel, Michael S. 2004. *The Gendered Society*, 2nd ed. New York: Oxford University Press.

Kinsman, Gary. 2001. "Gays and Lesbians: Pushing the Boundaries." In Dan Glenday and Ann Duffy (eds.). *Canadian Society: Meeting the Challenges of the Twenty-First Century*. Don Mills, ON: Oxford University Press.

Kinsman, Gary, Dieter K. Buse, and Mercedes Steedman, eds. 2000. *Whose National Security? Canadian State Surveillance and the Creation of Enemies*. Toronto: Between the Lines.

Klaffke, Pamela. 2003. *Spree: A Cultural History of Shopping*. Vancouver: Arsenal Pulp Press.

Koring, Paul. 2007. "China's Defence Spending Races to Match U.S." *Globe and Mail*, 12 June: A11.

Korten, David C. 1996. *When Corporations Rule the World*. West Hartford, CT: Kumarian Press.

Koskoff, David E. 1981. *The Diamond World*. New York: Harper and Row.

Krahn, Harvey J., Graham S. Lowe, and Karen D. Hughes. 2007. *Work, Industry and Canadian Society*. 5th ed. Toronto: Thomson Nelson.

Kuehn, Larry. 1998. "Schools for Globalized Business: The APEC Agenda for Education." *Our Schools/Our Selves* 9 (Feb.-March).

Laird, Gordon. 2007. *SHELTER—Homelessness in a growth economy: Canada's 21st century paradox*. Calgary: Sheldon Chumir Foundation. Available at <http://www.chumirethicsfoundation.ca/files/pdf/SHELTER.pdf> (accessed 26 June 2007).

Lasch, Christopher. 1991 [1979]. *The Culture of Narcissism*. New York: W. W. Norton.

Lavoie, Francois. 2005. "Canadian Direct Investment in 'Offshore Financial Centres'," Statistics Canada, Catalogue Number 11-621-MIE2005021. Available at <http://www.statcan.ca>.

Lawlor, James M. 1978. *IQ, Heritability and Racism*. New York: International Publishers.

Leacock, Eleanor Burke. 1972. Introduction to *The Origins of the Family, Private Property, and the State*, by Friedrich Engels. New York: International Publishers.

Leakey, Richard E., and Roger Lewin. 1977. *Origins*. London: E.P. Dutton.

Lee, Marc. 2002. "Inequality on the Rise, Both Between and Within Countries." *CCPA Monitor* 9(4) (September).

Lee, Richard. 1978. "Politics, Sexual and Nonsexual, in an Egalitarian Society." *Social Science Information* 17.

Lee, Richard, and Irven DeVore, eds. 1968. *Man the Hunter*. Chicago: Aldine.

Lee, Valerie E., and David T. Burkham. 2002. "Inequality at the Starting Gate: Social Background Differences in Achievement as Children Begin School." Available at <http://www.childcarecanada.org/research/complete/inequality_EPI_US.html> (accessed 14 October 2003).

Lemonick, Michael D., and Andrea Dorfman. 2006. "What Makes Us Different." *Time*, Canadian Ed., October 9.

Lenski, Gerhard E. 1966. *Power and Privilege*. New York: McGraw-Hill.

Lenski, Gerhard E., and Jean Lenski. 1978. *Human Societies: An Introduction to Macrosociology*. 3rd ed. New York: McGraw-Hill.

Lerner, Gerda. 1986. *The Creation of Patriarchy*. New York: Oxford University Press.

————. 1993. *The Creation of Feminist Consciousness: From the Middle Ages to 1870*. New York: Oxford University Press.

Lewis, David. 1972. *Louder Voices: The Corporate Welfare Bums*. Toronto: James Lewis and Samuel.

Lewis, Oscar. 1966. *La Vida: A Puerto Rican Family in the Culture of Poverty*. New York: Random House.

Lewontin, Richard. 2001. *It Ain't Necessarily So: The Dream of the Human Genome and Other Illusions*. New York: New York Review of Books.

Lewontin, R. C., Steven Rose, and Leon J. Kamin. 1984. *Not in Our Genes: Biology, Ideology and Human Nature*. New York: Pantheon.

Li, Chris, Ginette Gervais, and Aurélie Duval. 2006. *The Dynamics of Overqualification: Canada's Underemployed University Graduates*. Statistics Canada, April. Catalogue No. 11-621-MIE — No. 039. Available at <www.statcan.ca>.

Li, Peter, ed. 1990. *Race and Ethnic Relations in Canada*. Toronto: Oxford University Press.

Lichtenstein, Nelson. 2006. *Wal-Mart: The Face of Twenty-First-Century Capitalism*. New York: New Press.

Lima, Paul. 2006. "Are Women Shortchanging Themselves?" *Globe and Mail*, November 10: B7.

Little, Bruce. 2003. "Study Unearths Spending Data." *Globe and Mail*, 21 April: B4.

Livingstone, D.W. 1999. *The Education-Jobs Gap: Underemployment or Economic Democracy*. Toronto: Garamond.

Lorimer, Rowland, and Jean McNulty. 1996. *Mass Communications in Canada*. 3rd ed. Toronto: Oxford University Press.

Lowe, Graham S. 2001. "Quality of Work—Quality of Life," A Keynote Talk: Work/Life Balance and Employee Wellness Strategies Conference (May 14) Available at <http://www.cprn.com/cprn.html> (accessed 17 June 2003).

Luxton, Meg. 1990. "Two Hands for the Clock: Changing Patterns in the Gendered Division of Labour in the Home." In Meg Luxton, Harriet Rosenberg, Sedef Arat-Koc, *Through the Kitchen Window: The Politics of Home and Family*, 2nd ed. Toronto: Garamond.

MacDonald, Kevin, and Ross D. Parke. 1986 "Parental-Child Physical Play: The Effects of Sex and Age of Children and Parents." *Sex Roles* 15.

MacKinnon, Shauna. 2007. *Selling Our Soul for Lower Taxes*. January 4. Canadian Centre for Policy Alternatives–Manitoba. Available at <http://policyalternatives.ca/documents/Manitoba_Pubs/2007/FastFacts_Jan4_07_Selling_our_Soul.pdf> (accessed 29 March 2007).

Martin, M. Kay, and Barbara Voorhies. 1975. *Female of the Species*. Toronto: Methuen.

Marx, Karl, and Friedrich Engels. [1846] 1969. *The German Ideology*. In Karl Marx and Freidrich Engels, Selected Works, Vol 1. Moscow: Progress Publishers.

McBride, Stephen, and John Shields. 1997. *Dismantling a Nation: The Transition to Corporate Rule in Canada*. 2nd ed. Halifax: Fernwood.

McFarland, Janet. 2007. "Breaking the Boardroom Barrier." *Globe and Mail*, 22 May: B1.

McIlroy, Anne. 2007 "Walk Like an Orangutan." *Globe and Mail*, 1 June:A6.

McKenna, Barrie. 2007. "GM Strike a Harbinger of Future U.S. Health Care Battles." *Globe and Mail*, 25 September:B15.

McLaren, Angus. 1990. *Our Own Master Race: Eugenics in Canada, 1885–1945*. Toronto: McClelland and Stewart.

McNally, David. 2002. *A Better World Is Possible: Globalization and Anti-Capitalism*. Winnipeg: Arbeiter Ring.

McNish, Jacquie. 2007. "Deal Makers of 2006." *Globe and Mail*, online, 29 January.

Available at <http://www.theglobeandmail.com/servlet/story/RTGAM.20070128.
wdealsmain29/BNStory/Business/home> (accessed 31 January 2007).

McQuaig, Linda. 1992. *The Quick and the Dead: Brian Mulroney, Big Business, and the Seduction of Canada*. Toronto: Penguin Books.

———. 1999. *The Cult of Impotence*. Toronto: Penguin Books.

Mead, Margaret. [1935] 1963. *Sex and Temperament in Three Primitive Societies*. New York: William Morrow.

Mendelsohn, Matthew. 2003. "Birth of a New Ethnicity." *Globe and Mail*, 9 June:A6.

Mensah, Joseph. 2002. *Black Canadians: History, Experiences, Social Conditions*. Halifax: Fernwood.

Mensh, Elaine, and Harry Mensh. 1991. *The IQ Mythology: Class, Race, Gender, and Inequality*. Carbondale: Southern Illinois University Press.

Menzies, Heather. 2005. *No Time: Stress and the Crisis of Modern Life*. Vancouver: Douglas & McIntyre.

Milan, Anne, and Kelly Tran. 2004. "Blacks in Canada: A Long History." *Canadian Social Trends*, Spring. Statistics Canada Catalogue No. 11-008. Available at <http://www.statcan.ca/english/studies/11-008/feature/11-008-XIE20030046802.pdf> (accessed 26 June 2007).

Miles, Robert. 1989. *Racism*. London: Routledge.

Miliband, Ralph. 1969. *The State in Capitalist Society*. London: Quartet Books.

Mills, C. Wright. 1956. *The Power Elite*. New York: Oxford University Press.

———. 1961. *The Sociological Imagination*. New York: Grove Press, Inc.

Mithen, Steven. 2006. *The Singing Neanderthals: The Origins of Music, Language, Mind and Body*. Cambridge, MA: Harvard University Press.

Montagu, Ashley. 1975. Race and IQ. New York: Oxford University Press.

Mooers, Colin, ed. 2006. *The New Imperialists: Ideologies of Empire*. Oxford: Oneworld Publications.

Morissette, René, and Xuelin Zhang. 2006. "Revisiting Wealth Inequality." Perspectives on Labour and Income 7(12) (December). Available at <http://www.statcan.ca/english/freepub/75-001-XIE/11206/high-1.htm> (accessed 20 May 2007).

Morris, Marika. 2002. "Women and Poverty." Canadian Research Institute for the Advancement of Women. Available at <http://www.criawicref.ca/Poverty_fact_sheet.htm#Whoislikelytobepoor> (accessed 1 June 2003).

Murdock, George. 1937. "Comparative Data on the Division of Labour by Sex." *Social Forces* 15, 4 (May).

Nagler, Mark. 1972. "Minority Values and Economic Achievement: The Case of the North American Indian." In Mark Nagler (ed.), *Perspectives on the North American Indian*. Toronto: McClelland and Stewart.

National Council of Welfare. 1993. "Social Inequality in Health and Mortality." In James Curtis, Edward Grabb, and Neil Guppy (eds.), *Social Inequality in Canada: Patterns, Problems, Policies*. 2nd ed. Scarborough, ON: Prentice Hall.

National Farmers Union. 2005. "The Farm Crisis and Corporate Profits." November 30. Available at <http://www.nfu.ca/new/corporate_profits.pdf> (accessed 5 March 2007).

Nelson, Adie, and Barrie W. Robinson, 2002. *Gender in Canada*. 2nd ed. Toronto: Pearson Education Canada

Newman, Peter C. 1975. *The Canadian Establishment*. Toronto: McClelland and Stewart.

———. 1998. *Titans: How the New Canadian Establishment Seized Power*. Toronto: Viking.

Niosi, Jorge. 1981. *Canadian Capitalism: A Study of Power in the Canadian Business Establishment*. Toronto: Lorimer.

Nisbet, Robert A. 1959. "The Decline and Fall of Social Class." *Pacific Sociological Review* 2.

O'Connor, James. 1973. *The Fiscal Crisis of the State*. New York: St. Martin's Press.

O'Connor, Pauline. 1997. *Mapping Social Cohesion: CPRN Discussion Paper, Social Research Series*. Paper no. 2. Ottawa: Centre for International Statistics at the Canadian Council of Social Development, March.

Ogilvie, Megan. 2007. "Trying to Lose Pounds, Some Lose a Lot More." *Toronto Star*, 19 May. Available at <http://www.thestar.com/Life/article/215721> (accessed 19 May 2007).

O'Harrow, Jr., Robert. 2005. *No Place to Hide*. New York: Free Press.

OECD. 2006. *Society at a Glance: OECD Social Indicators 2006 Edition*. Available at <http://www.oecd.org/els/social/indicators/SAG> (accessed 1 May 2007).

Ornstein, Michael. 1985. "Canadian Capital and the Canadian State: Ideology in an Era of Crisis." In Robert J. Brym (ed.), *The Structure of the Canadian Capitalist Class*. Toronto: Garamond.

Panitch, Leo. 1977. "The Role and Nature of the Canadian State." In Leo Panitch (ed.), *The Canadian State: Political Economy and Political Power*. Toronto: University of Toronto Press.

Paxton, Robert. 2004. *The Anatomy of Facism*. New York: Knopf.

Parenti, Michael. 1993. *Inventing Reality: The Politics of the News Media*. 2nd ed. New York: St. Martin's Press.

———. 1995. *Democracy for the Few*. 6th ed. New York: St. Martin's Press.

Parsons, Talcott. 1955. "The American Family: Its Relations to Personality and to the Social Structure." In Talcott Parsons and Robert F. Bales (eds.), *Family, Socialization and Interaction Process*. Glencoe, IL: Free Press.

———. 1961. "The School as a Social System: Some of Its Functions in American Society." In A. H. Halsey, Jean Floud, and C. Arnold Anderson (eds.), *Education, Economy and Society*. New York: Free Press.

Perlo, Victor. 1976. *The Economics of Racism USA*. New York: International Publishers.

Philp, Margaret. 2003. "New Yardstick Places More People in Poverty." *Globe and Mail* 27 May: A1.

Picard, Andre. 1999. "Balancing Work and Home Tasks Raising Women's Blood Pressure." *Globe and Mail*, 29 March: A6.

Picot, Garnett, and Feng Hou. 2003. *The Rise in Low-Income Rates Among Immigrants in Canada*. Research Paper Series No. 198. Catalogue #11F0019. Ottawa: Statistics Canada.

Polanyi, Karl. 1957 [1944]. *The Great Transformation: The Political and Economic Origins of Our Time*. Boston: Beacon Press.

Pollack, William. 1998. *Real Boys: Rescuing Our Sons from the Myths of Boyhood*. New York: Owl Books.

Porter, John. 1965. *The Vertical Mosaic*. Toronto: University of Toronto Press.

Porter, John, Marion Porter, and Bernard Blishen. 1982. *Stations and Callings: Making It Through the Ontario Schools*. Toronto: Methuen.

Putnam, Robert D. 2000. *Bowling Alone: The Collapse and Revival of American Community*. New York: Simon & Schuster.

Rebick, Judy. 2005. *Ten Thousand Roses: The Making of a Feminist Revolution*. Toronto: Penguin Canada.

———. 2007. "Another U.S. Is Starting to Happen." July 9. rabble.ca. Available at <http://www.rabble.ca/news_full_story.shtml?x=60722> (accessed 15 July 2007).

Reguly, Eric. 2002. "Consumers Beware: Canada Is a Haven for Media Oligopolies." *Globe and Mail*, 28 February.

———. 2006. "Your Tax Dollars at Work." *Report on Business*, April: 19.

Reiman, Jeffery. 2006. *The Rich Get Richer and the Poor Get Prison*. 8th ed. Boston: Allyn & Bacon.

Reynolds, Neil. 2007. "Time to Weed out Agricultural Subsidies." *Globe and Mail*, 13 June: B2.

Rich, Adrienne. 1980. "Compulsory Heterosexuality and Lesbian Existence." *Signs* 5 (Summer).

Richardson, Ken, and David Spears, eds. 1972. *Race and Intelligence: The Fallacies Behind the Race-IQ Controversy*. Baltimore: Penguin Books.

Ridley, Matt. 2003. "What Makes You Who You Are." *Time*, 6 June.

Roberts, Paul Craig. 2006. "Wars, Debt and Outsourcing." *Counter Punch*, April 25. Available at <http://www.counterpunch.org/roberts04252006.html> (accessed 3 May 2006).

Roberts-Fiati, Gloria. 1996. "Effects of Early Marginalization on African Canadian Children." In Keren S. Brathwaite and Carl E. James (eds.), *Educating African Canadians*. Toronto: Lorimer.

Robinson, David. 1999. "Neo-liberalism Cancels Canada's Post-War Social Contract." *CCPA Monitor* 5 (March).

Rodney, Walter. 1972. *How Europe Underdevelops Africa*. London: Bogle-L'Ouverture.

Rosen, B. 1959. "Race, Ethnicity, and the Achievement Syndrome." *American Sociological Review* 24.

Ross, David, Katherine Scott, and Peter Smith. 2000. *The Canadian Fact Book on Poverty*. Ottawa: Canadian Council on Social Development.

Runk, David. 2006. "Ford to Borrow $18B." *Toronto Star* online, 27 November. Available at <http://www.thestar.com/NASApp/cs/ContentServer?pagename=thestar/Layout/Article_Type1&c=Article&cid=1164625145488&call_pageid=968350072197&col=969048863851> (accessed 28 November 2006).

Rushowy, Kristin. 2007. "Canada Is Failing Its Kids, MD Says." *Toronto Star*, 30 April. Available at <http://www.thestar.com/News/article/208734> (accessed 30 April 2007).

Ryan, William. 1971. *Blaming the Victim*. New York: Vintage Books.

Samuelson, Leslie. 1995. "The Canadian Criminal Justice System: Inequalities of Class, Race, and Gender." In B. Singh Bolaria (eds.), *Social Issues and Contradictions in Canadian Society*. 2nd ed. Toronto: Harcourt Brace.

Sanders, Richard. 2004. "Canada and the Big Business of War." *Canadian Dimension*, March/April. Available at <http://canadiandimension.com/articles/2004/03/01/150/> (accessed 1 April 2007).

———. 2007. "Ousting Aristide and Protecting the Illegal Regime." *Press for Conversion* 60, March: 15.

Sanderson, Steven K. 1999. *Macrosociology: An Introduction to Human Societies*. 4th ed. Boston: Allyn and Bacon.

Satzewich, Vic. 1995. "Social Stratification: Class and Racial Inequality." In B. Singh Bolaria (ed.), *Social Issues and Contradictions in Canadian Society*. 2nd ed. Toronto: Harcourt Brace.

———. 1999. "The Political Economy of Race and Ethnicity." In Peter S. Li (ed.), *Race and Ethnic Relations in Canada*. 2nd ed. Toronto: Oxford University Press.

Scarth, Todd. 2005. "The Worst Corporate Miscreant." *CCPA Monitor* 12, 1 May.

Schechter, Danny. 2007. "Manufacturing Indifference: Searching for a New 'Propaganda Model.'" CommonDreams.org. Available at <http://www.commondreams.org/archive/2007/05/19/1317/> (accessed 22 May 2007).

Sears, Alan. 2000. "Education for a Lean World." In Mike Burke, Colin Mooers, and John Shields (eds.), *Restructuring and Resistance: Canadian Public Policy in an Age of Global Capitalism*. Halifax: Fernwood.

———. 2003. *Retooling the Mind Factory: Education in a Lean State*. Aurora, ON:

Garamond.

——. 2005. *A Good Book, in Theory: A Guide to Theoretical Thinking*. Peterborough, ON: Broadview Press.

Seccombe, Wally, and David Livingstone. 1996. "'Down to Earth People': Revising a Materialist Understanding of Group Consciousness." In David Livingstone and J. Marshall Mangan (eds.), *Recast Dreams: Class and Gender Consciousness in Steeltown*. Toronto: Garamond.

Shaker, Erika. 2003. "Private Dollars in Canada's 'Public' Colleges and Universities: Who Really Pays?" *Our Schools/Our Selves* 12(4) (Summer).

Shepard, R. Bruce. 1991. "Plain Racism: The Reaction against Oklahoma Black Immigration to the Canadian Plains." In Ormond McKague (ed.), *Racism in Canada*. Saskatoon: Fifth House.

Shields, John, Susan Silver, and Sue Wilson. 2006. "Assessing Employment Risk: Dimensions in the Measurement of Unemployment, Research Note." *Socialist Studies: The Journal of the Society for Socialist Studies* 2, 2 (Fall).

Shutt, Harry. 1998. *The Trouble with Capitalism: An Enquiry into the Causes of Global Economic Failure*. London: Zed Books.

Sklar, Holly, ed. 1980. *Trilateralism: The Trilateral Commission and Elite Planning for World Management*. Boston: South End Press.

Slater, Philip. 1970. *The Pursuit of Loneliness: American Culture at the Breaking Point*. Boston: Beacon Press.

Smail, David. 1999. *The Origins of Unhappiness: A New Understanding of Personal Distress*. London: Constable.

Smith, Charlie. 2007. "Afghan Dangers Deepen." *Georgia Strait*, 7 April. Available at <http://www.straight.com/article-84662/afghan-dangers-deepen> (accessed 7 May 2007).

Smith, Mark. 2006. "How Do Teens Use the 'Net?" *Technology & Learning* 26, 6 (January).

Sorenson, John. 2003. "I'm Not a Racist, and Nobody I Know Is Either." In Judith Blackwell, Murray Smith, and John Sorenson (eds.), *Culture of Prejudice: Arguments in Critical Social Science*, Peterborough, ON: Broadview Press.

Stanford, Jim. 1999. *Paper Boom*. Toronto: CCPA and Lorimer.

——. 2007. "There's Blood on Factory Floors: Where's Ottawa?" *Globe and Mail*, 22 May: A15.

Staples, Steven. 2006. *Marching Orders: How Canada Abandoned Peacekeeping—and Why the U.N. Needs Us Now More Than Ever*. A report commissioned by the Council of Canadians. Available at <http://www.canadians.org/peace/issues/Marching_Orders/index.html> (accessed 1 April 2007).

Statistics Canada. 2002. *Health Indicators*, No. 2 (October). Available at <http://www.statcan.ca/English/freepub/82-221-XIE/01002/high/region/hdepres.htm> (accessed 9 May 2003).

——. 2003a. *Earnings of Canadians: Making a living in the new economy*. Catalogue No. 96F0030XIE2001013. Available at <http://www12.statcan.ca/ english/census01/Products/Analytic/companion/earn/pdf/96F0030XIE2001013.pdf> (accessed 25 May 2003).

——. 2003b. *Education in Canada, Raising the Standard*. Ottawa: Minister of Industry. Available at <http://www12.statcan.ca/english/census01/Products/Analytic/companion/educ/pdf/96F0030XIE2001012.pdf> (accessed 20 July 2003).

——. 2004a. *The Canadian Labour Market at a Glance 2003*. Cat. No. 71-222-XIE. Available at http://www.statcan.ca>.

——. 2004b. *Class of 2000: Profile of Postsecondary Graduates and Student Debt*. Cat. No.

81-595-MIE2004016. Available at <http://www.statcan.ca>.

———. 2005. "Study: Household spending and debt." *The Daily*, 22 March. Available at <http://www.statcan.ca/Daily/English/050322/d050322c.htm> (accessed 18 May 2007).

———. 2006a. "General Social Survey: Paid and unpaid work." *The Daily*, 19 July. Available at <http://www.statcan.ca/Daily/English/060719/d060719b.htm> (accessed 11 June 2007).

———. 2006b. "Women in Canada." *The Daily*, 7 March. Available at <http://www.statcan.ca/Daily/English/060307/d060307a.htm> (accessed 3 June 2007).

———. 2006c. *Women in Canada: A Gender-based Statistical Report*, 5th ed. No. 89-503-XPE. Ottawa: Ministry of Industry. Available at <http://www.statcan.ca/bsolc/english/bsolc?catno=89-503-X> (accessed 10 June 2007).

———. 2007a. "Average Earnings by Sex and Work Pattern." Available at <http://www40.statcan.ca/l01/cst01/labor01a.htm> (accessed 30 May 2007).

———. 2007b. *The Daily.* "General Social Survey: Navigating Family Transitions," 14 June. Available at <http://www.statcan.ca/Daily/English/070613/d070613b.htm> (accessed 14 June 2007).

———. 2007c. *Self-employment, Historical Summary*. Catalogue no. 89F0133XIE. Available at <http://www.statcan.ca>.

Stretton, Hugh, and Lionel Orchard. 1994. *Public Goods, Public Enterprise, Public Choice: Theoretical Foundations of the Contemporary Attack on Government*. New York: St. Martin's.

Sweeney, John. 2006. "Wal-Mart's Dirty Secret Is Out," *Seattle Post-Intelligencer*, 6 April.

Taylor, Paul. 1993. "Why the Rich Live Longer, Healthier." *Globe and Mail*, 16 Oct.

Teeple, Gary. 2000. *Globalization and the Decline of Social Reform: Into the Twenty-First Century*. Toronto: Garamond.

Thio, Alex. 1994. *Sociology: A Brief Introduction*. 2nd ed. New York: HarperCollins.

Toussaint, Eric. 2005. *Your Money or Your Life: The Tyranny of Global Finance*. Updated Edition (translated by Vicki Briault Manus with Raghu Krishnan and Gabrielle Roche). Chicago, IL: Haymarket Books.

Toynbee, Polly. 2003. *The Guardian*, 7 March Available at <http://www.guardian.co.uk/comment/story/0,3604,909025,00.html> (accessed 17 March 2007).

Trumbull, Mark. 2007. "Blitz of Mergers, Buyouts Sets a Record." *The Christian Science Monitor,* 16 January.

Turcotte, Martin. 2007. "Time Spent with Family During a Typical Workday, 1986 to 2005." *Canadian Social Trends*, February. Cat. No. 11-008-XWE Available at <http://www.statcan.ca/bsolc/english/bsolc?catno=11-008-X>.

Twenge, Jean M. 2006. *Generation Me: Why Today's Young Americans Are More Confident, Assertive, Entitled—and More Miserable Than Ever Before*. New York: Free Press.

UNCTAD. 2002. *World Investment Report 2002: Transnational Corporations and Export Competitiveness*. New York: United Nations.

United for a Fair Economy. 2007. "CEO Pay Charts." Available at <http://www.fair-economy.org/research/CEO_Pay_charts.html> (accessed 19 May 2007).

van der Gaag, Nikki. 2004. *The No-Nonsense Guide to Women's Rights*. Toronto: New Internationalist Publications.

Veblen, Thorstein. [1899] 1994. *The Theory of the Leisure Class*. New York: Dover.

———. [1904] 1932. *The Theory of Business Enterprise*. New York: Charles Scribner's Sons.

Veltmeyer, Henry. 1986. *Canadian Class Structure*. Toronto: Garamond.

Vosko, Leah F. 2006. "Precarious Employment: Towards an Improved Understanding of Labour Market Insecurity." In Leah F. Vosko (ed.), *Precarious Employment: Understanding Labour Market Insecurity in Canada*. Montreal & Kingston: McGill-Queen's University Press.

Walker, James W. St-G. 1980. *The History of Blacks in Canada: A Study Guide for Teachers and Students.* Ottawa: Minister of State for Multiculturalism.

Warner, W. Lloyd. 1949. *Social Class in America.* Chicago: Science Research Associates.

Watson, Jane Werner. 1980. *Dinosaurs.* Racine, WI: Golden Press.

Weber, Max. [1921] 1958. "Politics as a Vocation." In H.H. Gerth and C. Wright Mills (eds.), *From Max Weber: Essays in Sociology.* New York: Oxford University Press.

White, Leslie. 1965. "Summary Review." In J. N. Spuhler (ed.), *The Evolution of Man's Capacity for Culture.* Detroit: Wayne State University Press.

White, Patrick, and Matthew Trevisan. 2007. "Workin' 9 to 5? Yeah, Right." *Globe and Mail*, 6 June:L3.

Williams, Cara. 2003. "Sources of Workplace Stress. *Perspectives on Labour and Income* 4(6) (June). Available at <http://www.statcan.ca/english/indepth/75-001/online/00603/hi-fs_200306_01_a.html> (accessed 26 June 2003).

Willis, Andrew. 2007. "Bank CEOs' 2006 Pay Would Blow NHL Salary Cap." 23 February. Available at <http://www.theglobeandmail.com/servlet/story/RTGAM.20070223.wtd0223/BNStory/Business/home> (accessed 2 March 2007).

Wolf, Naomi. 1991. *The Beauty Myth.* Toronto: Vintage.

Wood, Ellen Meiksins. 1999. *The Origin of Capitalism.* New York: Monthly Review Press.

Wood, Julia. 1999. *Gender Lives: Communication, Gender, and Culture.* 3rd ed. Belmont, CA: Wadsworth.

Wright, Erik Olin. 1980. "Varieties of Marxist Conceptions of Class Structure." *Politics and Society* 9.

Xing, Lisa. 2007. "Is It Really MySpace?" *Globe and Mail*, 16 April: R3.

Yalnizyan, Armine. 1998. *The Growing Gap: A Report on Growing Inequality between the Rich and Poor in Canada.* Toronto: Centre for Social Justice.

————. 2007. "Canada's huge income gap has widened to a 30-year high." *CCPA Monitor*, April 2007, 13, 10.

Zerbesias, Antonia. 2007. "What Doesn't Make the News," *Toronto Star*, 18 May. Available at <http://www.thestar.com/article/215266> (accessed 18 May 2007).

Zimmer, Carl. 2001. Introduction by Stephen Jay Gould. *Evolution: The Triumph of an Idea.* New York: HarperCollins.

Zweig, Michael, ed. 2004 *What's Class Got to Do With It? American Society in the Twenty-First Century.* Ithaca, NY: Cornell U. Press.

Name Index

Abella, Irving, 266
Adams, Michael, 52, 70
Adler, Patricia A., 284
Alexander, Bruce K., 146
Alexander, Claire, 293
Allende, Salvador, 216
Ambachtsheer, Keith, 235
Anderson, Mitchell, 135
Anderssen, Erin, 137, 139
Anisef, Paul, 167
Arai, A. Bruce, 167
Arar, Maher, 196
Ardrey, Robert, 32
Aristide, Jean Bertrand, 219
Aristotle, 10, 278
Armstrong, Hugh, 282, 293
Armstrong, Pat, 282, 293, 297
Ashford, Mary-Wynne, 326
Atleo, Shawn, 273
Azmier, Jason J., 187
Azrieli, David, 110

Babbie, Earl, 25
Bacon, Sir Francis, 10
Bains, Camille, 111
Baldwin, James, 3
Banksy, 202
Baran, Paul A., 23, 275
Barber, Bernard, 102
Barlow, Maude, 168, 312, 314, 324
Barndt, Deborah, 302
Basran, G. S., 248
Bata, Thomas, 315
Beaud, Michel, 82, 98
Bentham, Jeremy, 150, 206
Berman, Morris, 307, 326
Berreby, David, 70
Bezanson, Kate, 224,
Bin Laden, Osama, 216, 217
Black, Errol, 204
Black family, 109
Blau, Peter M., 102
Blum, Jeffrey M., 30
Blum, William, 216-18, 224
Blumenbach, Johann Friedrich, 254
Bolaria, B. Singh, 256, 264
Bonacich, Edna, 269
Bowles, Samuel, 167-68
Boyd, Monica, 167
Boyko, John, 277
Brannigan, Augustin, 193
Brannon, Robert, 286
Brasfield, Charles R., 262
Brathwaite, Keren S., 236
Brent, Paul, 111, 159

Bronfman family, 109
Brown, Caroline, 200
Brown, Lester, 312
Brown, Lorne, 200
Brownlee, Jamie, 108-09, 121
Bunting, Madeline, 320
Burke, Mike, 127
Burkham, David T., 237
Buse, Dieter K., 200
Bush family, 217
Bush, George W., 197, 215, 217-18

Camara, Dom Helder, 241
Campbell, Kim, 182
Carey, Elaine, 188
Carroll, William K., 108, 113, 121, 173
Cavanagh, John, 308, 311-12
Cereseto, Shirley, 317
Chan, Wendy, 252
Chaplin, Ralph, 117
Charon, Joel M., 23, 25
Chase, Allan, 30, 33
Cheng, Maisy, 167,
Chernomas, Robert, 34
Chomsky, Noam, 157, 164
Chossudovsky, Michel, 249, 252
Chrétien, Jean, 182
Church, Elizabeth, 244
Clark, Terry N., 102
Clarke, George Elliott, 255
Clarke, Tony, 152, 324
Clement, Wallace, 101, 108, 115, 158
Cohen, Lizabeth, 161
Coleman, Marion Tolbert, 297
Collins, Randall, 19, 25
Comte, Auguste, 10-11, 21
Connell, R. W., 293, 295
Contenta, Sandro, 194
Conway, John, 299
Cooley, Charles Horton, 44
Corak, Miles, 236
Cortese, Anthony, 284
Cox , Oliver C., 258
Cribb, Robert, 197
Cullis-Suzuki, Severn, 326
Curry-Stevens, Anne, 244
Curtis, Bruce, 236

Daniels, Ronald J., 195
Dart, Raymond, 32
Darwin, Charles, 16, 31-32, 35-36, 46, 260, 336
Dauncey, Guy, 326
David, Deborah, 286
Davis, Kingsley, 232-33

Davis, William, 182
de Botton, Alain, 228-29
de Wolff, Alice, 125
Dennis, Lloyd, 168
Desmarais family, 109-10, 182
Diamond, Jared, 38, 61
Dicker, John, 122
Dillon, John, 91
Dobbin, Murray, 112, 121, 210, 314
Dobson, Charles, 326
Domhoff, G. William, 110
Dorfman, Andrea, 38
Dufour, Mathieu, 230
Duncan, Otis Dudley, 102
Durkheim, Émile, 2, 11, 21, 25, 141, 145, 263, 333-34

Eagleton, Terry, 173
Eaton family, 109
Ehrenberg, Margaret, 43
Eisenhower, Dwight D., 190
Engels, Friedrich, 14, 19, 64, 94, 98, 104-06, 149, 178, 287, 289-90, 302-03, 315-18, 323, 325, 330
Epps, Ken, 191
Erman, Boyd, 88

Fanon, Frantz, 277
Ferguson, Ian, 70
Ferguson, Will, 70
Ferrie, J.E., 133
Finkel, Alvin, 195
Finn, Ed, 163
Firestone, Shulamith, 287
Flavin, Christopher, 312
Fleming, James, 108
Forcese, Dennis, 236
Ford, Henry, 90, 126
Forrester, Alexander, 166
Foster, John Bellamy, 326
Fourier, Charles, 316
Francis, Diane, 108-09
Franklin, Benjamin, 79
Frenette, Marc, 237
Freud, Sigmund, 42, 44, 278
Frideres, James S., 260, 277
Frieden, Jeffry, 99
Friedman, Thomas, 215
Friesen, Joe, 155
Friscolanti, Michael, 313
Fudge, Judy, 93, 204

Gadacz, René R., 277
Galabuzi, Grace-Edward, 269-70, 277
Galton, Francis, 32, 331
Gaskell, Jane, 236
George, Susan, 250
Giddens, Anthony, 71
Gintis, Herbert, 167-68

Ginzberg, Effie, 269
Glasbeek, Harry J., 84, 152, 193, 200
Golding, William, 32
Goleman, Daniel, 44
Gordon, David M., 269
Gordon, Jaques, 90
Gosine, Kevin, 236
Gould, Stephen Jay, 30-31, 36-37, 46, 281
Graham, W. M., 262
Gramsci, Antonio, 150, 332
Gray, Jeff, 274
Gray, John, 278
Greider, William, 148
Grogan, Sarah, 173
Grusky, David B., 102
Guppy, Neil, 167
Gwyn, Richard, 88, 109

Hackett, Robert A., 173
Hall, Emmett, 168
Hamilton, Roberta, 287
Harding, Jim, 195-96
Harper, Stephen, 182, 186, 190, 219, 298, 314
Harris, Marvin, 54, 58, 65, 70
Harrison, Hunter, 111
Harrison, Trevor, 322
Harvey, David, 224
Heath, Joseph, 146
Hegel, Georg Wilhelm Friedrich, 14
Heisz, Andrew, 236
Henry, Frances, 269, 272, 277
Henton, Darcy, 33
Heraclitus, 14
Herman, Edward, 157, 164
Hesse-Beiber, Sharlene Naigy, 302
Higham, Charles, 198
Hitler, Adolf, 33, 198, 322
Hodgson, Maggie, 263
Hou, Feng, 241
Howe, P. 144
Hubbard, Ruth, 30, 35
Hurtig, Mel, 313
Hussein, Saddam, 216

Ighodaro, MacDonald E., 277
Innis, Harold, 157
Irving family, 109-10

Jackson, Andrew, 124, 246, 300
Jacobs, Jane, 307
Jaggar, Allison M., 288
James, Carl, 236
Jamieson, K., 274
Jang, Brent, 111
Jessop, John, 166
Jin, R. L., 133
Jiwani, Yasmin, 288
Johnson, Chalmers, 224
Johnson, Daniel, 182

Johnson, Leo, 108
Johnson, Olive Skene, 46
Joya, Malalai, 219

Kamin, Leon J., 46
Kassem, Abdul Karim, 216
Kealey, Gregory S., 121
Kendall, Diana, 103
Kennan, George, 216
Kerstetter, Steve, 110, 230, 240
Keynes, John Maynard, 204-05, 332
Khaldun, Ibn, 10
Kimmel, Michael, 296, 302
Kinsman, Gary, 194, 200, 337
Klaffke, Pamela. 137
Klein, Naomi, 224
Koring, Paul, 190
Korten, David C., 91, 108, 113, 213
Koskoff, David E., 41
Krahn, Harvey, 81, 134, 147, 297
Krawczyk, Betty, 111
Kuehn, Larry, 169

Laird, Gordon, 244, 247, 252
Lavoie, Francois, 186
Lawlor, James M., 30
Le Bon, Gustave, 281
Leacock, Eleanor Burke, 70, 290, 302
Leakey, Richard, 39-40, 253
Leape, James, 310
Leavy Patricia Lina, 302
Lebowitz, Michael A., 326
Lee, Marc, 250
Lee, Richard, 57-58
Lee, Valerie E., 237
Lemonick, Michael D., 38
Lenin, V. I., 95, 178
Lenski, Gerhard E., 61, 66
Lenski, Jean, 61
Lerner, Gerda, 290-91, 302
Lerner, Michael, 144
Levine-Rasky, Cynthia, 252
Lewin, Roger, 39-40, 254
Lewis, David, 188
Lewis, Oscar, 268
Lewontin, R. C., 30, 46
Lewontin, Richard, 30-31, 34, 36-37
Li, Chris, 167
Li, Peter, 256
Lichtenstein, Nelson, 127
Lima, Paul, 279
Linden, Rick, 103
Lipset, Seymour M., 102
Little, Bruce, 206
Livingstone, David, 271
Locke, John, 78-79, 150
Loiselle, Gilles, 182
Lombroso, Cesare, 30-31
Lorenz, Konrad, 32

Lorimer, Rowland, 165
Lowe, Graham, 134, 147
Lumumba, Patrice, 216
Luxton, Meg, 224, 297

MacDonald, Kevin, 284
MacKinnon, Shauna, 185-87
Macphail, Agnes, 33
Makowsky, Michael, 25
Mander, Jerry, 311
Mannix, Fred, 110
Mannix, Ron, 110
Marquardt, Richard, 147
Martin, M. Kay, 281
Martin, Paul, 182, 225
Marx, Karl, 14, 19-20, 22, 25, 55, 75-76, 81,
    83-84, 86, 92, 94-95, 98, 101, 104-06, 119,
    121, 125, 132-33, 141, 146, 149, 178, 303,
    315-18, 322-23, 325, 330
Mazankowski, Don, 182
McBride, Stephen, 165, 206, 210, 224
McCain family, 109
McChesney, Robert, 157, 174
McFarland, Janet, 279
McIlroy, Anne, 39
McKenna, Barrie, 190
McLaren, Angus, 33
McNally, David, 258, 260, 326
McNish, Jacquie, 88
McNulty, Jean, 165
McQuaig, Linda, 74, 206, 229
Mead, George Herbert, 44
Mead, Margaret, 47-48, 55, 68, 70, 284
Mendel, Gregor, 36
Mendelsohn, Matthew, 275
Mensah, Joseph, 264, 269, 277
Mensh, Elaine, 30
Mensh, Harry, 30
Menzies, Heather, 129, 147
Milan, Anne, 264
Miles, Robert, 259
Miliband, Ralph, 110, 157, 178
Mill, John Stuart, 150, 206
Milloy, John S., 277
Mills, C. Wright, 6, 23, 25, 110, 157, 318
Mirchandani, Kiran, 252
Mithen, Steven, 41
Mokhiber, Russell, 147
Montagu, Ashley, 30
Montbiot, George, 310
Mooers, Colin, 217, 224
Moore, Wilber E., 232-33
More, Thomas, 316
Morgan, Lewis Henry, 287
Morissette, René, 231
Morris, Desmond, 32
Morris, Marika, 243
Morrison, Ken, 25
Muir, Leilani, 34

Mulroney, Brian, 182, 314
Murdoch, Rupert, 154, 158-59
Murdock, George, 284
Murnighan, Bill, 118
Mussolini, Benito, 198, 322
Myles, John, 115

Nagler, Mark, 268
Newman, Peter C., 108-09
Newton, Isaac, 10, 14
Niosi, Jorge, 108
Nisbet, Robert A., 102

O'Connor, James, 178
O'Connor, Pauline, 144
O'Harrow, Jr., Robert, 194
Ogilvie, Megan, 161
Okihiro, Norman, 167
Orchard, Lionel, 136
Ornstein, Michael, 113
Owen, Robert, 316

Panitch, Leo, 110, 178, 189, 200
Parenti, Christian, 200
Parenti, Michael, 159, 163, 200
Parke, Ross D., 284
Parsons, Talcott, 21, 167, 282
Patterson, Lisa L., 274
Pattison, Jimmy, 110
Paxton, Robert O., 197
Perlo, Victor, 269
Philp, Margaret, 239
Picard, Andre, 298
Picot, Garnett, 241
Pinedo, Maria Rosa, 288
Pitfield, Michael, 182
Plato, 10
Polanyi, Karl, 60
Pollack, William, 293
Porter, John, 103-04, 108-09, 121, 157-58, 167
Posada Carriles, Luis, 219
Potter, Andrew, 146
Poulantzas, Nicos, 178
Putnam, Robert D., 143-45
Pynn, Larry, 111

Radwanski, George, 197
Rae, Bob, 182
Rae, John, 182
Rebick, Judy, 283, 323
Reguly, Eric, 158, 191
Reiman, Jeffrey, 193, 247, 252
Reynolds, Neil, 214
Ricardo, David, 150
Rich, Adrienne, 287
Richardson, Ken, 30
Ridley, Matt, 35
Robarts, John, 182
Roberts, Paul Craig, 217

Roberts-Fiati, Gloria, 237
Robertson, Grant, 165
Robertson, Heather-jane, 168
Robinson, Barrie, 285
Robinson, David, 199, 289
Rockefeller, John D., 32-33
Rodney, Walter, 249
Rogers, Ted, Jr., 110
Rose, Steven, 46
Rosen, B., 268
Rosenwein, Barbara H., 99
Ross, David, 241
Rothenberg, Paula, 288
Runk, David, 90
Rushowy, Kristin, 206
Russell, Ellen, 230
Ryan, William, 242-43, 245
Ryerson, Egerton, 166

Saint-Simon, Claude Henri, 316
Samuelson, Leslie, 193
Sanders, Richard, 191, 219
Sanderson, Steven K., 48, 55
Santinoli, Ana Maria, 288
Sarkozy, Nicolas, 182
Sasson, Jack M., 70
Satzewich, Vic, 255, 268, 270
Schechter, Danny, 164
Schellenberg, Grant, 300
Seabrook, Jeremy, 121
Sears, Alan, 17, 25, 30, 127, 170, 174, 295, 297
Seccombe, Wally, 271
Shadd, Adrienne, 253
Shaker, Erika, 138, 170
Shepard, R. Bruce, 264
Sherkin, Samantha, 288
Sherman, Barry, 110
Shields, John, 125, 127, 165, 206, 210
Shutt, Harry, 184, 304, 307
Sklar, Holly, 108, 110
Skoll, Jeff, 110
Slater, Philip, 142-44
Slee, Tom, 174.
Smail, David, 5, 6, 25, 145
Smith, Adam, 83, 86, 150
Smith, Charlie, 219
Smith, Mark, 144
Sorenson, John, 257
Spears, David, 30
Spencer, Herbert, 21, 32
Stanford, Jim, 123, 130, 133, 175, 235
Staples, Steven, 190-91
Steedman, Mercedes, 200
Stretton, Hugh, 136
Strong, Maurice, 182
Swanson, Jean, 252
Swartz, Donald, 200
Sweeney, John, 125

Sweezy, Paul M., 23, 275

Tator, Carol, 277
Taylor, Frederick Winslow, 126
Taylor, Paul, 133
Teeple, Gary, 105, 110, 130, 206, 213
Thio, Alex, 36
Thomson family, 109-10
Toussaint, Eric, 95, 224, 250
Toynbee, Polly, 138
Tran, Kelly, 264
Trevisan, Matthew, 128
Troper, Harold, 266
Trudeau, Pierre, 182, 194, 210-11, 273
Trumbull, Mark, 90
Tucker, Eric, 204
Tudiver, Neil, 174
Turcotte, Martin, 129
Twenge, Jean M., 143-44
Tyyskä, Vappu, 302

van der Gaag, Nikki, 280, 300, 302
Veblen, Thorstein, 137, 181, 228-29
Veltmeyer, Henry, 109, 114
Voorhies, Barbara, 281
Vosko, Leah F., 124, 147

Wald, Elijah, 30, 35
Walker, James W. St-G., 264
Walker, N., 1948
Warner, W. Lloyd, 102
Watson, Jane Werner, 36
Waugh, Neil, 111
Weber, Max, 11, 25, 79, 101-02, 175
Webster family, 109
Weissman, Robert, 147
Weston family, 109
Weston, Galen, 110
Wheen, Francis, 19
White, Leslie, 40
White, Patrick, 128
Williams, Cara, 129
Wolf, Naomi, 295, 296
Wollstonecraft, Mary, 150
Wood, Ellen Meiksins, 73-74, 82, 99
Wood, Julia, 163
Wright, Erik Olin, 115
Wright, Ronald, 99

Xing, Lisa, 154

Yakabuski, Konrad, 182
Yalnizyan, Armine, 230-31, 244, 252
Yankelovich, Daniel, 52
Yates, Michael, 99

Zawilski, Valerie, 252
Zerbesias, Antonia, 157, 164
Zhang, Xuelin, 231

Ziegler, Richard, 243
Zihlman, Adrienne L., 46
Zimmer, Carl, 42
Zinn, Howard, 34
Zweig, Michael, 109, 117

Subject Index

Aboriginal peoples, 56, 76, 78, 80, 177, 194, 202, 220, 255, 259, 272, 321
  and constitutional rights, 82, 261
  land claims, 273-74, 276
  marginalization of, 163, 233, 260-263, 266, 273, 276
  poverty among, 238, 240, 247, 251, 268-69
  self-government, 261, 276
  suicide, 2, 6, 262-63
  traditional societies in North America, 51, 53, 65, 261
  women, 269, 274-75, 280, 295
Absolute poverty, 238, 329
Addiction, 45, 129, 145
Advertisers, power of, 136-37, 159-161
Advertising, 41, 81, 89, 113, 136-39, 152, 155, 158-161, 164, 192, 202-03, 209, 229, 251, 284, 296, 305
African-Canadians, discrimination against, 194, 236, 264, 266, 271
Aggression, human, 26, 32, 45, 47-48, 55, 282, 285, 293-94
Agriculture, 58, 61-62, 76, 81, 214, 261, 309
  agrarian societies, 63-64, 66-68, 71, 81, 92, 139, 151, 153, 176, 181, 290-91, 33
  horticultural societies, 62, 64-67, 71
  Neolithic Revolution, 61-63, 333
Alienation, 144, 263
  in capitalist society, 132-33, 141-42, 146, 329
  worker alienation, 131-33, 329
Alliance Atlantis Communications, 159
Alliance of Manufacturers and Exporters of Canada, 112
American Union of Concerned Scientists, 12
Anarchy of production, 89-90, 98, 172, 329
Anti-Ballistic Missile Treaty, 215
Anti-globalization movements, 214, 311, 322-25
Anti-Semitism, 50, 256, 258, 266-67, 276, 322, 329
Anti-U.S. sentiment, 222, 308
Apartheid, 269
Arabs, 163, 220, 255
Arapesh, 47-48, 55
Arms industry, 190
Assimilationism, 267, 329
Astral Media, 159
The Australian, 158

Bands, in foraging societies, 55-58, 60
Barron's magazine, 158
Bata Shoes, 315
Beauty myth, 295
Berlin, Treaty of, 95

Bias, 18, 24, 149, 225, 267, 334
  media, 161-64
  in social science, 11-12, 18, 23-24
Bilderberg Group, 112-13, 213
Biological determinism, 20
  eugenics, 32, 45
  and human behaviour, 20, 26-27, 29-30, 32, 35, 329
  and social inequality, 31-32, 45, 242, 260
  theories of, 20-21, 26, 32, 329
Biopiracy, 312
Bipedalism, and human evolution, 38-39, 43, 45
Blue-collar jobs, 107, 120, 130
Bourgeoisie, 79, 80, 94, 106-10, 114, 151, 181, 283, 293, 316-17, 333
  consolidation of, 75, 226
  definition, 75, 329
  emergence of, 75
BP, 89
Brain development, 38-44
Bretton Woods conference, 213, 311
BSkyB, 158
Business Council on National Issues (BCNI), 112-13
Business-labour accord, 204-05, 212, 223
Business Roundtable, 112

Canada, 2, 6, 9, 13, 27, 32-33, 56, 70, 78, 80-82, 88, 90, 93-94, 97, 101-22, 130-35, 137-143, 144-48, 152-53, 156-60, 162-67, 169-73, 175-76, 178-80, 182-85, 187-88, 190-197, 199-211, 214, 217-21, 223-27, 229-41, 243-45, 247-48, 251-53, 255, 257-58, 260-80, 283, 285, 288, 292, 295, 296, 298-306, 312-14, 316, 319-21, 323, 328, 330
  arms industry, 190-92
  capitalism, development of, 81-83
  culture, 51-53, 70, 146, 165
  federal-provincial relations, 209, 239, 274, 298, 314
  immigration, 49, 51, 81, 128, 141, 166, 189, 194, 220-21, 231, 233, 240-41, 251, 255, 260, 265-67, 269-70, 272, 275, 277, 288, 294, 298, 322
  integration with United States, 182, 208-209, 313-14, 330
  owning class, 88, 108-14, 116, 118, 120, 128, 132, 146, 179, 192, 203-05, 211, 295, 314, 322
  racial equality initiatives, 237, 271-72, 275-76
  racism in, 153, 253, 255, 260-67, 269-76, 305

social spending, 115, 127, 166-67, 169-70,
172, 180, 184-86, 189-90, 202-03, 206-08,
210-12, 274, 288, 298, 304
tax system, 134, 154, 166, 176, 184-88,
199, 203, 208, 210, 235, 244
unemployment, 6, 105, 124-25, 134,
203-04, 210, 241, 262, 264, 300   .
    wages, 104, 106, 115-16, 124, 127-29,
146, 171, 188, 202, 206-07, 209-11, 230,
236, 241, 265, 270, 279, 298, 300, 316
Canada.com, 159
Canadian Alliance, 322
Canadian Association of Food Banks, 240,
244
Canadian Broadcasting Corporation (CBC),
99, 165, 177-78
Canadian Cancer Society, 192
Canadian Centre for Policy Alternatives, 146,
187, 207, 231, 246, 252, 327
Canadian Chamber of Commerce, 112
Canadian Council of Chief Executives,
112-13, 180
Canadian Council on Social Development,
239-40, 327
Canadian Federation of Independent
Business, 112
Canadian Federation of Students, 328
·Canadian National Railway, 111
Canadian Newspaper Association, 197
Canadian Pacific Railway, 202, 265
Canadian Radio-television and
Telecommunications Commission (CRTC),
165
Canadian Security and Intelligence Service
(CSIS), 194
Canadian Taxpayers Federation, 188-89
CanWest Global communications, 159
Capital, 75-77, 80-81, 83-85, 88, 90-92,
94-97, 102, 105-06, 108-10, 112-16,
122-23, 125, 129, 132, 135-36, 145-46,
157-59, 168-69, 172-73, 178, 181, 183-84,
189-91, 198, 203-06, 208-09, 211-13, 215,
219, 221-223, 243, 246, 270, 275, 293-94,
296, 307-09, 314-15, 324, 329-30, 332, 337
concentration and centralization of, 88,
146, 159, 175, 315, 324, 330
Capitalism, 59, 89-91, 97-98, 149, 152, 166,
168, 172, 180, 183-84, 197, 200, 202-03,
205, 226, 229, 233-34, 244, 247, 249, 251,
254, 258-59, 271, 275-76, 303-05, 313,
315-318, 324-25, 330-33, 335, 337
agrarian capitalism, 74-77
boom/bust cycles, 84, 91, 125, 127, 205
classes, 74-75, 80, 82-84, 100-121, 153,
161, 260
consequences of perpetual growth, 137,
309-13
contradictions of, 92-93, 98, 101, 149, 205,
215, 227, 275, 304-09, 323, 325, 335

corporate interests, 122-146, 170, 209
defined, 82, 328
and gender relations, 291, 293, 300
as global system, 94-96, 107-08, 122,
210-223
and instability, 91, 94-95, 98, 184, 205,
222, 307-09
limits of growth, 137, 309-10
mode of production, 74, 77, 82-83, 98, 336
monopolization, 86-88, 95, 133-34, 332-33,
337
profits, drive for, 75-77, 81, 84-86, 90,
92-93, 96, 98, 122, 128-29, 166, 179, 190,
204, 211, 214, 234, 307-09, 330
roots of, 71-80
and socioeconomic formations, 71, 73,
79-80, 82, 129, 260
structural basis of class struggle, 85-86
surplus value, 87, 92, 106, 112, 114, 119,
132, 179, 229, 249, 329, 337
and technological change, 73, 76-77, 81,
86, 105, 125, 129-31, 166, 206
Catholic Church, 10, 50, 75, 79
CAUT, 170
cbc.ca, 196, 247
C.D. Howe Institute, 113, 210
Center for Arms Control and Non-
Proliferation, 218
Central Intelligence Agency (CIA), 194, 216
Centralization of capital, 88, 315, 330
Change theories, 19, 21-24, 95, 104, 157, 168,
173, 188, 199, 228, 234, 236, 249, 251,
303, 329-30
and political left, 178, 226-27
Charter of Rights and Freedoms, 9, 152, 272,
275, 279
Cheakamus River, 111
Chevron, 89
Child poverty, 240
Chinese immigration, opposition to, 265
Christianity, 50, 79
Civil society groups, 320-21, 326
    Class (See Social class)
    Class struggle, structural basis of, 85-86
    Cold War, 119
Colonialism, 94-95, 212, 220, 258-61, 276-77,
324
    and transition to capitalism, 76, 78, 80
    and underdevelopment, 95, 249
Commodity, defined, 73, 330
commondreams.org, 164, 328
Commons, 72, 77, 201, 207, 312-13, 330
    commodification of, 202
Comprehensive Nuclear Test Ban Treaty, 215
Concentration of capital, 88, 97, 146, 158-59,
175, 315, 324, 330
Conglomerates, 96, 159, 182
ConocoPhillips, 89-
Conseil du patronat, le, 112

Constitution Act of 1982, 272
Consumerism, 90, 137-39, 145-46
Contingent labour, 118, 124-25, 300
Continuous Passage Act, 265
Convergence, defined, 159, 330
Co-operative Commonwealth Federation, 321-22
Core regions, 88
Corporate branding, 136, 155
Corporate Higher Education Forum, 170
Corporations, 86, 89-94, 97, 104, 107, 109-10, 113, 116, 137-38, 156, 160, 162, 169, 180-82, 184, 188-92, 197, 199, 202, 204, 207-08, 211-12, 223, 230, 249, 274, 292, 308-15, 322, 330-31, 335
    corporate concentration, 88, 97, 108, 122-23, 146, 158-59, 165, 173, 168, 315, 324, 330
    as "fictitious persons," 108, 152, 192
    foreign control of, 135, 314
    mergers, 88, 91, 212
    and Nazi Germany, 198
    power of, 6, 97, 122-23, 133, 136, 145, 146-47, 154-55, 158-59, 162, 169-74, 200, 205-06, 208-17, 237, 243-44
        and public interest, 184, 210, 222, 306, 312
        and taxation, 154, 185-86, 188, 208
    transnational corporations (TNCs), 96, 98, 113, 122-24, 126, 135, 145-46, 153, 155, 157, 169, 203, 205-06, 212-15, 217, 222, 224, 227, 322-24, 337
Council of Canadians, 320-21, 324, 328
Council on Foreign Relations, 112-13, 213
Credentialism, 166-67, 330
Criminalization of dissent, 195, 199, 308
Criminal justice system (*See also* Law and order, in capitalist societies), 193, 199, 246-48, 252, 266, 272, 275, 279
Crisis of overproduction, 89-91, 98, 205, 329-30
CTVglobemedia, 159
Cultural determinism, 20, 48
Culture, 2, 4-5, 9, 23, 25, 27, 40, 43, 45, 47-49, 51, 60, 66, 68-70, 78, 81-82, 142, 145, 150, 154-56, 166, 171, 173, 202, 220-21, 227, 236, 255, 257-59, 262-64, 267-68, 272-73, 277, 281, 284, 288-89, 294, 301, 304, 307, 320, 331, 333-34, 336
    Canadian culture, 51-53, 70, 122, 135, 146, 164
    of capitalism, 135-39, 304
    characteristics of, 48-49
    cultural integration, 219, 262, 313
    cultural universals, 50
    cultural values, 249
    defined, 1, 48, 330
    dialectic of, 54-56
    globalization of American culture, 203, 221

of narcissism, 142, 145-46
and socialization, 48-49, 53, 69, 154, 284, 336

Daimler-Chrysler, 89
Dark age, 306-07
De Beers Corporation, 41
Debt, 6, 134, 138, 143, 152, 170, 205, 229, 231, 240, 250, 337
Deep integration, 314, 330
Determinist theories, 20-21, 30, 46
Deficit scare, 210
Delaware Indians, 59
Democracy, 71, 79, 138, 160, 162, 165, 171-73, 179, 183, 196-99, 224, 227, 275, 304, 321, 331
    and capitalist states, 94, 179, 180-81, 198, 322
    and class relations, 151
    and electoral process, 180, 183
    limits to, 180, 183
    meaning of, 179-80
    neoliberal attack on, 208, 213-14
    property rights and, 180
Deregulation, 208
Dialectics, concept of, 14-15, 151, 330
DirectTV, 158
Discrimination, 125, 241, 256, 262, 264-70, 272-77, 284, 288, 322, 330
Dissent, 163, 194-95, 197-99, 308
Distal relations of power, 5-6, 21-22, 24, 122, 324, 330, 335, 337
Division of labour, 40, 57-58, 62, 68, 102, 104, 141, 232-33, 281-82, 284, 295, 298, 330-34
    in capitalist societies, 92, 100
    in foraging societies, 40, 57, 69
Domestic Abuse, 288, 292
Domestic femininity, 295
Dow Jones, 158
DuPont, 312

East Asians, 163, 255
Economic Council of Canada, 246
Economic cycles, 91, 125
Economic determinism, 20
Education, 92-93, 100-05, 114, 120, 126, 130, 153, 165-68, 171-74, 178, 184-87, 189, 202-03, 206, 208, 210-11, 219, 242, 267, 270-71, 274, 288, 298, 300, 307, 315, 322, 336-37
    and business/neoliberal agenda, 169-70, 174, 210-11
    change theories and, 168, 236
    corporate participation in, 169-70, 207, 237
    functionalist theories and, 167-68
    gender gap in, 296
    and meritocracy, 232, 236

order theories and, 167-68, 236
postsecondary/university, 115, 124, 143, 148, 166-67, 169-70, 203, 209, 236, 237, 239, 241, 244, 297
racial segregation, 264
residential schools, 262-63, 273,
and social inequality, 236, 237, 247, 251, 275
and socialization, 148, 154, 166-68, 171, 173, 284, 297
two-tiered system of, 170-71, 237
Elderly, the, 111, 129, 136, 187, 202, 240, 243, 280, 298-99
Elections, 177, 180, 183, 248, 253, 265, 274, 280
Elites (*See also* Owning class), 95, 250
Employment Equity Act, 255, 272
Employment/unemployment Insurance, 134, 203, 210, 241, 300, 336
Enclosure movement, 77
Enron, 123
Environmental degradation, 222, 308, 312, 323
Equality of opportunity, 152, 168, 172, 187, 226, 236, 251
Equity funds, 88, 109
Ethnic chauvinism, 256, 276, 331
Ethnicity, 119, 264, 289, 331
concept of, 253, 255-56
and economic success, 167
and occupational mobility, 234
Ethnocentrism, 51, 69, 255
Eugenics (*See also* biological determinism), 32-34, 45, 331
Evolution, 16, 35-38, 46, 302
bipedalism, 38, 45
of human brain, 41-42, 45
of humans, 26, 30, 35, 37-38
and language, 38, 45
meat eating and, 39-40, 45
natural selection, 36, 253
and sexuality, 42, 45
and sociability of humans, 38
and toolmaking, 39, 45
Exogamy, in foraging societies, 57, 331
Exxon Mobil, 89, 162

Facebook, 44, 144
Farming, decline of, 134, 220, 241
Fascism, 119, 175, 198-200, 322, 331
Feminism, 283-302, 322
definition, 283, 331
inclusive feminism, 289
liberal feminism, 284, 286, 289, 301
radical feminism, 283, 286-87, 289, 301, 334-36
socialist feminism, 287, 336
waves of, 283-89, 301
Feminization of poverty, 240

Feudalism, 72-81, 83, 94
decline of, 73-74, 97
definition, 72, 331
and roots of capitalism, 72-74, 79, 81, 97
Fishing industries, decline of, 105, 134-35, 241
Fish stocks, decimation/collapse of, 111, 314
Food taboos, culture and, 50, 54, 65
Foraging societies, 56-66, 69, 71, 139, 176
decline of, 61-62
description of, 56-58
division of labour, 40, 69
gender relations, 58, 289-90
kinship and sharing in, 59, 63-64, 69, 289
Ford Motor, 89
Fordism, 126-27, 138, 331, 334
Fortune 500, 89
Fox Television, 158
Fraser Institute, 113, 180, 210, 238
Freedom, 8-9, 62, 117, 139-40, 157, 160, 197, 216-17, 224, 227, 267, 296, 308, 316, 320, 322
liberal notions of, 150-53, 283, 333
and society, 8-9
Free enterprise, 86-87, 94, 123, 331-33
Free trade (*See also* North American Free Trade Agreement [NAFTA]), 206-07, 214-15, 308, 314, 321
Friends Committee on National Legislation, 218
Front de Libération du Québec (FLQ), 194-95
Functionalism, 21, 167, 232, 281, 331, 337

Gambling, 145, 187-88, 227
Gemeinshaft vs. Gesselschaft, 141, 331, 32
Gender, 2-3, 17, 46, 47, 67, 100, 104, 119-20, 143, 161, 163, 193, 274, 276, 281, 284, 286-87, 292, 296-97, 299-300, 302
core status, 278
difference, 253, 280-81, 284, 286, 301
division of labour, 57-58, 281, 282, 284, 295, 297-98, 331
and familial relations, 295
and functionalism, 281-82
and occupational mobility, 234, 286
and physiological differences, 279, 296
terminology, 279
Gender inequality, 66, 144, 251-52, 278-83, 289-91, 293, 295, 297, 299-302,
beneficiaries of, 287, 292-94
biological determinism and, 281, 289
extent of, 278, 294-95
liberal feminism and, 284, 286, 289, 301
Marxism and, 287, 289, 293, 301-02, 336
neoliberalism and, 300
radical feminism, 283, 286-87, 289, 301, 335-36
root causes of, 286-87, 289-90, 301
wage gap, 125, 293
Gender roles, 53, 70, 282, 295-96

men, 294
socialization of, 53, 284, 286, 295, 297
sports participation and, 285, 295
General Agreement on Tariffs and Trade
(GATT), 214
General Agreement on Trade in Services
(GATS), 214
General Electric, 159, 198
General Motors, 89-90, 189, 198
Genetic engineering, 312
Genetics, 22, 34, 35, 45
Generation me/me generation, 141, 143
Giveaway feasts, 65
Globalization, 6, 94, 96, 99, 118, 122, 164,
168, 199, 201, 203, 205, 209, 211-12, 219,
222, 224, 226, 249-50, 321, 326
cultural globalization, 52, 203, 221
and disease, 308
and ethnic tensions, 271
and inequality, 225
imperialism, 212, 250, 258
institutional agents of, 173
opposition to, 321-24
population movements, 141, 221, 308
and role of the state, 211-12
of trade, 94, 299
women, impact on, 299-302
Government (See State, the)
Green Granny, 111
Gross Domestic Product (GDP), 93, 96, 122,
186-87, 190, 206, 250, 309
Groupe Bruxelle Lamber (GBL), 182

HarperCollins, 158
Head tax, 265
Hedge funds, 88, 91, 109
Heterosexism, 284, 287, 295, 297, 332
Hip-hop, 155
HIV/AIDS, 280
Homosexuality, 45, 281-82, 300
Horticultural societies, 62, 64-67, 71
Housing market, 244
Hudson's Bay Company, 261
Human agency, 8, 14, 17, 21, 24, 179
Human behaviour, 1-2, 7, 9, 15, 22, 24, 26-27,
29, 45, 48, 54, 136, 229, 242, 278, 329
biological bases of, 20-21, 26-27, 29-30, 35,
45, 154
culture and, 20-21, 32, 45, 48
genetics and, 21, 26, 29, 32, 35
Human Genome project, 34-35
Human Resources Development Canada,
118, 132, 293
Hunting and gathering societies (See Foraging
societies)
Hypergrowth, 308

Idealism (See Philosophical idealism)
Ideology, 149, 150, 154, 157, 167, 171-73,

176, 197, 226, 242-43, 251, 255, 258, 260,
268, 270, 275, 283-84, 287, 303-04, 321,
326, 331-34
definition, 148, 172, 332
ideological hegemony, 150, 171, 211, 332
and power, 171, 217
igeneration, 141, 144
Immigrants, 49, 51, 81, 141, 166, 194,
220-21, 255, 260, 265-66, 269, 272, 275,
277, 294, 322
incomes of, 124, 128, 221, 231, 241,
269-70, 275, 298
poverty among, 124, 128, 233, 240, 251
women and domestic abuse, 288
Immigration, 189, 219, 265-66, 269, 288
Imperialism, 95, 212, 217, 224, 250, 322, 332
and colonial development, 95, 249
and racism, 258, 266
and underdevelopment, 249
Incarceration, poverty and, 247
Incest taboo, 42, 332
Indian Act, 261, 274
Indian and Northern Affairs Canada, 263
Indian immigration, discrimination against,
265-66
Industrial Revolution, 10, 228
origins of, 77
and roots of sociology, 303
and transformation of work, 125
Industrial Workers of the World (IWW), 117
Inflation, 92, 127, 205, 210
Inheritance taxes, 188
Institutional racism, 267-68, 272-73, 332, 337
Intergenerational mobility, 234
Intergovernmental Panel on Climate Change,
162
International Chamber of Commerce, 113
International Convention on the Elimination
of All Forms of Racial Discrimination, 272
International Monetary Fund (IMF), 206,
213, 337
International World Court, 215
Internet, 12, 113, 139, 144-45, 153, 158-59,
164, 170, 189, 202, 272, 323, 327
Intragenerational mobility, 234
Iraq, 61, 93, 164, 196, 215-16, 219, 222
Islamofascism, 197
Islamophobia, 256, 266-67, 332
Italy, fascism in, 197-98, 322

Japanese Canadians, discrimination against,
183, 265
Job creation, technological change and, 128,
130
Job stress, 130-31, 133
Just-in-time production, 127

Kelowna Accord, 274
Keynesianism, 204-05, 332

Kinship, 42, 140
  in agrarian societies, 67
  in foraging societies, 57, 59, 258
  in horticultural societies, 66
Kyoto Protocol, 215

Labour, 40, 57-58, 62, 64, 67-69, 73-77,
  81-86, 90, 92-93, 96, 98, 100, 102, 104-07,
  111, 115, 125-26, 128, 130, 132-33, 136,
  141, 162-63, 180, 198, 200, 204, 211, 214,
  220-21, 223, 229, 232-33, 246, 248-49,
  259, 261, 265, 270-71, 275, 279-82, 284,
  292, 296, 298, 308, 315, 328, 330-37
  as a commodity, 85, 132, 146
  domestic labour, 280, 290, 297-98, 300
  forced labour, 67, 76, 259, 264
  neoliberal attack on, 205, 208
  unionization, declining rate of,
Labour markets, 127-28, 130, 167, 173, 189,
  230,
  racial inequality and, 264, 269-70
  sexism and, 294-98, 300
  unemployment, effects of, 127
Labour unions, 96, 115, 117-18, 120, 130,
  163, 194, 204, 244, 270, 321, 323, 332
Laissez-faire capitalism, 94, 332
Language, and human evolution, 38, 41-42,
  44
Law and order, in capitalist societies, 248
Lean production, 127
Left, political, 194, 303, 306, 321-22, 325-26
Lesbian feminism, 287
Liberalism, 152, 171, 226-27, 267, 269, 273,
  275, 283, 333
  dominant ideology of capitalism, 148,
  150-51, 172, 173, 206, 251, 303-04
  and freedom of choice, 151-53
  and individualism, 153
  racial inequality, analysis of, 276
  values of, 150, 267, 276
Liberal Party, 182, 194, 219, 274
Lobbying, of interest groups, 180
Looking-glass self, 44
Low-income cut-offs (LICOs), 238-40, 251,
  300
Lumpenproletariat, 101, 120, 322, 333

Macrosociology, 21-22, 333
Mad cow disease, 309
Managers, and supervisors, 115
Manpower Inc., 124
Manufactory system, 76
Market Basket Measure, 238-39
Markets, 75-76, 78-79, 80, 82-84, 87, 89,
  91-93, 98, 106, 123, 127, 133-38, 146,
  151-54, 158-61, 165, 168-70, 183-84, 206,
  215, 224, 226-27, 244, 249, 264, 300,
  308-09, 321, 327, 329, 333, 337
  growth of, 73-76, 78, 89, 93-94, 96

pre-capitalist form, 73, 75
Marketwatch.com, 158
Marxism, 19, 22, 86, 98, 108, 114, 119-20,
  132, 173, 178, 269, 276, 304, 306-07,
  326-27, 329-33, 335-37
  and changing influence of, 19-20
  concept of class, 63, 69, 101-03, 105-06,
  119, 269
  development of, 19
  and gender relations, 283, 286-89, 293,
  301-02, 336
  material basis of, 119
  and revolution, 119, 305, 336
  and social transformation, 68, 119
  socialist society, 316-17
Material culture, 48, 56, 156
Materialism, 12, 16, 36, 54, 119, 143, 136,
  246, 287
  culture, analysis of, 54-55, 65, 70
  philosophical materialism, 12-15, 24, 317,
  334
McMaster University, 267
"Me generation," 141, 143
Means of production, 60, 62-63, 68-69, 80,
  82-84, 96, 98, 100, 104, 106-07, 115, 132,
  228, 300, 329, 333-36
Meat eating, 39-40, 45, 54, 57
Mechanical solidarity, 141, 333-34
Media, 3, 5, 12, 26, 52-53, 108, 110, 113-14,
  138, 148-49, 156-57, 171-74, 196, 214,
  218, 252, 257, 264, 267, 270, 280-82, 284,
  289, 296, 309, 323, 332
  Canadian programming, 160
  change theories and, 157
  functionalist theories and, 157
  government role regarding, 165, 173
  myth of objectivity, 161-65
  ownership and control of, 157-58, 161, 173
  promotion of capitalism, 149, 154, 157,
  173, 304
Mercantilism, 258
Mergers, 88, 91, 190, 198, 212-13, 322
Micmac Indians, 59
Microsociology, 21, 333
Middle class, 100, 103-06, 115, 120, 239, 247
"Middle fish" of society, 18
"Middle fish" theories, 18, 21, 198, 321
Military-industrial complex, 190-91, 194, 199
Misogyny, 291, 333
Model Eugenical Sterilization Law, 32
Mode of production, 55-56, 69, 71, 73-74, 77,
  82-83, 98, 290, 333, 336-37
Money economy, emergence of, 73
Monopolization, 86-88, 133, 165, 190, 333
Monsanto, 312
Mujahideen, 217
Multicultural feminism, 288
Multiculturalism, 273, 275
Multinational corporations (*See* Transnational

corporations)
Mundugumor, 47-48, 55
Muscular masculinity, 295
Music, 3, 30, 41, 50, 52, 152, 154-56, 165,
203, 227, 271
MySpace, 144, 154, 158

Nation, 78, 96, 122, 165, 181, 188, 206,
211-13, 220, 222, 248-50, 253, 263, 308,
312, 326, 328, 332
National Council of Welfare, 245, 327
National Farmers Union, 134
National Film Board, 165
National Geographic Channel, 158
National Rugby League, 158
Nation-state, 77-78, 88, 96, 98, 107, 110, 200,
207, 211-13, 219-20, 222-23, 251, 308, 314
Natural selection (See also Evolution), 33, 36,
253
Nazi Germany, 9
and eugenics, 33
fascism, 198
Neoconservatism (See Neoliberalism)
Neoliberalism, 94, 201, 208-10, 223-24, 226,
244, 313-14, 333, 335
agenda, 174, 206, 209-11, 222, 310, 323,
335
families, impact on, 224, 243
promotion of corporate agenda, 208, 210,
222, 308
and retreat of activist state, 205, 224
structural adjustment policies, 206, 335
women, impact on, 224, 299-301
Neolithic Revolution, 61, 333
New Democratic Party (NDP), 188, 306, 322
New middle class, 115
New York Post, 158
News Outdoor Group, 158
Non-status Indians, 261
Nortel Networks, 93
North American Competitive Council, 182
North American Free Trade Agreement
(NAFTA), 113, 165, 169, 209, 314
Novartis, 312

Olympics 2010, 111
One Big Union (OBU), 117
Ontario Hydro, 182
Opposable thumb, 39
Order theories, 18-21, 23-24, 102, 104, 141,
167-68, 173, 178, 199, 232, 236, 267, 303,
334
and political right, 303
and power, 22
and social inequality, 168, 225
Organic solidarity, 141, 333-34
Organization for Economic Co-operation and
Development (OECD), 187, 190, 210, 327
Osprey Media, 159

Outsourcing, 116, 118, 124-25, 310
Overproduction (See Crisis of overproduction)
Owning class, 63, 78, 83, 86, 88, 97, 106,
108-11, 114, 120, 122, 126, 128, 132, 151,
176, 179, 183, 199, 203-05, 211, 223, 250,
269, 293, 295, 307, 314-15, 322, 329
in Canada, 146, 179, 192
class consciousness, 107, 112-13, 116, 118,
120
composition of, 109-10, 226, 315
dominant position of, 125, 136
and maintenance of power, 96-97, 113, 301
nature of, 116, 326
separation of ownership from
management, 315
wealth, 86, 128, 132, 308

Paper economy, 91-92, 98
Paradigms (See Theories)
Pastoralism, 62
Patriarchy, 287-88, 290, 294, 301, 334
Peripheral regions, 88, 122
Petite bourgeoisie, 101, 106, 114-15, 120,
321, 334
Phillip Morris, 162
Philosophical idealism, 13, 334
Pioneer, 312
Pluralism, 177-79, 199, 334
Police, role of, 16, 30, 178, 192-95, 200, 208,
275, 277
Political economy, 19-20, 83, 317
Populism, 321-22, 326, 334
Post-Fordism, 126-27, 138, 334
Postmodernism (poststructuralism), 289
Potlatch, 65, 261
Poverty, 6, 32, 35, 103, 168, 172, 180, 187,
225, 227, 238, 240-41, 243, 245-47, 262,
269, 305, 316, 322, 329, 335
blaming the victim, 242, 251
capitalism and, 176, 243-44, 251
contributing factors of, 224, 241-44, 300
culture of, 243, 245-46, 268
global inequality, 219, 249
measures of, 238-40, 251, 300
policy options, 187, 299
social impact of, 246-47
victims of, 240-41, 246-47, 251, 279-80
Power, 5, 6, 21-25, 50, 56, 62, 78, 81, 82,
97, 104, 106-08, 123, 130, 133, 148-50,
153-54, 157, 159, 163-65, 168-69, 171-73,
175, 177-78, 181, 192, 195-97, 200-01,
204, 209, 211-14, 216-18, 220, 222,
226-27, 229, 233, 236, 247-49, 257, 261,
269-70, 273, 288-89, 298, 306-07, 315,
317-19, 322, 324-25, 330-32, 334-35
in agrarian societies, 66-67, 72, 76
in capitalist societies, 75, 78, 80, 83-84,
86, 95, 96, 98, 101-02, 112, 115-18, 120,
135-36, 154, 171, 173, 176, 181, 182-83,

198-99, 301, 306, 316-17, 324
of corporations, 96-97, 104, 108, 110, 113,
  121-23, 145-47, 168, 198, 203, 205-06,
  222, 233, 314, 322-24
in foraging societies, 58, 60, 176
gender and, 68, 97, 286-87, 291-95, 299,
  301, 334, 336, 337
in horticultural societies, 64, 66
ideology and, 107, 113, 118, 121, 150,
  171-72, 257, 332
in Marxist theory, 92, 119, 301, 317
in society, 5, 22, 62, 139, 157, 175, 192,
  260
and structured inequality, 68-69, 107
in theories of stratification, 102
Power Corporation, 110, 182
Pratt & Whitney Canada, 189, 191
Precarious employment, 124-25, 127, 334
Precision grip, 39
Prejudice, 253, 256, 262, 264, 267-68, 271,
  275-76, 284, 332, 334-35
Primates, evolution of, 41-42
Prime TV, 159
Private property, 62-63, 69, 223, 287, 289,
  291, 302
Privatization, 133, 143-44, 155, 176, 192, 202,
  207-09, 248, 298, 312, 323, 335, 337
Productive sector workers, 114
Profit, 55, 74-78, 80-81, 84-86, 88-94, 96, 98,
  105, 111, 122, 125-26, 128, 130, 132-34,
  136, 146, 156, 158, 160-61, 165-66,
  169-70, 183, 185, 189-90, 201, 204-05,
  207-08, 211, 222, 230, 243, 269, 294-95,
  308, 312-13, 315, 318, 329, 336
  maximization of, 75, 82, 85, 89, 91, 95,
    98, 110, 122, 128-29, 132, 161, 178, 190,
    204, 208, 211, 214, 234, 270, 307-09,
    329-30
  overproduction and, 89-90
Progress, meaning of, 81
Progressive taxation, 185-86, 208, 245, 335
Proletarianization, 115, 335
Proletariat, 75, 114, 335
Property tax, 186
Protestant ethic, 79
Proximal relations of power, 5-6, 21-22, 24,
  97, 123, 151, 213, 287, 292, 330, 335
Public choice theory, 136
Public private partnerships (P3s), 207, 335

Quebecor, 159

rabble.ca, 164, 328
Race, 46, 100, 104, 119, 125, 143, 161, 167,
  193, 251-57, 259-60, 264, 272, 274-76,
  281, 286, 289, 295
  concept of, 253-55, 276
  defined, 254-55, 335
  and occupational mobility, 234

and status, 100, 104, 119-20, 161, 193, 228,
  234, 251-52, 264, 276
  stereotyping, 30, 163, 272-73, 275
  struggle for equality, 272-75
  and wage discrimination, 241
Racial profiling, 30, 266, 277, 328
Racialized groups, 163, 236, 252, 255-58,
  264, 267, 269-72, 275-77, 288, 335
Racism, 20, 119, 143, 153, 228, 237, 253,
  257, 260, 264, 266-67, 269-73, 275-77,
  294, 305, 337
  Aboriginal experience, 273-74, 276
  African-Canadian experience, 236, 264,
    271
  Chinese-Canadian experience, 265, 270
  class perspective, 269
  defined, 254-56, 335
  and discriminatory immigration policies,
    266
  and hiring practices, 95
  historical roots of, 258-60, 267, 276
  ideology of, 260, 267-68, 270-71
  Indo-Canadian experience, 265-66
  institutional racism, 267-69, 272-73, 332
  Islamophobia and, 256, 266-67
  Japanese-Canadian experience, 183, 265
  liberal perspective, 268, 275
  persistence of, 275-76
  and slavery, 258, 260, 276
Radical feminism, 283, 286-87, 289, 292, 301,
  334-36
RadioShack Corp., 93
RCMP, 194-96, 200
Real economy, 91, 98
Reciprocity, 60, 143, 336
  Redistribution, 65-67, 244, 324
  reciprocity, 60
  surplus expropriation, 69
Red scare, 119
Reflex, 27
Reform, 35, 80, 168, 170, 174, 204, 208, 223,
  242, 252, 304-06, 310, 319, 325, 335
Reformism, 306, 325, 335
Reform Party, 322
Regionalism, 51-52, 82
Regressive taxation, 185-88, 199, 208, 335
Relations of production, 60, 64, 73, 304, 333,
  335
Relative poverty, 238, 335
Religion, and gender relations, 53, 279-80,
  282, 290-91, 295, 299, 301-02, 322
Rent system, 72, 74
Representative government, 180, 183, 248
Reserve army of the unemployed, 125, 269,
  335-36
Residential schools, 262-63, 273, 277
Retirement, 90, 110, 124, 185, 235
Revolution (*See also* Transformation), 31, 80,
  174, 264, 277, 283, 305, 318, 325, 336

Right (political), 320, 326
  politics of the, 302, 325
  populist political parties of the, 322
RJ Reynolds, 162
Rogers Communications, 159
RottenTomatoes.com, 158
Royal Commission on Equality in Employment, 271
Royal Commission on the Status of Women in Canada, 163, 279
Royal Dutch Shell, 89
Rule of law, 192, 195, 198, 307, 336
Ruling class (*See* Owning class)
Russian Revolution of 1917, 119, 305

Sales tax, 177, 186, 208
Scientific management, 126, 336
Scientific principles, and sociology, 10-11
Self-employment, 83, 133-35, 279, 321, 334
Serfs, 72, 179, 331
Service sector workers, 107, 114, 299
Sex, and gender, 28, 46, 279, 297-98
Sexism (*See also* Gender inequality), 119, 153
Sexuality, 28, 38, 42, 45-46
  regulation and control of, 42-43, 291
Sexual Sterilization Act, 34
Sharing (*See* Collective action, and social development)
Shaw Communications, 159
Slavery, 31, 67-69, 72, 74, 76, 82, 84, 94, 100, 104, 179, 181, 221, 245, 258-60, 264, 276, 290-91, 322, 331
Small businesses (*See* Self-employment)
Sociability, of humans, 44, 57
Social assistance, cut-off lines for,
Social class (*See also* Bourgeoise, Owning class, Working class), 17, 63, 69, 100-02, 104, 119, 120-21, 132, 175-76, 228, 305, 310, 325, 330, 332, 336-37
  class conflict, 67, 106, 330
  class consciousness, 100, 107, 112-18, 120, 330
  and gender relations, 289, 301
  Marxist concept, 106
  and middle class status, 104-06
    stratification theories of, 102-03, 120
  and structured inequality, 63
  Weberian concept of, 102-03
Social Credit, 322
Social Darwinism, 32, 260, 336
Social democracy, 306, 325
Social inequality (*See also* Class; Poverty), 17-18, 21-23, 26, 31-32, 34-35, 45, 58, 60, 68-69, 97, 100-03, 106-08, 152, 157, 171-72, 175, 225-29, 232-34, 241-44, 248-49, 251, 260-61, 268, 280, 290-91, 316, 325, 336-37
  biological determinism and, 31-32, 45, 47, 52, 55, 167, 225

education and, 167-68, 172, 236-37, 251, 269
income and wealth inequality, 225-26, 228-31, 250, 269
structured inequality, rise of, 32, 62-68
Social mobility, 234, 236-37, 251, 268, 336
Social movements, 32, 144, 283, 318, 321-22, 325-26, 331-32
  anti-corporatist movement, 322-23
  collective action and, 319, 322
  defined, 321
  populism, 321-22, 326, 334
  "public issues" and, 319
Social networking sites, 44, 144
Social safety net, 94, 205, 321, 337
  cuts to unemployment insurance, 210, 241
  deterioration of, 170
Social spending
  cuts in, 94, 155, 170, 190, 206, 208, 211, 299, 304
  myth of excessive spending, 210
Social stratification, 102, 232
Social structure, 4-6, 17-18, 21-22, 149, 243, 258, 268, 294, 337
Social wage, 203-04, 206, 208-09, 222, 336
Socialism, 105, 117, 184, 204-05, 219, 283, 306, 316-18, 326, 335
Socialist feminism, 287, 336
Socialization, 49, 69, 148, 154, 278, 282, 284, 286, 295, 297, 299, 301
  agents of, 53, 149, 154, 166, 171, 284,
  and capitalist culture, 193
  defined, 48, 336
  education and, 166-68, 171, 173
  of production, 317, 323
Society, 1-9, 11, 13, 15-25, 27, 32-35, 40, 42, 45, 47-49, 51-74, 76, 79-86, 91-92, 94, 96-98, 100-08, 114, 116, 118-20, 122-23, 130, 132, 135-37, 139-155, 157-58, 161, 163, 167-69, 171-81, 183-84, 188, 192-93, 196-202, 206, 210, 216-17, 223-29, 232-34, 241-42, 244-45, 247-49, 251, 253, 258, 260-61, 263-64, 266-69, 271, 275-77, 281-82, 284, 286-87, 289-94, 299-307, 309, 316-323, 325-27, 329-37
  defined, 1, 336
  and freedom, 8-9, 151-52
  and human behaviour, 3, 7-8, 24, 42-43, 118, 192, 267
  as process, 6-7
  as social structure, 3-4, 24
"Solidarity Forever," 117
South Asians, 266
Sociocultural system, 4, 54, 60, 336
Socioeconomic formation, 55-56, 60-61, 69, 71-73, 79-80, 82, 94, 97, 101, 108, 129, 135, 153-54, 165, 178, 181, 260, 305-06, 317-19, 325, 331, 335-36
Socioeconomic status (SES), 34, 100-01,

103-04, 119-20, 161, 167, 193, 251-52,
264, 276, 289, 295, 336-37
Sociology, 1-4, 6-12, 16-25, 29, 32, 35-36, 40,
44, 47, 56, 63, 71, 79, 97, 101-104, 120-21,
139-142, 153-54, 157, 167, 173, 225, 228,
232, 234, 236, 242-43, 254, 257, 263, 267,
302-03, 307, 318, 325, 327, 331, 333, 337
bias in, 11-12, 18, 23-24
boundaries of, 22-24
class, concepts of, 101, 103
macrosociological approach, 21-22, 333
major theoretical frameworks, 3, 17, 44,
225
microsociological approach, 21-22, 333
roots of, 10-11, 21, 23-24
sociological imagination, 6, 25, 71, 337
Speculative investments (*See* Paper economy)
Sports and gender, 285
Standard Oil, 198
State, the, 66, 68, 78, 95, 105, 153, 172,
174-81, 183-84, 187, 189, 192-205, 207-11,
214, 219, 221-24, 243, 249, 260-62, 267,
272, 276, 283-84, 287, 289-91, 294-95,
298-99, 301-02, 308, 316-17, 320, 326,
330, 332, 335-37
and arms industry, 190-92
coercive power of, 183, 192-97
and corporate sector, 188-90, 198, 210-11
defined, 66, 175, 337
democratic state, 179-81
early formations, 176
emergence of, 176
and fascism, 197-98, 331
functions of, 177-78, 212
and gender relations, 286, 291, 299, 301
globalization and, 205-15
intervention of, 94, 165, 173, 184
and nation-building process, 165, 211
nation-states, 77,-78, 88, 96,98, 107, 110,
201, 207, 211-14, 219-20, 222-23, 251,
308, 314
neoliberalism and, 204-11
and taxation, 184-87
welfare state, 94, 201-03, 205, 210, 223,
230, 244
Statistics Canada, 128, 131, 134, 138-40, 145,
167, 230-32, 234-35, 237-39, 241, 251,
269, 279-80, 288, 295, 297-300, 327
Status, 5, 58, 62, 66, 68, 100, 102, 104-05,
115, 119-21, 127, 136, 157, 163, 225-26,
228-29, 232-34, 236, 251, 274, 278, 286,
290, 292, 298, 301, 321, 335, 337
defined, 5, 100
middle class, 104
social status, 114, 137, 242
socioeconomic, 34, 100-01, 103-04, 119-20,
161, 168, 193, 251-52, 264, 276, 289, 295,
336-37
Status Indians, 183, 261, 274

Status symbols, 228-29, 337
Stereoscopic vision, 39
Stereotypes, 30, 163, 272-73, 275, 284
Stock ownership, 110
Streaming, in education system, 236-37, 297
Stress, 7-8, 14-17, 34, 116, 121, 127, 129-130,
133-34, 140, 145-47, 211, 233, 237, 251,
262, 287, 293, 297-99, 301, 321
Structural adjustment policies/programs, 206,
213, 252, 337
Structural functionalism (*See* Functionalism)
Subsistence-level economies, 60, 69
Suicide, studies of, 2, 145, 262
Sun Dance, 261
Sun Life, 160
Surplus value, 86, 92, 106, 112, 114, 119, 132,
179, 184, 203, 229, 249, 329, 336-37
Symbolic-interactionism, 44
Symbols, 40, 49, 100, 228-29, 251, 255, 337
and communication, 40-41
as non-material elements of culture, 48
Systemic racism (*See* Institutional racism)
The Sun, 158

Taxation (*See also*: Canada, tax system;
Corporations, powers of, and taxation;
Head tax; Inheritance taxes; Progressive
taxation; Property tax; Regressive taxation;
Sales tax; State, and taxation)
neoliberal reforms, 208, 210
Tchambuli, 47-48
Technological change, 20, 44, 52, 58, 61-62,
64, 73, 76-77, 79-81, 96, 106, 109, 129-30,
137, 139, 144, 147, 157, 166, 190-91, 194,
205, 212, 278, 305, 310, 323, 333
and industrialization, 77, 81, 125, 310
and work, changing nature of, 7, 62, 76-77,
86, 105, 114, 126-27, 129-30, 146, 166,
205, 334
Telefilm Canada, 165
Television, 16, 139, 143-44, 153, 156-61, 163,
172, 194, 203, 227, 271, 313
Canadian content, 160
Terrorism, 30, 125, 194-96, 217-19, 224, 267,
308, 326
war on, 3, 218-19
Theories, 1, 15-16, 18-23, 25-26, 30-33, 35,
39-42, 46, 48, 84, 95, 102, 119, 130, 133,
136-37, 150, 152, 157, 166-68, 174, 178,
184-86, 188, 192-94, 199, 206, 213, 234,
249, 251, 253, 260, 267-68, 283, 286-89,
301-02, 329, 331, 334-36
change, 19, 21-24, 95, 104, 157, 168, 173,
199, 225, 234, 236, 249, 302, 329-30
order, 18-24, 102, 104, 167-68, 173, 178,
199, 225, 232, 236, 302
Tobacco advertising, 192
Toolmaking, and human evolution, 39, 45
Trade, 48, 56, 75, 76, 78, 88, 91, 95, 124, 175,

189, 191, 201-02, 206, 212, 214-15, 217, 219, 221, 224, 233, 249-50, 261, 299, 308, 311, 314, 321, 330, 337
and accumulation of capital, 75-76
and markets, 73, 76
Transfer payments, 186, 239, 316, 337
Transformation, 20, 35-36, 40, 56, 66-67, 77-78, 109, 119, 122, 130, 140-41, 145, 151, 155, 169, 179, 199, 205, 209, 217, 273, 287, 296, 300, 302, 305, 318, 325
alternatives to capitalism, 304, 310
principles for anti-capitalist politics, 322
capitalism, transition to, 77-79, 125, 302
Neolithic Revolution, 61, 333
process of, 74
reform and, 304, 325
revolution and, 305, 325, 336
social movements and, 318-324
Transnational corporations, 96, 98, 122-24, 126, 135,145-46, 153, 155, 157, 169, 203, 212-13, 215-17, 224, 227, 312, 322-24, 337
Trilateral Commission, 113, 213
Tuition fee increases, 170, 209

Underdevelopment, 95, 248-49
Underemployment, 124-25, 129, 243, 269, 295, 309
Unemployment, 2, 6, 13, 77, 84, 101, 105, 124, 128-29, 134, 136, 172, 176, 192, 202-05, 210, 221, 247-49, 262, 264, 268-69, 295, 300, 333, 336
and poverty, 103, 241, 243,
stress of, 133, 309
threat of, 124
Unions (See Labour unions)
United for a Fair Economy, 234
United Nations (U.N.), 190, 201, 213, 215, 248, 263, 308, 327
International Convention on the Elimination of All Forms of Racial Discrimination, 272
Security Council, 215
United States, 11-12, 31-32, 51-52, 61, 70, 79, 81, 90, 93, 95-96, 102, 109, 112, 119, 122-23, 137, 146, 155-57, 159, 164-65, 169, 174, 190, 193, 196, 198, 200, 203, 205, 208-09, 212-19, 222-24, 234, 237, 245, 247-48, 260, 264, 269-70, 283, 307-08, 313-14, 323, 330, 336
as global police officer, 212, 215-19, 223
as global superpower, 212-13, 215-24, 250, 252, 307-08
health insurance, 189-90, 211
military activities, 212-13, 215-17, 222-24, 307-08
military spending, 190-92, 217-18
protectionism, 214
unilateral foreign policy decisions, 215, 222-23, 308

United Technologies, 191
Urbanization, 141
"Us" versus "them," 50, 257
User-pay services, 186, 208
Utopian socialism, 316-17

Values, 1, 3, 7, 9, 52, 55, 60, 66, 68, 70, 91, 112, 120, 141, 148-50, 154, 157, 166-67, 171-72, 198, 210, 217, 221, 238, 267, 270, 275, 286, 288, 293, 300, 308, 315, 331-34, 336
of capitalism, 59, 108, 110, 136, 144-46, 154, 276
cultural values, 48-49, 51, 69, 136, 249, 263, 268, 276
of liberalism, 151, 206, 267-68
Vertical mergers, 159
Violence, 31, 47-48, 50, 156, 163, 172, 175, 217, 219, 256, 263, 266, 298, 308, 326
masculinity and, 294
revolution and, 305
against women, 275, 280, 288, 292, 306
Visible minorities, poverty among,

Wages, real, 127, 146, 203
Wal-Mart, 89, 122-23, 125-26, 174, 328
The Wall Street Journal, 158
Warfare, in horticultural societies, 64-66, 69
War Measures Act, 194-95
Waste disposal, 313
Water, privatization of, 312
Wealth inequality (See Social inequality, wealth and income)
Welfare state, 201, 244, 337
decline of, 94, 205, 230, 244
expansion of, 94, 202-05, 210, 223, 316
Westray disaster, 193
White-collar jobs, 107, 130
"White man's burden," 259
White privilege, 257, 293
Women (See also Division of labour; Gender inequality), 2, 3, 28, 43, 47-48, 53, 57, 66, 97, 106, 120, 128, 140, 151, 161, 163, 173, 177, 179-80, 183, 187, 206, 230, 233, 237, 260, 265, 267, 269, 272, 274, 278-84, 286-93, 295-302, 304, 321-22, 327-28, 331-32, 335
domestic relations, 47, 68, 280, 282-83, 289-93, 295, 298
in foraging societies, 57-58, 60
impact of neoliberalism on, 224, 300
labour market participation, 107, 127, 166, 279-80, 283, 286, 292, 295-97
and poverty, 240-41, 245-46, 279-80
violence against, 275, 280, 288, 292, 306, wage discrimination against, 241, 279, 293-94, 334
work and status, 47, 124, 279, 297
and "work-family crunch," 298

Women's movements (*See* Feminism)
Work, 4, 13, 40, 54-56, 62, 64, 74, 77, 79,
    83-86, 88, 95, 102, 105 107-08, 110-11,
    114-15, 117, 122, 124-35, 140-41, 143,
    146-47, 160, 173, 204, 220-21, 223, 228,
    230-31, 233-34, 241-42, 248, 255, 259,
    265, 269, 290, 292, 294-95, 297-300, 302,
    309, 311, 321, 334
    dehumanization of, 132
    factory system, 125
    increased productivity, demand for, 77
    polarization of jobs, 127, 146, 230
    post-Fordism, 126-27
    restructuring of, 124-27
    technological change and, 7, 86, 105, 114,
    125-27, 129-30, 146, 166, 205
    unsafe workplaces, 132
Work ethic, 79, 268
"Work-family crunch," 298
Working class, 83, 101, 103, 106, 114, 116,
    119-21, 125, 154, 204-05, 223, 315, 317,
    323
    changing nature of, 105, 107, 120-21, 315,
    326, 333
    and class consciousness, 107, 116-118,
    120-21
    nature and composition of, 109, 114-116,
    120-21
Working poor, 103
World Bank, 206, 213, 252, 308, 337
World Business Council for Sustainable
    Development, 113
World Economic Forum, 113, 187, 323
World Social Forum, 323
World Trade Organization (WTO), 201, 206,
    209, 213-14, 222
World War I, 119, 198, 307
World War II, 21, 32-33, 91, 94-95, 102,
    104-05, 107, 117, 119, 121, 126-27, 130,
    142, 159, 190, 197-98, 201, 204-05,
    212-13, 216, 218, 223, 265-67, 272, 295,
    307, 318, 332, 337